Introduction to
Reading the Pentateuch

Introduction to Reading the Pentateuch

JEAN-LOUIS SKA

Translated by Sr. Pascale Dominique

Winona Lake, Indiana
EISENBRAUNS
2006

Published by agreement with Edizioni Dehoniane, Rome; this volume first published as *Introduzione alla lettura del Pentateuco: Chiavi per l'interpretazione dei primi cinque libri della Bibbia* (© 1998 Edizioni Dehoniane); this translation from the French edition: *Introduction à la lecture du Pentateuque: Clés pour l'interprétation des cinq premiers livres de la Bible* (Brussels: Editions Lessius, 2000). The translation was reviewed and updated by the author.

Imprimi potest.   *Imprimatur.*
Rome, 26 November 1999   Mechelen, Belgium, 7 February 2000
R. F. O'Toole, S.J., Rector   É. Goffinet, vicar general

Library of Congress Cataloging-in-Publication Data

Ska, Jean Louis, 1946–
   [Introduzione alla lettura del Pentateuco. English]
   Introduction to reading the Pentateuch / Jean-Louis Ska ; trans. by Sr. Pascale Dominique.
      p.   cm.
   Translation from the French version of a work first published in Italian.
   Includes bibliographical references and index.
   ISBN-13: 978-1-57506-122-1 (pbk. : alk. paper)
   1. Bible. O.T. Pentateuch—Criticism, interpretation, etc.   I. Title.
   BS1225.52.S53   2006
   222'.1061—dc22

                        2006025270

2018   2017   2016   2015   2014   2013
           5   4   3

Contents

Foreword to the English Translation

The first edition of *Introduction to Reading the Pentateuch* was written in Italian and published in 1998 by the Edizioni Dehoniane of Rome. A second, slightly revised edition was published two years later by the Edizioni Dehoniane of Bologna. The French translation, based on this second Italian edition, was published in the same year, 2000, by Lessius (Brussels). I reread the whole French translation, introduced some clarifications, and added some updates. The present translation into English is essentially a translation of the French version. I thank the publisher, Lessius, especially, because they kindly provided the translator, Sr. Pascale-Dominique Nau, with the electronic files she needed to facilitate the work. I also reread the English translation and introduced some minor modifications for the sake of clarity. However, I have not changed my basic opinions about the formation of the Pentateuch. On some points, such as the Persian Imperial Authorization and the Yahwist, my opinions have received support from various quarters (see, for instance, J. W. Watts [ed.], *Persia and Torah: The Theory of Imperial Authorization of the Pentateuch* [SBLSymS 17; Atlanta: Society of Biblical Literature, 2001]; and J. C. Gertz, K. Schmid, and M. Witte [eds.], *Abschied vom Jahwisten: Die Komposition des Hexateuch in der jüngsten Diskussion* [BZAW 315; Berlin: de Guyter, 2002]).

Of course, the discussion continues, especially with regard to the possible existence of a Yahwist who was either a Postexilic author (J. Van Seters) or a Postexilic redactor (C. Levin). The date proposed for the final formation of the Pentateuch—the Persian period—has become a kind of *opinio comunis* among scholars. That several important texts go back to the same period is an idea that is gaining support from various quarters. One problem that is still very much debated, with various solutions being proposed in recent years, is the identification of the end of the Priestly source. R. Achenbach, J. Blenkinsopp, C. Frevel, N. Lohfink, C. Nihan, E. Otto, T. Römer, and others have expressed their opinions on this topic. On another topic, more and more authors assert that the traditions about the ancestors of Israel and about the Exodus originate from different traditions and that the Priestly writer was the first to unite them in a coherent way (A. de Pury, T. Römer, and K. Schmid). The existence of post-Deuteronomistic and post-Priestly redactions—another major point of discussion in this *Introduction*—has been supported by several authors in the past decade, among them J. C. Gertz, M. Witte, E. Otto, and his pupil, R. Achenbach; and by the recent dissertation of F. Giuntoli. For this and other points still under discussion, as for other important works published in the field in the past five years, I refer the reader to the bibliography that I have prepared for this English edition.

I would like to thank all the colleagues, friends, and students who promoted the idea of this translation into English and encouraged its completion. First of all, my thanks go to Bernard M. Levinson for his constant support, for the careful reading of the manuscript of the translation, and for invaluable suggestions, especially with respect to the bibliography. He also helped correct my "European biases." I also express my gratitude to my diligent translator, Sr. Pascale-Dominique Nau. Jim Eisenbraun, the publisher, who was always accessible and ready to solve problems, and Beverly McCoy, the copy editor who was responsible for preparing the very accurate, competent, improved final form of this text, deserve my special thanks. The quality of the book owes much to their conscientiousness. Of course, I take full blame for any errors that remain.

Let me state, finally, that I hope the English *Introduction* will be as helpful to scholars and students as the other versions have been.

JEAN-LOUIS SKA
October 2006

Preface

In recent times, the number of studies on the Pentateuch has been increasing, and it is difficult to keep up with all the theories in a field where problems abound. This situation is new. At the end of the 1970s, the classic documentary hypothesis distinguished four sources in the Pentateuch: the Davidic-Solomonic Yahwist; the Elohist from the Northern Kingdom, who was close to the first prophets—Amos and especially Hosea; the Deuteronomist, from the time of the Josianic reform (622 B.C.E.); and finally, the Priestly Writer (P), from the Exilic and Postexilic period. This theory became, for all cultured readers of the Bible, a kind of "Gospel" reflected in introductions and in notes in Bibles commonly used from the 1950s on.

This theory made its official "entry" into the Catholic world in 1956, with the first French edition of the *Jerusalem Bible*. Exegetes, teachers, researchers, and students of religion, as well as preachers could be proud of a theory that explained in a simple and convincing way the problems raised by the Pentateuch. Then this consensus fell to pieces, and today no one knows when a new consensus, comparable to the one that existed 20 years ago, will be reached.

What can still be said about the Pentateuch today? The documentary hypothesis (which, by the way, took time to be accepted by the various confessions, especially by the Catholic Church) has once again been attacked, blockaded, and captured by groups on all sides. Is there now "nothing left of it but ruins," as some say? Or has the citadel withstood all the assaults and proved its invincible nature, because it has finally revealed that it is more solid than was thought and has repelled all enemies?

Even in Pentateuchal exegesis, all the war communiqués resemble each other, because each one claims victory. People who wish to read the Pentateuch in an intelligent, critical way find themselves in an impossible situation. Or to use still another analogy: each client is pressed by a crowd of salesmen who want to sell their (often-contradictory) theories. What may be done?

The primary aim of the present introduction is to help these "customers" gain their bearings in the difficult world of the Pentateuch. The confusion reigning today in the exegetical field requires drastic choices for the goal to be reached. Above all, it is necessary not to enter too hastily into the raging debates of our time. The reader must be prepared to face today's battles and, in order to do so, we need to give him or her the indispensable critical "weapons." This is why the present introduction does not begin with the history of research or a presentation of the historical-critical method. The starting point must be "neutral."

Consequently, the introduction begins by presenting the data, that is, by a description of the Pentateuch in its present form, as it stands, because diachronic, analytical readings always follow synchronic readings and synthesis of the data. If the whole is greater than the sum of its parts, it is important to consider the whole before looking at the "sum."

The first two chapters deal exclusively with the canonical form of the Pentateuch and of the five books that compose it. In the following chapters (3 to 5), I thought it would be useful to review at length the various fields of the Pentateuch in order to discover, bit by bit, the "forms" of its variegated landscapes. The texts have a "third dimension" that appears clearly in the course of chaps. 3–5, which deal first with the legislative texts and then with the narratives. I wanted to present the problems before considering how they may be solved. Of course, it has been impossible not to propose, already in the first reading, some simple solutions. For this reason, "sources" and questions of the "redaction" of composite texts, written by different authors at various periods, are dealt with there. However, I do not propose a global theory.

Chapter 5 is probably the most innovative chapter, because it presents various examples of redactional activity. Some of the passages dealt with are well known, while others are less familiar. This chapter also presents the techniques generally used by the editors when they wanted to insert an addition into an existing text.

Only after this comprehensive survey do I present, in two chapters (6 and 7), a summary of the research history. Instead of starting with Baruch Spinoza and Richard Simon, I thought it necessary to consider this history once again from its beginning, that is, from the period of the Rabbis and the Church Fathers, because this will help to explain better the problem of modern exegesis, which, as we shall see, continues and corrects various trends that already existed in preceding periods.

This history of the research does not present a long list of names, dates, and theories. I want instead to point out the cultural and religious background of each era and each exegetical school so that their questions and answers may be understood better. If the Bible has a context, exegesis has a historical setting. Specific questions are asked in specific contexts and not in other contexts.

At the end of chap. 7, the book reaches a critical point. It becomes necessary to take a stance and to propose some solutions to the problems enumerated in the course of the preceding chapters. Among the possible approaches, I have chosen to present a study of ancient literature before dealing with the formation of the Pentateuch. How did authors write? Why did they write? What was written? What principles did the authors, redactors, and editors of the Pentateuch follow in the process of their work? These are the main questions we will try to answer in chap. 8.

Chapter 9 then proposes not precisely a theory of the Pentateuch's formation but a solid foundation for the elaboration of such a theory. The reader will perhaps be surprised to see me abandoning (after careful reflection) the idea of a Preexilic Yahwistic document without disproving the existence of Preexilic texts. I advance reasons that I believe to be convincing. The chapter also attempts to distinguish the most convincing theories from those that are more conjectural.

The last chapter seeks to situate the formation of the Postexilic Pentateuch in its historical setting. In the end, I had to choose between the hypothesis of the imperial authorization and that of a community of citizens assembled and organized around the temple. This choice was not an easy one even if, *a posteriori*, the theory chosen is in my opinion the most valid and enlightening. A few final considerations on the relationship between the Pentateuch and the New Testament follow.

From a methodological viewpoint, this book seeks to convince its readers that it is impossible today to read the Pentateuch without recourse to the historical-critical method. The reader encounters too many problems, and the problems are too complex to be dealt with "naïvely." I do not at all discount synchronic views—the stylistic and narrative analysis of multifarious texts. This kind of approach turns out to be more profitable than some studies on the sources, which atomize texts without actually making their reading any easier.

Be that as it may, the choice of a method is mainly dictated by one's subject. If the Pentateuch, like the Bible as a whole, is a historically situated text that came into being in a milieu very different from our own, one necessarily needs "to move" in order to understand it better.

There is another even more compelling reason to choose the path of the historical-critical method in this introduction to the Pentateuch. The synchronic studies themselves, when they are conducted honestly and rigorously, cannot avoid the difficulties, "jumps," or "fractures," and the attempts to resolve problems of continuity, tension, or contradictions in various texts. These difficulties appear less readily to those who study isolated texts and "superficial" structures than to those who, for legitimate reasons, prefer to look for the most general meaning of the texts. Anyone who enters into the heart of these texts and tries to understand the details and the "function" of narratives and laws in order to explain how the details were introduced into the final composition cannot avoid the difficulties that only a study of the genesis of the Pentateuch can solve.

Today's reader, whether a believer or a nonbeliever, cannot ignore the problems that a text written more than 20 centuries ago presents. Ignoring these problems would mean denying the sense of history and the meaning of the "Incarnation of the Word." It would mean overlooking the profound depth of Scripture, which speaks to us chiefly because it has a rich history.

I would like to say this in a simple way: the history of the Pentateuch's formation constitutes the very message of the Pentateuch precisely because its history is a history of death and resurrection, the history of the people of Israel resuscitated after the Exile. The Pentateuch is the primary witness of Israel's survival, or more precisely of its resurrection after the traumatizing experience of the Exile. Like Jacob after the fight with the angel, the Pentateuch still bears the scars of the wounds received during its painful history. It is not useless to consider the ancient books carefully in order to retrace the various stages of the journey. The journey also reveals the message this history has to offer us.

I must also add that I do not exclude, *a priori*, any method. The reader will see, for example, that the first chapters make good use of B. S. Child's canonical reading, although it is employed somewhat differently. The first reading is, in any case, synchronic. Only after this first step do problems appear that should be dealt with in a diachronic manner. In any case, as I already said, the choice of a method must be determined by the nature of the problems to be studied. In my view, it is not useful to set methods one against the other and certainly not to reject one method or another just for generic or philosophical reasons. The most useful method is the one that helps us to understand the texts better, the one that offers the surest way to grasp the meaning and presents the simplest solutions to problems of interpretation. My choice will therefore be rather pragmatic, but it is based on long reflection on the aim of exegesis, its duties, and its limits. I would only like to give, or to restore, a taste for surveying the Pentateuch attentively and discovering its marvelous landscapes. I would be happy if I were to reach this goal.

This book, in its present structure, preserves the marks of its genesis. It was worked out over the course of more than ten years of teaching at the Biblical Institute in Rome. In order to be as clear as possible, I have all along retained a "teaching" tone and style.

I dedicate this book to today's students and to the alumni of the Biblical Institute who have followed and encouraged me in the delineation of these reflections on the foundational documents of the Jewish and Christian faiths, a monument of our Western culture and of universal literature.

Abbreviations

Some Common Textual Abbreviations

*	An asterisk following a chapter/verse reference indicates that the intent is not to refer to the entire verse or chapter but only to the part of the verse, pericope, or chapter that belongs to a given source or redaction. For example, Exod 14:21* refers only to the part of the verse under discussion (either the Priestly source or the non-Priestly source).
D	Deuteronomy (Pentateuchal source)
Dt	original Deuteronomist (generally connected with the reform of Josiah [622 B.C.E.]; used in the same context as the abbreviation Dtr)
Dtr	Deuteronomistic work (subsequent to the work of the original Deuteronomist and composed in the same spirit; generally speaking, and based on the theory of M. Noth, this refers to some more-recent chapters or pericopes in Deuteronomy, such as Deuteronomy 1–3, and the texts composed by the Deuteronomistic editors in the section Joshua– 2 Kings, such as, for example, 2 Kings 17)
E	Elohist source
H	Holiness Code (Leviticus 17–26; from German *Heiligkeitsgesetz*)
J	Yahwist source (from German *Jahwist*)
P	Priestly source/Writer
Pg	narrative part of the Priestly source (from German *Priesterliche Geschichtserzählung*)
Ps	supplements to the "Priestly narrative" (see theory of M. Noth)
Rp	abbreviation used by some scholars to designate the last editor(s)/ redaction(s) of the Pentateuch

General Abbreviations

FS	Festschrift
LXX	Greek translation of the Hebrew Bible (Alexandria, Egypt, ca. 250–150 B.C.E.)
MT	Masoretic Text
NT	New Testament
OT	Old Testament
par(s).	parallel(s)

Reference Works

AB	Anchor Bible
ABD	Freedman, D. N. (editor). *The Anchor Bible Dictionary*. 6 vols. Garden City, N.Y.: Doubleday, 1992
ABRL	Anchor Bible Reference Library
AJBI	*Annual of the Japanese Biblical Institute*
AnBib	Analecta Biblica
AOAT	Alter Orient und Altes Testament
ATANT	Abhandlungen zur Theologie des Alten und Neuen Testaments
ATD	Das Alte Testament Deutsch
ATLA	American Theological Library Association
BA	*Biblical Archaeologist*
BASOR	*Bulletin of the American Schools of Oriental Research*
BBB	Bonner biblische Beiträge
BETL	*Bibliotheca ephemeridum theologicarum lovaniensium*
BHS	Elliger, K., and W. Rudolph. *Biblica Hebraica Stuttgartensia*. Stuttgart: Deutsche Bibelgesellschaft, 1984
Bib	*Biblica*
BibInt	*Biblical Interpretation*
BIOSCS	*Bulletin of the International Organization for Septuagint and Cognate Studies*
BJS	Brown Judaic Studies
BKAT	Biblischer Kommentar: Altes Testament
BN	*Biblische Notizen*
BWANT	Beiträge zur Wissenschaft vom Alten und Neuen Testament
BZ	*Biblische Zeitschrift*
BZAW	Beihefte zur Zeitschrift für die Alttestamentliche Wissenschaft
CahRB	Cahiers de la Revue biblique
CBQ	*Catholic Biblical Quarterly*
ConBOT	Coniectanea Biblica, Old Testament
DBSup	Pirot, L., and A. Robert (editors). *Dictionnaire de la Bible, Supplément*. Paris: Letouzey & Ané, 1928–
DJD	Discoveries in the Judaean Desert
EB	Echter Bibel
EstBib	*Estudios bíblicos*
ETL	*Ephemerides theologicae lovanienses*
EvT	*Evangelische Theologie*
FAT	Forschungen zum Alten Testament
FRLANT	Forschungen zur Religion und Literatur des Alten und Neuen Testaments
HAT	Handbuch zum Alten Testament
HKAT	Handkommentar zum Alten Testament
HSM	Harvard Semitic Monographs
HTR	*Harvard Theological Review*

HUCA   *Hebrew Union College Annual*
ICC   International Critical Commentary
IDB   Buttrick, G. A. (editor). *Interpreter's Dictionary of the Bible*. 4 vols.
           Nashville: Abingdon, 1962
Int   *Interpretation*
JAOS   *Journal of the American Oriental Society*
JBL   *Journal of Biblical Literature*
JJS   *Journal of Jewish Studies*
Joüon-Muraoka   Joüon, P. *Grammar of Biblical Hebrew*. Translated and revised by
           T. Muraoka. 2 vols. Rome: Pontifical Biblical Institute, 1991
JPS Torah Commentary   Jewish Publication Society Torah Commentary
JQR   *Jewish Quarterly Review*
JSOT   *Journal for the Study of the Old Testament*
JSOTSup   Journal for the Study of the Old Testament Supplement Series
KD   *Kerygma und Dogma*
LD   Lectio Divina
NEchtBib   Neue Echter Bibel
NICOT   New International Commentary on the Old Testament
OBO   Orbis biblicus et orientalis
OBT   Overtures to Biblical Theology
OTG   Old Testament Guides
OTL   Old Testament Library
OtSt   *Oudtestamentische Studiën*
PEQ   *Palestine Exploration Quarterly*
RB   *Revue biblique*
RivB   *Rivista biblica*
RSR   *Religious Studies Review*
RTL   *Revue théologique de Louvain*
RTP   *Revue de théologie et de philosophie*
SB   Sources bibliques
SBLDS   Society of Biblical Literature Dissertation Series
SBLMS   Society of Biblical Literature Monograph Series
SBLSP   Society of Biblical Literature Seminar Papers
SBS   Stuttgarter Bibelstudien
SJOT   *Scandinavian Journal of the Old Testament*
SOTSMS   Society for Old Testament Study Monograph Series
SSN   Studia semitica neerlandica
StudBib   Studia Biblica
SubBi   Subsidia Biblica
SWBA   Social World of Biblical Antiquity
TBü   Theologische Bücherei
TDOT   Botterweck, G. J., and H. Ringgren (editors). *Theological Dictionary of
           the Old Testament*. Grand Rapids, Mich.: Eerdmans, 1974–
TLZ   *Theologische Literaturzeitung*

TRev	*Theologische Revue*
TRu	*Theologische Rundschau*
TWAT	Botterweck, G. J., and H. Ringgren (editors). *Theologisches Wörterbuch zum Alten Testament.* Stuttgart: Kohlhammer, 1973–
TynBul	*Tyndale Bulletin*
TZ	*Theologische Zeitschrift*
VT	*Vetus Testamentum*
VTSup	Vetus Testamentum Supplements
WBC	Word Biblical Commentary
WMANT	Wissenschaftliche Monographien zum Alten und Neuen Testament
ZABR	*Zeitschrift für altorientalische und biblische Rechtsgeschichte*
ZAW	*Zeitschrift für die Alttestamentliche Wissenschaft*
ZTK	*Zeitschrift für Theologie und Kirche*

Chapter 1

Basic Questions about the Pentateuch

This first chapter presents the Pentateuch as a whole. First of all, we must ask what the word *Pentateuch* means. Then, we will see why the first five books of the Hebrew Bible form a whole and why this unity is important from the point of view of the revelation and largely differs from the rest of the Old Testament. The hiatus separating the end of Deuteronomy from the beginning of the book of Joshua is not only situated in time. It also marks a transition from the first stage of the history of the revelation to the next.

A. The Origin of the Word *Pentateuch* and Its Usage

In the rabbinic tradition, the *Tôrah* ("Teaching," "Law") comprises the first five books of the Bible, which end with Moses' death (Deuteronomy 34). These five books are called *ḥămišâ ḥumšê hattôrâ*, "the five-fifths of the teaching/law." This Hebrew expression is probably the source of the Greek term *hē pentateuchos (biblos)*. The Greek word *pentateuchos (biblos)*, translated in Latin as *pentateuchus (liber)*, "Pentateuch," is composed of *pente* (five) and *teuchos* (a kind of "instrument," "tool," or "utensil").[1] The latter term first designates the box or cylinder containing the scrolls, and second, by extension, its contents—that is, the "scroll."[2] So, Pentateuch means "five books" or, more specifically, "five scrolls."

The Pentateuch is the first part of the Old Testament and of the Hebrew Bible. It contains the first five books of the Bible: Genesis, Exodus, Leviticus, Numbers, and Deuteronomy. These five titles come from the Greek translation, the Septuagint, reproduced in the Latin Vulgate. The Hebrew titles of these books, in turn, derive from the first significant words of each book: *bĕrē'šît* ("In the Beginning": Genesis), *šĕmôt* ("The Names": Exodus"); *wayyiqrā'* ("And He Called": Leviticus); *bĕmidbar* ("In the Wilderness [of Sinai]": Numbers); *dĕbārîm* ("The Words": Deuteronomy).

---

1. In specific contexts, the Greek noun *teuchos* can have four different meanings: the plural, in Homer: "weapons," "tackle" (sails, ropes, rudders); after Homer: "vase," "container" ("jug," "pitcher," "barrel," "kneading trough," "box," "hive"); "scroll," "book."
2. C. Houtman, *Der Pentateuch* (Contributions to Biblical Exegesis and Theology 9; Kampen, 1994) 1; M. Z. Brettler, "Torah," in *Jewish Study Bible* (ed. A. Berlin and M. Z. Brettler; Oxford, 2004) 1.

1

The word *Pentateuch* appears less frequently in the writings of the Church Fathers,[3] who prefer to talk about "the Law" or "the Law of Moses," in order to distinguish it from the "Prophets," as do Jews and the New Testament.[4] Other ancient writings also mention the "five books" of the Law.[5] One of the first references is perhaps found in the Qumran texts, in a fragment where the expression *kwl [s]prym ḥwmšym* may be translated precisely "all the books of the Pentateuch."[6] A five-part division is also found in the Psalter of the Hebrew Bible: Psalms 1–41, 42–72, 73–89, 90–106, and 107–50. The Psalter was probably designed to be a meditation on the five books of the Torah ("Law"). Psalm 1 certainly leads the way (see Ps 1:2).

The Gospel of Matthew contains five discourses that end with formulas similar to each other (Matt 7:28, 11:1, 13:53, 19:1, 26:1). In fact, for Matthew, Jesus is a "doctor of the Law," and it is not impossible that he wanted his Gospel to be a kind of "New Pentateuch." The first words of this Gospel, *biblos geneseōs* ("book of the genealogy") correspond to the translation of Gen 2:4 and 5:1 in the Septuagint. Likewise, the first words of John's Gospel, *en archēi*, are also the first words of the Greek version of Genesis (LXX) as well as the Greek translation of its Hebrew title *(běrē'šît)*.

Philo of Alexandria (ca. 20 B.C.E.–ca. 50 C.E.), who wrote before the Gospels were set into writing, said that the first of the five books containing the holy laws was called "Genesis" by Moses himself: "Moses, the legislator of the Hebrews, said in the holy books that the world was created and incorruptible; these books are five in number; to the first of them he gave the title 'Genesis.'"[7] Elsewhere, Philo quotes the first verse of Leviticus and calls this book by its name, "Leviticus."[8] Finally, he frequently quotes the book of Deuteronomy but calls it *Protrepticus*, "Exhortation," a title that is also quite appropriate for this book.

---

3. See J.-P. Bouhout and H. Cazelles, "Pentateuque," *DBSup* 7.687–858, especially p. 687 (J.-P. Bouhout). We again encounter the term "Pentateuch" in Origen, *Comm. on John* 2; Epiphanius, *Pan.* 33.4; *Weights and Measures* 4.5; Ptolemy, *Flor.* 4.1 (gnostic author); Athanasius, *Letter to Marcell.* 5. Among the Latin Fathers, we first encounter it in Tertullian, *Against Marcion* 1.10; then in Jerome, *Letter LII to Paulina* 8; *Preface to Joshua*. Finally, in Isidor of Seville, *Etymologies* 6.2.1–2.

4. See Matt 5:17; 7:12; 11:13; 22:40; Luke 16:16; cf. 24:27 ("Moses and the Prophets"); 24:44 ("the Law of Moses, the Prophets, and the Psalms"); Acts 13:15; 24:14; 28:23; Rom 3:21.

5. Concerning this point, see J. Blenkinsopp, *Pentateuch: An Introduction to the First Five Books of the Bible* (ABRL; New York, 1992) 42–44.

6. D. Barthélemy and J. T. Milik, *Qumran Cave I* (DJD 1; Oxford, 1955) 132–33.

7. See Philo of Alexandria, *Aet.* 19; cf. *Opif.* 12; *Post.* 127. Quoted in Blenkinsopp, *Pentateuch*, 44.

8. Philo, *Plant.* 26.

We find the name "Deuteronomy" in the Septuagint, where it is used to translate the Hebrew words *mišnēh hattôrâ hazzōt* (Deut 17:18), "a copy of the Law," which the king must acquire for himself and read daily. Now, the usual translation of this expression would be *deuteros nomos* and not *deuteronomion*. But we can understand the choice of the Septuagint, if we understand that the book was already called "Deuteronomy" at that time.

Toward the end of the first century B.C.E., Josephus clearly mentions "the five books of Moses" in *Against Apion* 1.8.37–41:[9]

> (Seeing that with us it is not open to everybody to write the records, and that there is no discrepancy in what is written; seeing that, on the contrary, the prophets alone had this privilege, obtaining their knowledge of the most remote and ancient history through the inspiration which they owed to God, and committing to writing a clear account of the events of their own time just as they occurred)—it follows, I say, that we do not possess myriads of inconsistent books, conflicting with each other. Our books, those which are justly accredited, are but two and twenty, and contain the record of all time.
>
> Of these, five are the books of Moses, comprising the laws and the traditional history from the birth of man down to the death of the lawgiver. This period falls only a little short of three thousand years. From the death of Moses until Artaxerxes, who succeeded Xerxes as king of Persia, the prophets subsequent to Moses wrote the history of the events of their own times in thirteen books. The remaining four books contain hymns to God and precepts for the conduct of human life.
>
> From Artaxerxes to our own time the complete history has been written, but has not been deemed worthy of equal credit with the earlier records, because of the failure of the exact succession of the prophets.

These witnesses confirm that, around the time of Christ's birth, the Jewish tradition had established this: there are five fundamental books of the Law; they are the work of Moses; and finally, the authority of the five books of Moses is greater than the authority of the books attributed to the prophets.

B. Tetrateuch, Pentateuch, Hexateuch, or Enneateuch?[10]

1. Hexateuch

The age-old tradition limiting the number of the books of the Law to five was questioned in studies concerning the origin of the Pentateuch and the people of Israel. H. Ewald, in his *Geschichte Israels*, proposed that Israel's first

---

9. Josephus, *Against Apion* (trans. H. St. J. Thackeray; LCL; Cambridge: Harvard University Press, 1926) 177–78; cf. Blenkinsopp, *Pentateuch*, 43.

10. Concerning this question, see R. Smend, *Entstehung des Alten Testaments* (Theologische Wissenschaft 1; Stuttgart, 1978) 33–35.

historical work was "the book of the origins" (*Das Buch der Ursprünge*). This work included the Pentateuch and the book of Joshua.[11] The same idea had already been proposed by Bonfrère (1625), Spinoza (1670), and Geddes (1792). After Ewald, it became conventional to unite the book of Joshua and the Pentateuch. This is why the expression *Hexateuch* ("Six Scrolls") came into use, replacing *Pentateuch*. The classic work by Wellhausen, for example, is entitled *Die Composition des Hexateuchs und der historischen Bücher des Alten Testaments* ("The Composition of the Hexateuch and of the Historical Books of the Old Testament").[12]

The famous exegete G. von Rad also speaks of a Hexateuch in his fundamental study *The Problem of the Hexateuch*.[13] For von Rad, the core of the traditions concerning Israel's origins is to be found in Israel's "small historical creed": for example, in Deut 6:21–23 and especially in Deut 26:5–9; also see Josh 24:2–13. Now, this "creed" ends with the mention of the gift of the land. For this reason, von Rad concludes that one should not speak of a Pentateuch but of a Hexateuch, because the tradition of Israel's history must end with the account of the conquest, which is found in the book of Joshua, the sixth book of the Hebrew Bible.

2. Tetrateuch

Von Rad's idea was challenged by one of his own students, Martin Noth, in his famous work *A History of Pentateuchal Traditions*.[14] The term *Tetrateuch* ("Four Scrolls") originated with Noth's work, because it excluded the book of Deuteronomy from the Pentateuch. His thesis is based on three observations:[15]

1. No "Deuteronomic" texts are found in the first four books of the Bible, with the exception of some minor additions. There is, then, no literary bond reaching from the unit Genesis–Numbers, on the one hand, to Deuteronomy, on the other.

2. The sources of the Pentateuch do not figure in the book of Joshua. In other words, the narratives that begin in Genesis–Numbers are not continued in the book of Joshua. This makes it difficult to talk about a Hexateuch.[16]

---

11. H. Ewald, *Die Geschichte des Volkes Israel* (2 vols.; 3rd ed.; Göttingen, 1864) 1.94. For the English translation, see the bibliography at the end of this volume.

12. J. Wellhausen, *Die Composition des Hexateuchs und der historischen Bücher des Alten Testaments* (Berlin, 1866; 3rd ed., 1899).

13. G. von Rad, *The Problem of the Hexateuch and Other Essays* (New York, 1966) 1–78.

14. M. Noth, *A History of Pentateuchal Traditions* (Englewood Cliffs, NJ, 1972; repr. Chico, CA, 1981).

15. Ibid., 6; cf. S. Mowinckel, *Tetrateuch—Pentateuch—Hexateuch: Die Berichte über die Landnahme in der drei altisraelitischen Geschichtswerken* (BZAW 90; Berlin, 1964) 3.

16. Noth, *History of Pentateuchal Traditions*, 6; cf. idem, *Das Buch Josua* (HAT 1/7; Tübingen, 1938) xiii–xiv.

3. Deuteronomy is the preface to the "Deuteronomistic History" (Joshua–2 Kings). The "Deuteronomic Code" is preceded by a short summary of Israel's history (Deuteronomy 1–3), which repeats what the reader has already learned from the book of Numbers. This repetition can only be understood if Deuteronomy was intended to introduce a work that continues in the historical books, that is, Joshua–2 Kings. Deuteronomy 1–3 would indeed be meaningless if Deuteronomy were the conclusion of a work containing the book of Numbers.

The Deuteronomistic History should be read "in the light of Deuteronomy." For example, Joshua was able to conquer the land because he was faithful to the "Law of Moses" (Josh 1:7–8, 23:6). The Lord punished the unfaithful people by allowing them to lose the land (2 Kgs 17:7–23; especially 17:13, 19). The "Deuteronomistic History" is, to a large extent, the story of Israel's faithfulness and unfaithfulness to the Law of Moses contained in Deuteronomy.

For Noth, the Pentateuch came into existence when the two units Genesis–Numbers, on the one hand, and Deuteronomy—with its Deuteronomistic History—on the other, were brought together to form one great work. At that moment, Deuteronomy became the conclusion of the Pentateuch, and so it became necessary to separate it from the book of Joshua and from the rest of the Deuteronomistic History. However, Noth did not go so far as to assert the existence of a "Tetrateuch" because, in his view, the ancient sources as well as the current books of Genesis–Numbers require a continuation, that is, an account of the Conquest. The Swedish exegete Engnell was to take the decisive step by speaking in favor of the existence of an independent Tetrateuch.[17] According to Engell, the current Tetrateuch, that is, Genesis–Exodus–Leviticus–Numbers, is the work of P (Priestly Writer), who collected and compiled ancient oral traditions. The primitive Deuteronomy (Dt) and the Deuteronomistic History should be distinguished from this Priestly Tetrateuch.[18] Unfortunately, Engnell was content with proposing his thesis and did not develop complete arguments to support it.

3. Enneateuch

a. The Thesis

Some exegetes think that the section Genesis–2 Kings should be seen as a single literary work that begins with the Creation of the world and ends with

---

17. I. Engnell, *Gamla Testamentet: En tradistionshistorisk inledning* (Stockholm, 1945) 209–12; idem, "The Pentateuch," *A Rigid Scrutiny* (Nashville, 1969) = *Critical Essays on the Old Testament* (Nashville, 1969) 50–67.

18. Cf. Mowinckel, *Tetrateuch*, 3–4.

the Exile in Babylonia.[19] The central theme of this story is the land. At the beginning, YHWH promises it to the patriarchs; in Exodus and Numbers, Israel travels toward it through the wilderness; Joshua conquers it; the judges defend it; under David and Solomon, it becomes a kingdom that is at first united and then is divided into North and South; finally, at the moment of the Exile in Babylonia, Israel loses this land.

According to D. N. Freedman, this long account is Israel's "Primary History."[20] This "Primary History" needs to be differentiated from the "History of the Chronicler," which is composed of 1–2 Chronicles and Ezra–Nehemiah. The second historical account, by the Chronicler, sums up in a very sweeping way the story of the origins from the Creation to David and then centers its attention on David's reign and on the reigns of his son Solomon and their successors. The books of Ezra and Nehemiah describe the reconstitution of Israel's community after the Exile.

The "Primary History" ends with the destruction of the temple and the Exile; the "History of the Chronicler" culminates with the reconstruction of the temple and the Postexilic community.

b. The Arguments

• Some exegetes think that "Israel's history" does not end with the conquest of the land. For example, Judg 2:8, 10 is connected to Exod 1:6, 8:[21]

Exodus 1: [6]Then Joseph died, and all his brothers, and that whole generation. [. . .] [8]Now a new king arose over Egypt, who did not know Joseph.

Judges 2: [8]Joshua son of Nun, the servant of YHWH, died at the age of one hundred ten years. [. . .] [10]Moreover, that whole generation was gathered to their ancestors, and another generation grew up after them, who did not know YHWH or the work that he had done for Israel.[22]

These literary "brackets" create ties between the different narrative blocks and also mark the transition from one period of Israel's history to another. Exod 1:6, 8 marks the transition from the age of the patriarchs to the age of the Exodus, and Judg 2:8, 10 the shift from Joshua's time to the time of the Judges (see Josh 24:29, 31).

---

19. "Enneateuch" means "nine scrolls": Genesis, Exodus, Leviticus, Numbers, Deuteronomy, Joshua, Judges, 1–2 Samuel, 1–2 Kings. In the Hebrew Bible, the book of Ruth is one of the "Writings"; the two books of Samuel are considered to be a single work; this is also the case with the two books of Kings.

20. D. N. Freedman, "Pentateuch," *IDB* 3.712–13.

21. Blenkinsopp (*Pentateuch*, 36–37) follows R. Rendtorff, *Das überlieferungsgeschtliche Problem des Pentateuch* (BZAW 147; Berlin, 1977) 166–69.

22. See Josh 24:29, 31.

• The chronology of the books provides another indication of this global vision of Israel's history. For example, according to Exod 12:40–41, Israel lived in Egypt for 430 years (Gen 15:13: 400 years). Solomon began to build the temple 480 years after the Exodus (1 Kgs 6:1), that is, 430 + 50. Now, if we count the years from this date on, that is, from the fourth year of Solomon's reign until the end of the Kingdom of Judah, we again come up with 430 years.[23] By adding the 50 years of exile, the sum is once again 480 years. In order to reach this number, it is necessary to calculate the information given in 1–2 Kings without any corrections.

There are other analogous facts. For example, according to the chronology of the Priestly Writer, the Exodus took place 2,666 years after the Creation of the world. This number of years is equivalent to 2/3 of 4,000 years, a number that is probably symbolic. The year 4,000 could correspond to the purification and the new dedication of the temple by the Maccabees (164 B.C.E.).[24] However, I must add that this information is far from univocal. Moreover, is chronology alone sufficient to establish that the Pentateuch is a unified history?

• Blenkinsopp gives three reasons for asserting that the Pentateuch cannot end with Moses' death (Deuteronomy 34):[25]

1. Without the book of Joshua, the promise of the land made to the patriarchs remains unfulfilled.[26] Furthermore, Josh 21:43–45 considers the Conquest to be the fulfillment of a promise made much earlier to Israel's "ancestors":

> Thus YHWH gave to Israel all the land that he swore to their ancestors that he would give them; and having taken possession of it, they settled there. And YHWH gave them rest on every side just as he had sworn to their ancestors; not one of all their enemies had withstood them, for YHWH had given all their enemies into their hands. Not one of all the good promises that YHWH had made to the house of Israel had failed; all came to pass.

2. There are correspondences between the work of Creation (Genesis 1), the construction of the sanctuary in the wilderness (Exodus 35–40), and the installation of the sanctuary in the Promised Land (Joshua 18–19). Finally, Solomon's temple was built 480 years after the Exodus (1 Kgs 6:1).

3. A major theme in Israel's history is that of faithfulness to the Covenant and the Law. According to the Deuteronomistic History, the people are exiled because of their unfaithfulness. Now, this theme already appears in Genesis 2–3 with a universal sense. The Garden of Eden corresponds to the land, the

---

23. Blenkinsopp, *Pentateuch*, 48.

24. Ibid. For other data, see pp. 47–50.

25. Ibid., 34–35.

26. Otherwise, it would be necessary to speak of a "partial realization of the promise" or of a "deferral of the promise." Cf. D. J. A. Clines, *The Theme of the Pentateuch* (JSOTSup 10; Sheffield, 1978).

commandment not to eat of the fruit of the tree of the knowledge of good and evil corresponds to the Law of Moses, and the expulsion of Adam and Eve from the Garden after the fall corresponds to the Exile.[27]

However, these arguments are not totally convincing. The vocabulary in Josh 21:43–45 is typically Deuteronomistic and is only found in certain late texts, for example in Gen 15:7, 18; 26:3:

> 15:7: [YHWH said to Abraham:] "I am YHWH who brought you from Ur of the Chaldeans, to give you this land to possess."

> 15:18: On that day YHWH made a covenant with Abram, saying, "To your descendants I give this land."

> 26:3: [YHWH said to Isaac:] "to you and to your descendants I will give all these lands, and I will fulfill the oath that I swore to your father Abraham."

However, there is discussion today about whether the "fathers" are the patriarchs or the Israelites in Egypt.[28] Moreover, the promises evoked by Josh 21:44 do not figure in Genesis but in Deut 12:10b, 25:19, where the expression "give rest from all enemies on every hand" appears, just as it does in Josh 21:44. In these last two texts, the promise is made to the exiled people, not to the patriarchs. If there is a connection, it is vague and, in any case, late.

The congruence of Genesis 1 and Exodus 24–25, 39–40 is well known.[29] For example, the structure of the week in Gen 1:1–2, 4a reappears in Exod 24:16. However, this theme does not appear in Josh 18:1; 19:51. The analogies between Genesis 2–3 and the theme of the land in Joshua are barely perceptible. The vocabulary is different and the Deuteronomistic History does not refer explicitly to the history of Genesis. Furthermore, Genesis 2–3 contains no clear references to the theology of Covenant. In Gen 2:16–17, the punishment pending for those who do not observe the commandment is not expulsion from the Garden but death (2:17b). Finally, Genesis 2–3 itself is quite likely a relatively late text.[30]

---

27. See L. Alonso Schökel, "Motivos sapienciales y de alianza en Gen 2–3," *Bib* 43 (1962) 295–316; N. Lohfink, "Die Erzählung vom Sündenfall," *Das Siegeslied am Schilfmeer: Christliche Auseinandersetzung mit dem Alten Testament* (Frankfurt, 1965) 81–101.

28. T. Römer, *Israels Väter: Untersuchungen zur Väterthematik in Deuteronomium und in der deuteronomistischen Tradition* (OBO 99; Fribourg and Göttingen, 1990); on Josh 21:43–45, see pp. 358–63; N. Lohfink, *Die Väter Israels im Deuteronomium: Mit einer Stellungnahme von Thomas Römer* (OBO 111; Fribourg and Göttingen, 1991); on Josh 21:43–45, see pp. 81–85.

29. See, for example, P. J. Kearney, "Creation and Liturgy: The P Redaction of Exod 25–40," *ZAW* 89 (1977) 375–87.

30. See, for example, E. Otto, "Die Paradieserzählung Genesis 2–3: Eine nachpriesterschriftliche Lehrerzählung in ihrem religionshistorischen Kontext," in *"Jedes Ding hat seine Zeit . . .": Studien zur israelitischen und altorientalischen Weisheit—Diethelm Michel zum 65. Geburtstag* (ed. A. A. Diesel et al.; BZAW 241; Berlin, 1996) 167–92.

To conclude, it is necessary to clarify the situation and to define more closely the object of the discussion. Although, from a canonical viewpoint, we may talk about the "Enneateuch" or "Primary History," it is not possible from a literary viewpoint. A critical study of these different books reveals, for example, connections between Deuteronomy and Joshua, or between Deuteronomy and 1–2 Kings. However, no literary activity has assembled in an organic unit the books containing the "Primary History" of Israel, that is, Genesis–2 Kings. These connections remain on the thematic level and have no real influence on the literary structuring of the different books.

C. Moses, the Pentateuch, and the Canon of the Hebrew Bible [31]

There are good reasons to continue talking about the "Pentateuch." Of course, as we shall see further on, this way of organizing the books of the Old Testament does not exclude other possibilities. But it does have special merit because it takes into account the definitive and normative canonical form of the Bible for the faith community—first of all, the people of Israel and, then, the Christian churches. [32]

1. The Pentateuch: Deut 34:10–12

With regard to the Pentateuch, there is a fundamental text that marks the "dividing line" and permits us to distinguish the first five books of the Bible from those that follow (Joshua–2 Kings). This text is Deut 34:10–12: [33]

> Never since has there arisen a prophet in Israel like Moses, whom YHWH knew face to face. He was unequaled for all the signs and wonders that YHWH sent him

31. In this section, we are following, with some minor changes, E. Zenger (ed.), *Einleitung in das Alte Testament* (Studienbücher Theologie 1/1; 4th ed.; Stuttgart, 2004) 24–26.

32. Concerning the question of the canon, see J. A. Sanders, *Torah and Canon* (Philadelphia, 1972); idem, "Adaptable for Life: The Nature and Function of Canon," in *Magnalia Dei: Essays on the Bible and Archeology in Memory of G. Ernest Wright* (Garden City, NY, 1976) 531–60; B. S. Childs, *Introduction to the Old Testament as Scripture* (Philadelphia, 1979). For his method, see P. R. Noble, *The Canonical Approach: A Critical Reconstruction of the Hermeneutics of Brevard S. Childs* (Biblical Interpretation Series 16; Leiden, 1995).

33. On this text, see F. García López, "De la antigua a la nueva crítica literaria del Pentateuco," *EstBib* 52 (1994) 7–35, esp. 25–35; idem, "Deut 34, Dtr History and the Pentateuch," in *Studies in Deuteronomy: In Honour of C. J. Labuschagne, on the Occasion of His 65th Birthday* (VTSup 53; Leiden, 1994) 47–61; C. Dohmen and M. Oeming, *Biblischer Kanon: Warum und wozu?* (Quaestiones disputatae 137; Freiburg-im-Breisgau, 1992); T. C. Römer and M. Z. Brettler, "Deuteronomy 34 and the Case for a Persian Hexateuch," *JBL* 119 (2000) 401–19; J. H. Tigay, "The Significance of the End of Deuteronomy (Deuteronomy 34:10–12)," in *Texts, Temples, and Traditions: A Tribute to Menahem Haran* (ed. M. V. Fox et al.; Winona Lake, IN, 1996) 137–43.

to perform in the land of Egypt, against Pharaoh and all his servants and his entire
land, and for all the mighty deeds and all the terrifying displays of power that
Moses performed in the sight of all Israel.

Three important things are asserted here:

1. Moses is greater than the other prophets. This is why the "Mosaic Law"
is superior to all other forms of revelation. His Torah is incomparable and its
value is permanent. In other words, the revelation through Moses is superior to
all other revelation attributed to the prophets. Because of this, Moses comes
before the "Former Prophets" (Joshua–2 Kings) and the "Latter Prophets"
(Isaiah–Malachi) in the canon. For the same reason, he also precedes the
"Writings," or Books of Wisdom. The authority of the Pentateuch in the final
analysis depends on the greater authority of Moses.[34]

2. Moses' superiority also comes from the preeminence of his relationship
to YHWH (see Exod 33:11, Num 12:6–8; cf. John 1:18, 3:11).[35] YHWH and
Moses were in "direct contact," without an intermediary or a "screen" (as in
dreams or visions; cf. Num 12:6–8).

3. The Exodus is the foundational event of Israel's history. No other event
can be compared with it. The institution of Israel therefore goes back to Moses,
not to David or Solomon. Israel is in fact older than the Monarchy or even than
the Conquest of the Promised Land.

2. The Second Part of the Hebrew Bible: The Former and Latter Prophets

a. Joshua 1:1–8

Josh 1:1–8 clearly ties the figure and work of Joshua to the figure and work
of Moses:

[1]After the death of Moses the servant of YHWH, YHWH spoke to Joshua son of
Nun, Moses' assistant, saying, [2]"My servant Moses is dead. Now proceed to cross
the Jordan, you and all this people, into the land that I am giving to them, to the
Israelites. [3]Every place that the sole of your foot will tread upon I have given to
you, as I promised to Moses. [4]From the wilderness and the Lebanon as far as the
great river, the river Euphrates, all the land of the Hittites, to the Great Sea in the
west shall be your territory. [5]No one shall be able to stand against you all the days
of your life. As I was with Moses, so I will be with you; I will not fail you or forsake you. [6]Be strong and courageous; for you shall put this people in possession
of the land that I swore to their ancestors to give them. [7]Only be strong and very

---

34. B. S. Childs, *Introduction to the Old Testament as Scripture* (Philadelphia, 1979) 134–35.

35. For the figure of Moses in the NT, see, among others, D. C. Allison, *The New Moses:
A Matthean Typology* (Minneapolis, 1993); M.-E. Boismard, *Moïse ou Jésus: Essais de Christologie Johannique* (BETL 84; Leuven, 1988).

courageous, being careful to act in accordance with all the law that my servant Moses commanded you; do not turn from it to the right hand or to the left, so that you may be successful wherever you go. [8]This book of the law shall not depart out of your mouth; you shall meditate on it day and night, so that you may be careful to act in accordance with all that is written in it. For then you shall make your way prosperous, and then you shall be successful.

In this text we encounter at least four basic assertions about the book of Joshua and the books of the Former and Latter Prophets:

• Joshua is Moses' successor. He has the task of conquering the land promised to the fathers.

• Moses is YHWH's servant (*ʿebed yhwh*); Joshua has a different designation: he is "Moses' minister" (*mĕšārēt mōšeh*). While Moses defines himself on the basis of his relationship with YHWH, Joshua is defined in relation to Moses. We are at another stage of the "revelation" and of relations with YHWH. In other words, Joshua is the successor of Moses, but he does not replace him as "YHWH's servant."

• There is continuity between Joshua and Moses: YHWH will be with Joshua as he was with Moses (v. 5). YHWH will fulfill the promise made to Moses by giving Israel possession of the land (v. 3). But this means that Moses, not Joshua, is the beginning and the foundation of Israel.

• Joshua's success depends on his faithfulness to the "Mosaic Law" (vv. 7–8). This law is "written" (*hakkātûb*; v. 8) in a "book" (*sēper*; v. 7). Henceforth, this book will be the cornerstone of the whole enterprise of Israel's history. It will also be the criterion for judging this history. Israel's history will be the history of the people's faithfulness or unfaithfulness to the Law/Teaching of Moses.[36]

b. Malachi 3:22–24

The conclusion of the prophetic books (Mal 3:22–24) contains a series of similar assertions:

Remember the teaching of my servant Moses, the statutes and ordinances that I commanded him at Horeb for all Israel. Lo, I will send you the prophet Elijah before the great and terrible day of YHWH comes. He will turn the hearts of parents to their children and the hearts of children to their parents, so that I will not come and strike the land with a curse.

This text closes the prophetic books (*nĕbîʾîm*) like an inclusio. There are four essential elements to the relationship between the prophetic books and the Law of Moses (the Pentateuch):

---

36. See 1 Kgs 17:7–23, especially 17:13–16, which explains the end of the Northern Kingdom on the basis of this principle: unfaithfulness to the Law caused the downfall of the Kingdom of Samaria.

- The prophets should be read with "reference" to the Law of Moses. According to this "canonical" interpretation of the Bible, prophecy fulfills the Law and keeps it alive in Israel's memory.
- The Law of Moses is a divine law. Its authority is not of human origin. In more modern terms: the Mosaic Law is the product of revelation, not of human reason.
- This Law is found, above all, in Deuteronomy. In this book, YHWH appears on Mount Horeb, not on Mount Sinai. We see this, for example, in Deut 5:2 and in Exod 19:1. The expression "statutes and ordinances" is typically Deuteronomic (see Deut 5:1, 11:32, 12:1, 26:16).
- Of all the prophets, Elijah alone is mentioned, because he most resembles Moses. Like Moses, Elijah went to Horeb (1 Kings 19) and heard God in the cave (cf. Exod 33:22: "the cleft of the rock"). See also "forty days and forty nights" in Exod 24:18, 34:28; Deut 9:9; and 1 Kgs 19:8.[37]

3. The Third Part of the Hebrew Bible: "The Writings" (kĕtûbîm)

a. Psalm 1

The first psalm, which introduces the entire third part of the Hebrew Bible, also mentions the Law/Teaching:

> [1] Happy are those who do not follow the advice of the wicked, or take the path that sinners tread, or sit in the seat of scoffers;
> [2] but their delight is in the law of YHWH, and on his law they meditate day and night.
> [3] [. . .] In all that they do, they prosper.

Some of the assertions of this psalm aim at situating the Psalter and the Writings in relationship to the Law:

- The criterion that distinguishes the righteous man from the impious one is meditation on the Law. The Law also constitutes the criterion for judgment (Ps 1:5−6). This psalm applies to the individual what the "Former Prophets" said about the people.
- The Law is called "Law of YHWH" (tôrat yhwh).
- Psalm 1 is an invitation to read all the Psalms and all the "Writings" as a meditation on YHWH's Law.[38]

---

37. This is why Moses and Elijah appear together in the scene of Jesus' Transfiguration (Matt 17:3 and parallels).

38. There are many similarities between Psalm 1 and Josh 1:1−8, such as the expressions "meditate on the law day and night" and "prosper in all you do." Both texts have an undeniable Deuteronomistic flavor.

b. 2 Chronicles 36:22–23

The conclusion of the Hebrew Bible, which coincides with the conclusion of the "Writings," is situated in many manuscripts in 2 Chr 36:22–23. This text provides an additional key for understanding the sense of the Bible according to the Hebrew canon:

> ²²In the first year of King Cyrus of Persia, in fulfillment of the word of YHWH spoken by Jeremiah, YHWH stirred up the spirit of King Cyrus of Persia so that he sent a herald throughout all his kingdom and also declared in a written edict: ²³"Thus says King Cyrus of Persia: YHWH, the God of heaven, has given me all the kingdoms of the earth, and he has charged me to build him a house at Jerusalem, which is in Judah. Whoever is among you of all his people, may YHWH his God be with him! Let him go up."

We can make three important observations about this text:

1. Here, Moses and the Law/Teaching are no longer mentioned but, rather, Jeremiah and Jerusalem. The Hebrew Bible closes with an invitation to "go up" (*wĕyāʿal*). This verb may contain an allusion to the Exodus, given that the expression used to describe the departure from Egypt contains this same verb, "go up" (*ʿlh*, Hiphil; cf. Exod 3:8).

2. The temple of Jerusalem as such is not mentioned in the Pentateuch. However, texts such as Exodus 25–31, 35–40, the ritual prescriptions of Leviticus, and the Law concerning the centralization of the cult in Deuteronomy 12 are to be read in association with the temple.

3. In any case, among the last books of the Hebrew Bible we find the books of Ezra and Nehemiah, which in an earlier period probably were located after the books of the Chronicles. The order 1–2 Chronicles–Ezra–Nehemiah best reflects the chronology of the events. Now, the books of Ezra and Nehemiah reach a climax with the solemn proclamation of the "Mosaic Law" before the people (Nehemiah 8; cf. 8:1). This Law becomes the cornerstone of the whole Postexilic community. It is difficult to imagine the temple without reference to the Law and the ritual prescriptions contained in the Pentateuch. In the most sacred part of the temple, the Holy of Holies, we find the ark, and the ark contains only one object: the two tablets that YHWH gave to Moses on Horeb (2 Chr 5:10). The "Law" is at the heart of the temple, and worship is performed there according to the prescriptions of the Mosaic Law (2 Chr 8:13). We also find many references to the Law of Moses in the books of Ezra and Nehemiah (Ezra 3:2; 6:8; 7:6; Neh 1:7, 8; 8:1, 14; 9:14; 10:30; 13:1).

The Hebrew canon concludes with a call to all the Hebrews of the diaspora, inviting them to return to Jerusalem to help rebuild the temple. This invitation requires a response that each reader of the Bible must write with his or her own life. In the Hebrew canon, the Bible has a structure that opens out onto the future. The last verb is jussive, that is, a form of imperative, not an indicative.

4. Conclusion

From these observations we can draw some key conclusions about reading the Pentateuch within the canon of the Hebrew Bible:

• The texts that have been presented and that frame the three main sections of the Hebrew Bible are important because of their contents and especially because of their position at strategic points of the Bible. The division brings out the unique position of the "Law," which according to biblical tradition bears the mark of Moses' exceptional personality. The Pentateuch is unique because Moses occupies a unique place in the history of revelation.

• The five books of the Pentateuch therefore have a "normative" character that the other biblical texts do not have.[39]

• Moreover, the Pentateuch largely appears to be the "life of Moses," from his birth in Exodus 2 to his death in Deuteronomy 34. However, this is essentially a "life of Moses in the service of YHWH and of the people." Genesis, which precedes this "life of Moses," describes the origin of the world (Genesis 1–11) and the origin of Israel as a people (12–50).[40]

• From a canonical point of view, this particular grouping of the books is more important than others. Likewise, the connections between Deuteronomy and Moses are more important than the ties linking Deuteronomy to the Deuteronomistic History. This fact raises serious problems with regard to the Promised Land, which essentially remains outside the Pentateuch. The Promised Land, and not the possession of it, constitutes a fundamental element of Israel's faith. In other words, according to the Pentateuch, it is possible to belong to the people of Israel without living in the Promised Land. This sort of assertion is more understandable after the experience of the Exile and at the time of the diaspora.[41]

• Another element should be emphasized. According to the canon of the Hebrew Scriptures, the Monarchy is subordinate to the Law. While the Mosaic institutions are central to Israel's existence, the people can do without the Monarchy. This truth grows out of the hard, tragic experience of the Exile. At that moment, Israel discovered itself older than David or even than Joshua's Conquest. Israel began to exist as a people much earlier, when the Lord brought them out of Egypt, the house of slavery.

• In order to rediscover the oldest traces of its ancestors, Israel must go even further back, to the patriarchs, Abraham, Isaac, and Jacob. To them the Lord

---

39. Blenkinsopp, *Pentateuch*, 51–52.

40. See Blenkinsopp, *Pentateuch*, 52; Zenger (ed.), *Einleitung*, 36, and many others.

41. On this point, see Sanders, *Torah and Canon*; summary in Childs, *Introduction*, 131–32.

promised the land that Moses contemplated before he died, unable to enter there (Deut 34:1–4). The Pentateuch contains two elements that are absolutely indispensable for defining the identity of Israel: the patriarchs and Moses. Israel is the people that descends from the patriarchs and that has lived through the experience of the Exodus under Moses' guidance.

From a theological point of view, the two key elements are the promises made to the ancestors and the related terms Exodus/Law (cf. Exod 20:2–3). Israel's Lord defines himself as the "God of Abraham, of Isaac and of Jacob" (Exod 3:6) and as the "Lord who brought [Israel] out of Egypt, the house of slavery" (Exod 20:2). These two assertions constitute the two main pillars that support the entire Pentateuch, setting aside the history of origins (Genesis 1– 11). The first chapter of Genesis adds another element: the God of the patriarchs and the God of the Exodus is also the Creator of the universe.

The structure of the Pentateuch and the organization of the Hebrew canon are essential for understanding the New Testament. Jesus' public life, in the four Gospels, begins on the banks of the river Jordan, where John the Baptist was baptizing. What is the reason for this scene? Anyone who has read the Pentateuch will immediately find the answer to this question. Moses arrived at the Jordan with the people and he died without having been able to cross this last boundary. So, his work was left unfinished. The conclusion of the Pentateuch is an opening in the direction of the land that Moses contemplated. Joshua achieves the work that had been begun.

When Jesus appears in the Gospels, his mission is similar: he proclaims the coming of the "kingdom," that is, the moment when Israel may finally take possession of its land. The beginning of the New Testament presents itself as the achievement of Moses' unfinished work. Jesus is another Joshua. In fact, the two names are identical: Joshua is the Hebrew form and Jesus the Aramaic form. John 5, which tells of the healing of the paralytic at the pool of Bethesda, alludes to this theme when Jesus says: "Moses spoke about me" (5:46). Moses announced that YHWH would choose Joshua to accomplish the promise made to the patriarchs to give the land to the people.[42] According to John 5, Jesus is the announced Joshua. This is why the Gospels begin on the banks of the Jordan, where the people are still assembled in Deuteronomy 34 when the curtain falls on the Pentateuch and on Moses.[43]

---

42. See J.-L. Ska, "Dal Nuovo all'Antico Testamento," *Civiltà cattolica* 147/2 (1996) 14–23, especially pp. 20–23; idem, "Il canone ebraico e il canone cristiano dell'Antico Testamento," *Civiltà cattolica* 148/3 (1997) 213–25.

43. The prophetic books end with the proclamation of the return of Elijah, who is identified by the New Testament with John the Baptist (Mal 3:23–24; cf. Luke 1:17; Matt 11:14, 17:12–13). Moreover, Jesus' arrival gives an opportunity to respond to Cyrus's invitation in 2 Chr 36:23. See John 2:10: Jesus is the new temple (cf. 4:21–24), and he will gather together all of God's dispersed children (John 10:16, 11:51–52).

Chapter 2

The Five Books of the Pentateuch: Content and Structure

How and why was the Pentateuch divided into five books? Was this division purely physical, or did it have significance? This is the first question I treat in the present chapter. I then consider how these "five-fifths of the Law/Teaching" (*ḥămîšâ ḥûmšê hattôrâ*) are structured.

A. The Division into Five Books

1. The Physical Reasons[1]

The five books of the Pentateuch vary in length. The shortest book is Leviticus (25 chapters, 859 verses, 11,950 words, 51 pages in BHS) and the longest is Genesis (50 chapters, 1,534 verses, 85 pages in BHS). The books of Exodus and Numbers are approximately the same length. Exodus has 40 chapters, 1,209 verses and 16,713 words, 71 pages in BHS, while Numbers has 36 chapters, 1,288 verses (but many of the verses are very short, such as Num 1:2, 7, 26, 29, 33), 16,413 words, and 74 pages in BHS. Deuteronomy is slightly longer than Leviticus (34 chapters, 955 verses, 71 pages in BHS, but the critical apparatus is more voluminous than in the other books). In all, the Pentateuch has 5,845 verses (353 pages in BHS). In the edition without notes, the count is as follows: 88 pages for Genesis, 73 pages for Exodus, 52 pages for Leviticus, 73 pages for Numbers (as for Exodus), 64 pages for Deuteronomy.

There are authors who maintain that it would have been physically difficult to write the entire Pentateuch on one scroll. The scroll would have had to be approximately 33 meters long. This was of course not completely impossible, because it is said that the complete works of Homer (*Iliad* and *Odyssey*) were written on a single scroll measuring 50 meters. However, a long scroll would not have been practical for reading at home or in the synagogue. At Qumran, the longest scrolls are the *Temple Scroll*, which measures 8.75 m, and 1QIsa (the *Great Isaiah Scroll*), which is 7.35 m long. The average length of the scrolls of the Pentateuch was probably between 6 and 7 meters.

---

1. I am following Blenkinsopp, *Pentateuch*, 45–47.

The division between the different books seems totally arbitrary and artificial. For example, Jacob's family settled in Egypt in Genesis 46, but the book of Exodus begins further on. The Sinai pericope begins in Exodus 19 and ends in Num 10:10. So, it covers a whole book (Leviticus) and parts of two others (Exodus and Numbers) but does not correspond to any particular division. The Israelites arrive on the plains of Moab in Num 21:20, where they stay until Moses' death. But the division between Numbers and Deuteronomy does not correspond to that moment.

2. The Theological Criteria[2]

What then were the criteria for the partitioning of the five books?

a. Genesis

The book of Genesis begins with the Creation of the world and the well-known expression *běrē'šît bārā' 'ĕlōhîm* (*"in the beginning God created . . ."*),[3] and it ends with the deaths of Jacob and Joseph. This is the conclusion of the patriarchal period, that is, the family history of Israel's ancestors. From here on, Israel is no longer a family but a people. Furthermore, before dying, Joseph announces the return of his descendants to the land promised to Abraham, Isaac, and Jacob (Gen 50:24). So the conclusion of Genesis prepares for the future and ties Genesis to Exodus–Deuteronomy. In the language of narrative analysis, Gen 50:24 contains a "proleptic summary" of the later account.

b. Exodus

The book of Exodus starts with a review of the Joseph story, which provides a link between "the history of the patriarchs" and "the history of the people of Israel" (Exod 1:1–7). Exod 1:8, "Now a new king arose over Egypt, who did not know Joseph," marks the transition from one period of Israel's history to another. The conclusion of the book of Exodus (40:34–38) describes the moment when, after much wandering, the "glory of YHWH" enters and fills the "tent of meeting." This moment is important because from now on YHWH resides in the midst of his people (40:34–35), so that he can accompany and guide them (40:36–38).

c. Leviticus

The beginning of the book of Leviticus alludes to this filling and residence: "YHWH summoned Moses and spoke to him from the tent of meeting,

---

2. See, among others, Childs, *Introduction*, 128–30; Zenger (ed.), *Einleitung*, 34–36.

3. The translation of Gen 1:1 has been discussed, for example, by G. J. Wenham, *Genesis 1–15* (WBC 1; Waco, TX, 1987) 11–13.

saying. . . ." From this moment on, Yʜᴡʜ speaks to Moses from the tent of meeting and no longer from the summit of Mount Sinai (cf. Exod 19:3). The original conclusion of the book of Leviticus was Lev 26:46: "These are the statutes and ordinances and laws that Yʜᴡʜ established between himself and the people of Israel on Mount Sinai through Moses." This is without doubt a "concluding summary," which follows a chapter of blessings and maledictions (Lev 26:3, 14). Leviticus 27 is a later addition, and the last verse of this chapter repeats the conclusion of 26:46: "These are the commandments that Yʜᴡʜ gave to Moses for the people of Israel on Mount Sinai." Both conclusions indicate Mount Sinai as the site of the revelation. For Israel's tradition, the Laws promulgated by Yʜᴡʜ on Mount Sinai and transmitted by Moses have unique normative value. These assertions are therefore very important, because they make a distinction between the Laws that are incorporated in the "Mosaic canon" and the others.

d. Numbers

The book of Numbers also has its own introduction and its own conclusion. The introduction is similar to the introduction of Leviticus (Num 1:1; cf. Lev 1:1): "Yʜᴡʜ spoke to Moses in the wilderness of Sinai, in the tent of meeting, on the first day of the second month, in the second year after they had come out of the land of Egypt." We are still in the wilderness of Sinai, and Yʜᴡʜ continues to speak from the tent of meeting (cf. Exod 40:34–35; Lev 1:1). The conclusion of the book of Numbers recalls Lev 26:46 and 27:34: "These are the commandments and the ordinances that Yʜᴡʜ gave through Moses to the Israelites in the plains of Moab by the river Jordan at Jericho" (Num 36:13). Between the introduction and the conclusion, the people are led from Mount Sinai into the plains of Moab, where they prepare themselves to enter the Promised Land. The laws promulgated in the plains of Moab also have a special canonical value. Deut 28:69 even mentions another covenant that Yʜᴡʜ concludes here with Israel (subsequent to the Covenant made on Mount Horeb). These assertions create a parity between the Laws of Moab and those of Horeb/ Sinai.[4]

e. Deuteronomy

Deuteronomy has its own setting. Like the book of Numbers, it begins with a formula indicating the place from which Moses spoke (Deut 1:1–3): "These

---

4. Concerning the covenant on the plains of Moab, see N. Lohfink, "Der Bundesschluß im Lande Moab: Redaktionsgeschichtliches zu Dt 28,69–32,47," *BZ* n.s. 6 (1962) 32–56 (= *Studien zum Deuteronomium und zur deuteronomistischen Literatur* [Stuttgarter biblische Aufsatzbände 8; Stuttgart, 1990] 53–82); idem, "Bund als Vertrag im Deuteronomium," *ZAW* 107 (1995) 215–39.

are the words that Moses spoke to all Israel beyond the Jordan—in the wilderness . . . in the fortieth year, on the first day of the eleventh month." All Moses' discourses are pronounced on the same day, and on that day Moses dies (Deut 32:38; 34:5). Then, after Moses' death, Deuteronomy ends and so does the Pentateuch (34:1–12).

3. Conclusion

The five books of the Pentateuch are clearly divided by linguistic and structural markers. Nonetheless, there is a major hiatus between the first book (Genesis) and the four books that follow (Exodus–Deuteronomy). The first book narrates the origins of Israel, and the others, the organization of the people under Moses' leadership. They constitute a kind of "life of Moses" in the service of YHWH and of all Israel.[5]

From a structural viewpoint, the end of Deuteronomy corresponds to the end of Genesis. Joseph's death marks the end of the patriarchal period (Gen 50:26), and Moses' death, the conclusion of another period, that is, the time of Israel's wanderings in the wilderness and the formation of the people of Israel into YHWH's people. Jacob's blessings in Genesis 49 correspond to the blessings of Moses in Deuteronomy 33. The introductions and conclusions of the books of Leviticus and Numbers as well as of Deuteronomy thus emphasize the legislative character of these books, the figure of Moses (the intermediary between YHWH and the people), and the importance of Sinai/Horeb and the plains of Moab as "theological sites" of the Law.

B. The Structure of the Book of Genesis[6]

1. The Tôlĕdôt ("Generations") Formula

A large majority of exegetes consider the *tôlĕdôt* formula to be the structuring element of the book of Genesis. The formula appears ten times in the book (or even eleven, if we include 36:9, which repeats 36:1): 2:4; 5:1; 6:9; 10:1; 11:10, 27; 25:12, 19; 36:1 (9); 37:2.[7]

---

5. See R. P. Knierim, "The Composition of the Pentateuch," *The Task of Old Testament Theology: Substance, Method and Cases* (Grand Rapids, 1995) 351–79.

6. See especially Blenkinsopp, *Pentateuch*, 57–59 and 98–100. See also Childs, *Introduction*, 145; R. B. Robinson, "The Literary Function of the Genealogies of Genesis," *CBQ* 48 (1986) 595–608. R. N. Whybray (*Introduction to the Pentateuch* [Grand Rapids, 1995] 31–32) is opposed to this view, but his arguments are quite weak.

7. Much has been written about this formula. See, among others, N. Lohfink, "Die Priesterschrift und die Geschichte," in *Congress Volume: Göttingen, 1977* (ed. W. Zimmerli; VTSup 29; Leiden, 1978) 189–255, especially p. 205 (= Lohfink, *Studien zum Pentateuch* [Stuttgarter biblische Aufsatzbände: Altes Testament 4; Stuttgart, 1988] 213–54, mainly

a. A Problem of Interpretation

Whybray does not recognize this formula as the structuring element of the book of Genesis.[8] He advances two objections:

1. The word *tôlĕdôt* does not have the same meaning in all contexts. In some cases, it means "list of descendants," "descendants of . . . ," "what was gendered by . . ." (5:1; 10:1; 11:10, etc.). Then again, elsewhere, it means "history of . . ." and refers to specific events (2:4).

2. In Gen 2:4 the formula serves to conclude a narrative (1:1–2, 4a), while in other cases it serves as an introduction, for example, in 37:2.

We can reply to these objections by noting that:

1. The term *tôlĕdôt* has the same meaning in all contexts. It means "what was engendered by. . . ." Now and again this formula is followed by a simple list of names, that is, a genealogy (5:1; 10:1; 11:10; 25:12; 36:1, 9). In other cases, it is followed by narratives (2:4, 6:9, 11:27, 25:19, 37:2). Whatever the case may be, these narratives are always referring to the descendants of the personality mentioned in the formula. For example, in 6:9 the formula introduces the history of Noah and his family; in 11:27, the history of the descendants of Terah, that is, chiefly Abraham; 25:19 the history of Esau and Jacob, the son of Isaac; 37:2, the history of Joseph and his brothers, the sons of Jacob.

A distinction must be made between the *meaning* of a word and its *use* in different contexts. The term *tôlĕdôt* has lexical meanings that we find enumerated in dictionaries and significations that we need to differentiate on the basis of its *usage* in context. Let us recall the well-known distinction made by the Swiss linguist F. de Saussure between "language" and "speech" on an abstract level (regarding the possibilities of language) and on a concrete level (in discourse and texts, that is, in usage).[9] On a concrete level, the *meaning* of the *tôlĕdôt* formula remains the same, that is, "engenderment of. . . ." But there are two *uses* of this same term: in certain cases, it introduces genealogies, and in others, narratives. While its use differs, its *meaning* remains the same.

---

p. 230); S. Tengström, *Die Toledotformel und die literarische Struktur der priesterlichen Erweiterungsschicht im Pentateuch* (Lund, 1982); M. D. Johnson, *The Purpose of the Biblical Genealogies* (2nd ed.; Society for New Testament Studies Monograph Series 8; Cambridge, 1988); B. Renaud, "Les généalogies et la structure de l'histoire sacerdotale dans le livre de la Genèse," *RB* 97 (1990) 5–30.

8. Whybray, *Introduction*, 23–24.

9. F. de Saussure, *Course in General Linguistics* (trans. R. Harris, ed. C. Bally and A. Sechehaye; 3rd ed.; LaSalle, IL, 1983) 77. For the distinction between *meaning* and *significance*, see E. D. Hirsch, *Validity in Interpretation* (New Haven, CT, 1967); idem, *The Aims of Interpretation* (Chicago, 1976).

2. All the formulas are introductory, including Gen 2:4a: the term *tôlĕdôt* is consistently followed by the name of the genitor and never by the person engendered.[10] Consequently, the formula in Gen 2:4 *does not* mean: "the story of the origin of heaven and earth" ("how heaven and earth were engendered or created") but "the story of what was engendered by heaven and earth." Now, what was engendered by heaven and earth is described in Gen 2:4–25: from the earth—that is, the soil—YHWH formed the first human being (2:7), produced trees (2:9), and then made animals (2:19).[11] It is (to return to Whybray's point) not likely that the formula in Gen 2:4 is a conclusion to Genesis 1, the first narrative of Creation, with the meaning "what was engendered by heaven and earth." In addition to the difficulty mentioned in no. 1 above, it should be mentioned that Genesis 1 does not describe the "engenderment" of the universe but its creation.[12]

b. Subdivisions

The most important events.   As we have already said, certain formulas introduce genealogies (5:1; 10:1; 11:10; 25:12; 36:1, 9) while others introduce narratives (2:4, 6:9, 11:27, 25:19, 37:2). The latter correspond to the most important moments of Genesis: the creation of man and woman (2:4), the Flood (6:9); the stories of Abraham (11:27), of Jacob (25:19), and of Joseph and his brothers (37:2).

Before and after the Flood.   The formula covers the entirety of the book of Genesis and, at first glance, it does not appear to mark the boundary between the history of origins (Genesis 1–11) and the history of the ancestors (the patriarchs: Genesis 12–50), the division traditionally presented by commentaries and introductions. However, the book of Genesis seems to emphasize another division: before and after the Flood (see the formula *'aḥar hammabbûl* in 10:1 and 11:10, "after the Flood"). This criterion indicates that the two parts of Genesis are Genesis 1–9 and 10–50.[13]

---

10. J. Skinner, *Genesis* (ICC; Edinburgh, 1910) 41; cf. B. Jacob, *Das erste Buch der Tora: Genesis* (Berlin, 1934) 71; Childs, *Introduction*, 145.

11. For more details, see T. Stordalen, "Genesis 2,4: Restudying a *locus classicus*," *ZAW* 104 (1992) 163–71 (with bibliography); E. Blum, *Die Komposition der Vätergeschichte* (WMANT 57; Neukirchen-Vluyn, 1984) 451–52; idem, *Studien zur Komposition des Pentateuch* (BZAW 189; Berlin, 1990) 280; D. M. Carr, *Reading the Fractures of Genesis: Historical and Literary Approaches* (Louisville, 1996) 74–75 (with bibliography); F. M. Cross, *Canaanite Myth and Hebrew Epic* (Cambridge, MA, 1973) 302.

12. It is quite likely that the formula is redactional in origin and that it serves to integrate Gen 2:4a with the "genealogies" of Genesis.

13. See R. Rendtorff, "Gen 8,21 und die Urgeschichte des Jahwisten," *KD* 7 (1961) 69–78.

Between the Flood and Abraham, the book of Genesis contains few narratives. The various elements of 10:1–11:10 have a single aim: they show how the transition from Noah to Abraham occurred. Even accounts such as Noah's drunkenness (9:18–29) and the Tower of Babel (11:1–9) prepare for Abraham's coming. Gen 9:18–29 explains why Canaan, the son of Ham, was cursed and lost all his privileges, while Shem, Abraham's ancestor, was blessed and therefore occupies a preeminent position in the history of salvation (Gen 9:26; cf. 10:21–31; 11:10–26). Gen 11:1–9 (the Tower of Babel) prepares for the migrations of Terah and of Abraham. From Gen 9:20–29 on, the text no longer shows an interest in the history of the universe as such but introduces a principle of selection that reaches its highpoint in Abraham's calling (Gen 12:1–3). For example, the "Table of Nations" (Genesis 10) begins with the genealogy of Japheth, then Ham, and finally Shem, although Shem is the oldest son. After that, Gen 11:10–26 presents the genealogy of Shem alone, because he is the ancestor of Terah and Abraham. These are deliberate choices made to highlight the figure of Shem and to prepare for Abraham's arrival.

Consequently, there are good reasons for introducing a break between Gen 1:1–9:19 and 9:20–50:26. The ancient texts are less inclined to divide and structure than to unify: they cultivate "the art of transition." In the specific case of Genesis, they progressively pass from the history of the universe (Genesis 1–9) to the history of Abraham and his descendants (12–50), with the "transition" in Gen 9:20–11:26.[14]

2. Other Structural Elements in the Patriarchal History (Genesis 12–50)

Under the general heading of the *tôlĕdôt*, we need to introduce some more important subheadings. The first one, as we have seen, is the distinction between the antediluvian universe and the postdiluvian one. In the second section, the patriarchal history, or history of Israel's ancestors (Genesis 12–50), occupies a special place. Here, the structural elements are different. Some divine discourses are placed on the horizon of the history of Israel or the history of one of the patriarchs. In the technical language of narrative analysis, these are "narrative programs."[15] The most important of these are Gen 12:1–3, 26:2–5, 28:13–15, and 46:1–5a; also see 50:24.

In Gen 12:1–3, "the call of Abraham" introduces the first major break in the great genealogies (*tôlĕdôt*) of Genesis:

---

14. In any case, it is necessary to insist on the fact that the *tôlĕdôt* formulas make the book of Genesis a literary unit. See the reflections of Childs, *Introduction*, 146.

15. See my "Sincronia: Analisi narrativa," in *Metodologia dell'Antico Testamento* (ed. H. Simian-Yofre; Studi biblici 25; Bologna, 1994; 2nd ed., 1997) 157 and 230.

[1] Now YHWH said to Abram, "Go from your country and your kindred and your father's house to the land that I will show you. [2] I will make of you a great nation, and I will bless you, and make your name great, so that you will be a blessing. [3] I will bless those who bless you, and the one who curses you I will curse; and in you all the families of the earth shall be blessed."

Up to this point, God took care of the universe and all humanity. From now on the narrative is centered only on the people and the land. In what follows, when other peoples or other countries are mentioned, it is only in relationship to the people and to the land. This radical change in the narrative development certainly indicates that something new begins in Gen 12:1–3.

The problem is no longer humanity's destiny on earth but the destiny of Israel's ancestors. Gen 12:1–3 contains the divine "program" for Abraham's descendants without any limits; it therefore reaches far beyond the book of Genesis. This program is everlasting. A second divine discourse is addressed to Abraham, a little further on, and the account indicates the boundaries of the land (Gen 13:14–17). After the separation of Abraham and Lot, God allows the ancestor to "see" the land he will give him.

Isaac's program is presented in Gen 26:2–5. Essentially, God repeats to him the promises made to Abraham: the promise of the land and the promise of countless descendants. Furthermore, the discourse establishes continuity between the God of Abraham and the God of Isaac.

As the narrative moves on to Jacob, a key passage is the "vision of Bethel" (Gen 28:10–22). In this vision, God reveals himself as the God of Abraham and of Isaac, again emphasizing the continuity between the patriarchs. In addition to the promises of land and large lineage, Gen 28:13–15 introduces a new element: the promise to "bring Jacob back" to the land of his fathers (28:15). The return begins in Gen 31:3, when Jacob receives the explicit order, "Return to the land of your ancestors and to your kindred." Gen 31:13 and 33:10 refer to the same set of themes. Gen 46:1–5a is situated at the beginning of Jacob's journey to Egypt, where he will once again find Joseph. With him, the entire family immigrates to Egypt. Here begins Israel's long stay in Egypt, the stay that will end with the Exodus (Exodus 12–15). At this moment, the divine oracle promises the patriarch that God will accompany him on the second important journey of his life and then "bring him up" from Egypt. So, Israel does not settle in Egypt forever.

Finally, before dying, Joseph returns to this idea and states that one day God will lead the people into the land promised to Abraham, Isaac, and Jacob (50:24). The interest in the "land" constitutes an important thread in this framework. YHWH shows the land to Abraham, promises it once again to Isaac, brings Jacob back to it after his "exile" in the household of his Uncle Laban, and promises to lead his descendants back to it after the descent to Egypt. Joseph reiterates this idea in the conclusion of the book of Genesis. In this way the patriarchal story is largely, but not exclusively, an account centered on the itinerary of the patriarchs, and this is one of the elements that most strongly unites the narratives in the book of Genesis.

Although it is more apparent in Jacob's case than for Abraham and Isaac, the message of these narratives is clear: the land promised to Israel is the land of Canaan. With this goal, these narratives interpret Abraham's life as a departure for and an exploration of the Promised Land. Jacob's life constitutes a circular itinerary because he leaves the country and finally returns with his entire family. The story of Joseph, in this context, explains why Israel settled only temporarily in Egypt. The narratives in 46:1–5a and 50:24 stress the transitory character of this stay in a foreign country.[16]

3. The Function of the Tôlĕdôt Formula in the Patriarchal History

The patriarchal narrative merges the concerns for the lineage and the land. The problem is to discern who is the heir of the promise. This problem is also connected with the *tôlĕdôt* formula and its function. The questions of genealogy and territory are intertwined, and in this context we could even talk about geopolitical theology.

One of the aims of a genealogy is, of course, to define who belongs to a family, race, or people.[17] In the case of Genesis, the *tôlĕdôt* formula is intended to mark the boundaries of the people of Israel and to situate Israel in the world, that is, in creation. The various formulas are related to the most important moments of this "history of the definition of Israel."[18] Actually, in antiquity, "genealogies" often served to "legitimate" the prerogatives of individuals, of groups, and of peoples. Certain formulas introduce these genealogies and accounts, which are the two means used in the book of Genesis to determine who belongs and who does not belong to the chosen people.

Genesis 1–9 describes the origin of the universe and of humanity. Sin and violence are the causes of the Flood (Genesis 6–9). So, Israel belongs to the postdiluvian nations. After the Flood, the genealogies focus on the figure of Shem, the remote ancestor of the people of Israel.

The Abraham story (Genesis 12–25) is organized around a central question: who will inherit the promise? There is a succession of candidates: Lot (Genesis 13), Eliezer (Genesis 15), and Ishmael (Genesis 16 and 21). They are all elimi-

---

16. On this, see, among others, Blum, *Komposition der Vätergeschichte*, 297–300.

17. Concerning the various functions of the genealogies, see, among others, R. R. Wilson, "The Old Testament Genealogies in Recent Research," *JBL* 94 (1975) 169–89; idem, *Genealogy and History in the Biblical World* (New Haven, CT, 1977); Johnson, *The Purpose of Biblical Genealogies*; Childs, *Introduction*, 152–53.

18. See Blum, *Komposition der Vätergeschichte*, 479–91 and 505–6.

nated in favor of Isaac (Gen 21:1–7; cf. Gen 15:1–6; 17; 18:1–15).[19] Ishmael will have his own genealogy (the *tôlĕdôt* in Gen 25:12–18), but this is a collateral lineage, not the main one. Abraham's genealogy and his story help us to understand and to define more closely the position of neighboring peoples, such as the Moabites and the Ammonites (descendants of Lot), the Ishmaelites, and the Israelites (descendants of Ishmael and of Isaac). In addition, Genesis 12–25 shows that the Promised Land is the land of Canaan. Therefore, Isaac inherits the land of Canaan, while Lot's descendants settle in Moab and Ammon (Genesis 19) and Ishmael's descendants in the wilderness, to the south of Beer-sheba, not far from Egypt (Gen 25:18; cf. 16:14; 21:14, 21).

The Jacob story (Genesis 25–35) defines Israel in relationship to Esau and the Edomites, Esau's descendants, and to Laban, the Aramean. Once again, the text is concerned with the "related" populations who occupy the neighboring territories. Esau is Jacob's twin and Laban is his uncle, but Jacob alone will inherit the promise, although he obtains the blessing in a rather dishonest way (Genesis 25 and 27). The story fixes the precise delimitation of the boundaries between the territories occupied by each one. The oath of Laban and Jacob (31:51–54) that concludes the events recounted in Genesis 28–31 has precisely the task of marking the boundaries between the respective territories. Gen 36:6–8 states quite clearly that Esau did not settle in the land of Canaan but in the hill country of Seir. The land of Canaan belongs to Jacob (28:13–14; 31:3, 13; 32:10).

The Joseph story answers the final question: why are there twelve tribes? In Genesis 37 a new conflict arises between "brothers." Will Joseph, like Isaac and Jacob, be the sole heir? The account explains why all the brothers (or most of them) are blessed in Genesis 49 and are thus all ancestors of the people of Israel. After the reconciliation between the brothers, the entire family goes down to Egypt. However, the last verses of this story contain the promise of a return to the land of Canaan (50:24).[20] Thus, the Joseph story serves as the transition between the book of Genesis and the book of Exodus.[21]

4. The Importance of the Patriarchal History

The patriarchal history (Genesis 12–50) constitutes, by far, the most important part of the book of Genesis. According to the chronology of Genesis, Abraham was born in the *anno mundi* (since creation) 1946. He left his country

19. See L. R. Helyer, "The Separation of Abraham and Lot: Its Significance in the Patriarchal Narratives," *JSOT* 26 (1983) 77–88.

20. From Gen 12:1–3 on, the "land" becomes the central theme of the patriarchal narrative.

21. For other presentations, see Blenkinsopp, *Pentateuch*, 57–59 and 98–100; Whybray, *Introduction*, 29–40 and 49–62.

to immigrate to the land of Canaan in *anno mundi* 2021 (cf. Gen 12:4b). Jacob and his family went down to Egypt in *anno mundi* 2236 (Gen 47:9).[22] Consequently, chaps. 1–11 of Genesis cover 2,021 years, and the chapters dedicated to the patriarchs cover 215, without counting the years between the arrival in Egypt and the deaths of Jacob and of Joseph. Now, if we add this number to more or less 70 years in order to arrive at Joseph's death, we get the sum of 285/290 years.[23]

Proportionally, the "narration time" is much longer in Genesis 12–50 than in Genesis 1–11. Or to put it more simply, the narrative of Genesis 12–50 is far richer and more detailed than the account of Genesis 1–11. In the first case, the proportion is approximately 200 years per chapter but, in the second, $7\frac{1}{2}$ years per chapter.

C. The Structure of the Book of Exodus

1. The Subdivisions[24]

The structure of Exodus differs greatly from the structure of Genesis. We do not encounter any linguistic markers comparable to the "*tôlĕdôt* formula" to help us grasp the composition of the book.[25] There are, however, some recurring formulas of Priestly origin (P) that mark the various phases of Israel's wandering in the wilderness (Exod 12:37a, 40–42; 13:20; 14:2; 15:22a; 16:1; 17:1; 19:2). The formula of wandering reappears in the book of Numbers (10:11–12; 12:16; 20:1, 22; 21:4, 10–13; 22:1).[26] Numbers 33 contains a complete list of the stages of wandering. However, the formula is not found in all sections of Exodus (it does not appear in Exodus 19–40) and does not correspond to the principal divisions of Exodus. Moreover, the wandering continues in Numbers, structuring a unit that goes far beyond the single book of Exodus.

---

22. See Blenkinsopp, *Pentateuch*, 48.

23. Joseph was 17 years old at the beginning of the story (Gen 37:2) and 30 in Gen 41:46. To this it is necessary to add at least 7 years of abundance (41:53) and 2 years of famine (45:6). When Jacob and his family arrived in Egypt, Joseph was at least 39 years old. He died at 110 (50:26). The difference is more or less 70 years.

24. See Childs, *Introduction*, 170–71. Other exegetes leave aside study of the "canonical form" of Exodus, preferring to study Exodus–Numbers. Cf. Blenkinsopp, "From Egypt to Canaan," in *Pentateuch*, 134–82. Blenkinsopp divides the books of Exodus–Numbers into three sections: (1) "Israel in Egypt" (Exod 1:1–15:21); (2) "Israel in the wilderness" (Exod 15:22–18:27 + Num 10:11–36:13); (3) "Israel at Sinai" (Exod 19:1–Num 10:10); Whybray (*Introduction*, 63–64) adopts a similar division.

25. Childs, *Introduction*, 170; Blenkinsopp, *Pentateuch*, 135.

26. See Lohfink, "Priesterschrift," 206 (= *Studien zum Pentateuch*, 231); Blenkinsopp, *Pentateuch*, 135–36.

Generally, exegetes distinguish at least three parts to Exodus: (1) the departure from Egypt (Exod 1:1–15:21); (2) the journey from Egypt to Sinai (15:22–18:27); (3) Israel in Sinai: the Covenant and the Laws (19–40). In this last section, a distinction is normally made between the Covenant (Exodus 19–24), the breach of the Covenant, and its renewal (32–34); and, finally, the instructions for the building of the sanctuary and their execution (25–31; 35–40).[27] But there is no clear linguistic signal to support this way of structuring the text. We therefore need to look elsewhere.

2. Attempt at a Solution

The book of Exodus ends with the consecration of the tent of meeting (Exod 40:34–38). This text may provide the key for interpreting the book in its canonical form.

a. The Literary and Historical Context

What happens in Exod 40:34–38? YHWH takes possession of the tent of meeting, and this implies that he comes to live in the midst of his people (40:35; cf. 29:43–46). The eminent symbols of the Presence are the "glory" and the "cloud." This moment anticipates 1 Kgs 8:10–13, where YHWH takes up residence in the temple of Solomon (cf. 2 Chr 5:11–6:2).

Ezek 43:1–7 is another text that needs to be connected with Exodus 40. There, we see the "glory of YHWH" entering the temple it had abandoned in Ezek 10:18–22. The temple destroyed by the Babylonians will be rebuilt after the Exile (Ezra 5–6). This second temple will be purified by Judas Maccabeus in 1 Macc 4:36–61. For the Postexilic community, the consecration of the tent was the key moment of Israel's history. It should probably be seen in relationship to the reconstruction of the temple of Jerusalem and the restoration of the cult during the Persian period.[28]

b. Significance of the Construction of the Temple[29]

In the ancient Near East, the consecration of a temple is the moment when a divinity affirms his or her sovereignty. The creation accounts often conclude with the construction of a temple for the creator-god. Marduk, for example, has a sanctuary built for himself at the end of the poem *Enùma Elish*. At Ugarit, there is a long poem telling about the construction of the temple of

---

27. Childs, *Introduction*, 170–71.

28. Blenkinsopp, *Pentateuch*, 218.

29. See above all M. Weinfeld, "Sabbath, Temple, and the Enthronement of the Lord: The Problem of the *Sitz im Leben* of Gen 1:1–2:3," in *Mélanges bibliques et orientaux en l'honneur de M. Henri Cazelles* (ed. A. Caquot and M. Delcor; AOAT 212; Neukirchen-Vluyn and Kevelaer, 1981) 501–12.

Baal. Likewise, YHWH, who comes to live in the midst of Israel, affirms his
sovereignty over the people of Israel (and the world). Israel is the people of
YHWH and of no other divinity or power. The consecration of the tent corresponds to the categorical illustration of the first commandment: *"I am YHWH*
your God, who brought you out of the land of Egypt, out of the house of slavery; you
shall have no other gods before me" (Exod 20:2–3).[30]

Exodus 40 completes the story of the Creation (Genesis 1). Genesis 1 ends
with the consecration of a sacred time (the seventh day, the Sabbath). YHWH
will not have a residence in the created world until Exodus 40, when Israel will
have become his people (Exod 6:7) and YHWH their God (29:45–46).[31]

c. The Structure of the Book of Exodus

The question of YHWH's sovereignty over Israel runs throughout the entire
book of Exodus.

• In Exodus 1–15, the fundamental problem is to discern who the true sovereign of Israel is and whom Israel should "serve": Pharaoh or YHWH? The
question appears even more clearly in the plague narrative (Exodus 7–11) and
in the narrative of the crossing of the sea (Exodus 14). In these chapters, YHWH
reveals his sovereignty. The plagues of Egypt and the crossing of the sea prove
who "YHWH is" because Pharaoh said, "I do not know YHWH" (Exod 5:2).
This is why the "recognition formula" is frequently repeated in this part of Exodus (see 7:5, 17; 8:6, 18; 9:14, 29; 10:2; 11:7; 14:4, 18): "by this you shall /
they shall know that I am YHWH." Compare 14:18: "and the Egyptians shall
know that I am YHWH."[32]

• Exod 15:18, the last verse of the "Song of Moses," proclaims after the final
victory in Exodus 14: "YHWH will reign forever and ever." YHWH reigns and
he will make his residence in the midst of his people. These two themes of the
sovereignty and the residence (sanctuary) are already connected in the concluding verses of the "Song of Moses."[33]

---

30. The translation of the expression *ʿal-pānāya* (translated "before me" above) is disputed. See the commentaries.

31. On the correspondences between Genesis 1 and Exodus 25–40, see, among others,
Blenkinsopp, *Pentateuch*, 217–18; P. Weimar, "Struktur und Komposition der priesterschriftlichen Geschichtsdarstellung," *BN* 24 (1984) 151 n. 179; idem, "Sinai und Schöpfung: Komposition und Theologie der priesterschriftlichen Sinaigeschichte," *RB* 95 (1988) 138–62.

32. See M. Greenberg, *Understanding Exodus* (New York, 1969) 164–67, 169–70, and
181; D. J. McCarthy, "Moses' Dealings with Pharaoh: Exod 7:8–12:27," *CBQ* 27 (1965)
336–47; J.-L. Ska, *Le passage de la mer: Étude de la construction, du style et de la symbolique*
d'Exod 14,1–31 (AnBib 109; Rome, 1986) 57–60 and 75.

33. On Exodus 1–15, also see G. Fischer, "Exodus 1–15: Eine Erzählung," in *Studies in*
the Book of Exodus: Redaction—Reception—Interpretation (ed. M. Vervenne; BETL 126; Leuven, 1996) 149–78.

• Exod 15:22–18:27 forms a transition that leads Israel from Egypt to Mount Sinai. From this moment on, YHWH is the "sovereign" of Israel and must resolve the problems of his people: thirst (Exod 15:22–27, 17:1–7); hunger (chap. 16); belligerent enemies (17:6–16). In addition, these chapters allude to the Law (15:25b; 16:4–5, 28) and to the organization of the people (chap. 18). The only stylistic element uniting these chapters is the "wandering formula" (15:22, 27; 16:1; 17:1; cf. 19:1–2), which contains the verbs *nsʿ* ("to move around," "to journey," "to travel"), *bwʾ* ("to arrive"), and *ḥnh* ("to camp"); and various place-names, especially the points of departure and arrival.

• Exod 19:1–24:11 is one of the most intense moments in the book of Exodus.[34]

The style.　　The corresponding phrases in 19:7–8 and 24:3, 7 frame the entire section:[35]

> 19:7–8: [7]So Moses came, summoned the elders of the people, and set before them all these words that YHWH had commanded him. [8]The people all answered as one: "Everything that YHWH has spoken we will do." Moses reported the words of the people to YHWH.

> 24:3: Moses came and told the people all the words of YHWH and all the ordinances; and all the people answered with one voice, and said, "All the words that YHWH has spoken we will do."

> 24:7: [Moses] took the Book of the Covenant, and read it in the hearing of the people; and they said, "All that YHWH has spoken we will do, and we will be obedient."

With regard to YHWH, the *central assertion* appears in Exod 20:2–3, "I am YHWH your God, who brought you out of the land of Egypt, out of the house of slavery; you shall have no other gods before me." The Exodus is the foundational event in Israel's history, the event on which YHWH bases all his prerogatives. The first consequence of this fact—that is, the "first commandment"— is that Israel must have no other gods: YHWH alone has freed Israel; YHWH alone has rights over Israel.

Israel's status.　　The first part (Exod 19:3–8) contains the "program" for the whole section. In this oracle, which introduces the Sinai section, YHWH reminds Israel of the Exodus (19:4) and invites them to become his exclusive possession (*sĕgullâ*) among the peoples of the earth, a "priestly kingdom"

---

34. On these difficult chapters, see Blum, *Studien*, 88–99 (with bibliography). Also see T. B. Dozeman, *God on the Mountain: A Study of Redaction, Theology and Canon in Exodus 19–24* (SBLMS 37; Atlanta, 1989); B. Renaud, *La théophanie du Sinaï—Exod 19–24: Exégèse et théologie* (CahRB 30; Paris, 1991).

35. See L. Perlitt, *Bundestheologie im Alten Testament* (WMANT 36; Neukirchen-Vluyn, 1969) 192.

(*mamleket kōhănîm*) and a "holy nation" (*góy qādôś*).[36] After the proclamation of
the Decalogue and the "Covenant Code" (20:22–23:19), the various rituals,
especially the ritual of the Covenant in Exod 24:3–8, seal the new relations between YHWH and his people. From now on, Israel is the exclusive possession of
YHWH, a "holy nation" and a "priestly kingdom." The rituals in Exod 24:3–8,
especially the sprinkling with blood, "consecrate" Israel. The same rite of as-
persion consecrates the priests in Exodus 29 and Leviticus 8. The vision and
the meal in Exod 24:9–11 are intended to confirm the authority of the priests
and of the elders, the legitimate representatives of YHWH in the midst of the
"holy nation."[37] However, the "sanctuary" with its indispensable elements, the
altar and the priesthood, is still missing (cf. 29:43–46). This will be the topic of
discussion in the next section.

• Exod 24:12–31:18, especially 24:15–31:17, are the chapters in which
YHWH reveals to Moses his plan for construction of the sanctuary: "Have them
make me a sanctuary, so that I may dwell among them" (25:8–9). YHWH will
be even more the "sovereign" of Israel when he has a sanctuary permitting him
to live in the midst of his people. This section is set off by an inclusio marked
by two references to the "stone tablets" containing the Law (24:12, 31:18).
These tablets play an important role in the chapters that follow because they
represent the basic conditions of the relationship between YHWH and his
people. YHWH will be able to live in the midst of his people only if Israel respects this Law.[38]

• Exodus 32–34. However, Israel does not respect the basic Law inscribed
on the stone tablets. The episode of the golden calf provokes a serious crisis that
endangers Israel's existence as the people of YHWH. The golden calf is considered to be a rival divinity (cf. Exod 20:3; 32:1, 8). One question dominates
chaps. 32–34: after the incident of the golden calf, will YHWH continue to reside

---

36. This text has been the object of much study and debate. For the discussion and the
bibliography, see ibid., 167–81; B. S. Childs, *Exodus: A Commentary* (OTL; London, 1974)
340 and 360–61; J. Durham, *Exodus* (WBC 3; Waco, TX, 1987) 256 and 261–63; D. J. Mc-
Carthy, *Treaty and Covenant: A Study in Form in the Ancient Oriental Documents and in the Old
Testament* (AnBib 21A; Rome, 1978) 270–73; J.-L. Ska, "Exod 19,3b–6 et l'identité de l'Israël postexilique," in *Studies in the Book of Exodus: Redaction—Reception—Interpretation* (ed.
M. Vervenne; BETL 126; Leuven, 1996) 289–317.
37. Exod 24:1–2, 9–11 and 24:3–8 are also largely discussed. See Perlitt, *Bundestheologie*,
181–90 and 190–203; McCarthy, *Treaty and Covenant*, 264–69; Blum, *Studien*, 51–52 (with
bibliography); J.-L. Ska, "Exod 19,3–8 et les parénèses deutéronomiques," in *Biblische Theologie und gesellschaftlicher Wandel: Für Norbert Lohfink SJ* (ed. G. Braulik, W. Gross, and S. Mc-
Evenue; Freiburg-im-Breisgau, 1993) 307–14, notably pp. 311–12; idem, "Le repas de Exod
24,11," *Bib* 74 (1993) 305–27.
38. On these chapters, see H. Utzschneider, *Das Heiligtum und das Gesetz: Studien zur Bedeutung der sinaitischen Heiligtumstexte (Ex 25–40, Lev 8–9)* (OBO 77; Fribourg, 1988); Weimar, "Sinai und Schöpfung," 138–62.

in the midst of his people and guide them in the wilderness? (see 33:3, 5, 14). Moses intercedes and finally YHWH concedes (33:14, 17). From this moment on, the God who accompanies Israel will be a God of forgiveness and mercy (Exod 34:6–7). The renewal of the Covenant (Exodus 34) is symbolized by the granting of two new tablets of the Law. Moses destroyed the first tablets in Exod 32:15–16, 19. The "words" are written on the new tablets in 34:1, 27–28.[39]

• Exodus 35–40. It is now possible to build the sanctuary in which YHWH will take up residence in 40:34–35. After having eliminated the human power of Pharaoh and the other divinities, symbolized by the golden calf, YHWH has now shown that he is the only real sovereign of Israel.

From a stylistic point of view, the last section of these chapters (40:34–38) is linked to the first section (35:1–3) by the word "work" (*mĕlā'kâ*), which appears in 35:2 and 40:33. There are allusions to Gen 1:1–2, 4a in both cases, and notably to Gen 2:1–3. Exod 35:1–3 mentions the week and the rest of the seventh day (cf. Gen 2:1–3), and Exod 40:33 says that Moses finished his work exactly as God had finished his work in Gen 2:2:

Gen 2:2: And on the seventh day God finished the work that he had done.

Exod 40:33: So Moses finished the work.

In the last chapter of Exodus, there are two key elements: YHWH dwells in the midst of his people (40:34–35), and it is necessary to organize the people in relation to the divine presence. This will be the task of Leviticus. From the tent, YHWH guides his people (Exod 40:36–38). The book of Numbers describes Israel's journey under the guidance of YHWH, present in the cloud.

One last remark concerning these chapters needs to be added. The beginning of the book of Exodus describes Israel's slavery in Egypt (Exodus 1). At the end of the book, Israel "serves" YHWH. However, "serving YHWH" is not another form of slavery. The "liturgy" (in Hebrew this word means "service," "work," or "worship") is spontaneous and voluntary "service," not "forced labor." See Exod 35:4–29, where the Israelites act "willingly" ("of a generous heart," 35:5, 22; "everyone whose heart was stirred, and everyone whose spirit was willing," 35:21).[40] Moreover, the rest on the Sabbath (Exod 35:1–3)

---

39. Concerning the problems of this very complex section, see Blum, *Studien*, 73–75; R. W. L. Moberly, *At the Mountain of God: Story and Theology in Exodus 32–34* (JSOTSup 22; Sheffield, 1983); B. Renaud, "La formation de Exod 19–40. Quelques points de repère," in *Le Pentateuque: Débats et recherches. XIVᵉ Congrès de l'ACFEB, Angers, 1991* (ed. P. Haudebert; LD 151; Paris, 1992) 101–3.

40. On this point, see, among others, N. Lohfink, "Freizeit: Arbeitswoche und Sabbat im Alten Testament, insbesondere in der priesterlichen Geschichtsdarstellung," *Unsere grossen Wörter: Das Alte Testament zu Themen dieser Jahre* (Freiburg-im-Breisgau, 1977) 190–208; J.-L. Ska, "Il lavoro nella Bibbia," *Firmana* 8 (1995) 47–62.

introduces a difference between "voluntary work" and slavery. The book of Leviticus also describes it as the Israelites' "free service" for YHWH, their God.

D. The Structure of the Book of Leviticus [41]

1. The Problem

YHWH's presence in midst of his people requires a special organization of their entire life around the basic requirement of "purity" and holiness." This is the primary aim of the book of Leviticus.

2. The Structure

Interpreters agree on the division of Leviticus into four important sections and an appendix. Leviticus 1–7 deals with sacrifices; 8–10 with the inauguration of the cult; 11–16 with the laws of purity and impurity; 17–26 with the "Holiness Code"; and chap. 27 is an appendix concerning various offerings in the sanctuary.

Let us look at the evidence for the structuring.

• Leviticus 1–7 ends with a characteristic "concluding summary" (7:37–38): "This is the ritual of the burnt offering, the grain offering, the sin offering, the guilt offering, the offering of ordination, and the sacrifice of well-being, which YHWH commanded Moses on Mount Sinai, when he commanded the people of Israel to bring their offerings to YHWH, in the wilderness of Sinai." The other sections of Leviticus do not have an introduction or conclusion of this sort. The formulas in Lev 26:46 and 27:34 close the entire book. The division is therefore based on other criteria.

• Leviticus 8–10 describes the consecration of the priests, Aaron and his sons, and the inauguration of the cult. Moses, Aaron, and his sons are the central figures here (8:2, 9:1, 10:1).

• Leviticus 11–16 are chapters in which the vocabulary of purity and impurity is dominant—*tāmēʾ* ("impure"); *ṭāhor* ("pure"); *šeqeṣ* ("abomination"); and the corresponding verbs. Chapter 11 has its own conclusion (11:46–47). Other conclusions of this kind also appear in 12:7 (law of parturition); 13:59 (law concerning leper spots); 14:54–57 (law concerning leprosy); 15:32–33 (law concerning sexual impurity).

• Leviticus 16 does not precisely belong to the law of impurity. Actually, it deals with the ritual to be observed for the "Day of Expiation" (*yôm hakkippurîm*), one of the theological pivots of Leviticus. This chapter has a double conclusion (16:29a and 16:34).

---

41. See, above all, Childs, *Introduction*, 182.

- Leviticus 17–26 contains what convention calls the "Holiness Code." Unfortunately, the linguistic markers that would have permitted singling out this section are not clear. For example, the expression "Holiness Code" derives from the well-known phrase: "You shall be holy, for I YHWH your God am holy" (Lev 19:2). But this phrase is not found at the beginning of the Holiness Code, in Lev 17:1, and furthermore it already appears in Lev 11:44. Many exegetes think that Leviticus 17 is a part of the "Holiness Code" because this chapter refers to the blood, the sacred element (17:11) present in many rituals of consecration.

Some chapters have their own conclusions, that is, an exhortation to observe the Law. See 18:30, 19:37, 20:22–26, 22:31–33, 26:2. Elsewhere, the conclusion only states that Moses communicated to Israel (or to Aaron) the prescriptions promulgated by YHWH (Lev 21:24, 23:44). See also 24:23 (conclusion of a historical interlude). As we have already said, Lev 26:46 and 27:34 conclude the entire book.

More simply, one could even say that the book of Leviticus has two main sections. In the first section (1–10), the cult is organized (1–8) and inaugurated (9–10). In the second, Leviticus indicates what YHWH expects from the "cultic community of Israel": purity (11–15) and holiness (17–26, 27). The liturgy of the Day of Atonement in Leviticus 16 is the means given to Israel to be reconciled with the Lord on a regular basis.

3. The Meaning of the Book [42]

In order to understand the book of Leviticus, it is necessary to consider its context. Israel has just left Egypt and is now at the foot of Mount Sinai. The people are living in the wilderness and have not yet entered the Promised Land. What legal foundations do the people of Israel have? Israel cannot take possession of any territory and, consequently, it is not possible to apply property law. The only basis for the existence of Israel at this moment is the experience of the Exodus: YHWH brought Israel out of Egypt, and he liberated them from slavery. The Israelites are therefore a free people, although they do not yet possess land.

In the book of Leviticus, the experience of the Exodus is interpreted in a new way: when YHWH led Israel out of Egypt, he "separated" them from the other nations, especially from Egypt, and "sanctified" them. This "theological

---

42. See especially W. Zimmerli, "'Heiligkeit' nach dem sogenannten Heiligkeitsgesetz," *VT* 30 (1980) 493–512; F. Crüsemann, "Der Exodus als Heiligung: Zur rechtsgeschichtlichen Bedeutung des Heiligkeitsgesetzes," in *Die hebräische Bibel und ihre zweifache Nachgeschichte: Festschrift für Rolf Rendtorff zum 65. Geburtstag* (ed. E. Blum, C. Macholz, and E. W. Stegemann; Neukirchen-Vluyn, 1990) 117–29.

basis" of the Israelites' existence has consequences for their legal status. The most important of these consequences are the following:

• The Exodus is not a human feat, the action of a great hero or a well-organized group; it is not even due to the intervention of some divinity: it is the achievement of YHWH alone. Because Israel owes its existence as a people to YHWH, it "belongs" to YHWH. See, for example, Lev 25:55: "For to me the people of Israel are servants; they are my servants whom I brought out from the land of Egypt: I am YHWH your God."

• This fact defines the relations between the various members. The freedom of all the members of the people is "sacred" because they belong to YHWH alone. See Lev 25:42 (law regarding the redemption of slaves): "For they are my servants, whom I brought out of the land of Egypt; they shall not be sold as slaves are sold."

• Because Israel is a "holy" people, all the aspects of its existence are characterized by "holiness" (Lev 19:2; 22:31–33). Consequently, Leviticus insists on the cult and the observance of "religious" rules—for example, the distinction between "pure" and "impure." See Lev 11:44–47 (law on permitted and prohibited food):

> [44]For I am YHWH your God; sanctify yourselves therefore, and be holy, for I am holy. You shall not defile yourselves with any swarming creature that moves on the earth. [45]For I am YHWH who brought you up from the land of Egypt, to be your God; you shall be holy, for I am holy. [46]This is the law pertaining to land animal and bird and every living creature that moves through the waters and every creature that swarms upon the earth, [47]to make a distinction between the unclean and the clean, and between the living creature that may be eaten and the living creature that may not be eaten.

Israel was sanctified by YHWH when he brought the people out of Egypt. This is why, according to the same text in Leviticus 11, Israel must "make a distinction between the pure and the impure," in other words, remain "holy" and "pure" (cf. 18:1–4, 20:24–25).

• The land that will be given to the people belongs exclusively to YHWH, who will be its sole owner.[43] This means that there will be no "property rights" in Israel. The Israelites will have the usufruct of the land, but they will not be able to own it: Lev 20:24; 25:23, 38. Lev 25:23 is particularly significant (law regarding the redemption of the land): "The land shall not be sold in perpetuity, for the land is mine; with me you are but aliens and tenants."

• The Exodus, as "separation" and "sanctification," also defines Israel's relations with other nations.[44] The people that have been "sanctified" cannot live

---

43. Ibid., 124–25.
44. Ibid., 118–19.

as do the other nations from which they have been "separated." See Lev 11:47, 18:3–5, 20:22–26, 22:32–33; especially Lev 22:32–33 (conclusion of a law concerning the sacrifices): "You shall not profane my holy name, that I may be sanctified among the people of Israel: I am YHWH; I sanctify you, I who brought you out of the land of Egypt to be your God: I am YHWH." This text establishes a precise correspondence between two divine actions: the sanctification of Israel and the departure from Egypt. The participle *mĕqaddišĕkem* ("who sanctifies you") is followed by the participle *hammôṣîʾ* ("who led you out"). The two participles have the same value and, consequently, the departure from Egypt is the sanctification of Israel.

Also see Lev 18:3–4, which introduces the laws regarding sexuality: "You shall not do as they do in the land of Egypt, where you lived, and you shall not do as they do in the land of Canaan, to which I am bringing you. You shall not follow their statutes. My ordinances you shall observe and my statutes you shall keep, following them: I am YHWH your God." If the Israelites are "separated" and "sanctified," they cannot follow the laws and customs of peoples from whom they have been "separated" in order to be "sanctified."

4. Conclusion

This introduction is not the place to attempt a full evaluation of the theology of Leviticus, which definitely has limits. The emphasis on the cult, "separation," and Israel's distinctive character is not without danger. The Old Testament—for example, the books of Ruth and Jonah—manifests a critical attitude toward this mentality. The New Testament will judge it severely. Nonetheless, we need to elucidate its merits. Without this theology, Israel would not have been able to survive and transmit its faith when, after having lost its political autonomy, it no longer possessed its own territory. This is all the more true for the Jews of the diaspora.

E. The Structure of the Book of Numbers [45]

1. The Problem

As many authors have noted, it is especially difficult to determine the structure of the book of Numbers. Generally, a three-part division prevails, but with

---

45. I am primarily following R. P. Knierim, "The Book of Numbers," in *Die hebräische Bibel und ihre zweifache Nachgeschichte: Festschrift für Rolf Rendtorff zum 65. Geburtstag* (ed. E. Blum, C. Macholz, and E. W. Stegemann; Neukirchen-Vluyn, 1990) 155–63, esp. 155–56 on the problem. See also R. Rendtorff, *The Old Testament: An Introduction* (trans. J. Bowden; London, 1985) 147; also see the commentaries and studies of G. B. Gray, *Numbers* (ICC; Edinburgh, 1903); N. H. Snaith, *Leviticus and Numbers* (Century Bible; London, 1967); M. Noth,

a large variety of opinions. These three parts are: Israel at Sinai; the journey from Sinai to the plains of Moab; Israel in the plains of Moab. For many scholars, the first section ends in 10:10. But according to Noth and Coats, it ends in 10:36, and Budd argues for 9:14. The conclusion of the second part is located, according to these authors, in 20:13 (most), 21:9 (Noth), 22:1 (Coats), and 25:18 (Budd). Similarly, no agreement has been reached on the conclusion of the book. Almost all the authors think that the conclusion of the third section coincides with the end of the book, 36:13. For Budd, however, chap. 36 is an addition.

Thus, most scholars divide the book into three parts. However, some prefer two sections (D. T. Olson),[46] chaps. 1–25 and 26–36. The first section mainly discusses the generation that experienced the Exodus and the Sinai, while the second section deals with the new generation that replaced the first 40 years later. The two censuses, in chap. 1 and chap. 26, mark the beginning of each of the two sections.

2. The Bipartite Structure

The book of Numbers contains several indicators that may help us determine its structure: for example, the chronological data in Num 1:1, 7:1, 10:11, and 33:38; the topographical information distinguishing the various stages of Israel's wanderings in the wilderness: Sinai (1:1–10:10), Paran (10:11–12:16), Edom (20:23–21:4), Negeb (21:1), Moab (21:11, 13, 20; 22:1), the land of the Amorites (21:13, 21, 31), and, finally, the plains of Moab (chaps. 22–36). However, these chronological and topographical indicators are not conclusive with regard to the structure of the book because they do not converge. In order to obtain more satisfying results, we must study both the form and the content.

This is why Knierim suggests beginning with a three-part division. However, he goes on to note that there is no reason to distinguish the second part

---

Numbers (trans. J. D. Martin; Philadelphia, 1968); G. W. Coats, *Rebellion in the Wilderness: The Murmuring Motif in the Wilderness Traditions of the Old Testament* (Nashville, 1968); J. de Vaulx, *Les Nombres* (SB; Paris, 1972); B. A. Levine, *Numbers 1–20* (AB 4A; New York, 1993); idem, *Numbers 21–36* (AB 4B; Garden City, NY, 2000); J. Milgrom, *Numbers* (JPS Torah Commentary; New York, 1989); P. J. Budd, *Numbers* (WBC 5; Waco, TX, 1984); A. Schart, *Mose und Israel in Konflikt: Eine redaktionsgeschichtliche Studie zu den Wüstenerzählungen* (OBO 98; Fribourg and Göttingen, 1990); T. R. Ashley, *The Book of Numbers* (NICOT; Grand Rapids, 1993); R. K. Harrison, *Numbers: An Exegetical Commentary* (Grand Rapids, 1992); J. Scharbert, *Numeri* (NEchtB 27; Würzburg, 1992); K. D. Sakenfeld, *Journeying with God: A Commentary on the Book of Numbers* (International Theological Commentary; Grand Rapids, 1995); cf. Childs, *Introduction*, 194–99.

46. D. T. Olson, *The Death of the Old and the Birth of the New: The Framework of the Book of Numbers and the Pentateuch* (BJS 71; Chico, CA, 1985).

from the third part on the basis of form and content. From 10:11 on, Israel is journeying in the wilderness. Moab is only a "stage for Israel in the wilderness," one among others, even if the stay there is the longest one. Consequently, it seems most reasonable not to distinguish more than two sections in the book: Num 1:1–10:10 and 10:11–36:13.

What is the factor that unites and distinguishes these two parts on the highest structural level?[47] In 1:10–10:10, Israel prepares itself for the march in the wilderness. This preparation is both religious and military, and it differs from the preparations in the following chapters because it takes into consideration the entire march in the wilderness, not just one particular stage. The second part of the book (10:11–36:13) describes the execution of the plan contained in the first chapters. The fundamental structure of the book of Numbers is therefore: plan / execution of the plan. The book as a whole belongs to the literary genre of military campaign.[48]

There are, however, good reasons to introduce another subdivision, without modifying the structure proposed by Knierim. The second part of the book of Numbers (10:11–36:13) describes the march through the wilderness on the model of a military campaign. But there are two distinct stages in this campaign. In the first stage, Israel journeys from Sinai toward the Promised Land. Then, in a second section, the conquest of the territory begins. The "campaign" is no longer exactly the same, because, for the first time, the text says that Israel has "taken a territory" and has "settled" there. These verbs appear in Num 21:21–26, in the account of the campaign against Sihon, the king of the Amorites; see 21:25: "Israel took all these towns, and Israel settled in all the towns of the Amorites, in Heshbon, and in all its villages." See also 21:31: "Thus Israel settled in the land of the Amorites." In addition, in 21:24, a key verb related to the conquest occurs, *yrš* ("to conquer, take possession"): "Israel put him to the sword, and took possession (*wayyíraš*) of his land from the Arnon to the Jabbok."

From this moment on, the account centers around the conquest. For example, Numbers 32 contains instructions for the distribution of the territory of Transjordan and Numbers 34 for Cisjordan. Num 21:10–20 serves as a transition between the two stages of the march in the wilderness. The oracles of

---

47. Knierim, "Numbers," 156–60. Here, see esp. p. 159. From the methodological viewpoint, Knierim's observation is very important. The structure helps us to understand the entire book and the articulation of the two parts.

48. G. W. Coats, "The Wilderness Itinerary," *CBQ* 34 (1972) 135–52; G. I. Davies, "The Wilderness Itineraries: A Comparative Study," *TynBul* 25 (1974) 46–81; idem, *The Way of the Wilderness: A Geographical Study of the Wilderness Itineraries in the Old Testament* (SOTSMS 5; Cambridge, 1979); J. Van Seters, *The Life of Moses: The Yahwist as Historian in Exodus–Numbers* (Contributions to Biblical Exegesis and Theology 10; Louisville, 1994) 153–64. For the Mesopotamian parallels, see Davies, "Wilderness Itineraries," 52–78.

Balaam (Numbers 22–24) occupy a key position in this structure, at the beginning of the conquest. They do indeed show that no one can stand in the way of the divine plan.

To *conclude*, I propose the following structure for the book of Numbers:

1. Preparation for the campaign—1:1–10:10
2. Execution of the campaign—10:11–36:13
   a. The march in the wilderness—10:11–21:20
   b. The beginning of the conquest—21:21–36:13.

3. The Meaning of the Book of Numbers[49]

The problem presented in the book of Numbers is to know how to "march with YHWH," who resides in the tent, in the midst of Israel. The first part of the book (1:1–10:10) is primarily dedicated to the organization of the tribes around the tent (Numbers 2) and to the charge to the Levites in the service of the tent (Numbers 3–4). Numbers 7–8 contains other religious prescriptions that are also connected to the sanctuary. Numbers 10 deals with the immediate preparation for the departure. The second part of the book (10:11–36:13) shows what it actually means to "march with YHWH." YHWH is ready to help his people, but he is above all a God who punishes all rebellion (11; 12; 13–14; 16–17; 20:1–13; 21:4–9; 25). In the most cases, all the people rebel against YHWH as well as against Moses and Aaron. However, in certain cases, YHWH punishes individuals: Aaron and Miriam in Numbers 12; Dathan, Abiram, and the sons of Korah in Numbers 16; Moses and Aaron in Num 20:1–13.

The most important episode is found in Numbers 13–14, where the whole generation of the Exodus is condemned to die in the wilderness because they refused to conquer the Promised Land. The message is clear: the failure was not in any way due to the preparation of the campaign: YHWH had foreseen everything. The wanderings result from Israel's sins. However, when the Israelites follow the instructions that YHWH gives to Moses, they succeed in all of their undertakings. This is also the case, for example, in the first wars of conquest (21:21–32; 21:33–35; 31). If the Pentateuch was composed for Israel after the Exile, the book of Numbers explains under what conditions they may regain the Promised Land.

F. The Structure of the Book of Deuteronomy

The structure of Deuteronomy is based on four "titles," the construction and contents of which are analogous:

---

49. Knierim, "Numbers," 160–63.

1:1: These are the words that Moses spoke to all Israel beyond the Jordan.

4:44: This is the law that Moses set before the Israelites.

28:69: These are the words of the covenant that YHWH commanded Moses to make with the Israelites . . .

33:1: This is the blessing with which Moses, the man of God, blessed the Israelites before his death.[50]

This book requires special treatment.[51] Briefly, the book of Deuteronomy is to be distinguished from Exodus–Numbers for one main reason: it contains "words of Moses" (Deut 1:1), whereas Leviticus and Numbers explicitly present their content as "words of YHWH" (Lev 1:1–2, 26:46, 27:34; Num 1:1, 36:13; see also Exod 20:1, 22; 21:1; 24:3). Therefore, we have in the book of Deuteronomy the first "commentary" on the Law/Teaching by the most dependable and most competent commentator, Moses himself.[52]

Thus, the books of the Pentateuch are not all structured in the same way, and they do not all present a clear structure. Nonetheless, it is possible to elucidate the structure of the canonical text of each book. We now need to study this canonical text more closely to see if it is unified or if it bears marks that reveal it to be a composite work based on older elements.[53]

---

50. See P. Kleinert, *Das Deuteronomium und die Deuteronomiker: Untersuchungen zur alttestamentlichen Rechts- und Literaturgeschichte* (Bielefeld and Leipzig, 1872) 167; Lohfink, "Der Bundesschluss im Lande Moab, 32–56, especially pp. 32–33 (= *Studien zum Deuteronomium*, 1.53–82, especially pp. 53–54); idem, "Bund als Vertrag im Deuteronomium," 219; G. Braulik, *Deuteronomium 1–16,17* (NEchtB; Würzburg, 1986) 5–6.

51. See my *Introduzione al Deuteronomio: Struttura, storia, teologia* (Rome, 1995).

52. Idem, "La structure du Pentateuque dans sa forme canonique," *ZAW* 113 (2001) 331–52.

53. Complementary bibliography on the canonical reading of the OT: J. Barton, *Oracles of God: Perceptions of Ancient Prophecy in Israel after the Exile* (Oxford, 1986); R. T. Beckwith, *The Old Testament Canon of the New Testament Church and Its Background in Early Judaism* (Grand Rapids, 1985); J. Blenkinsopp, *Prophecy and Canon: A Contribution to the Study of Jewish Origins* (Notre Dame, IN, 1977); W. Brueggemann, *The Creative Word: Canon as a Model for Biblical Education* (Philadelphia, 1982); R. E. Clements, *Prophecy and Tradition* (Atlanta, 1975); L. M. McDonald, *The Formation of the Christian Biblical Canon* (2nd ed.; Peabody, MA, 1995); D. F. Morgan, *Between Text and Comunity: The "Writings" in Canonical Interpretation* (Minneapolis, 1990); P. R. Noble, *The Canonical Approach: A Critical Reconstruction of the Hermeneutics of Brevard S. Child* (Biblical Interpretation Series 16; Leiden, 1995); J. H. Sailhamer, *Introduction to Old Testament Theology: A Canonical Approach* (Grand Rapids, 1995); G. T. Sheppard, "Canonical Criticism," *ABD* 1.961–66.

Works of B. S. Childs: Exodus; Introduction to the Old Testament as Scripture; Biblical Theology of the Old and New Testaments: Theological Reflection on the Christian Bible (London, 1992).

Works of J. A. Sanders: Torah and Canon; Canon and Community: A Guide to Canonical Criticism (Philadelphia, 1984); From Sacred Story to Sacred Text: Canon as Paradigm (Philadelphia, 1987); "Canon," *ABD* 1.837–52; "The Integrity of Biblical Pluralism," in *"Not in Heaven": Coherence and Complexity in Biblical Narrative* (ed. J. P. Rosenblatt and J. C. Sitterson; Indianapolis, IN, 1991) 154–69.

Chapter 3

Literary Problems of the Pentateuch I: The Legislative Texts

The reading of the Pentateuch in its "canonical form" has already brought to light the variety of contents in the first five books of the Bible. In this chapter I would like to show that is impossible to attribute the Pentateuch to a single "author." On the one hand, many of the legislative and narrative texts are quite similar and, on the other hand, they contain undeniable differences. These comparative texts are the famous "doublets" of the Pentateuch. The simplest explanation is to say that different authors wrote these texts at different times.

Here we will first look at examples of legislative texts,[1] and then, in the following chapters, we will analyze some narrative texts. The legislative texts have special value because they are presented as the "Words" of YHWH, revealed directly to Moses and transmitted by him to the people of Israel (see Exod 20:18–21, Deut 5:23–31). Although all of the legislative texts have the same authority, obvious discrepancies may be noted between the various laws, above all between the three major codes: the "Covenant Code" or the "Book of the Covenant" (Exod 20:22–23:33), the "Deuteronomic Code" (Deut 12:1–26:15), and the "Holiness Code" (Leviticus 17–26). Analysis shows that certain laws were written in reference to others, which they correct. The laws about slaves, loans, the love of enemies, and the Decalogue provide the clearest examples of this phenomenon.

A. The Laws with Regard to Slaves[2]

1. The Covenant Code (Exod 21:2–11)

The law regarding slaves in the Covenant Code distinguishes the case of a male slave from the case of a female slave:

---

1. For a brief presentation, see Zenger (ed.), *Einleitung*, 54–61.

2. On this point, see I. Cardellini, *Die biblischen "Sklaven"—Gesetze in Lichte des Keilschriftlichen Sklavenrechts: Ein Beitrag zur Tradition, Überlieferung und Redaktion der alttestamentlichen Rechtstexte* (BBB 55; Bonn, 1981); G. C. Chirichigno, *Debt-Slavery in Israel and in the Ancient Near East* (JSOTSup 141; Sheffield, 1993); B. S. Jackson, "Biblical Laws of Slavery: A Comparative Approach," in *Slavery and Others Forms of Unfree Labour* (ed. L. J. Archer; London,

[2]When you buy a male Hebrew slave, he shall serve six years, but in the seventh he shall go out a free person, without debt. [3]If he comes in single, he shall go out single; if he comes in married, then his wife shall go out with him. [4]If his master gives him a wife and she bears him sons or daughters, the wife and her children shall be her master's and he shall go out alone. [5]But if the slave declares, "I love my master, my wife, and my children; I will not go out a free person," [6]then his master shall bring him before God. He shall be brought to the door or the doorpost; and his master shall pierce his ear with an awl; and he shall serve him for life.

[7]When a man sells his daughter as a slave, she shall not go out as the male slaves do. [8]If she does not please her master, who designated her for himself, then he shall let her be redeemed; he shall have no right to sell her to a foreign people, since he has dealt unfairly with her. [9]If he designates her for his son, he shall deal with her as with a daughter. [10]If he takes another wife to himself, he shall not diminish the food, clothing, or marital rights of the first wife. [11]And if he does not do these three things for her, she shall go out without debt, without payment of money.

The law in Exod 21:1–11 concerns people who have been given or acquired to pay debts; the text does not deal with the question of "permanent slaves" such as prisoners of war, for example.

It is not always easy to interpret the details of this law.[3] One thing, however, is clear: this law emphasizes the rights and the duties of masters toward their male and female servants. Its first aim is to protect the rights of families. This is why it begins by settling questions about marriage.

2. The Deuteronomic Code (Deut 15:12–18)

Deut 15:12–18 is similar to the Covenant Code on certain points, yet on others it substantially diverges. In the following translation, I have italicized the passages common to the two laws:

1988) 86–101; J. M. Hamilton, *Social Justice and Deuteronomy: The Case of Deuteronomy 15* (SBLDS 136; Atlanta, 1992); N. P. Lemche, "The Hebrew Slave," *VT* 25 (1975) 129–44; idem, "The Manumission of Slaves—The Fallow Year—The Sabbatical Year—The Jobel Year," *VT* 26 (1976) 38–59; I. Mendelsohn, *Slavery in the Ancient Near East* (New York, 1949); A. Phillips, "The Laws of Slavery: Exod 21,2–11," *JSOT* 30 (1984) 51–66; J. P. M. van der Ploeg, "Slavery in the Old Testament," in *Congress Volume: Uppsala, 1971* (VTSup 22; Leiden, 1972) 72–87; B. M. Levinson, "The Birth of the Lemma: Recovering the Restrictive Interpretation of the Covenant Code's Manumission Law by the Holiness Code (Lev 25:44–46)," *JBL* 124 (2005) 617–39; idem, "The Manumission Laws of the Pentateuch as a Challenge to Contemporary Pentateuchal Theory," in *Congress Volume: Leiden, 2004* (ed. André Lemaire; VTSup 109; Leiden: Brill, 2006) 281–324.

3. See the commentaries for a detailed discussion; also see my *Il codice dell'alleanza: Il diritto biblico e le leggi cuneiformi. Esegesi di Es 21,2–32* (Rome, 1996).

¹² If a member of your community, whether a *Hebrew* man or a *Hebrew* woman, is sold to you and *works for you six years, in the seventh year* you shall set that person *free*. ¹³ And when you send a male slave out from you a free person, you shall not send him out empty-handed. ¹⁴ Provide liberally out of your flock, your threshing floor, and your wine press, thus giving to him some of the bounty with which YHWH your God has blessed you. ¹⁵ Remember that you were a slave in the land of Egypt, and YHWH your God redeemed you; for this reason I lay this command upon you today. ¹⁶ But *if he says to you, "I will not go out from you,"* because he *loves* you and your household, since he is well off with you, ¹⁷ then you shall take an *awl* and thrust it through his *earlobe* into *the door*, and *he shall be your slave forever.* You shall do the same with regard to your female slave. ¹⁸ Do not consider it a hardship when you send them out from you free persons, because for *six years* they have given you services worth the wages of hired laborers; and YHWH your God will bless you in all that you do.

A comparison of Exod 21:2–11 and Deut 15:12–18 reveals four essential items: [4] certain points of the laws converge; but in some cases the law of Deuteronomy corrects the Covenant Code; generally, the law of Deuteronomy is less detailed than the Covenant Code; however, Deuteronomy 15 also contains new elements.

a. Similarities

Exodus 21 and Deuteronomy 15 converge on three important points: both laws deal with Hebrew slaves (*'ibrî*); the length of the servitude is fixed at six years, and the slave is freed in the seventh year; if the slave wishes to remain with his master, the same procedure is performed: the earlobe of the servant is pierced with an awl against a door.

b. Differences

• The first and most important difference concerns the treatment of female servants. The Covenant Code treats male and female servants in contrasting ways, because a female servant *cannot* be freed after six years ("she shall not go out as the male slaves do"; Exod 21:7), whereas in the Deuteronomic Code the law is applied to a male as well as to a female slave: "If a member of your community, whether a *Hebrew* man or a *Hebrew* woman, is sold to you." Both serve for six years and are freed the seventh year (Deut 15:12). The same rule also applies to the servant who wants to remain with his master and has his earlobe pierced with an awl, regardless of gender: "You shall do the same with regard to your female slave" (Deut 15:17).

• Male and female servants are not just insignificant people; they are "brothers" and "sisters" ("your brother"; Deut 15:12). The Deuteronomic

---

4. On this Deuteronomistic law, see Hamilton, *Social Justice and Deuteronomy.*

Code insists on the fraternity and solidarity that should unite all members of the people of Israel.

• When the male and female servants have completed their time of service, the Deuteronomic Law introduces the right to an "end-of-service indemnity."[5] This right stipulates that the slave (man or woman) be given certain goods permitting him or her to survive after the end of the time of service. The slaves have worked for their master for six years, and they therefore have little at their disposal. If they do not receive help, they are almost certainly condemned to misery.

• The "ritual of the door" in Deuteronomy presents something new: it does not take place "before God" (Exod 21:6)—that is, probably at a local sanctuary—but at the door of the master's house (Deut 15:16), because in Deuteronomy there can only be one central sanctuary (Deuteronomy 12).

c. Omissions in the Deuteronomic Law

The Deuteronomic Law is simpler than the Covenant Code: it only deals with the length of service and the conditions of liberation, leaving out all of the clauses regarding the marriage of slaves (men or women) that occupy a great deal of space in the law of Exod 21:1–11.

d. Additions in the Deuteronomic Law

The Deuteronomic Law is more theological than the Covenant Code. Thus, Deuteronomy 15 mentions YHWH three times (15:14, 15, 18). Twice it speaks about blessing (15:14, 18). In addition, it connects the law regarding slaves to the experience of the Exodus, that is, to salvation history (15:15). Just as the Israelites were slaves in Egypt and were liberated by YHWH their God, so they must now liberate their own slaves and must not send them away empty-handed.

Conclusion. The main problem treated by the Deuteronomic Law is the liberation of male and female slaves. Deuteronomy insists much more than the Covenant Code on the rights of male and female servants.

3. The Holiness Code (Lev 25:39–55)

This law does not have the same strong connections with Exod 21:2–11 or Deut 15:12–18 that the two of them have with each other. Nevertheless, the relations between the law in Leviticus and the others are undeniable. The first part of the law in Leviticus (Lev 25:39–43) deals with Hebrew slaves and has several similarities to the other two laws. In the following translation, the expressions in italic appear in both the law of Leviticus and the law of Deuteronomy:

---

5. The indemnity paid at the end of a work contract, at the moment of "settlement."

[39] If any *who are dependent on you* become so impoverished that *they sell themselves to you*, you shall not make them serve as slaves. [40] They shall remain with you as hired or bound laborers. They shall serve with you until the year of the jubilee. [41] Then they and their children with them *shall be free from your authority*; they shall go back to their own family and return to their ancestral property. [42] For they are my servants, whom I brought out of the land of Egypt; they shall not be sold as slaves are sold. [43] You shall not rule over them with harshness, but shall fear your God.

• This law once again evokes the "brother" concept, as does Deut 15:12, but it does not mention female servants. Moreover, in the context of Leviticus 25, "brother" primarily means "Hebrew" and "non-foreigner" (cf. 25:44). Just like the law of Deuteronomy, the law of Leviticus refers to people who are obliged to "sell" themselves in order to pay their debts and to their eventual liberation. There is one major contrast with the preceding laws: the law of Leviticus actually abolishes slavery among the people of Israel. Anyone who cannot repay a debt is employed as a worker or resident alien, not a "slave" (*ʿebed*), as Lev 25:39–40 [6] clearly stipulates.

• However, liberation only occurs every 50 years, during the year of Jubilee (Lev 25:40b). At that moment, the worker returns to his clan and, what is even more important, to his heritage.

• As in Deut 15:15, the law recalls the experience of the Exodus to justify its norms: because all of the members of the people of Israel are God's "servants," they cannot be "servants" of one another (25:42; cf. 25:55). In the presence of the God of the Exodus, all members of the people of Israel are equal.

The other laws in Leviticus 25 deal with cases of foreign slaves and a Hebrew who becomes the slave of a foreigner. These situations exist neither in the Covenant Code nor in the Deuteronomic Code, or at least they do not raise any legal problems:

[44] As for the male and female slaves whom you may have, it is from the nations around you that you may acquire male and female slaves. [45] You may also acquire them from among the aliens residing with you, and from their families that are with you, who have been born in your land; and they may be your property. [46] You may keep them as a possession for your children after you, for them to inherit as property. These you may treat as slaves, but as for your fellow Israelites, no one shall rule over the other with harshness.

Lev 25:39–43 and 25:44–46 make a clear distinction between a Hebrew, who can become a "worker" but not a slave, and a foreigner, who will be a "permanent slave." Lev 25:47–55 provides for an Israelite who becomes the slave of a foreigner and for the modes of his redemption. Like the laws of Deuter-

---

6. See, among others, Crüsemann, "Exodus," 124–25.

onomy, Leviticus above all attempts to protect Israelites against the perils of getting into debt. This is why Leviticus emphasizes the rights of poor Israelites more than the rights of masters.

4. Conclusion

The similarities with and differences between these laws are clear. This presents a serious legal problem: which law prevails as far as slavery is concerned? Should the slave be freed after six years (Exodus and Deuteronomy) or during the celebration of the Jubilee year (Leviticus)? After six years, must only the male slaves be freed (Exodus) or may female slaves also be freed (Deuteronomy)? Is one permitted to acquire a Hebrew slave (Exodus, Deuteronomy), or is this prohibited (Leviticus)?

Contradictory laws appear in the same Pentateuch and have the same divine and Mosaic authority because YHWH transmitted them all to Moses on Mount Sinai. Were these laws written by the same author in the same period? If this was the case, Israel's legislation is confusing and cannot be applied.

B. The Laws regarding Loans: Exod 22:24, Deut 23:20–21, Lev 25:35–36[7]

The primary goal of the laws regarding loans is to reduce the effects of the indebtedness and impoverishment of weaker classes in the population.

1. The Covenant Code (Exod 22:24)

If you lend money to my people, to the poor among you, you shall not deal with them as a creditor; you shall not exact interest from them.

This law is simple and clear: it only deals with lending money and prohibits loans with interest among the people of Israel, especially to the weak.

2. The Deuteronomic Code (Deut 23:20–21)

You shall not charge interest on loans to another Israelite, interest on money, interest on provisions, interest on anything that is lent. On loans to a foreigner you may charge interest, but on loans to another Israelite you may not charge interest, so that YHWH your God may bless you in all your undertakings in the land that you are about to enter and possess.

---

7. See Zenger (ed.), *Einleitung*; for more details, see the commentaries and E. Neufeld, "The Prohibitions against Loans at Interest in Ancient Hebrew Laws," *HUCA* 26 (1955) 355–412.

Three points deserve attention. The Deuteronomic Law is more detailed and more precise than the Covenant Code because it excludes all kinds of interest, while Exod 22:24 only refers to money. Furthermore, the law introduces a distinct difference between the Israelites (the famous "brother" of the Deuteronomic legislation) and the foreigner (23:21a). Finally, the law introduces a theological incentive: "so that YHWH your God may bless you" (23:21b).

3. The Holiness Code (Lev 25:35–36)

> If any of your kin fall into difficulty and become dependent on you, you shall support them; they shall live with you as though resident aliens. Do not take interest in advance or otherwise make a profit from them, but fear your God; let them live with you.

The law of Leviticus introduces a fundamental change: not only is lending with interest prohibited, *helping* a brother who is in difficulty is required. The interpretation of the words "stranger or guest" is not clear. However, it seems that the law applies to Israelites in difficulty norms that were applied to "guests," that is, immigrants. Finally, the law of Deuteronomy, like the law of Leviticus, contains a theological motive.

The three repetitions of the law converge on one essential point: a prohibition of loans with interest. On other points, there are differences. For example, what is the creditor's duty: not to lend with interest (Exodus, Deuteronomy) or, more than that, to help the debtor (Leviticus)? Does the law apply only to Israelites (Deuteronomy) or does it also apply to immigrants and resident aliens (Leviticus)? Does the prohibition against loans at interest apply only to money loans (Exodus) or also to any other kind of loan (goods) (Deuteronomy)?

The repetitions and differences create problems that are not minor for those who must apply the law.

C. The Laws concerning the Enemy's Donkey or the Love of One's Enemies: Exod 23:4–5; Deut 22:1–4; Lev 19:17–18 [8]

1. The Covenant Code (Exod 23:4–5) [9]

> When you come upon your enemy's ox or donkey going astray, you shall bring it back. When you see the donkey of one who hates you lying under its burden and you would hold back from setting it free, [you must help to set it free].

---

8. See Zenger (ed.), *Einleitung*, 54–58. On these laws, also see G. Barbiero, *L'asino del nemico: Rinuncia alla vendetta e amore del nemico nella legislazione dell'Antico Testamento (Es 23,4–5, Dt 22,1–4, Lv 19,17–18)* (AnBib 128; Rome, 1991).

9. The translation is uncertain. See the commentaries and the work by Barbiero indicated in the preceding note.

The "enemy" mentioned in this text must be a neighbor, and he is probably an adversary in a lawsuit or the member of a rival clan. The law shows that, in certain circumstances, solidarity must be stronger than "feuds" or the desire for vengeance. It is only a question here of the enemy's donkey because whoever encounters the "donkey of a friend" would certainly lead it back to him voluntarily. The donkey and the ox are two essential animals in an agricultural and pastoral economy.

2. The Deuteronomic Code (Deut 22:1–4)

> [1]You shall not watch your neighbor's ox or sheep straying away and ignore them; you shall take them back to their owner. [2]If the owner does not reside near you or you do not know who the owner is, you shall bring it to your own house, and it shall remain with you until the owner claims it; then you shall return it. [3]You shall do the same with a neighbor's donkey; you shall do the same with a neighbor's garment; and you shall do the same with anything else that your neighbor loses and you find. You may not withhold your help. [4]You shall not see your neighbor's donkey or ox fallen on the road and ignore it; you shall help to lift it up.

• The "enemy" or "the one you hate" in the Covenant Code becomes a "brother" in Deuteronomy. The law in Exod 23:4–5 is an exhortation to help one's enemy, whereas the Law in Deut 22:1–4 contains an invitation to brotherly love.[10] In Deut, this duty of solidarity is extended to all of the people.

• The law provides for the case of an animal that does not belong to someone living in the neighborhood. Deuteronomy legislates at a time of much population movement, while the Covenant Code deals with problems of local communities. Like the law on loans, the Deuteronomic law is more precise: it extends the duty to restoring a cloak or any lost object.

3. The Holiness Code (Lev 19:17–18)

> You shall not hate in your heart anyone of your kin; you shall reprove your neighbor, or you will incur guilt yourself. You shall not take vengeance or bear a grudge against any of your people, but you shall love your neighbor as yourself: I am YHWH.

The law of Leviticus no longer mentions animals or lost objects. It deals with duties within the community. Among brothers and compatriots, hate should never exist. On the contrary, it is important to correct any who do not walk in righteousness. Even vengeance and wrath must be eliminated. The law aims at creating a kind of solidarity between people that will help them to overcome

---

10. Against Barbiero, see A. Schenker's review of Barbiero in *Bib* 73 (1992) 263–65, especially p. 264.

disruptive social behavior, up to and including the desires for "vengeance" and "feuds." National solidarity becomes a primary obligation for each person.

4. Conclusion

These laws are not contradictory, but it is difficult to attribute them to a single author because the settings and phraseology are so different. Why, for example, are there three laws on the same topic in three different passages of the Pentateuch?

D. The Decalogue[11]

The Decalogue is the core text of the whole Law of the Old Testament. This text is the only one that YHWH transmitted directly to the people, without Moses' mediation (Exod 20:1; see especially Deut 5:4). Moreover, according to various witnesses, God himself inscribed it on two stone tablets (Exod 24:12, 31:18, 32:15; Deut 5:22).

Two forms of this "ethical Decalogue" figure in the Pentateuch: Exod 20:1–17 and in Deut 5:6–21. Considering the fact that in both cases YHWH himself proclaims the same Decalogue at the same point in time and on the same mountain, Sinai/Horeb, before the same Israelites, one would expect to encounter the same text. But this is not the case! Exegetes have enumerated approximately 20 differences between Exodus 20 and Deuteronomy 5.[12] The passage in Deuteronomy contains a series of "additions" in comparison with Exodus 20; in 7 cases, this only concerns a coordinating conjunction *wĕ* ("and"). Three of these variations, however, appear to be more significant.

---

11. See Zenger (ed.), *Einleitung*, 58–60; for a recent bibliography on the Decalogue, consult W. H. Schmidt, H. Delkurt, and A. Graupner, *Die Zehn Gebote im Rahmen alttestamentlicher Ethik* (Erträge der Forschung 281; Darmstadt, 1993). For a comparison of the two forms of the Decalogue, see F.-L. Hossfeld, *Der Dekalog: Seine späten Fassungen, die originale Komposition und seine Vorstufen* (OBO 45; Fribourg and Göttingen, 1982); C. Levin, "Der Dekalog am Sinai," *VT* 35 (1985) 165–91; A. Graupner, "Zum Verhältnis der beiden Dekalogfassungen Exod 20 und Dtn 5: Ein Gespräch mit Frank-Lothar Hossfeld," *ZAW* 99 (1987) 308–29; F.-L. Hossfeld, "Zum synoptischen Vergleich der Dekalogfassungen: Eine Fortführung des begonnenen Gesprächs," in *Vom Sinai zum Horeb: Stationen alttestamentlicher Glaubensgeschichte* (ed. F.-L. Hossfeld; Würzburg, 1989) 73–118; J. Loza, *Las Palabras de Yahve: Estudio del Decálogo* (Biblioteca Mexicana; Mexico City, 1989); B. Z. Segal (ed.), *The Ten Commandments in History and Tradition* (Jerusalem, 1990); R. G. Kratz, "Der Dekalog im Exodusbuch," *VT* 44 (1994) 205–38.

12. See, for example, J. J. Stamm, *Der Dekalog im Lichte der neueren Forschung* (Berne, 1958) 5 (20 differences); Loza, *Palabras de Yahve*, 99–102 (22 differences); Schmidt, Delkurt, and Graupner, *Zehn Gebote*, 34–35 (synopsis).

1. The Commandment regarding the Sabbath (Exod 20:8–11, Deut 5:12–15)

In Exod 20:8–11 the motivation is different from that in Deut 5:12–15. Exod 20:8–11 ties the commandment regarding the Sabbath to God's resting on the seventh day of Creation (20:11), while Deut 5:15 relates it to the experience of the Exodus. Exodus 20 uses the theology of Creation as an argument, and Deuteronomy 5 prefers the theology of salvation history.

2. The Structure of the Decalogue [13]

The Decalogue in Exod 20:1–17 distinguishes ten commandments, each of which begins with an imperative verb or what grammars call a "vetitive" (*lō'* "not" followed by a *yiqtol* verb). Exod 20:2 is a "title." So we have the following progression:

20:2:	Title
20:3:	Prohibition of worshiping other gods
20:4–6:	Prohibition of making images
20:7:	Prohibition of using the divine name in vain
20:8–11:	Commandment of the Sabbath
20:12:	Commandment to honor one's parents
20:13:	Prohibition of killing
20:14:	Prohibition of committing adultery
20:15:	Prohibition of stealing
20:16:	Prohibition of giving false witness
20:17:	Prohibition of coveting what belongs to others

The Decalogue in Deuteronomy is not structured the same way; it is divided into three sections.[14] The commandment of the Sabbath is placed at the core of

---

13. See Zenger (ed.), *Einleitung*, 60; for other proposals, see R. Meynet, "Les dix commandements, loi de liberté: Analyse rhétorique d'Exod 20,2–7 et Dt 5,6–21," *Mélanges de l'Université Saint-Joseph* 50 (Beirut, 1984) 405–21; H. J. Koorevaar, "De opbouw van de tien woorden in Exodus 20:1–17," *Acta Theologica* 15 (1995) 1–15.

14. Cf. N. Lohfink, "Zur Dekalogfassung von Dt 5," *BZ* 9 (1965) 17–32 (= *Studien zum Deuteronomium*, 1.193–209), who divides the text into five parts (p. 203):

    I. Worship of Yhwh—5:6–10 (long)
    II. The name of Yhwh—5:11 (short)
    III. The Sabbath—5:12–15 (long)
    IV. The parents—5:16 (short)
    V. Moral commandments—5:17–21 (long)

The difficulty with this outline comes from the fact that there is no stylistic reason to separate 5:11 from the rest of the text. The construction of Deut 5:6–11 is identical to that of Exod 20:3–7.

the text and tied to the introduction and conclusion by a series of verbal references. The verb "to bring out" appears in 5:6 ("I brought you out") and in
5:15 ("and [YHWH your God] brought you out"). This verb links the beginning of the Decalogue to the commandment of the Sabbath. In addition, this
same commandment of the Sabbath and the final commandment, the prohibition of coveting what belongs to others, have two common terms: "your male
and female slave" (*ʿebed, ʾāmâ*; Deut 5:14, 21). These two terms are also present
in the Exodus 20 version.

The second part of the Deuteronomic Decalogue (Deut 5:16–21) constitutes a chain of coordinated clauses. Deuteronomy repeats *wĕlōʾ* ("neither shall
you . . .") seven times after the initial *lōʾ* ("you shall not . . .") in Deut 5:17,
whereas in Exod 20:13–17 the five repetitions of *lōʾ* follow one another without coordination. In Deuteronomy 5, this second part appears as a positive
commandment, honoring one's parents, within a series of six prohibitions. The
first part (Deut 5:6–11) also begins with an assertion (5:6) that is followed by
five interdictions, all of which are related to YHWH.

We therefore have the following macrostructure:[15]

   A.   Deut 5:6–11:   the commandments concerning YHWH
    X.   Deut 5:12–15:   the Sabbath
   A′.   Deut 5:16–21:   the social commandments

The text of Deuteronomy is more structured and more organized, especially in
the second part, where major differences in style and content distinguish it
from Exodus 20. The structure of Deuteronomy 5 emphasizes the commandment of the Sabbath, which is both a commandment relative to YHWH and a
social commandment. Centered on the experience of the Exodus, this commandment becomes the symbol of responsibilities to YHWH, who is the God-
liberator (5:6, 15), and to one's "freed" neighbor (5:14, 21).

3. The Second Part of the Decalogue[16]

The major differences between the two versions of the Decalogue are particularly noticeable in the second part. It is useful to study this matter more
closely. The text of Exod 20:13–17 contains five social commandments that are
not connected and have no apparent order. However, in Deut 5:17–21, the six
commandments are coordinated and form two successive, mutually corresponding series (5:17–19 and 5:20–21ab). The first series deals with violations

---

15. I do not rule out subdividing the text. I just maintain that it is important to note its
main points of emphasis.

16. Zenger (ed.), *Einleitung*, 59.

as such and the second with their main causes.[17] Moreover, the first series includes short prohibitions (two words in Hebrew), while the second contains longer formulations:

Violations	*Principal causes*
Assassination, 5:17	False witness, 5:20
Adultery, 5:18	Coveting a neighbor's wife, 5:21a
Stealing, 5:19	Coveting the possessions of others, 5:21b

False witness in a trial is one of the simplest ways to take vengeance on one's enemy or adversary. This often leads to homicide, as in the famous case of Naboth (1 Kgs 21: "Naboth's vineyard"). Coveting another man's wife leads to adultery, and coveting his belongings naturally ends in theft. In comparison with Exod 20:13–17, Deuteronomy evidences deeper reflection and a greater pedagogical sense.[18]

4. The "Cultic Decalogue" (Exod 34:11–26)[19]

After the episode of the golden calf (Exodus 32), during which Moses destroyed the tablets of the Law (32:15–16, 19), he intercedes for the people and obtains divine forgiveness. In order to seal this reconciliation, YHWH orders Moses in Exod 34:1, saying: "Cut two tablets of stone like the former ones, and I will write on the tablets the words that were on the former tablets, which you broke." After this declaration, the reader expects to find a Decalogue identical to the words of Exod 20:1–17. But this is not the case. The "Decalogue" in Exod 34:11–26 contains prescriptions that only concern the cult owed to YHWH alone: the prohibition of having other gods, laws concerning the sacrifices, and the liturgical calendar. This is why it is called the "cultic Decalogue."

---

17. Zenger (*Einleitung*, 59) instead speaks of secret violations and public violations. But it seems to me that this distinction does not correspond exactly to what differentiates the two series. Are desiring another man's wife and coveting his belongings public violations of the law?

18. In Deuteronomy, the Decalogue is the law that must be observed by each person belonging to Israel, wherever he or she may be. Conversely, only the inhabitants of the land are obliged to observe the other laws (cf. 5:1 and 6:1).

19. See Zenger (ed.), *Einleitung*, 60; on Exod 34:11–26, see J. Halbe, *Das Privilegrecht Jawhes (Ex 34,10–26): Gestalt und Wesen, Herkunft und Wirken in vordeuteronomischer Zeit* (FRLANT 14; Göttingen, 1975); E. Blum, "Das sog. 'Privilegrecht' in Exodus 34,11–26: Ein Fixpunkt der Komposition des Exodusbuches?" in *Studies in the Book of Exodus: Redaction—Reception—Interpretation* (ed. M. Vervenne; BETL 126; Leuven, 1996) 347–66; B. M. Levinson, "Goethe's Analysis of Exodus 34 and Its Influence on Julius Wellhausen: The *Pfropfung* of the Documentary Hypothesis," *ZAW* 114 (2002) 212–23.

In Exodus 34, even the prohibition of having other gods is expressed differently from Exod 20:3. Moreover, Exod 34:11–26 has a parallel in the final part of the "Covenant Code" (Exod 23:10–19).[20] There are verbal correspondences but also differences in the order of the commandments and their formulation. Lastly, there are many ties between the "cultic Decalogue" and the second part of the "Covenant Code" and the "Deuteronomic Code."

5. Conclusion

These repetitions, tensions, and contradictions between the "divine discourses" raise serious problems for critics. From a literary point of view, it is difficult to attribute all of these texts to the same author. Indeed, a single author would have avoided these difficulties. It is simpler to argue that these laws were written in different periods and correspond to different situations and concerns.

From a theological point of view, the number of laws that correct one another raises another problem: that of the divine authority of the Law as such. In Israel, YHWH alone could change the Law he had sealed by his authority and transmitted through Moses. A modification to the divine Law was accepted only if YHWH had promulgated it through the mediation of Moses and if it harked back to revelation on Mount Sinai. The problem of interpretation is to discern which "divine Law" is currently valid.

For the same reason, a new law did not abolish an older one: the Law was of divine origin, and its validity was therefore "permanent"; it could not be abrogated. Consequently, a "new law" was considered to be a form of an old law. It was both identical and different. In practical terms, only a new, "updated" formulation was valid.[21] Even the New Testament is to be understood, in certain areas, as an updating of the Old Testament (cf. Matt 5:17).

There are two reasons for this phenomenon. On the one hand, the Law was not valid unless it was founded on divine authority. Therefore, it had to be ancient and derived from the Mosaic, "Sinai" revelation. On the other hand, in order to be applicable, the Law had constantly to be updated and interpreted in accordance with the changing situations that Israel experienced throughout its history.[22]

---

20. See Exod 34:18 and 23:15; 34:20 and 23:15; 34:23 and 23:14, 17; 34:25 and 23:15; 34:26 and 23:19.

21. On this point, see M. Fishbane, *Biblical Interpretation in Ancient Israel* (Oxford, 1985) 91–277.

22. B. M. Levinson demonstrates the hermeneutical issues involved in "'You Must Not Add Anything to What I Command You': Paradoxes of Canon and Authorship in Ancient Israel," *Numen: International Review for the History of Religions* 50 (2003) 1–51.

Chapter 4

Literary Problems of the Pentateuch II: The Narrative Texts

"Introductions" to the Pentateuch more often deal with the narratives than with the legislative texts. The great variety of theories proposed by exegetes regarding the analysis of narratives may overwhelm the novice and create confusion. Moreover, there is a tendency to "caricature" a certain type of analysis that succeeds in distinguishing diverse sources and editions even within a single verse. One gets the impression that the only tools that exegetes use are "scissors and paste." But, this is not really true.[1]

Before confronting various theories on the composition of the Pentateuch, however, we need to look at the problems that actually exist and that no serious reader can ignore. No attentive reader can deny the presence of repetitions, tensions, and contradictions in the Pentateuch. Disagreement only arises in the way these phenomena are interpreted. In this chapter, I will therefore present two kinds of problems: double and triple versions of the same event and the presence of doublets within a single narrative.

A. Different Versions of the Same Event

1. The Double Narrative of the Creation (Gen 1:1–2:4a and 2:4b–3:24)[2]

Anyone who reads the book of Genesis is undoubtedly surprised to note that God, after having created the universe in Gen 1:1–2:4a, appears to begin the whole process once again in Gen 2:4b–25. Furthermore, he does not create the same world the second time. There are many distinct differences between

---

1. For a good presentation of the historical-critical method, see H. Simian-Yofre, "Diacronia: I metodi storico-critici," in *Metodologia dell'Antico Testamento* (ed. H. Simian-Yofre; Bologna, 1994) 79–119; P. Guillemette and M. Brisbois, *Introduction aux méthodes historico-critiques* (Héritages et Projets 35; Montreal, 1987).

2. Notably see Zenger (ed.), *Einleitung*, 49; also see K. Koch, "P—kein Redaktor! Erinnerung an zwei Eckdaten der Quellenscheidung," *VT* 37 (1987) 446–67; Blenkinsopp, *Pentateuch*, 60–67; A. F. Campbell and M. O'Brien, *Sources of the Pentateuch: Texts, Introductions, Annotations* (Minneapolis, 1993) 22–23 and 92–94; Carr, *Reading the Fractures of Genesis*, 62–68.

the two accounts, notably in the way they present Creation, but also in their theology.

a. The Narrative

• In Genesis 1, the universe rises out of waters and primordial darkness (Gen 1:2). The picture suggested by this account is that of a world submerged by water, similar to the flooding that occurred each year in Mesopotamia and Egypt, although not in Israel. After the flood, the earth slowly reemerges from the waters, vegetation begins to cover it, and then living beings populate it. The description of the Creation in Genesis 1 largely follows this order. First God creates light (1:3–5), then the firmament (the heavens; 1:6–8), and finally he raises the earth out the waters and causes plants to grow (1:14–19). After that, he creates the living beings: birds, animals, plants, and human beings (1:20–31). All of this happens in the course of one week.

In Genesis 2, quite on the contrary, before divine intervention, the earth is a wilderness without water. In Genesis 1 there is nothing but water, while in Genesis 2 there is no water at all. It has not yet rained, and only a "river" waters the land (2:6).[3] God forms the first human being, and then he plants the garden that springs up like an oasis in the middle of a barren steppe. This depiction of Creation reflects the climatic and geographic context of Palestine.[4]

• In Genesis 1, God creates the first couple on the sixth day (1:26–27), while in Genesis 2 he first creates ʾādām (the "human being," "man"; 2:7), and then at the end of the story, a woman (2:22).

• Genesis 1 contains a complete account of the Creation of the universe: the heavens, the sea, and the earth. Genesis 2, on the other hand, does not mention the creation of the heavens and of the sea, nor does it say anything of the stars. The second account of Creation only considers the earth and the living beings that thrive there.

According to Gen 1:11, God made plants grow on the surface of the earth without any distinction. But in Gen 3:18 there is a big difference between the garden full of trees giving good fruit (2:9) and the land outside the garden, where only "thorns and thistles" (3:8) grow.

• Of the plants and trees, Genesis 1 does not mention any special examples. Contrariwise, Genesis 2 notes the presence of the tree of knowledge of good and evil as well as the tree of life in the garden (2:11b).

---

3. The translation of this verse, especially the term ʿēd, is heavily disputed.

4. See O. Keel and M. Küchler, *Synoptische Texte aus der Genesis* (Biblische Beiträge 8; Fribourg, 1971) 49–103.

• According to Gen 1:29–30, all living beings are vegetarians, and it is forbidden to kill animals. After the Flood, in Gen 9:2–3, God changes this norm and allows, under certain conditions, the killing of animals in order to eat their meat. In Gen 3:21, God clothes the man and the woman with "skin tunics," and this, of course, implies that he has killed animals.[5]

b. Theology

The divinity who created the world does not have the same name in the two narratives. In the first one, he is simply called "God" (*ʾĕlohîm*; 35 times in 1:1–2:4a), whereas in the second account he has a double name: Yhwh God (*yhwh ʾĕlohîm*). The God of Genesis 1 is transcendent: he plans Creation with all its details, then calls forth the elements; everything he says comes to be, while he himself remains invisible and separate from what has been created.[6]

However, in Genesis 2–3, the divinity is more "anthropomorphic": Yhwh God forms the first human being out of clay and breathes the breath of life into his nostrils. Then he plants the trees and places the human being in the garden. After that, he recognizes that the human being is in need of something: he is alone. God searches for a solution to the problem of the first human being's solitude, first by creating the animals and then by creating the woman. In Genesis 3, God comes for an evening walk in the garden: he notices something strange and discovers, after investigation, the fall of the man and of the woman. This divinity does not seem to be "omniscient" or "all-powerful," and he differs significantly from the God of Genesis 1.

c. The Perspective

• Genesis 1 describes the Creation of the universe. First of all, God creates and organizes the essential elements of the universe: the light, darkness, heavens, earth, sea, and stars. The vegetation will serve to feed the living beings that live in the three parts of the world: the birds of the sky, the fish of the sea, and the animals and humans on earth. However, Genesis 2 primarily deals with the creation of humanity and with the conditions of life on earth. The earth needs human beings to cultivate it. The fertility of the soil depends on water. The trees must provide food for the human being, who also needs company in order to survive. This is why God first creates the animals and then the woman.

• The universe of Genesis 1 is entirely positive, to such an extent that the text of Gen 1:1–2:4a contains no negatives. It repeats seven times "and God

---

5. This problem greatly preoccupied the rabbis and the Church Fathers.

6. The distinction between the two divine appellations Yhwh and God (*ʾĕlohîm*) must be dealt with prudently. Following Rendtorff, Blum (*Komposition*, 471–77) has severely criticized the indiscriminate use of this criterion.

saw that it was good" (Gen 1:4, 10, 12, 18, 21, 25, 31). The first negative element appears in Genesis 2–3 with the "the tree of the knowledge of good and
evil" (Gen 2:11, 17; cf. 3:3).

d. Conclusion

These differences prevent us from attributing the two texts to a single author, just as they rule out a purely synchronic reading.[7]

2. The Triple Narrative about the Wife/Sister (Gen 12:10–20, 20:1–18, 26:1–11)[8]

In the book of Genesis, we find three narratives that present a patriarch, his
wife, and a foreign sovereign. The three accounts follow the same plotline:

1. The patriarch arrives in a foreign land.
2. He fears for his life and pretends that his wife is his sister.
3. The ploy is discovered by the land's sovereign.
4. This sovereign summons the patriarch and reproaches him for his
   deceit.

Despite the common structure, the three versions contain many differences.

The *first narrative* (Gen 12:10–20) unfolds in three successive phases, each of
which deals with a particular problem. The first problem is the famine, and its
solution is emigration to Egypt (12:10). However, this emigration raises another problem: Abraham fears for his life because Sarah is very beautiful, and he
fears that the inhabitants of the land may try to eliminate the husband in order
to get the wife (12:11–12). The solution to this is a ploy: Sarah must say that
she is Abraham's sister and not his wife (12:13). The subterfuge partially succeeds because Abraham is well treated by Pharaoh, but it also creates a further
problem: Sarah finds herself in Pharaoh's harem (12:14–16). Yнwн then intervenes and afflicts Pharaoh with plagues (12:17). He finally discovers the
truth—though we do not know exactly how—summons Abraham, directs re-

---

7. Even scholars attempting to read synchronically must recognize the differences between the two narratives. See, for example, T. C. Eskenazi ("Torah as Narrative and Narrative as Torah," in *Old Testament Interpretation: Past, Present, Future* [ed. J. L. Mays, D. L.
Petersen, and K. H. Richards; Edinburgh, 1995] 13–30), who refers, among others, to
R. Alter, *The Art of Biblical Narrative* (New York, 1981) 141–47.

8. Much has been written about this phenomenon. For a recent study, see I. Fischer, *Die
Erzeltern Israels: Feministisch-theologische Studien zu Genesis 12–36* (BZAW 222; Berlin, 1994);
also see S. Niditch, *Underdogs and Tricksters: A Prelude to Biblical Folklore* (San Francisco, 1987)
23–69; cf. Simian-Yofre, "Diacronia: I metodi storico-critici," 99–100; for the structure, see
R. C. Culley, *Studies in the Stucture of Hebrew Narrative* (Semeia Supplements; Philadelphia,
1976) 33–41. For a short presentation of the texts, see Campbell and O'Brien, *Sources of the
Pentateuch*, 99, 108–9, and 167.

proaches at him, gives him back his wife, and has him escorted to the border (12:18–20).

The *second version* takes place not in Egypt but in Gerar, the land of Abimelech, king of the Philistines. The first part of the account is very short, almost partial (20:1). The narrator does not tell, among other things, why Abraham goes to settle in Gerar, in the Negeb. There is no explanation for Abraham's pretension that his wife is his sister or for Abimelech's taking Sarah for himself (20:2). The God who intervenes in this story is called *ʾĕlōhîm*, except in v. 18, where *Yhwh* steps in. The divine intervention, very briefly described in 12:10–20, is much more developed in Genesis 20. Here, God appears to Abimelech in a dream and has a long discussion with him (20:3–7). After this takes place, the servants (20:8) and then Abraham (20:9–13) are summoned, which also takes a relatively long time.

In the epilogue (20:14–18), all of the problems are resolved: Abimelech gives Sarah back to Abraham, showers him with gifts, and invites him to live in his country (20:14–15); in addition, the king offers compensation for the offense to Sarah (20:16); finally, Abraham intercedes for Abimelech and for his family so that all may be healed of an illness that the reader only learns about at the end of the story (20:17–18).

The *third version* is shorter (Gen 26:1–17). This time, the central figures are Isaac, Rebekah, and, once again, Abimelech, the king of Gerar (cf. 20:1–2). The reason for Isaac and Rebekah's stay in the area is a famine, just as in 12:10 (cf. 26:1). Like Abraham, Isaac says that his wife is his sister (26:7). But this time nothing happens: Rebekah and Isaac live in peace. Simply by accident the king commits an indiscretion and discovers the truth: while looking out the window, he sees Isaac "playing" with Rebekah (26:8). The king reproaches him for his lack of honesty and forbids anyone to "touch" Rebekah, on pain of death (26:10–11).

The intent of the first narrative is to show how God protects and saves Sarah, Abraham's wife, by revealing her true identity: Sarah is not just a "woman" or a "beautiful woman"; nor is she Abraham's "sister"; she is "Abraham's wife." She is at the center of the entire story, although she does not say a word.

The second narrative probably presupposes that the reader knows the first account or, at least, its general theme.[9] The first two verses (20:1–2) correspond to six verses in the first account (12:10–16) and say nothing of the circumstances of the trip or of Sarah's entry into Abimelech's harem. The main part of the narrative deals with the legal problem of guilt. Each person tries to

---

9. The most important representative of this theory is J. Van Seters, *Abraham in History and Tradition* (New Haven, CT, 1975) 167–91.

justify his own behavior: God, Abimelech, and Abraham. Then, in the epilogue, all show concern for "reestablishing justice."

The third narrative shows how YHWH protects Rebekah from a danger that only exists in her husband's imagination. Abimelech does not take Rebekah for himself; on the contrary, as soon as he has discovered the truth, he proclaims a decree of matrimonial inviolability.

In each of these narratives, "the foreign king" manifests that he is very different from the notion that the patriarchs have of him. Pharaoh and Abimelech both have a deep sense of justice and of their duty to protect foreigners. The "fear of God" exists in foreign countries, although Abraham does not believe it does (20:11), and men do not necessarily follow their instincts. From a critical and literary point of view, it is difficult to attribute these three narratives to a single author. Why indeed would someone repeat himself so blatantly? Why would he use two different divine names? Why does Abraham make the same mistake twice? The second time, neither Sarah nor God seems to remember the first episode. Isaac, in Genesis 26, does not appear to have learned much from his father's experience. Similarly, Abimelech reacts as if he had no previous experience of this kind of thing.

3. The Double Narrative of the Episode at Meribah
(Exod 17:1–7, Num 20:1–13)[10]

The two episodes at Meribah are constructed on the basis of the same plotline and have many common elements:

1. The lack of water.
2. The people complain to Moses.[11]
3. Moses speaks to YHWH.
4. YHWH indicates the solution: make water spring from the rock.
5. The order is executed.

There are also many differences, however.

a. The Purpose of the Narrative

The most obvious difference between the accounts is found in the conclusion. In Exod 17:1–7, there is no trace of any sin that the people or its leaders might have committed. In Numbers 20, on the other hand, Moses and Aaron

---

10. For the texts, see Campbell and O'Brien, *Sources of the Pentateuch*, 86–87 and 144. For an analysis of the texts, see N. Lohfink, "Die Ursünden in der priesterlichen Geschichtserzählung," in *Die Zeit Jesu: Festschrift für Heinrich Schlier* (ed. G. Bornkamm and K. Rahner; Freiburg-im-Breisgau, 1970) 38–57 (= Lohfink, *Studien zum Pentateuch*, 169–89, especially pp. 187–89); Blum, *Studien*, 271–78.

11. In Numbers 20 Aaron accompanies Moses.

are punished for not having trusted and not having shown YHWH's holiness (20:12). Exod 17:1–7 explains how YHWH saved his people from thirst. Faced with the people's need and attentive to Moses' prayer, YHWH answers and offers a solution to the problem. Numbers is more complex. In addition to the problem of thirst and its solution, the text introduces a narrative concerning sin/punishment.[12]

b. The Narrative Framework

• *Lamentation of the people.*   At the beginning, the complaining of the people is more developed in Num 20:3–5 than in Exod 17:2a. The lack of water, which is the only problem in Exod 17:2a, is expanded by the people with another accusation: they assert that their leaders want to kill them and express doubt about the Exodus as such (Num 20:3–5).

• *Moses' reaction.*   In Exod 17:2b–3, Moses answers that the people are criticizing not their leader but God himself. Then he speaks directly to YHWH. In Numbers 20, he is content with bowing down before the tent of meeting in the company of Aaron.

• *YHWH's reply.*   In Exod 17:5–6a, YHWH answers Moses' prayer and gives him orders to make the water spring from the rock by striking it with the staff. The elders must be present. In Num 20:6b, the "glory of YHWH" appears. YHWH's orders (20:7–8) mention the staff, as in Exod 17:5–6, but Moses must only speak to the rock.

• *The solution to the problem.*   In Exod 17:6b everything ends very quickly with a "completion formula," whereas Numbers contains an elaborate report: the "completion formula" (20:9) is followed by a reproach discourse that Moses addresses to the people (20:10). Then Moses strikes the rock from which the water springs two times (20:11). In Numbers 20, the elders are absent. Both accounts end with an etiology (Exod 17:7; Num 20:13). However, before the etiology, Num 20:12 contains a final discourse in which YHWH accuses Moses and Aaron of not having trusted in him and not having shown his holiness to the people ("sanction").[13]

c. Characters and Other Details

• The *elders* only appear in Exodus 17, and Aaron only in Numbers 20.

---

12. On Numbers 20, see, among others, F. Kohata, "Die priesterschriftliche Überlieferungsgeschichte von Numeri xx,1–31," *AJBI* 3 (1977) 3–34; L. Schmidt, *Studien zur Priesterschrift* (BZAW 214; Berlin, 1993) 45–72; H. Seebass, "Biblisch-theologischer Versuch zu Num 20,1–13 und 21,4–9," *Altes Testament: Forschung und Wirkung—Festschrift für Henning Graf Reventlow* (ed. P. Mommer and W. Thiel; Frankfurt, 1994) 219–29.

13. On the concept of "sanction," see my "Sincronia," 158 and 231.

• Exod 17:7 concludes the episode with an etiology of *Massah and Meribah*, whereas Num 20:13 mentions only *Meribah* and alludes to *Kadesh* (20:1, 13b).

• The *staff* appears in both accounts. However, its function differs, and it seems almost superfluous in Numbers 20.

Conclusion

The second episode (Num 20:1–13) is easier to understand if we consider it to be a second, revised version of the same event and not another similar event. If it were a different event, occurring after the first and told by the same author, it would be impossible to understand why no one knows how to solve the problem of the water. The people, Moses, Aaron, and even Yhwh have no memory of the preceding episode.

B. Doublets within a Single Narrative

In addition to different versions of a single event, there are other even more complex problems when tensions and discrepancies appear within a single narrative. There are many examples of texts in which two or even more narrative plotlines cross. The following narratives belong to the group of classic examples: Genesis 6–9 (the Flood); Genesis 37 (the beginning of the Joseph story); Exodus 14 (the miracle of the sea); and Numbers 13–14 (the exploration of the Promised Land). I will briefly present the problems of Genesis 6–9, Genesis 37, and Exodus 14.

1. The Account of the Flood (Genesis 6–9)[14]

Someone who reads this narrative for the first time perhaps does not recognize the problems inherent to its composition, because the narrative actually hides its duality behind a unified composition. Unity and duality are both present in this text.[15]

---

14. For an overview, see Campbell and O'Brien, *Sources of the Pentateuch*, 211–23; Zenger (ed.), *Einleitung*, 51; for a recent analysis, see my "Relato del diluvio: Un relato sacerdotal y algunos fragmentos redaccionales posteriores," *EstBib* 52 (1994) 37–62; P. J. Harland, *The Value of Human Life: A Study of the Story of the Flood (Genesis 6–9)* (VTSup 64; Leiden, 1996); Carr, *Reading the Fractures of Genesis*, 48–62; also see my "Nel segno dell'arcobaleno: Il racconto biblico del diluvio (Gen 6–9)," in *La natura e l'ambiente nella Bibbia* (ed. M. Lorenzani; Studio biblico teologico aquilano (L'Aquila, 1996) 41–66; see the analysis by B. M. Levinson, "'The Right Chorale': From the Poetics of Biblical Narrative to the Hermeneutics of the Hebrew Bible," in *"Not in Heaven": Coherence and Complexity in Biblical Narrative* (ed. J. P. Rosenblatt and J. C. Sitterson; Bloomington: Indiana University Press, 1991) 129–53 (esp. pp. 136–42).

15. This presentation essentially follows Campbell and O'Brien, *Sources of the Pentateuch*, 211–23.

a. The Narrative's Unity[16]

The account of the Flood follows a sufficiently clear narrative line. At first glance we feel no difficulty in reading the text. We can summarize the events as follows:

1. God discovers humanity's perversity.
2. God decides to destroy the earth.
3. Noah is presented as the only righteous man at this time.
4. God asks Noah to build an ark.
5. Noah enters this ark with his family and representatives of all the animals of the world.
6. The Flood arrives. All the living beings perish in the water, with the exception of Noah and those who are with him in the ark.
7. After the Flood, the land dries. Noah, his family, and all the other passengers leave the ark.
8. God guarantees the existence of the world after the Flood.

b. The Duality of the Narrative[17]

• *The most important tensions.* If we read the text attentively, it is impossible not to notice certain surprising tensions. Generally, exegetes enumerate six major contradictions.[18]

> *The reason for the Flood*: the perversity of the human heart (6:5), or the corruption of the earth and of "all flesh" (every living being) and the presence of violence (6:11–13).
>
> *The divine orders*: God asks Noah to take with him a pair of each animal species (6:19–20), or seven pairs of clean animals and one pair of unclean animals (7:2).
>
> *The length of the Flood*: 40 days and 40 nights (7:4, 12), or an entire year (7:6, 11; 8:13, 14).
>
> *The nature of the Flood*: heavy rain (7:12; 8:2b), or a cosmic cataclysm caused by the opening of the abyss and the cataracts of heaven (7:11; 8:1–2a).
>
> *The departure from the ark*: after sending out various birds (8:6–12), or after a divine order (8:15–17).
>
> *The divine names*: YHWH (*yhwh*) or God (*ʾĕlohîm*).

---

16. Ibid., 214–15.

17. Ibid., 215–16. Also see the excellent analysis of S. E. McEvenue, *The Narrative Style of the Priestly Writer* (AnBib 50; Rome, 1971) 2–36.

18. See Zenger (ed.), *Einleitung*, 51; cf. C. Westermann, *Genesis 1–11* (trans. J. J. Scullion; Minneapolis, 1984) 395–98; Wenham, *Genesis 1–15*, 163–64.

• *The two parallel narratives.*   In the view of many exegetes, it is possible to reconstruct two parallel accounts of the Flood. Each one is complete—or seems so at first glance—and all the elements are present in both narratives.[19]

  1. The wickedness of humans, 6:5, 6:11–12
  2. The divine decision to destroy the world, 6:7, 6:13
  3. Announcement of the Flood, 7:4, 6:17
  4. The order to go into the ark, 7:1, 6:18
  5. The order concerning the animals, 7:2, 6:19–20
  6. The aim: save them from the Flood, 7:3, 6:19
  7. The entry into the ark, 7:7–9, 7:13–16
  8. The beginning of the Flood, 7:10, 7:11
  9. The rising of the waters, 7:17, 7:18
  10. The destruction of all living beings, 7:22–23, 7:20–21
  11. The end of the Flood, 8:2b, 8:2a
  12. The ebb of the waters, 8:3a, 8:3b, 5
  13. Preparations before leaving the ark, 8:6–12, 8:15–17
  14. The divine promise never again to send a flood, 8:20–22, 9:8–17

These elements permit us to distinguish the two narrative lines.

In the *first narrative* (A), God's name is YHWH. The Flood is caused by the perversity of the human heart. YHWH asks Noah to take seven pairs of clean animals and one pair of unclean animals with him. The Flood lasts 40 days and 40 nights and ends when the rain stops. Noah leaves the ark and offers a sacrifice, obviously of clean animals. This fact helps us to understand why Noah had to take along *seven* pairs of clean animals. YHWH smells the odor of the sacrifice, resigns himself to human wickedness, and promises never again to devastate the earth by a flood.

In the *second narrative* (B), God is called *'ĕlohîm*, just as in Genesis 1. The reason for the Flood is more generic: the world is corrupt, and violence reigns everywhere. God asks Noah to build an ark and to bring one pair of each animal species living on earth into it. The chronology of the second narrative is remarkably precise: the text contains a genuine "calendar" of the Flood, with dates from Noah's life (7:6, 11; 8:13).[20] The Flood occurs when the cataracts of heaven and the abyss open up. The cosmology is the same as Genesis 1 (cf. Gen 1:2). At the end of the Flood, after the waters have receded, God blesses Noah

---

19. See, among others, Zenger (ed.), *Einleitung*, 51.

20. The chronology of the Flood presents many problems. See, for example, L. M. Barré, "The Riddle of the Flood Chronology," *JSOT* 41 (1988) 3–20; F. H. Cryer, "The Interrelationships of Gen 5,32; 11,10–11, and the Chronology of the Flood (Gen 6–9)," *Bib* 66 (1985) 241–61; N. P. Lemche, "The Chronology in the Story of the Flood," *JSOT* 18 (1980) 52–62. For the data, see Skinner, *Genesis*, 167–69; McEvenue, *Narrative Style*, 54–59.

and his family, changes the instructions concerning food (making allowance, under certain conditions, for eating meat; cf. 1:29–30), and concludes a Covenant with Noah, promising never again to send a flood. The rainbow symbolizes this Covenant.

• *Some problems.* Despite the many correspondences, the two parallel narratives are not complete. In narrative A, two fundamental elements are missing: the construction of the ark and the departure from the ark. It is indeed possible to understand why the construction of the ark is only recounted once. The "compiler" or "editor" perhaps did not want to repeat himself and chose the narrative best adapted to his intent.

The second problem is more serious: Why is the departure from the ark not described two times, given that the entry is recounted twice? This question prompts some interpreters to cast doubt on the previous reading and to revise the "parallels" proposed by the analysis. Thus, the double entry is perhaps not a "doublet" but a way of stressing a decisive moment in the history of the world through the double repetition of crucial phases of the event.

• Other "doublets" are questionable, however, particularly the beginning of the Flood, the rising of the water, and its receding. Systematic reflection undoubtedly led some exegetes to "discover" doublets that would permit them to construct two complete accounts despite a lack of justification for it.[21]

In spite of these difficulties, we must admit that it is not entirely possible to harmonize the two versions of the Flood, especially in the case of the two series of divine orders concerning the animals to be taken on the ark, the nature of the Flood, its length, and the double divine promise never again to destroy the world.[22]

c. The Different Solutions

According to most exegetes, the account of the Flood is the product of redactional work that combined two parallel, complete narratives of the same event. Except for a few aspects (see above), the redactional work includes the complete versions of the previous texts.

---

21. See B. D. Eerdmans, *Alttestamentliche Studien I: Die Komposition der Genesis* (Giessen, 1908) 81–82; more recently, see Wenham, *Genesis 1–15*, 167–69; Blenkinsopp, *Pentateuch*, 77–78; Blum, *Studien*, p. 282 n. 206; Ska, "Diluvio," 40–51; B. Gosse, "La tradition yahviste en Gn 6,5–9,17," *Henoch* 15 (1993) 139–54; J. Blenkinsopp, "P and J in Genesis 1–11: An Alternative Hypothesis," in *Fortunate the Eyes That See: Essays in Honor of David Noel Freedman in Celebration of His Seventieth Birthday* (ed. A. B. Beck et al.; Grand Rapids, 1995) 1–15.

22. The cause of the Flood may be added to this list. But in this case, the two versions are more accurately described as complementary. Each has its own vision and its own vocabulary, but they are not contradictory.

A small minority of exegetes propose a different solution.[23] There was one complete account, narrative B, while narrative A constituted a series of later additions. These additions were quite likely intended to complete the preceding account on the basis of Mesopotamian narratives as a response to new concerns. The key element of this "completed" account is Noah's sacrifice after the Flood. This element is found in parallel versions: the *Epic of Gilgamesh* (XI 159–161) and *Atrahasis* (3.5.34–35).[24] After having "smelled" the pleasant odor of the sacrifice offered by Noah, Yʜᴡʜ decides never again to destroy living beings or disrupt the order of the universe (Gen 8:20–22).

These "complements" stress the importance of the cult: the universe now exists thanks to Noah's sacrifice after the Flood. For this sacrifice, God had asked Noah to load seven pairs of clean animals (7:2), because only these animals are authorized for sacrifice. Since for the ancients the older an institution is, the more venerable, the editor of these additions wanted to trace this religious institution back to Noah's time and in this way give it its "credentials." Other elements, such as the torrential rain and the sending out of the birds, have parallels in Mesopotamian narratives.[25]

The complete account (our narrative B), attributed to the Priestly source (P), has a more cosmological intention. The Flood represents a partial regression to the chaos that preceded Creation (cf. Gen 1:2). The event is cosmic and concerns the world as described in Genesis 1. For example, the waters that covered the earth are also those that are above the firmament and in the primordial abyss (Gen 7:11; 8:2; cf. Gen 1:2, 6–7, 9).

The Flood is intended to eliminate the "violence" that threatens to destroy the world. In other words, the waters purify the world. After the Flood, a new world appears, comparable to the world in Genesis 1: the earth dries again (8:14; cf. 1:9); God blesses humanity a second time in the person of Noah, the new Adam, with his family (9:1; cf. 1:28); and, finally, he changes the instructions concerning food (9:2–3; cf. 1:29–30). The existence of a new world, purified by the Flood, depends entirely on "divine grace," because God concludes a unilateral Covenant with Noah, his family, and all the living beings who were in the ark (9:8–17). God will remember this Covenant when he sees its sign: the rainbow (9:13–15). This message is particularly significant for Israel after its experience of the Exile.

---

23. See the authors mentioned in n. 21.

24. See Wenham, *Genesis 1–15*, 159–64.

25. Concerning the violent downpour, see *Gilgamesh* XI 96–109 and *Atrahasis* 3.2.53–4.27; for the sending of the birds, see *Gilgamesh* XI 145–54.

d. Conclusion

The final text succeeds in giving the impression of a harmonious narrative. Nevertheless, tensions remain in this text that cannot be ignored if one wants to respect all the facts. It is difficult to harmonize the divine decrees in 6:19–20, where God orders Noah to take only one pair of the various animals with him into the ark, and 7:2, which mentions seven pairs of clean animals and one pair of unclean animals. In 7:9, the same problem reappears, because it says that Noah led the animals into the ark two by two. Does this mean that Noah did not hear the order in given in 7:2? Or should we understand that Noah brought in "pairs" of animals, seven pairs in certain cases and only one pair in others? Finally, why does God change his request?[26] Why did he not immediately communicate his will to Noah? Such phenomena require an explanation, and they are not compatible with the idea of a single author.[27]

The present account of the Flood is like a cantata sung by two or more voices. The universe could only be destroyed once, and it was therefore difficult to relate the event two times.[28] The message, nevertheless, is "polyphonic." A reading that would attempt to eliminate the different voices in order to defend the unity of the composition would not only risk abolishing certain facts in the texts but also leaving an important part of the message out.[29]

2. The Beginning of the Joseph Story (Genesis 37)[30]

Genesis 37 constitutes another classic example presented by handbooks in order to show that more than one hand worked on the composition of the

---

26. The theory of complementary episodes helps us to understand this phenomenon. Only YHWH may correct himself. For this reason, Gen 7:1–5 comes *after* Gen 6:13–22.

27. For criticism of certain attempts to defend the literary unity of Genesis 6–9, see J. A. Emerton, "An Examination of Some Attempts to Defend the Unity of the Flood Narrative in Genesis," *VT* 27 (1987) 401–20; *VT* 28 (1988) 1–21. For attempts in favor of a unitary and structural reading of the Flood, see above all B. W. Anderson, "From Analysis to Synthesis: The Interpretation of Gen 1–11," *JBL* 97 (1978) 23–39; M. Kessler, "Rethorical Criticism of Gen 7," in *Rhetorical Criticism: Essays in Honor of J. Muilenburg* (ed. J. J. Jackson and M. Kessler; Pittsburgh, 1974) 1–17; G. J. Wenham "The Coherence of the Flood Narrative," *VT* 28 (1978) 336–48; idem, *Genesis 1–15*, 156–57; idem, "Method in Pentateuchal Criticism," *VT* 41 (1991) 84–109; G. Borgonovo, "Gen 6,5–9,19: Struttura e produzione simbolica," *La scuola cattolica* 115 (1987) 321–48, 28. See Campbell and O'Brien, *Sources of the Pentateuch*, 236; C. Levin, *Der Jahwist* (FRLANT 157; Göttingen, 1993) 439–40.

28. See Campbell and O'Brien, *Sources of the Pentateuch*, 236; Levin, *Der Jahwist*, 439–40.

29. "In the combination of both (the sources J and P), two voices have joined in the singing of one song, and the song is the more powerful for their harmony. Two witnesses give the testimony of the faith of Israel; in such a matter of life and death, at least two witnesses are required. The compiler of our composite final text has done marvelously well" (Campbell and O'Brien, *Sources of the Pentateuch*, 223).

30. See ibid., 223–37.

Pentateuch.[31] Usually, authors highlight the presence of doublets and parallel plotlines: the patriarch has two names, Jacob in 37:1–2, 34 and Israel in 37:3, 13; two brothers try to save Joseph, Reuben in 37:21–24, 29–30 and Judah in 37:26–27; for the sale of Joseph, the text mentions the Ishmaelites (37:25, 28; cf. 39:1) and the Midianites (37:28, 36).

a. The Difficulty

We encounter the main difficulty of the narrative of Genesis 37 in vv. 28 and 36 (cf. 39:1). We do not know exactly how Joseph was sold. Indeed, many readings of the passage are possible: Joseph could have been sold to the Ishmaelites by his brothers, or kidnapped by the Midianites who then sold him to the Ishmaelites, or abducted by Midianites who sold him to Potiphar in Egypt.

The development of the action is not clear. According to Gen 37:17–20, the brothers see Joseph coming, in the distance, and decide to kill him (37:20). Reuben then intervenes to save his brother and suggests that they put him into an empty cistern (37:21–22). Reuben's plan is accepted, and Joseph finds himself in a pit, stripped of his tunic (37:23–24). Then his brothers sit down to eat (37:25). A caravan of Ishmaelites comes by, and Judah suggests that they sell Joseph to these merchants (37:26–27). Once again, the brothers agree on the proposal (37:27b). At this point, the narrative is complicated. According to the final version of the text, (a possible reading) another group of merchants—Midianites, this time—pull Joseph out of the pit and sell him to the Ishmaelites, who take him to Egypt (37:28). The text implies that all of this remains unknown to the brothers, who are eating and discussing. Then Reuben goes back to the pit and discovers that Joseph has disappeared (37:29). He returns to announce the news to his brothers (37:30). Together they decide to lie to their father and to convince him that a wild beast has devoured Joseph (37:31–35). In fact, according to the final version of the narrative, none of the brothers knows exactly what has happened to Joseph. Reuben wanted to save him, and Judah suggested that they sell him. While the brothers were eating and conversing, the Midianites came by, abducted Joseph, and sold him to the Ishmaelites that Judah and his brothers had seen shortly before these events. This sequence presents few problems, at least at first sight.

A critical reader might ask himself why the brothers did not see the Midianites come and were not conscious of the fact that they sold their brother to the Ishmaelites. In any case, the reader is truly surprised by v. 36, which states that the Midianites—and not the Ishmaelites—sold Joseph in Egypt. Gen 39:1 re-

---

31. In addition to Campbell and O'Brien, ibid., see Blenkinsopp, *Pentateuch*, 107; Whybray, *Introduction*, 57; N. Marconi, "Contributi per una lettura unitaria di Gn 37," *RivB* 39 (1991) 277–303.

peats 37:28b but attributes this action to the Ishmaelites. It is impossible to harmonize the two versions entirely.

b. The Solutions

Exegetes have presented various solutions.

According to one opinion, which seems reasonable enough, the actual text combines two parallel versions. In the first version, Reuben is the main figure, and he decides to save Joseph (37:21–22). He convinces his brother not to kill the "dreamer" but simply to put him in a pit (37:22), and this is what they do (37:23–24). When the brothers have gone away, the Midianites approach and secretly pull Joseph out of the pit and take him to Egypt (37:28a). Reuben returns to the pit to deliver Joseph and take him back to his father (cf. 37:22b), but he finds the pit empty and, quite astonished, goes to announce the news to his brothers (37:29–30). In Gen 40:15, Joseph seems to confirm this version of the story when he says that he had been "abducted," "stolen," "secretly kidnapped" from the land of the Hebrews.

In the second version, only Judah intervenes. While the brothers are eating, they see a caravan of Ishmaelites on its way to Egypt (37:25). Judah then proposes that they sell Joseph (37:26–27). The brothers agree with the idea and sell him to the Ishmaelites (37:28aß, b). In this scenario, the subject of the verb "to sell" in 37:28aß is "brothers" and not "the Midianites." In Gen 45:4–5, Joseph supports this version: his brothers sold him ("you sold me").

Gen 37:36 concludes the "Reuben version," according to which the Midianites sell Joseph in Egypt, while 39:1 is tied to the "Judah version."

Most exegetes agree with these facts. However, they part ways on some other questions. Two problems are more significant and more difficult to resolve: Are these two versions, the Reuben version and the Judah version, complete? In other words, is the present text a combination of two versions that existed separately, or was there actually only one version that an editor completed by adding some supplementary elements? The second question is tied to the first: Is it possible to date the two versions and discern which is the oldest?[32]

c. Coherence and Incoherence of the Final Text

The synchronic readings attempt to reduce the difficulties in this case just as in others.[33] But the explanations are rarely satisfying. It is not enough, for

---

32. For a recent opinion on this argument, with an updated bibliography, see C. Paap, *Die Josephsgeschichte Genesis 37–50: Bestimmungen ihrer literarischen Gattung in der zweiten Hälfte des 20. Jahrhunderts* (Europäische Hochschulschriften 23; Frankfurt, 1994).

33. See Marconi, "Contributi," 277–303; R. E. Longacre, *Joseph: A Story of Divine Providence* (Winona Lake, IN, 1989; 2nd ed., 2003) 31; idem, "Who Sold Joseph into Egypt?" *Interpretation and History: Essays in Honour of Allan A. MacRae* (ed. R. L. Harris et al.; Singapore,

example, to assert that "Ishmaelites" and "Midianites" are two names for one people (cf. Judg 8:24), because insurmountable difficulties remain. I will mention two of them: Why would one use two different names to designate one people in the same verse (37:28) and elsewhere (37:36; 39:1)? In order to solve this problem, some exegetes argue that in the present text the "brothers" sell Joseph to the Ishmaelites/Midianites.[34] But in this case, we must ask ourselves where Reuben was at that moment. If he was not with the brothers, why does the text not explain this? If he is with his brothers when Joseph is sold, why does he go to look for him in 37:29?[35]

The hypothesis of "two versions" that must be attributed to two different authors is the simplest and most "economical," because it helps to explain the present text without creating any further problems. In exegesis, the best solution is the one that explains most simply the greatest amount of data.

d. Conclusion

In the case of Genesis 37, two contradictory, incompatible versions coexist in the final text, which therefore can hardly be attributed to the same author.[36]

3. The Crossing of the Sea (Exodus 14)[37]

Along with Genesis 6–9, Exodus 14 constitutes one of the rare examples of a double parallel version of the same event.[38] The reason for this is simple: the Egyptians could only drown in the sea once, just as the generation of the Flood could only disappear in the waters one time. Consequently, it was difficult to tell the same story twice.

1986); W. L. Humphreys, *Joseph and His Family: A Literary Study* (Columbia, SC, 1988); and the criticism of Campbell and O'Brien, *Sources of the Pentateuch*, 233 n. 59.

34. See Longacre, *Joseph*, 31; idem, "Who Sold Joseph?" 75–92.

35. See Campbell and O'Brien, *Sources of the Pentateuch*, 231–36.

36. Campbell and O'Brien (ibid., 235–37) propose an interesting explanation. According to them, Genesis 37 wished to maintain two different accounts of Joseph's "sale" in the same text. The ancient manuscripts had no notes, nor did they have our modern typographical possibilities, such as different sets of characters. The narrative therefore had to contain, if this can be said, both the text and the notes. Moreover, Joseph could only be sold once, and so it was difficult to present two successive texts relating the same event.

37. See ibid., 238–54; Blenkinsopp, *Pentateuch*, 157–60; E. Zenger, *Einleitung*, 51–52; for some recent studies of this pericope, see M. Vervenne, "The Sea Narrative Revisited," *Bib* 75 (1994) 80–98.

38. According to Levin (*Jahwist*, 439–40), these are the only true examples of this type of literary phenomenon. In my view, Genesis 6–9 does not contain two complete versions of the Flood. One could also discuss Numbers 13–14. For Noth (*History of Pentateuchal Traditions*, 249), these cases occur "only very seldom" (*ziemlich selten*); cf. Campbell and O'Brien, *Sources of the Pentateuch*, 210 n. 22.

a. The Difficulties

Exodus 14 presents four main difficulties that prevent reading the text as a unified, coherent narrative. These difficulties concern Moses' attitude in 14:13–14 and the divine discourse of 14:15; the location of the Egyptians before the "miracle"; the nature of the "miracle"; and the death of the Egyptians.

• Confidence or a cry of distress? Should one stay calm or move? (Exod 14:13–14 and 14:15).[39]

α. *Confidence or a cry of distress?* In Exod 14:13–14, Moses speaks to the Israelites who are disturbed about the presence of the Egyptian army that has just caught up with them on the seashore (14:8–10). The man of God tells the people not to fear, because YHWH will save his own. Then he announces that YHWH himself will fight against the Egyptian army, that Israel will no longer see the Egyptians, and that the people should remain calm (14:14). However, in 14:15 YHWH speaks to Moses and seems to reproach him: "Why do you cry to me?" In the preceding verse, Moses did not cry to YHWH but, quite the contrary, he exhorted the people to remain calm and be confident.

β. *Watch, keep still, or move?* In his exhortation to the Israelites, Moses said: "stand firm, and see the deliverance that YHWH will accomplish for you today" (14:13a) and then he added, in 14:14: "YHWH will fight for you, and you have only to keep still." Although the interpretation of certain verbs is difficult, the most obvious meaning of the phrase is that Israel should remain still, where they are, without moving, and look to YHWH, who will act. The verb *yṣb/nṣb* primarily means "take a position," "stand firm," which does not exclude the possibility of movement, for example, in a military context, as in a maneuver before attacking an enemy.[40] Be this as it may, the rest of Exod 14:13 says more explicitly that Israel should prepare to "watch" (*rʾh*) and not to act. The verb *ḥrš* only means "be silent," "keep still." It does not allude to any kind of movement, even if this is not to be excluded *a priori*. In this context, it is difficult to understand why, in 14:15, YHWH quite unexpectedly asks Moses to have Israel change their position: "Tell the Israelites to go forward."

• Chronology and topography of the narrative (Exod 14:15–20, 28–29).[41]

α. *Chronology.* When did the "miracle" occur? According to 14:20, the cloud separates the two camps "during the whole night." On the other hand, 14:23 says that the Egyptians were pursuing Israel. But in this context there is no mention of the night.

β. *Topography.* Where are the Israelites and the Egyptians? In 14:19–20, the cloud changes its position: instead of advancing at the head of the people to

---

39. Ibid., 241.

40. Cf. J. Reindl, "צצנ/צי *nṣb/yṣb*," *TDOT* 9.519–29, esp. pp. 522–24.

41. Campbell and O'Brien, *Sources of the Pentateuch*, 243–44.

lead them (cf. 13:21–22), it places itself between the camp of the Israelites and the Egyptians, so they are separated all night long and unable to draw near to one another (14:19–20). Thus, the column of cloud constitutes an impassable obstacle that prevents the Egyptians from catching up with Israel.

According to this description, the Israelites and the Egyptians remain stationary, motionless, during the entire night. Because the cloud prevents them both from moving, the two camps stay where they met before the night, on the seashore (14:9–10). Furthermore, nothing in this text indicates that the cloud moved after 14:19–20 (cf. 14:19b and 14:24).

So these verses do not refer to a nighttime crossing of the sea. The maneuver would be hard to imagine: the cloud is no longer in front of the Israelites to shed light on their path (13:21–22), and the Egyptians are blocked behind the cloud that keeps them from reaching Israel. Only the final text suggests a different scene.

• The nature of the miracle [42]

Exod 14:21 contains one of the greatest difficulties of the text as a whole. For many exegetes, this verse is also the starting point for the theory of a redactional activity that combined two different versions of the same story. The verse says this: "Then Moses stretched out his hand over the sea. YHWH drove the sea back by a strong east wind all night, and turned the sea into dry land; and the waters were divided." [43] This verse presents several problems. How can we imagine the phenomenon? Moses extends his hand, and YHWH makes a strong wind blow from the east that separates the water into two parts, thus opening a passage in the middle of the sea. The wind must indeed have blown in an exceptional way to produce this result—that is, always straight in the same direction, in a discrete zone, not over the entire surface of the sea. However, the text does not say that "YHWH made a strong east wind blow and opened a passage in the sea." It only states that the wind dried the sea.

Verse 16b allows us to go a step further. In his instructions to Moses, YHWH says three things: Moses must lift his staff, stretch his hand out over the sea, and divide it in two. The first element (the staff) is perhaps an addition, or it may be one of the "slight variations" that are frequent in biblical texts, especially in the Priestly source (P). [44] Two other elements are found at the beginning and end of the verse:

---

42. Ibid., 242.

43. Some translations miss the point because they do not distinguish the terms "sea" and "waters" accurately, as in the original Hebrew text.

44. See McEvenue (*Narrative Style*, 51), who states, concerning the style of the repetitions in the Priestly text: "Its essence is variety within system."

v. 16a, stretch out your hand over the sea and divide it

v. 21, Moses stretched out his hand over the sea . . . , and the waters were divided

The picture is clear: Moses stretches his hand out and the waters obey: that is, they divide themselves in two. In this way, "the dry land" appears in the middle of the sea and the passage lies open so the Israelites can cross to the other shore. The Egyptians immediately follow them (cf. 14:22–23). The waters form high walls to the right and to the left of these two marching groups (14:22 and 14:29).

However, the rest of v. 21 describes a different phenomenon: YHWH makes the east wind blow all night long so that the sea as such is dried up and there is a large dry area, not just a narrow "passageway" between the waters.[45]

- The death of the Egyptians[46]

α. *The waters or the sea?* Here also it is difficult to harmonize the descriptions in the text. According to v. 26, the Israelites have arrived on the other shore. At that moment, YHWH tells Moses to extend his hand for the second time and to make the waters cover the Egyptians. Moses executes this order in 14:27–28. However, the verses once again contain new elements that were not originally mentioned in the divine order. Only the beginnings of v. 27 and v. 28 are compatible with v. 26. The verbal correspondences are clear:

v. 26, Stretch out your hand over the sea, so the water may come back

v. 27, So Moses stretched out his hand over the sea

v. 28, The waters came back . . .

The rest of v. 27 does not mention the receding "waters" (as do vv. 26 and 28); it talks about the "sea" (v. 27: "and at dawn the *sea* returned to its normal place"). This slight difference of vocabulary appears in addition to other significant divergences. For example, the divine order in v. 26 mentions chariots and their drivers (v. 26b).[47] These reappear in v. 28 but not in v. 27.

β. *The dawn.* Verse 27 contains the last temporal indication, "at dawn," in a series that began in vv. 20 and 21 with "all night" and continued in v. 24 with "at the morning watch." On the other hand, in v. 26, YHWH did not tell Moses to extend his hand or to make the sea return at dawn.[48] There is no indication of time in v. 26.

---

45. Many commentators discuss yet another problem: Where exactly are the Israelites and the Egyptians at that moment? Some authors suggest that the Egyptians move in order to occupy the part of the sea dried by the wind. This is possible, but the text does not say so explicitly. See F. Kohata, *Jahwist und Priesterschrift in Exodus 3–14* (BZAW 166; Berlin, 1986) 281–83. For discussion, see Blum, *Studien*, 257 n. 96.

46. Campbell and O'Brien, *Sources of the Pentateuch*, 244–45.

47. The usual translation, "horseman," is not correct. The *paraš* is an armed soldier mounted on a chariot but not a horseman. See H. Niehr, "פָּרָשׁ *pārāš*," *TDOT* 12.124–28.

48. Campbell and O'Brien, *Sources of the Pentateuch*, 243.

γ. *The wind.* Verse 21 mentions the wind. However, in the order that YHWH gives to Moses in v. 26, he does not tell him to make it stop. We can suppose that the wind, having blown all night, falls by itself in the morning.[49]

δ. *Do the Egyptians flee in the direction of the sea or are they covered by the waters?*[50] According to v. 27, the sea returns to its usual place shortly before dawn. The verse must be related to v. 21, which says that YHWH pushed the sea back with a strong east wind all night and dried the seabed. Then, in v. 27 the wind diminishes and the sea flows back to the place it occupied the previous evening. The same v. 27 states that the Egyptians fled "into the sea." The sense of the verse does not require a long explanation: the sea flowed back into place, and the Egyptians, in the panic provoked by YHWH in v. 24, flee in the direction of the sea, which is coming toward them. In other words, the Egyptians, in general confusion, begin to flee toward the zone usually occupied by the sea and uncovered by the wind during the night. They encounter the sea, which is returning to its place, and they are carried away by the tide (v. 27b). So the Israelites will be able to contemplate their corpses thrown onto the seashore by the waters (v. 30).

It is difficult to reconcile this scene with the second picture, which appears in vv. 26, 28, 29. According to these verses, the Israelites have crossed the sea on "dry land," through the passage opened by Moses in 14:21*. The waters formed walls to their right and to their left (vv. 22, 29), and the Egyptians followed them into this "corridor" laid open in the middle of the sea (vv. 23, 28). When Israel gets to the other shore, YHWH tells Moses to stretch his hand out for the second time so that the waters will flow back over the Egyptian army (v. 26). This happens at the beginning of v. 27* and in vv. 28 and 29. In this case, the waters that had formed two walls "collapse" on the Egyptians who are, consequently, covered by them.

Here we have, on the one hand, the sea flowing back to its place in a "horizontal" movement and, on the other hand, the waters falling down in a "vertical" movement. On one hand, the Egyptians flee away from Israel (vv. 25, 27): "Let us flee from the Israelites"; on the other hand, the Egyptians pursue Israel (vv. 23, 28), even when the waters cover them: "The waters returned and covered the chariots and the chariot drivers, the entire army of Pharaoh that had followed them into the sea." If, at this moment, they are pursuing Israel, how can they flee away from them? And how can the waters simultaneously accomplish two movements? How can they flow back and, at the same time, fall onto the Egyptians?

In order to reconcile these two descriptions, we need to use our imagination. The panicking Egyptians, who are pursuing the Israelites, have turned

---

49. Ibid., 246.
50. Ibid., 244–45, 251.

back toward the shore from which they started. At this moment YHWH orders Moses to stretch his hand out over the sea. The waters, first, fall on the Egyptians from both the right side and the left and, second, they come back into the "passageway" by flowing from the other shore in the direction of the Egyptians, who are fleeing to the same shore. Although this is not impossible, nowhere does the text say this explicitly and, furthermore, this is certainly not the simplest way of interpreting the phenomenon.

The current text of Exodus 14 has preserved two descriptions of the "miracle of the sea." The very simple means permitting us to reconstruct these two narratives are the following: the correspondences in vocabulary, especially the correspondences between the divine discourses and their implementation (execution of the orders by Moses). Each narrative has its own logic.

b. The Two Narratives[51]

According to most exegetes, the current text combines two parallel, complete versions of the "miracle" of the sea. In the *first*,[52] which we could call "the version of the drying of the sea," the Egyptians catch up with the Israelites in the evening on the seashore. The cloud steps in, moves, and keeps the Egyptians from getting any closer. This situation of "balance" lasts all night long. During this same night, YHWH makes a strong east wind blow until it has dried up the sea (or at least a part of it).

Toward morning (at the morning watch, between two and six o'clock, v. 24) YHWH creates panic among the Egyptians. The cause of this panic is not really described. The wind has perhaps fallen, and the Egyptians, facing the cloud (heavy fog), suppose that the sea is flowing back into its bed. They want to flee but have difficulty moving their chariots. Here as well, we need to make some suppositions; for example, we can imagine that the Egyptians are on very wet ground and that their chariots have sunk into the mud. Finally, they take flight, probably without thinking, in the direction of the sea, which is flowing back into its place in the morning. The waters carry them away, and the sea throws their corpses on the shore where the Israelites are camping.

---

51. For a more detailed study, see the commentaries, for example, Childs, *Exodus*, 218–24; see also K. von Rabenau, *Die beiden Erzählungen vom Schilfmeerwunder in Exod. 13,17–14,31* (Theologische Versuche 1; Berlin, 1966) 7–29; P. Weimar and E. Zenger, *Exodus: Geschichten und Geschichte der Befreiung Israels* (Stuttgarter Bibelstudien 75; 2nd ed.; Stuttgart, 1975); P. Weimar, *Die Meerwundererzählung: Eine redaktionskritische Analyse von Exod 13,17–14,31* (Ägypten und Altes Testament 9; Wiesbaden, 1985); Kohata, *Jahwist und Priesterschrift*, 278–95; idem, "Die Endredaktion (Rp) der Meerwundererzählung," *AJBI* 14 (1988) 10–37; Blum, *Studien*, 256–62; L. Schmidt, *Studien zur Priesterschrift*, 19–34.

52. Campbell and O'Brien, *Sources of the Pentateuch*, 246.

According to the *second description*[53]—we will call it "the narrative of the division of the waters"—the miracle happens during the day, because no temporal indication is given. After the Egyptians have caught up with the Israelites close to the sea—probably a wide lake—YHWH tells Moses to stretch his hand out over the sea in order to divide the waters. Moses obeys, and the Israelites go into the passage between the waters, while the Egyptians pursue them.

When the Israelites have arrived on the other shore of the sea, or lake, YHWH tells Moses to extend his hand over the waters a second time to make the waters "come back" over the Egyptian army. Moses executes this order as he did the first time, and the waters cover the Egyptians, who are still in the seabed. In this second account, the Israelites serve as bait to lure the Egyptians into a trap.

Exegetes generally attribute the first account to the so-called Yahwist (J) and the second to the so-called "Priestly Writer" (P). The *first account* ("the drying of the sea") is structured around three references to "fear": 14:10, 13, 31. When the Israelites see the Egyptians, they experience "great fear." Moses reacts and exhorts them by saying: "Do not be afraid" (14:10). YHWH throws the Egyptian army into panic and confusion (14:24), thus saving the Israelites (14:13, 30), who "fear YHWH and believe in YHWH and in his servant Moses." The account describes, by and large, Israel's transition from fear of the Egyptians to the fear of YHWH and to faith.[54]

The *second account* ("the division of the waters") precisely describes the first manifestation of YHWH's "glory" (14:4, 17–18) and the acknowledgment of YHWH's personal sovereignty over the Egyptians (14:4, 18).[55] YHWH shows his "glory" in two correlative ways: as Lord of Creation and as Lord of history. He shows that he is the Lord of Creation by making "the dry land" appear, as in Gen 1:9–10 (cf. 8:14). He shows that he is the Lord of history when he reveals himself as the Judge of the nations by making the Egyptians drown in the waters, just as he did the perverse generation in the Flood.[56]

---

53. Ibid., 245–46.

54. See Weimar and Zenger, *Exodus*, 56–58; Ska, *Passage de la mer*, 136–45.

55. On the "glory," see C. Westermann, "Die Herrlichkeit Gottes in der Priesterschrift," *Wort, Gebot, Glaube: Beiträge zur Theologie des Alten Testaments. Walther Eichrodt zum 80. Geburtstag* (ed. H. J. Stoebe; ATANT 59; Zurich, 1970) 227–29 (= *Forschung am Alten Testament: Gesammelte Studien* [TBü 55; Munich, 1974] 2.115–37); U. Struppe, *Die Herrlichkeit Jahwes in der Priesterschrift: Eine semantische Studie zu kᵉbôd JHWH* (Österreichische Biblische Studien 9; Klosterneuburg, 1988). Also see the recognition formula in 14:4, 18: "the Egyptians shall know that I am YHWH."

56. See my "Séparation des eaux et de la terre ferme dans le récit sacerdotal," *La nouvelle revue théologique* 103 (1981) 512–32; idem, *Passage de la mer*, 96–97.

c. The Final Account[57]

• *From a stylistic point of view*, the final account is structured by the three divine discourses in Exod 14:1–4, 15–18, and 25, and by Moses' discourse in 14:13–14. The latter reaches its fulfillment in 14:25 (cf. 14:14) and in 14:30–31 (cf. 14:13). So, there are three parts: 14:1–14, 15–25, and 26–31. The first of these sections describes the crisis and the other two the solution. Each of the three sections corresponds to a particular moment and a specific place. Exod 14:1–14 happens at night, in the wilderness between Egypt and the sea. Exod 14:15–25 is situated at the sea and at night. Exod 14:26–31 describes the events that occur at dawn, on the other seashore.

• *From a theological point of view*, the narrative is a song executed by two voices, just like Genesis 6–9 and Genesis 37. One of the voices sings the "glory" of YHWH (14:4, 17–18), and the other sings the "salvation of Israel" (14:13, 30–31), because YHWH reveals his glory when he forces the Egyptians to recognize him, and he "saves" his people Israel. After the miracle, Israel responds by putting its faith in YHWH and in Moses, his servant (14:31).

A synchronic reading that did not respect the polyphonic diversity of the text would only diminish the message of this narrative.[58]

---

57. On this point, see ibid., 24–37; also see U. F. W. Bauer, *kl hdbrym h'lh—All diese Worte: Impulse zur Schriftauslegung aus Amsterdam. Expliziert an der Schilfmeererzählung in Exodus 13,17–14,31* (European University Studies 13; Theology 442; Berne, 1992); Vervenne, "The Sea Narrative Revisited," 80–98.

58. See Campbell and O'Brien, *Sources of the Pentateuch*, 251–54.

Chapter 5

Literary Problems of the Pentateuch III: Some Redactional Interventions

A. Two Examples of Redactional "Insertions"

1. Exodus 14:11–12[1]

In Exod 14:8–10, the Egyptians catch up with the Israelites, who are setting up camp for the night by the sea. This moment is dramatic: after three days of freedom, the Israelites realize that the Egyptians have pursued them and are now near. There is no possibility of being saved: the Israelites are trapped between the Egyptians and the sea. Fear immediately spreads throughout the camp: "In great fear the Israelites cried out to Yнwн" (14:10b).

In Exod 14:11–12, immediately after this event, the Israelites cry out to Moses, but in their speech there is no mention of the Egyptian army or of Pharaoh; instead, they express their fear of the perils of the wilderness and their desire to return to Egypt because they prefer living in slavery in Egypt to dying in the wilderness. The language of this discourse has legal connotations. The phrase "What have you done to us?" (14:11b) is an accusation formula.[2] The Israelites accuse Moses of wanting to destroy them (14:11), and they do it in such a way that the reader expects the "scores to be settled" between Israel and the man of God.

However, the following verses (14:13–14) do not show Moses responding to this serious accusation. As we saw in the previous chapter, his discourse in vv. 13–14 exhorts the people to remain calm and to be confident. His first words are tied to v. 10b and not to vv. 11–12: they contain the exhortation not to fear; the instruction "do not be afraid" (v. 13a) echoes v. 10b, "in great fear."

---

1. See M. Vervenne, "The Protest Motif in the Sea Narrative (Exod 14,11–12): Form and Structure of a Pentateuchal Pattern," *ETL* 63 (1987) 257–71; T. Römer, "Exode et Anti-Exode: La nostalgie de l'Égypte dans les traditions du désert," in *Lectio difficilior probabilior? L'exégèse comme expérience de décloisonnement* (FS F. Smyth-Florentin) (ed. T. Römer; Dielheimer Blätter zum Alten Testament und seiner Rezeption in der Alten Kirche 12; Heidelberg, 1991) 155–72.

2. H. J. Boecker, *Redeformen des Rechtslebens im Alten Testament* (WMANT 14; Neukirchen-Vluyn, 1964; 2nd ed., 1970) 26–31; P. Bovati, *Re-establishing Justice: Legal Terms, Concepts and Procedures in the Hebrew Bible* (trans. M. J. Smith; JSOTSup 105; Sheffield, 1994) 76–77.

Therefore, we have good reason to consider vv. 11–12 a later addition. The three strongest arguments in favor of this hypothesis are: the common vocabulary in vv. 10b and 13a (the verb "to fear"); the thematic unity between v. 10 and vv. 13–14 (the problem of Israel's fear of the Egyptians); the isolation of vv. 11–12 in their context, from a stylistic point of view as well as on account of the content (legal vocabulary; dangers in the wilderness; longing for Egypt; the problem of slavery).

2. Exodus 24:3–8[3]

After having delivered the "Covenant Code" to Moses (Exod 21–23), Yhwh instructs him to climb the mountain with Aaron, Nadab, Abihu, and 70 of Israel's elders (24:1). The next verse adds a few details (24:2). However, in 24:3, Moses does not climb the mountain with the men mentioned in 24:1. The reader discovers a quite different scene: Yhwh's words are read, a book is written, there are sacrifices, blood sprinkled, the reading of the book, and the solemn rite of the Covenant (24:3–8).

The command in 24:1 is not carried out until 24:9: the imperative verb "come up" in 24:1 corresponds to the past form (*wayyiqtol*) of "went up" in 24:9. Moses is accompanied by Aaron, Nadab, Abihu, and 70 of Israel's elders—that is, the men mentioned by Yhwh in his instructions in 24:1. However, in 24:3–9 Moses is with the people and some "young men" who assist him (in v. 5) at the moment of the sacrifice. Verses 3–8 quite clearly interrupt the narrative line of vv. 1–2, 9–11.

There are many examples of this kind of procedure in the Pentateuch. However, they are not all as obvious as in the two cases presented above. Consequently, it is not always easy to prove the existence of a redactional addition with decisive, irrefutable arguments. In the following sections, I will attempt to analyze some of the redactional techniques most frequently encountered in the Pentateuch.

B. The "Resumptive Repetition"[4]

Resumptive repetition is a literary technique that consists of repeating, after an interruption, one or more of the words that immediately preceded the digression or addition, so that the reader may continue from the point of

---

3. For the bibliography, see my "Repas de Ex 24,11," especially p. 307 n. 9; see, above all, E. W. Nicholson, "The Interpretation of Exodus xxiv 9–11," *VT* 24 (1974) 77–97, especially pp. 78–79. Cf. Campbell and O'Brien, *Sources of the Pentateuch*, 199 and n. 37.

4. Basic studies: C. Kuhl, "Die "Wiederaufnahme": Ein literarkritisches Prinzip?" *ZAW* 64 (1952) 1–11; M. Anbar, "La 'reprise,'" *VT* 38 (1988) 385–98. The word *Wiederaufnahme*

the interruption.[5] In the case of redactional additions, the first text was original and the resumption—that is, the repetition of one or several words—was inserted by the editor, who wanted to "sew up" his addition to the original text in this way.

This is a well-known phenomenon, but it is not limited to redactional work. Authors themselves use this technique: for example, when they want to introduce a digression or describe two similar, simultaneous scenes. Consequently, a resumption as such is not sufficient evidence for affirming the presence of a redactional addition. Other indications, such as a change of vocabulary or topic, must also be present.[6] Many examples appear in the Pentateuch and elsewhere in the Bible and in ancient literature.[7]

1. Genesis 6:22, 7:5 [8]

At the beginning of the account of the Flood, God commands Noah to build an ark. This first series of divine instructions ends with a "completion formula" (Gen 6:22):

Noah did this; he did all that God commanded him.

("resumption"; cf. Kuhl) was already used by A. Dillmann, *Die Bücher Numeri, Deuteronomium und Josua* (2nd ed.; Leipzig, 1886) 465; A. Dillmann and V. Ryssel, *Die Bücher Exodus und Leviticus* (3rd ed.; Leipzig, 1897) 63; C. Steuernagel, *Deuteronomium und Josua* (Göttingen, 1900) 169, 172; Wellhausen, *Composition des Hexateuchs*, 64. See Anbar, "Reprise," 385 n. 1. For bibliography, see A. Rofé, *The Book of Balaam* (Jerusalem, 1979) 55 n. 106. See the discussion of this and other editorial devices in B. M. Levinson, *Deuteronomy and the Hermeneutics of Legal Innovation* (New York: Oxford University Press, 1997) 17–20.

5. See Kuhl, "Wiederaufnahme," 2–3; Anbar, "Reprise," 385.

6. See W. Richter, *Exegese als Literaturwissenschaft: Entwurf einer Literaturtheorie und Methodologie* (Göttingen, 1971) p. 70 n. 81.

7. For more information, see Anbar, "Reprise"; G. Braulik, *Die Mittel deuteronomischer Rhetorik erhoben aus Deuteronomium 4,1–40* (AnBib 68; Rome, 1978) 85 and 144–45; C. Conroy, *Absalom, Absalom! Narrative and Language in 2 Sam 13–20* (AnBib 81; Rome, 1978) 54 and 110 n. 57; Kuhl, "Die Wiederaufnahme," 1–11; idem, *Die drei Männer im Feuer* (BZAW 55; Berlin, 1930) 163; B. Lang, "A Neglected Principle in Ezekiel Research: Editorial Criticism," *VT* 29 (1979) 39–44, especially p. 43; B. O. Long, "Framing Repetitions in Biblical Historiography," *JBL* 106 (1987) 385–99; H. V. D. Parunak, "Oral Typesetting: Some Uses of Biblical Structure," *Bib* 62 (1981) 153–68, especially pp. 160–62; P. A. Quick, "Resumptive Repetition: A Two-Edged Sword," *Journal of Translation and Textlinguistics* 6 (1993) 289–316; Richter, *Exegese als Literaturwissenschaft*, 70–71, with n. 81; I. L. Seeligmann, "Hebräische Erzählung und biblische Geschichtsschreibung," *TZ* 18 (1962) 305–25, especially p. 318; S. Talmon, "The Presentation of Synchroneity and Simultaneity in Biblical Narrative," in *Studies in Hebrew Narrative Art throughout the Ages* (Scripta Hierosolymitana 27; Jerusalem, 1978) 12–25; J. Trebolle Barrera, "Redaction, Recension, and Midrash in the Books of Kings," *BIOSCS* 15 (1982) 12–35; H. M. Wiener, *The Composition of Judges II 11 to 1 Kings II 46* (Leipzig, 1929) 2.

8. Kuhl, "Wiederaufnahme," 9. See also my "Relato del diluvio," 56; cf. Westermann, *Genesis 1–11*, 429.

A second series of instructions, which introduces the distinction between pure and impure animals, ends in the same way (7:5):

> And Noah did all that Yʜwʜ had commanded him.

This formula is short, and it uses the divine name Yʜwʜ instead of *ʾĕlōhîm* (God). However, the procedure is clear: the second conclusion indicates that the addition of 7:1–4 is to be understood as a divine order of the same type as the order in Gen 6:13–21. This command is given with the same authority and requires the same obedience. After 7:5, the story line can resume.

In the present case, as we have already seen, there are at least two arguments to support the hypothesis that 7:1–4 is an addition: a contradiction exists between the two series of divine commands concerning the number of animals; and God is not called by the same name (God/Yʜwʜ).

2. Genesis 21:27b, 32a [9]

Gen 21:22–34 describes the conclusion of a covenant between Abraham and Abimelech. At the end of the account, Abraham offers oxen and sheep to Abimelech (21:22–27, 32b–34). The narrator concludes the description with the following formula: "the two men made a covenant" (21:27b).

At this point, an editor, or perhaps two, introduced two etymologies of the name *Beer-sheba*, "well of the seven ewe lambs" (21:28–31a) and "well of the oath" (21:31b). In Hebrew "seven" is *šebaʿ* and the verb "to make an oath" is *šābaʿ*. In popular thinking, both roots may explain the name *bĕʾēr šebaʿ*, "Beersheba." After this addition, the reader finds, in 21:32a, the same formula as in 21:27b, with a slight alteration: "they made a covenant at Beer-sheba." The narrative then quickly comes to an end (21:32b–34). Here, the addition interrupts the narrative to introduce a new topic—an "explanation" or "etiology"—just before the end of the account.

3. Genesis 37:36, 39:1 [10]

This example has already been discussed in the analysis of Genesis 37. The "resumption" of Gen 39:1 ties Genesis 39 to the plotline of chap. 37, while chap. 38 deals with a subject that is not related to the Joseph story: the episode of Judah and Tamar. The resumption is obvious, despite the fact that it replaces

---

9. Anbar, "Reprise," 386. For a different explanation, see Campbell and O'Brien, *Sources of the Pentateuch*, 169 (20:27b and 32 are additions). Also see C. Westermann, *Genesis 12–36* (trans. J. J. Scullion; Minneapolis, 1985) 348–49 (Gen 21:32a "is a resumption of the same sentence in v. 27b").

10. See, among others, H. Gunkel, *Genesis* (trans. M. E. Biddle; Mercer Library of Biblical Studies; Macon, GA, 1997) 407; C. Westermann, *Genesis 37–50* (trans. J. J. Scullion; Minneapolis, 1986) 61.

the Midianites with the Ishmaelites of 37:36, probably in an attempt to recon-cile the two versions of Joseph's sale in Genesis 37 as much as possible:

> 37:36: The Midianites had sold [Joseph] in Egypt to Potiphar, one of Pharaoh's officials, the captain of the guard.

> 39:1: Now Joseph was taken down to Egypt, and Potiphar, an officer of Pharaoh, the captain of the guard, an Egyptian, bought him from the Ishmaelites who had brought him down there.

4. Exodus 6:10–12, 29–30; 6:13, 26–28[11]

The genealogies of Reuben, Simeon, and Levi (6:14–25) are enveloped by two sets of repetitions: vv. 10–12 and 29–30, which mention Moses' objection to the mission YHWH has entrusted to him; vv. 13 and 26–28 deal with the mission of Moses and Aaron. The genealogy in 6:14–25 introduces a subject that has little to do with the rest of the chapter. The verbal correspondences be-tween the original text and the resumption are irrefutable, despite some slight differences between them.

• The first resumptive repetition:

> 6:10–12: [10]Then YHWH spoke to Moses, [11]"Go and tell Pharaoh king of Egypt to let the Israelites go out of his land." [12]But Moses spoke to YHWH, "The Israelites have not listened to me; how then shall Pharaoh listen to me, poor speaker that I am?"

> 6:29–30: [29]he said to him, "I am YHWH; tell Pharaoh king of Egypt all that I am speaking to you." [30]But Moses said in YHWH's presence, "Since I am a poor speaker, why would Pharaoh listen to me?"

• The second resumptive repetition:

> 6:13: Thus YHWH spoke to Moses and Aaron, and gave them orders regarding the Israelites and Pharaoh king of Egypt, charging them to free the Israelites from the land of Egypt.

> 6:26–28: [26]It was this same Aaron and Moses to whom YHWH said, "Bring the Israelites out of the land of Egypt, company by company." [27]It was they who spoke to Pharaoh king of Egypt to bring the Israelites out of Egypt, the same Moses and Aaron. [28]On the day when YHWH spoke to Moses in the land of Egypt. . . .

---

11. Anbar, "Reprise," 386–87. Also see W. H. Schmidt, *Exodus 1,1–6,30* (BKAT 2/1; Neukirchen-Vluyn, 1988) 295–96; Campbell and O'Brien (*Sources of the Pentateuch*, 36–37, with n. 27) follow Noth, with an excellent description of the phenomenon of resumption. Cf. Childs, *Exodus*, 111.

The first series of repetitions (6:10–12, 29–30) only mentions Moses, while the second (6:13, 26–28) adds Aaron. In addition, it should be noted that in 6:28 the editor attempts to create a transition between his resumption and the discourse that follows (7:1–5).

5. Leviticus 26:46, 27:34 [12]

Originally, Leviticus ended at Leviticus 26, which contains a series of benedictions and maledictions analogous to those in vassal treaties of the ancient Near East. Chapter 26 concludes at 26:46, as we saw above. The resumptive repetition of the conclusion, in 27:34, signifies that another passage has been "added" to the already existing text. As in the cases above, the contents of chap. 27 provide enough arguments for affirming with certainty that there actually is a later addition:

> 26:46: These are the statutes and ordinances and laws that YHWH established between himself and the people of Israel on Mount Sinai through Moses.

> 27:34: These are the commandments that YHWH gave to Moses for the people of Israel on Mount Sinai.

6. Numbers 22:21b, 35b [13]

The episode of Balaam's donkey (Num 22:22–34) is well known. This is, in fact, a long interpolation that contains a variant of the seer's mission. In Num 22:7–21, the king of Moab, Balak, sends two groups of messengers to convince Balaam to come and prophesy against Israel. The first time, obeying God's order, Balaam refuses. But the second time, God suggests to Balaam that he should go with the legation (22:20), and Balaam sets out with Balak's messengers (22:21). However, in 22:21, God becomes angry with Balaam. The reader cannot help being surprised by this after the divine discourse in 22:20: if God allows Balaam's departure, why does he then get angry with him in 22:22?

The simplest explanation is to admit that the episode of the donkey is an addition. This argument based on the contents—there is a contradiction between the two versions of Balaam's mission—is confirmed by the resumptive repetition of 22:21b in 22:35b:

> 22:21b: [Balaam] went with the officials of Moab.

> 22:35b: Balaam went on with the officials of Balak.

---

12. Anbar, "Reprise," 387; see also Levinson, "The Right Chorale," 150.
13. Ibid., 388. Also see Budd, *Numbers*, 256–57.

Moreover, 22:35a is connected to 22:20. In 22:20, after the episode of the donkey, YHWH's angel repeats the order God gave to Balaam the first time in 22:20.

> 22:20: Get up and go with them [the officials]; but do only what I tell you to do.

> 22:35a: The angel of YHWH said to Balaam, "Go with the men; but speak only what I tell you to speak."

7. Conclusion

The technique of resumptive repetition appears frequently in the Hebrew Bible.[14] We must emphasize again the fact that a resumption is not by itself proof of editing. If there are no other arguments or clear indications of the presence of an addition, then the resumption may be just a technique used by the author himself—for example, to describe two simultaneous events.[15]

C. Some "Linguistic Markers" of Redactional Work

1. Divine Discourses

a. Genesis 22:15–18[16]

"Abraham's trial" or "the sacrifice of Isaac" (Gen 22:1–19) has one conclusion in 22:14, after the angel has come to keep the patriarch from sacrificing his son and Abraham has named the site of this "trial." Then the angel speaks a second time to "ratify" Abraham's obedience and reconfirm the promises made previously; among these promises is the promise of numerous offspring. Afterward, Abraham goes back to Beer-sheba (22:19).

The angel's second discourse is surprising for several reasons:

1. Why does YHWH's angel call "a second time" (*šēnît*; 22:15)? Why does he not just say everything at once (22:11–12)?
2. Gen 22:15–18 adds nothing that is indispensable for understanding the narrative. The first "confirmation" in 22:12 ("Now I know that you fear God") adequately enough concludes the "trial" of 22:1–10, and the reader does not expect anything else.

---

14. See the examples presented in the articles cited in the bibliography.

15. See Long, "Framing Repetitions," 385–99; disputed examples: 2 Kgs 4:12b, 15; 4:25a, 27a; 1 Kgs 20:12a, 16; 2 Kgs 5:11a, 12b; 2 Kgs 4:8a, 11a; 1 Sam 1:3a, 7a; 2 Kgs 7:5b, 8a; 1 Kgs 1:1, 4 and 1:15b; 1 Sam 18:5, 14, 30; to frame an *excursus*: 2 Kgs 17:6b, 23b; 17:33–34, 40–41.

16. For a commentary on this text, see R. W. L. Moberly, "The Earliest Commentary on the Akedah," *VT* 38 (1988) 302–23.

3. The angel's second discourse repeats various elements from the first discourse in completing it, notably with regard to the introduction: "the angel of YHWH called to [Abraham] from heaven, and said . . ." (22:11, 15); and with regard to Abraham's obedience: "since you have not withheld your son, your only son" (22:12, 16).
4. The vocabulary and contents of Gen 22:15–18 repeat, in another form, the promises of 12:1–3; 13:14–17; and 15:1–7, 21.[17]

For all these reasons, many exegetes think that Gen 22:15–18 is a later addition.[18] In 22:15 the "linguistic marker" is the adverbial phrase "a second time." This addition attempts to tie the divine promises to the episode of the trial of Abraham.

b. Exodus 3:15

From a critical point of view, the scene of the burning bush is a very complex text.[19] In this narrative, one of the most difficult passages is the text in which God answers Moses' question about his name (3:13–15). After the "revelation of the name" in 3:14, God "again" (*'ôd*) speaks, with more information (3:15). The word "again" suggests that there is an addition:

God again said to Moses, "Thus you shall say to the Israelites, 'YHWH, the God of your ancestors, the God of Abraham, the God of Isaac, and the God of Jacob, has sent me to you': This is my name [by which you shall invoke me] forever, and this my title for all generations."

---

17. See Westermann, *Genesis 12–36*, 217–31; also see Moberly's article cited in n. 16.

18. See, among others, Gunkel, *Genesis*, 236. A different opinion is represented by G. W. Coats, "Abraham's Sacrifice of Faith: A Form-Critical Study of Genesis 22," *Int* 27 (1973) 389–400; Van Seters, *Abraham*, 227–40, especially pp. 230–31; T. D. Alexander, "Gen 22 and the Covenant of Circumcision," *JSOT* 25 (1983) 17–22; G. J. Wenham, *Genesis 16–50* (WBC 2; Dallas, 1994) 102–3. Their argumentation seems weak. Thus Wenham (ibid., 102) writes: "For God to spare Isaac's life, which would not have been a risk without Abraham's submission to the test, and then merely to say 'now I know you fear God' is somewhat an anticlimax. Surely God should say more to Abraham after putting him through such a traumatic experience." However, does this reaction correspond to ancient or to modern sensibilities? Who could say with certainty: "Surely God should say more"? Is there any particular reason?

19. For a literary study of this pericope, see G. Fischer, *Jahwe unser Gott: Sprache, Aufbau und Erzähltechnik in der Berufung des Mose (Exod 3–4)* (OBO 91; Fribourg and Göttingen, 1989); for a study on the composition of the passage, see B. Renaud, "La figure prophétique de Moïse en Exod 3,1–4,17," *RB* 93 (1986) 510–34; also see P. Weimar, *Die Berufung des Mose: Literaturwissenschaftliche Analyse von Exodus 2,23–5,5* (OBO 32; Fribourg and Göttingen, 1980); Kohata, *Jahwist und Priesterschrift*, 17–18; W. H. Schmidt, *Exodus 1,1–6,30*, 107–23; Blum, *Studien*, 22–28; J. C. Gertz, *Tradition und Redaktion in der Exoduserzählung: Untersuchungen zur Endredaktion des Pentateuch* (FRLANT 186; Göttingen, 2000) 254–334.

Many exegetes consider Exod 3:15 to be a later addition.[20]

1. The introduction combines elements from v. 14a: "God said to Moses" and v. 14b: "Thus you shall say to the Israelites." Now, the adverb *'ôd* ("again") clearly indicates that v. 15 is to be understood as a "supplement" given by God.

2. Verse 15 contains an explanation about what preceded. It repeats elements from v. 6: "I am the God of your father, the God of Abraham, the God of Isaac, and the God of Jacob"; and from v. 13: "the God of your fathers has sent me to you." However, v. 15 replaces the difficult "I am" (*'ehyeh*, v. 14b) with the better-known Tetragrammaton (*yhwh*). Thus, the verse elucidates the quite enigmatic content of v. 14.

3. Although v. 15a is indeed well anchored in its context, v. 15b not only answers the question asked in v. 13 but goes well beyond it because God speaks to all the generations of the people of Israel who will call on him in prayer. From a stylistic perspective, there is a transition from the third person in v. 15a, "YHWH . . . sends me to you," to the first person in v. 15b, "This is *my* name. . . ."

c. Genesis 16:9, 10, 11[21]

Genesis 16 recounts the conflict between Hagar and Sarai and Ishmael's birth. When Hagar flees into the wilderness (16:6), she meets "the angel of YHWH." After a short "introduction" (16:7–8), the angel speaks to her three times and each time his words are introduced by the same formula: "The angel of YHWH said to her" (16:9a, 10a, 11a). How do we explain these three introductions since Hagar does not interrupt the discourse in any way? The simplest explanation is to conclude that one or more editors added two other divine discourses to the primitive oracle in vv. 11–12 in order to reconcile the present text with other narratives in Genesis 12–25.

In 16:9 the angel of YHWH tells Hagar to return to Sarai. This command allows us to understand why Ishmael is born in Abraham's (and Sarah's) house, in vv. 16:15–16, and why he is present when Isaac is born (21:1–3). Similarly, it will be easier to understand why, in 21:8–21, Hagar will again be sent away

---

20. See W. H. Schmidt, *Exodus 1,1–6,30*, 132–33.

21. See, among the first to have dealt with this question, Wellhausen, *Composition des Hexateuchs*, 19–20; also see, among others, Gunkel, *Genesis*, 183; Westermann, *Genesis 12–36*, 244–45; Blum, *Komposition der Vätergeschichte*, 316–17, 365. As usual, Wenham (*Genesis 16–15*, 5–6) shows great prudence before admitting the presence of sources or redactional additions. However, his arguments are primarily formal, because he tends to base them on his own structuring of the text. Van Seters (*Abraham*, 194–95) thinks that only v. 10 is an addition. However, his analysis of v. 9 is problematic. If the angel of YHWH ordered Hagar to return to *Sarai*, why is there no allusion to this in what follows?

with her son, Ishmael. The second discourse (16:10) contains the promise of numerous offspring for Ishmael. This promise reappears in 17:20 and 21:13, 18. Later editors were constantly trying to unite and harmonize isolated narratives with other passages in the same book or in other parts of the Bible.[22]

2. Explanatory Glosses Introduced by *hû'* or *hî'* ("he/this" or "she/this")

a. Genesis 36:1, 8, 19[23]

Genesis 36 contains the genealogy of Esau (36:1). To the title "These are the descendants of Esau," the text adds the following explanation: "that is, Edom" / "who is Edom" (*hû' 'ĕdôm*). Because Esau's name reappears in vv. 2, 4, 6, 9, 15, etc., without this clarification, we assume that the words "that is, Edom," were added by an editor who wished to dispel all doubt concerning the identification of Esau and Edom. This idea is confirmed by vv. 8 and 19, where the same addition reappears, but this time it is not perfectly integrated into the context. Verse 8 says: "So Esau settled in the hill country of Seir; Esau is Edom." Verse 19 contains a rather awkward grammatical construction: "These are the sons of Esau (that is, Edom), and these are their clans." In all three cases, the scribe used the same technique: he introduced an explanatory gloss with the pronoun *hû'* ("he").

b. Genesis 14:2, 3, 7, 8, 17[24]

Genesis 14 is a difficult text that contains several little-known proper names and place-names. In many cases, the text provides explanations that begin with the pronouns *hî'* and *hû'* ("she" or "he"). In 14:2, 8 the city of Bela is

---

22. The double *wayyō'mer* is not always an indication of redactional work. In other words, there are many cases in which we must attribute to a single author a double *wayyō'mer* that introduces two successive discourses of the same speaker without the interruption of an interlocutor. This is the case, for example, when someone asks a rhetorical question or provokes someone's thinking, allows the interlocutor to reflect briefly, and then continues his/her discourse (Gen 19:9; 37:21–22). Likewise, someone may give a command and wait for it to be executed before speaking again (see Gen 15:5; Exod 3:5–6). On this phenomenon, see M. Shiloh, "And He Said . . . and He Said," *Sefer Korngreen* (Tel Aviv, 1963) [Hebrew]; Conroy, *Absalom*, 130 n. 65; S. Bar-Efrat, *Narrative Art in the Bible* (JSOTSup 70; Bible and Literature Series 17; Sheffield, 1989) 43–45; G. Fischer, *Jahwe, unser Gott*, 41–45; S. A. Meier, *Speaking of Speaking: Marking Direct Discourse in the Hebrew Bible* (VTSup 46; Leiden, 1992) 73–81.

23. For the redactional technique in this passage and in those that follow, see Fishbane, *Biblical Interpretation*, 44–46; G. R. Driver, "Glosses in the Hebrew Text of the Old Testament," in *L'Ancien Testament et l'Orient* (Orientalia et biblica lovaniensia 1; Leuven, 1957) 123–61; for Gen 36:1, 8, 19, see pp. 45–46. Cf. Gunkel, *Genesis*, 376.

24. Fishbane, *Biblical Interpretation*, 45, 80–81.

identified as the city of Zoar: "[and the king of] Bela, [that is,] Zoar." According to 14:3, the "the Valley of Siddim" is the Dead Sea. In 14:7, which depicts the campaign of the four kings, En-mishpat is equated with Kadesh: "that is, Kadesh." In 14:17, which talks about the place where the king of Sodom comes to meet Abraham, the text explains that this "Valley of Shaveh"[25] is "the King's Valley" (see 2 Sam 18:18).

These explanations are intended to help the reader identify the places referred to in the biblical text, places that probably no longer had the same names. The original addressees of the text did not need these explanations, and this is why they are often considered to be additions. The frequency of these phenomena in the course of one chapter is confirmation of editing. Additions reveal a desire to "update" the text so that it may be easily understood by readers of a more recent time. This method shows the vitality of the biblical tradition.[26]

3. Explanatory Glosses that Repeat One or More Terms from the Original Text

a. Genesis 13:13[27]

In the account of the separation of Abraham and Lot, Lot goes and sets up his tent close to Sodom (13:12b). Verse 13 repeats the word "Sodom" in order to add information concerning the town. The verse says: "Now the people of Sodom were wicked, great sinners against YHWH." This information has no function in the immediate context, but it prepares the reader to understand Genesis 18–19, where the perversity of the Sodomites will be manifest—the perversity that will be punished by the destruction of the town.

b. Genesis 16:7[28]

In Gen 16:7, Hagar meets the angel of YHWH "by a spring of water in the wilderness." An editor who wanted to specify which "spring" this was added the words: "the spring on the way to Shur." This addition repeats two terms

---

25. A. Wieder ("Ugaritic-Hebrew Lexicographical Notes," *JBL* 84 [1965] 160–64) suggests interpreting the Hebrew *šwh/šwy* on the basis of the Ugaritic word *ṯwy*, which means "reign"; see Ps 89:20. In this case, the expression "the King's Valley" would only be the translation of an ancient term whose meaning was no longer known. See Fishbane, *Biblical Interpretation*, 45. "The King's Valley" is mentioned in 2 Sam 18:18. For others, however, the word *šāwâ* means "valley," and if so, it would be a pleonasm. Cf. Wenham, *Genesis 1–15*, 315.

26. For other examples, see Gen 23:2, 19; outside the Pentateuch: Josh 18:13; 1 Kgs 6:38, 8:2; 1 Chr 11:4; Esth 2:16, 3:17, 8:12, 9:24. See Fishbane, *Biblical Interpretation*, 44–45.

27. See Gunkel, *Genesis*, 174; Westermann, *Genesis 12–36*, 178; Blum, *Komposition der Vätergeschichte*, 283; Levin, *Jahwist*, 143.

28. See Gunkel, *Genesis*, 185.

from the original text, "by the spring," to introduce the clarification. If the original text had wanted to mention "the way to Shur," it would have done so at the end of v. 6, which describes Hagar's flight.

c. Exodus 16:36

In Exodus 16 ("the miracle of the manna") the name of a measurement, the "omer," appears several times (16:16, 18, 22, 32, 33). Each family gathered one omer of manna each day. Now, at the end of the narrative, after the conclusion, the text continues with a precise explanation of what an "omer" is: a tenth of an ephah ("measure," v. 36). This is probably a redactional addition. The editor felt a need to explain this term because his contemporaries no longer knew about or used the omer. The author of the original text, however, did not think this was necessary when he used the term the first time in v. 16.

d. Numbers 13:22

In Numbers 13, Moses sends explorers into the Promised Land on a reconnaissance mission. In Num 13:22a the men explore the area of Hebron. At this point, the text adds a piece of information concerning the city of Hebron—information that has no direct connection with the story itself: "Hebron was built seven years before Zoan in Egypt." Verse 22b repeats the word "Hebron," which already appears in v. 22a. In a modern text, the editor would have inserted a footnote. This is why the exegetes consider Num 13:22a to be a redactional addition or the "gloss" of an erudite editor.

e. Deuteronomy 3:9

The first territory conquered by the Israelites on the other side of the Jordan extends, according to Deut 3:8, from Wadi Arnon to Mount Hermon. Verse 9 contains a "scholarly" note concerning this mountain: "the Sidonians call Hermon Sirion, while the Amorites call it Senir." The text is perfectly comprehensible without this information, which must therefore be attributed to an editor.

D. Important "Divine Discourses" of Redactional Origin

In the course of recent decades, scholars have drawn our attention to the presence of "divine discourses" introduced in strategic places, notably at the beginning of the most important stages of salvation history. These discourses are frequently "narrative agendas" placing the foundations for Israel's future history in its distant past. The origin of these discourses is still disputed. However, certain exegetes think that there can be no doubt about their redactional origin. These texts are late additions to preexisting narratives or to narrative

cycles in order to "update" them, reinterpret them, and deduce a new meaning
from them on the basis of the concerns of the Postexilic period. This is how Israel wanted to redefine its identity after the Babylonian Exile.

These are "divine discourses" because, in the Bible, YHWH is the supreme
authority, and only the divine voice can give these affirmations the unquestion-
able value that everyone recognizes. But who had the authority to write a text
of this sort and attribute it to YHWH? It is quite likely that these texts derived
from people who were entrusted with preserving and interpreting the tradition
after the disappearance of the Preexilic institutions that were tied to the monarchy. These religious authorities should first be sought within the priestly families and the chief landowners of Judah and Jerusalem.

In the following paragraphs, I will simply identify these passages and provide
the main arguments that support their redactional origin. In the footnotes, I
will refer the reader to sources for further information.

1. Genesis 12:1–4a [29]

Abraham's calling was long considered to be one of the key texts of the most
ancient source of the Pentateuch, the Yahwist. Now, more and more exegetes
tend to think that this is actually a text dating to the Exilic or Postexilic period.
Three important reasons lead us to believe that the text is later and that it was
inserted into its present context.

• Gen 12:1–4a interrupts a chronicle of the migrations of Terah's clan. This
chronicle begins in 11:31, where Terah leaves Ur of the Chaldeans "to go into
the land of Canaan," but stops in Haran, where he dies (11:32). Abraham continues the journey in 12:5 and this time arrives at the original destination—the
land of Canaan (cf. 11:31). The correspondences between 11:31 and 12:5 show
clearly that these verses are the work of the same author. The exegetes attribute
these verses to the "Priestly Writer":

> 11:31: Terah took his son Abram and his grandson Lot son of Haran, and his
> daughter-in-law Sarai, his son Abram's wife, and they went out together from Ur
> of the Chaldeans to go into the land of Canaan; but when they came to Haran,
> they settled there.

> 12:5: Abram took his wife Sarai and his brother's son Lot, and all the possessions
> that they had gathered, and the persons whom they had acquired in Haran; and
> they set forth to go to the land of Canaan. When they had come to the land of
> Canaan. . . .

---

29. See Blum, *Komposition der Vätergeschichte*, 349–59; Carr, *Reading the Fractures of Gene-
sis*, 183–96; J.-L. Ska, "L'appel d'Abraham et l'acte de naissance d'Israël (Gn 12,1–4a)," in
Deuteronomy and Deuteronomic Literature: Festschrift C. H. W. Brekelmans (ed. M. Vervenne and
J. Lust; BETL 133; Leuven, 1997) 367–89.

An oracle in 12:1–3 and a reference to Abraham's obedience in 12:4a are inserted between two episodes in the chronicle of this journey. Furthermore, the indication of Abraham's age (12:4b: "Abram was seventy-five years old when he departed from Haran") does not follow v. 5 but precedes it. This information was probably transferred and inserted into its new context. Abraham's departure is described for the first time in 12:4a, and the reference to Abraham's age (12:4b) is connected to the departure "by obedience" instead of being in the more "natural" location, in v. 5.

• The oracle in 12:1–3 gives another picture of Abraham's migration. Gen 18:18 and 22:18 (both late additions) aside, no text is related to the oracle, which remains totally isolated in the whole of the Abraham and Sarah Cycle. The portrait of Abraham, the man of faith, who accomplishes a long migration is largely dependent on Gen 12:1–3. The other, more ancient, narratives present migrations that are much less important. Abraham moves from Bethel to Hebron (13:18); then in the direction of Gerar, in the country of the Philistines (20:1); and finally to Beer-sheba (21:33). The trip to Egypt is an exception (12:10–20), but it is necessitated by a famine (12:10).

• The aim of Gen 12:1–3 is to show that Abraham is the ancestor of the exiled people who have come back from Babylon to Israel and to legitimize their rights in the eyes of the people who remained in the country. The two groups are fighting for possession of the land, as we can see clearly, particularly in Ezek 33:24.[30] The exiled group—those of the *gôlâ* (Hebrew for "exile")—win the case and give a theological interpretation to Abraham's "migration" by asserting that Israel's ancestor obeyed YHWH's order (12:1, 4a). The exiles are therefore considered to be Abraham's spiritual heirs because, like him, they came back from Babylon in response to a divine call, such as the one we find in Isaiah 40–55. Over the course of their history, the people of Israel constantly seek new reasons in their tradition to live and to hope.

2. Genesis 13:14–17

There are fewer problems with the redactional origin of this oracle. The arguments are quite convincing.[31]

• The oracle in Gen 13:14–17 interrupts a description of the migrations of both Abraham and Lot after their decision to go separate ways. The original text in Gen 13:12 is clearly repeated in 13:18. In 13:13 the intrusion of the narrator directly precedes the oracle:[32]

---

30. Also see the contrast between Abraham and Moses in Isa 63:11, 16.

31. See Wellhausen, *Composition des Hexateuchs*, 23–24; Gunkel, *Genesis*, 175; Noth, *History of Pentateuchal Traditions*, 28; Westermann, *Genesis 12–36*, 178; Campbell and O'Brien, *Sources of the Pentateuch*, 100; Blum, *Komposition der Vätergeschichte*, 290; Levin, *Jahwist*, 145–46; Carr, *Reading the Fractures of Genesis*, 163–66.

32. This is also thought to be a late, redactional text.

¹²Abram settled in the land of Canaan, while Lot settled among the cities of the Plain and moved his tent as far as Sodom. . . . ¹⁸So Abram moved his tent, and came and settled by the oaks of Mamre, which are at Hebron; and there he built an altar to YHWH.

From the stylistic viewpoint, the passage has a chiastic structure:

A. Abraham lives in the land of Canaan.
       B. Lot settles in the valley.
       B′. Lot moves his tents to Sodom.
A′. Abraham moves his tents and goes to live by the oaks of Mamre.

This construction is interrupted in 13:13 by the intrusion of the narrator, who explains to us the perversity of the inhabitants of Sodom, and especially by the intrusion of the oracle in vv. 14–17.

• The oracle in 13:14–17 is not closely tied to its context. First, the promise of the land (13:14–15) sanctions Abraham's choice *a posteriori* because YHWH gives him the land on which he has already settled, according to 13:12. Second, the promise of numerous offspring is awkwardly inserted into a narrative that deals primarily with the land. Third, the command to traverse the length and the breadth of the land (13:17) is not carried out. Abraham only moves from Bethel to Hebron (13:18).

• The oracle in Gen 13:14–17 places the first promise of land and numerous offspring after the separation of Abraham and Lot (13:14a). This context is very important because, in this way, Lot and his descendants, the Moabites and the Ammonites (19:29–38), are excluded from the divine promises.

3. Genesis 28:13–15 [33]

Only recently have some scholars come to the conclusion that Gen 28:13–15 is also a later addition. However, the reasons advanced to support this hypothesis are convincing.

• From the narrative and stylistic points of view, the account of the vision at Bethel (28:10–22) is centered around the discovery of a "sacred place": Bethel (28:19). The word "place" (*māqôm*) is a key word of this text (28:11 [3×], 16, 17, 19). The stone is another important element (28:11, 18; cf. v. 22). The narrative ends when Jacob sets up the stone for a pillar and gives the name *Bethel* to the "sacred place" that he has just discovered (28:18–19).

The oracle in vv. 13–15, on the other hand, deals with a quite different question: YHWH, the God of Abraham and of Isaac, will also be the God of Jacob (28:13b). He also promises land to the fugitive (28:13b) as well as numer-

---

33. See R. Rendtorff, "Jakob in Bethel: Beobachtungen zum Aufbau und zur Quellenfrage in Gen 28,10–22," *ZAW* 94 (1982) 511–23; Blum, *Komposition der Vätergeschichte*, 1–35.

ous offspring (28:14a) and then adds that Jacob will become a "blessing" (28:14b); finally, YHWH pledges to protect him throughout his journey and to bring him home one day (28:15). These themes are not related to the story about "the discovery of the sacred place."

• When Jacob wakes up from his sleep during the night in 28:16 or in the morning in 28:18, he does not mention the oracle at all. He seems to remember only the vision. The only element of the account that is attached to the oracle is the oath in vv. 20–22, which follows the narrative's conclusion in 28:19 and, for this reason, must also be a later addition.

The oracle functions as a transition: it connects Genesis 28 to the Abrahamic Cycle (28:13–14) and presents a proleptic summary of the Jacob cycle up to the patriarch's return to his land (28:15).

• The connections with Gen 13:14–17 are obvious.[34] The oracle in Gen 28:13–14 repeats to Jacob essentially what was said to Abraham in Gen 13:14–15:

Gen 13:14–15	Gen 28:13–14
All the land that you see I will give to you and to your offspring forever.	The land on which you lie I will give to you and to your offspring.
I will make your offspring like the dust of the earth,	Your offspring shall be like the dust of the earth,
northward and southward	spread abroad to the west and to the east
and eastward and westward.	and to the north and to the south.

The promise to make Jacob a "blessing" (28:14b) is similar to the promise made to Abraham in 12:3, 18:18, and 22:18 and to Isaac in 26:4. The affinity between these different texts is undeniable despite slight characteristic variations of the Hebrew style. Gen 28:15 unites all the episodes of Jacob's stay in the household of his uncle, Laban, into a single story that unfolds under the benevolent eye of YHWH until Jacob returns, safe and sound, to Bethel (Gen 33:18–19, 35:1–7).[35]

Conclusion. The main function of the oracle is to unite various parts of the book of Genesis: to attach the Jacob cycle to the Abrahamic cycle (and to the Isaac cycle) and to organize the narratives about Jacob around the journey that will lead him back home after a prolonged adventure.

---

34. See ibid., 290; Carr, *Reading the Fractures of Genesis*, 181.

35. Cf. L. A. Turner, *Announcements of Plot in Genesis* (JSOTSup 96; Sheffield, 1990) 137–38.

4. *Exodus 19:3–8*[36]

Another example of this kind of redactional insertion is found in Exod 19:3–8. Here the indications are clear.

• In Exod 19:3a Moses goes up the mountain to God, while in 19:3b YHWH calls to him from the mountain to give him a message to be communicated to Israel. In 19:7 Moses carries out the order, transmits the message, and then communicates to YHWH the people's answer in 19:8b. After a final divine message addressed to Moses and a resumptive repetition in 19:9b, the text continues with a series of instructions to prepare for the theophany (19:10–13). In 19:14, Moses comes down from the mountain.

It is not easy to follow all of Moses' "ups and downs" in this chapter. However, there are two incompatible movements that become apparent: on the one hand, Moses goes up the mountain (19:3a); and, on the other, YHWH speaks to him from the mountain (19:3b), and all the action happens in the plain at the foot of Mount Sinai. Nowhere in 19:3b–8 does it say that Moses goes down to speak to the people. In 19:7, he approaches those who are closest. So, the man of God stays at the foot of the mountain, despite what is said in 19:3a.

The text becomes clearer when we separate 19:3b–8, 9 from the preceding and following passages. In 19:3b–8 YHWH calls to Moses from Mount Sinai, and Moses responds without going up the mountain. He only goes back and forth between the people and YHWH, who talks to him from the summit of Mount Sinai. In 19:3a, on the other hand, he climbs the mountain, where he receives the instructions given in 19:10–13; then he goes back down, in 19:14, and prepares for the theophany in accordance with the instructions that YHWH has given him.

• The oracle in Exod 19:3b–6 is not directly tied to the theophany in 19:16–19 and does not mention it. Verses 3b–6 are primarily concerned with the covenant sealed in 24:3–8, another later text. Thus, Exod 19:3b–6 introduces the entire section about the revelation at Mount Sinai and reveals its significance: YHWH invites the people to become his "possession" (*sĕgullâ*), a "holy nation" (*gôy qādôš*), and a "priestly kingdom" (*mamleket kōhănîm*). In other words, YHWH defines Israel's status as a nation, and the oracle contains important elements of "Israel's constitution." The text presents itself as an interpretation of the entire Law of the chosen people.

---

36. See B. Baentsch, *Exodus–Leviticus–Numeri* (HAT 1/2; Göttingen, 1903) 170–71; Childs, *Exodus*, 360–61; my "Exode 19,3b–6 et l'identité de l'Israël postexilique," in *Studies in the Book of Exodus: Redaction–Reception–Interpretation* (ed. M. Vervenne; BETL 126; Leuven, 1996) 289– 317, with bibliography.

E. Moses' Intercessions:
Exod 32:7–14, Num 14:11b–23a

Moses has to intercede many times for the people during their wanderings in the wilderness. Critics have identified two intercessions, which are more developed and are situated in two key contexts in Exodus and Numbers, as being later additions. The first, Exod 32:7–14, appears in the account of the golden calf, which describes Israel's first sin after the Sinai Covenant. In the second, Num 14:11b–23a, Moses intercedes after the people have refused to conquer the land (Numbers 13–14). Both texts are characterized by Deuteronomistic theological language.

1. Exodus 32:7–14 [37]

In Exod 32:7–10, YHWH informs Moses about what is happening in the camp during his absence, and he tells him that he has decided to destroy the rebellious people. Moses intercedes, and YHWH grants forgiveness. This account was inserted into an older text. There are many grounds for this conclusion:

• In 32:7–10 YHWH tells Moses about the construction of the golden calf, while in 32:15–19 Moses and Joshua discover the transgression when they come down from the mountain.

• In 32:14 YHWH changes his mind and gives up the idea of punishing the people. However, in 32:35 YHWH sends a plague to punish Israel.

• Moses intercedes in 32:11–13 and then again in 32:30–34. The second prayer does not mention the first one.

• Certain themes and vocabulary are similar to themes and words used in Deuteronomy 9, a chapter that recalls the same event. The most significant are the references to the patriarchs (Exod 32:13 and Deut 9:27; cf. 9:5); the promise made to the fathers (with the verb *šbʿ*);[38] the verb "to remember" (Exod 32:13; Deut 7:18; 8:18; 9:7, 27); the expression "stiff-necked" (Exod 32:9; Deut 9:6, 13).

• The ancient narrative most likely went directly from 32:6 to 32:15. The passage is connected to Exod 24:12–15a, where we encounter the two main characters, Moses and Joshua (24:13, 32:17), and the reference to the two tablets of the Law that YHWH prepared and gave to Moses on the mountain (24:12; 32:15–16, 19).

---

37. For a bibliography and analysis of the text, see E. Aurelius, *Der Fürbitter Israels: Eine Studie zum Mosebild im Alten Testament* (ConBOT 27; Stockholm, 1988) 41–44 and 91–100.

38. See Deut 1:8, 35; 4:31; 6:10, 18; 7:8, 12, 13; 8:1, 18; 9:5; 10:11; 11:9, 21; 13:18; 19:8; 26:3, 15; 28:11; 29:12; 30:20; 31:7, 20–21; 34:4.

2. Numbers 14:11b–23a [39]

In Num 14:11b–12, just as in Exod 32:7–14, YHWH threatens to destroy the rebellious people and to make Moses the ancestor of a greater and more powerful nation. Moses intercedes and once again obtains divine clemency. This text, which is heavily theological, is a later insertion. Two arguments support this view.

1. The theology and the style of this passage are different from the older layers in Numbers 13–14 and from the other narratives about Israel's wandering in the wilderness. The vocabulary of Num 14:11b–23a shows acquaintance with other texts of various origins, especially Exod 32:7–14 and some Deuteronomistic passages. [40]
2. The verb "reject" appears in 14:11a and in 14:23b, but it is missing in 14:11b–23a. We are uncertain how to delineate the addition (Num 14:11b–23a), and we do not know what precisely constituted the ancient text before the insertion of the passage. Despite these uncertainties, most exegetes think that there is indeed an addition in Num 14:10–25*.

F. Conclusion

We could extend the list of these redactional interventions. [41] Their presence in the Pentateuch—as well as elsewhere in the Old Testament—precludes the possibility that a single author wrote the first five books of the Bible or even the idea that these books form a literary unit, the product of a single structural design. In fact, polyphony is one of the basic characteristics of the text and must be respected as such. The legislative texts and the narratives have been reread, corrected, reinterpreted, and updated several times in accordance with new situations and the need to answer new questions.

---

39. See Aurelius, *Fürbitter*, 132–33; Noth, *Numbers*, 108–10.

40. The following are the most significant parallels: (1) the "signs": Num 14:11, 22; Deut 4:34, 6:22, 7:19, 11:3, 26:8, 29:2, 34:11; (2) YHWH wants to make Moses into a great nation: Num 14:12b, Exod 32:10, Deut 9:14; (3) the motif of "YHWH's renown" in Moses' intercession: Num 14:13–16, Exod 32:12, Deut 9:28; (4) the cloud; Num 14:14, Deut 1:33; (5) the description of YHWH, the merciful God: Num 14:18; Exod 20:6, 34:7; Deut 5:10; 7:9–10; (6) the people put YHWH to the test: Num 14:22; Exod 7:2, 7; Deut 6:16; (7) "listen to the voice": Num 14:22b; Deut 4:30, 8:20; 9:23; 13:5, 19; 15:5; 26:4, 17; 28:1, 2, 15, 45, 62; 30:2, 8, 10, 20.

41. See, for example, Gen 26:2–6, 31:3, 46:1–5. The interventions are more frequent in the book of Genesis, perhaps because the stories of the patriarchs required more profound reinterpretation.

Redactional activity must therefore never be disdained. On the contrary, this activity proves the great vitality of a tradition that was capable of adapting and renewing itself in all circumstances.[42]

---

42. On the importance of redactional activity and ways to interpret it, see, for example, M. V. Fox, *The Redaction of the Books of Esther: On Reading Composite Texts* (SBLMS 40; Atlanta, 1991) 142–54; and above all Fishbane, *Biblical Interpretation*.

Chapter 6

Exegesis of the Pentateuch:
A History of Research
from Ancient Times to 1970

In the context of this introduction, it is impossible to present an exhaustive overview of the exegetical history of the Pentateuch from the time of its composition up to today. In the bibliography, I have noted some works on this subject. The present chapter only shows how exegetes from the Church Fathers up to our day have read the Pentateuch and solved the various critical problems that were enumerated in the preceding chapters.

A. Antiquity and the Middle Ages

1. The Reading of the Church Fathers[1]

During the Patristic period, Moses was commonly deemed, both in the Synagogue and in the Church, to be the author of the entire Pentateuch. At that time, no one paid attention to critical problems because the chief preoccupation was theological and apologetic. It was necessary to defend Christianity against Classical culture and in controversies with Judaism. Judaism was also defending the authority and reliability of its Scriptures against the attacks of "pagan" authors. The attribution of the Pentateuch to Moses was probably due to the influence of Hellenism, for which no great work could be anonymous. Great works and great names went together.[2]

At least three major schools distinguish themselves at the time of the Church Fathers: the Alexandrian school, the Antiochene school, and the Syriac school. Of these schools, the best known—because it prevailed in the history of the Church—is the Alexandrian school. Nevertheless, the other two schools also had great masters and exercised notable influence during certain periods and in particular regions of Christianity.

---

1. For this section, see J.-P. Bouhout, "Pentateuque chez les Pères," 687–708, in the article by Bouhout and H. Cazelles, "Pentateuque," *DBSup* 7.687–858; also see M. Sæbø (ed.), *Hebrew Bible. Old Testament: The History of Its Interpretation*, vol. 1: *From the Beginnings to the Middle Ages (until 1300)*. Part 1: *Antiquity* (Göttingen, 1996).

2. See Blenkinsopp, *Pentateuch*, 1.

The Alexandrian reading, following Origen, was principally allegorical, while the school of Antioch gave more attention to the historical context and preferred a more literal approach, which was called *theoria*.[3] The Syriac Fathers, such as Ephraim and Aphraates, were greatly influenced by the Semitic world, and their works are largely liturgical.

All of the Eastern and Western Fathers were influenced by the Greek philosophy of Plato. The allegory of the Alexandrian Fathers was already practiced by Platonic philosophers in their reading of the Greek classics. In the Jewish world, the allegorical readings of the Old Testament proposed by Philo greatly influenced Origen and, through him, the other Fathers of the Alexandrian school.

The principles of allegorical reading are very clearly explained by St. Augustine in his work *De doctrina Christiana* (*Christian Instruction*).[4] The basis of Augustinian exegesis is the Platonic distinction between the Latin *signum*, "sign," and *res*, "reality or a real thing." Each "sign" refers back to a "real thing." Because Scripture is composed of words, that is, "signs," the signs refer back to the only true reality, the Trinity. The exegete has the task of showing how one may move from signs, or words (narratives, prayers, oracles, etc.), to reality: the unique Triune God.

In another work, the *De catechizandis rudibus* (*Catechizing the Uninstructed*), Augustine defines the *res* ("reality") of the Bible in a different way: the Bible reveals God's love for the world. This revelation reaches its high point with the incarnation of Jesus Christ. The more "pastoral" vision of *De catechizandis rudibus* is also more dynamic because it introduces the notions of history and development.

In their exegesis of Old Testament texts, the Fathers seek above all the "figure" of Christ. They see people and events as announcing and prefiguring the person and life of Christ. In more technical terms, there is a transition from the "type" to the "antitype," from the *signum* to the *res*, from the "letter" to the "spirit."[5]

---

3. The main representatives of this school are Theodore of Mopsuestia, John Chrysostom, and Theodoret of Cyrus.

4. For a critical analysis, see, for example, E. V. McKnight, *Postmodern Use of the Bible: The Emergence of Reader-Oriented Criticism* (Nashville, 1988) 29–44.

5. The basic distinction between "letter" and "spirit" is found in the doctrine of the four "meanings of Scripture," especially in the exegesis of the Old Testament: the literal meaning, the allegorical or christological meaning, the tropological or moral meaning, and the anagogical or mystical meaning. The allegorical, tropological, and anagogical meanings are only subdivisions of the spiritual meaning. See the fundamental work of H. de Lubac, *Medieval Exegesis: The Four Senses of Scripture* (2 vols.; Grand Rapids, 1998) vol. 1; idem, *Scripture in the Tradition* (New York, 2000).

The world of the Latin and Greek Fathers is by and large overshadowed by the hierarchical representation of reality inherited from Plato. According to the "myth of the cave" presented by the great philosopher, the material world only contains "shadows" of authentic reality—that is, of "eternal ideas." Furthermore, in Platonic philosophy, language as such does not have any consistency: it is only an "imitation of reality," *mimēsis.*[6]

2. From Plato to the Middle Ages[7]

During the Middle Ages, society and culture slowly moved from being an economy based on agriculture and landowning to an economy in which artisanship, especially the textile industry, and commerce became progressively more important. The cities took precedence over the countryside; the urban bourgeoisie contested the power of the rural aristocracy. In addition to the Benedictines, who had built great abbeys in the countryside, new religious orders were founded, especially the Dominicans and the Franciscans (the Mendicant Orders), who preferred to settle in the cities.

Corresponding to these political, social, and cultural changes were developments in the philosophical and theological world. The most important of these developments was a gradual transition from the "idealistic" and "hierarchical" philosophy of Plato to the more "realistic" philosophy of Aristotle. The latter was introduced to European universities by Muslim philosophers in Spain, particularly Averroès. The shift is apparent in the writings of authors such as Albert the Great and Thomas Aquinas.

The exegetical world experienced a similar evolution. The reading of the Bible slowly became separate from doctrinal studies. More attention was given to the "literal" meaning, which was less and less frequently set in opposition to the "spiritual" meaning, in contrast to the tendency of the preceding period. For the first time, someone questioned the idea that Moses was the originator of the Pentateuch. This voice spoke from Spain, which at that time truly was a cultural melting pot, where Muslims, Jews, and Christians lived together in peace. The author in question was the great rabbi Abraham Ibn Ezra (b. Toledo, ca. 1092, d. Calahorra, ca. 1167) who in his commentary on Deuteronomy drew attention to the fact that it is difficult to attribute certain texts to Moses.[8] Ibn Ezra was afraid of being censured and even of being persecuted. Consequently, he spoke enigmatically and cautiously.[9] For example, he consid-

---

6. See E. Auerbach, *Mimesis: The Representation of Reality in Western Literature* (Princeton, 1968); M. H. Abrams, *The Mirror and the Lamp* (New York, 1953).

7. See H. Cazelles, "L'époque médiévale," 687–858 in the article by J.-P. Bouhout and Cazelles, "Pentateuque," *DBSup* 7.687–858.

8. See Blenkinsopp, *Pentateuch*, 2.

9. Ibid.

ered it strange that Moses would have said: "At that time the Canaanites were in the land" (Gen 12:6); he should have said, "the Canaanites are now in the land," because they were still there when he traveled from Egypt with the people of Israel.

In Gen 22:14, after the "trial," Abraham gives a name to the site of the "sacrifice": "YHWH will see/provide." The narrator (that is, Moses, according to the tradition), adds: "As it is said to this day, 'On the mountain YHWH appears.'" For Ibn Ezra, this mountain was Mount Zion, where the temple in which YHWH appears was built. Consequently, Moses could not have said, "as it is said *to this day* . . . ," because the temple was built long after his lifetime, under Solomon.

The book of Deuteronomy is full of difficulties. When, Deut 1:1 says: "These are the words that Moses spoke to all Israel *beyond* the Jordan" the author must be in the Promised Land, that is, in today's West Bank. However, Moses never left Transjordan. Deut 3:11 mentions the bed of Og, the king of Bashan, a descendant of the Rephaim, the giants of ancient times. This bed was iron, and it was nine cubits long and four cubits wide. Furthermore, the text notes that "it can still be seen in Rabbah of the Ammonites." If Moses lived at the same time as Og, why would he say this? This sentence was written by someone making reference to a long-standing tradition. Deut 31:9 states, "Moses wrote down this law." Why did Moses not say: "I wrote . . ." (using first-person singular)? Finally, it is also difficult, again according to Ibn Ezra, to imagine that Moses was able to write the entire Law on plastered stones, as YHWH commanded him to do in Deut 27:2–3 (cf. Deut 27:1–8).

Ibn Ezra was to remain isolated for a long time and, until the time of Spinoza, he had only a few followers.[10]

B. Humanism and the Beginning of Modern Exegesis[11]

1. New Interest in the Original Languages

In modern times, biblical exegetical studies generally attach great importance to Protestantism, especially the principle *Sola Scriptura*. Its influence on biblical exegesis, notably exegesis of the Pentateuch, is undeniable. However, the exegetical traditions of the various confessions is also indebted to another, larger cultural movement that left its mark on this period: the Renaissance. The rediscovery of Classical Antiquity, humanism, and a taste for both philology

---

10. See A. Lods, *Histoire de la littérature hébraïque et juive* (Paris, 1950) 86–87.

11. See H. Cazelles, "L'exégèse des temps modernes," 728–36 in the article "Pentateuque," by J.-P. Bouhout and Cazelles in *DBSup* 7.687–858.

and ancient Near Eastern languages have had a deep influence on the way the Bible is read.

After several centuries of reading and interpreting the Bible in its Latin version, Western Christians returned to the original languages. The movement began in Spain, where Cardinal Francisco Jiménez de Cisneros founded the university of Alcalá in order to promote (among other things) the teaching of Greek and Hebrew, and he commissioned the edition of the Complutensian Polygot Bible of Alcalá (*Biblia complutensis*), which was printed in 1514–1517 and published in 1520–1522. The Complutensian Polygot Old Testament is printed in Hebrew, Greek, and Latin, with the Aramaic Targum of the Pentateuch, and the New Testament in Greek (for the first time since the ancient manuscripts) and in Latin.

Fifty years later, Christoph Plantin published another renowned polyglot Bible, the *Biblia regia* (1569–1572), in Antwerp in the Netherlands. The invention of the printing press in 1434 by Gutenberg (Mainz, ca. 1440–1468) and the publication of the first printed Bible under his auspices (1454–1456) made possible these new editions of the sacred text in the original languages.[12]

In France, in 1530, William Budé obtained permission from Francis I to found the Collège des Trois Langues in Paris, where Greek, Hebrew, and Classical Latin were taught, while the Sorbonne continued to teach a less-polished form of Medieval Latin. After the Restoration (1815), this institution became the Collège de France.

Erasmus (b. ca. 1469, Rotterdam; d. 1536, Basel), one of the fathers of modern exegesis, published his Greek Testament in Basel, in 1516, shortly before the Complutensian Polygot (1521) came out.[13] Erasmus's text, which had many defects, was then partly corrected and used as the basis for Robert Estienne's edition (1546 and 1549); it was to become the *textus receptus* until the 19th century.

Because Luther preferred *sola Scriptura* to the most recent "tradition," he demonstrated that he was a faithful disciple of the humanists of his time by

---

12. The Gutenberg Bible is called the "Bible with forty-two lines." The first printed edition of the Hebrew Bible was the Soncino edition (1477). In 1518, the printer D. Bomberg published the first *Biblia rabbinica* (a Bible with the masorah, the targum, and a selection of medieval commentators) and a second, more important edition, in 1524/1525, edited by Jacob ben Chayyim, which for several centuries was considered the *textus receptus*. This edition was not replaced until 1929, when *Biblia Hebraica* was published by R. Kittel and P. Kahle. With regard to the LXX, the first two printed editions were the *Aldina* (Venice, 1518) and the Complutensian Polygot (Alcalá, 1521).

13. Among the most famous of the humanists, we should mention Melanchton (Philipp Schwartzerd, 1497–1560), the disciple and successor of Luther, as well as Thomas More (1478–1535), a friend of Erasmus. Of the many humanists in Italy, we should mention at least Giovanni Pico della Mirandola (b. Mirandola, 1463, d. Florence, 1494) and Marsilio Ficino (b. Figline Valdarno, 1433, d. Careggi, 1499).

sharing their interest in "origins" and Antiquity and by showing a certain aversion to the Middle Ages. The distinction in Protestant Bibles between "original" books, which were written in Hebrew, and "apocryphal" books, which were written in Greek, is another manifestation of this same trend.

2. Baruch Spinoza and Richard Simon[14]

Two personalities stand out during this period: Baruch Spinoza (Netherlands) and Richard Simon (France). Baruch Spinoza (b. Amsterdam, 1632, d. The Hague, 1677) was a Jew of Portuguese origin.[15] He already knew the Hebrew Bible very well when he discovered the philosophy of Descartes and the science of Galileo. In chap. 8 of his *Tractatus theologico-politicus*, he again takes up the questions that Abraham Ibn Ezra had advanced concerning certain verses of the Pentateuch, and he affirms quite clearly what Ibn Ezra had said in guarded terms. Adding some arguments of his own, Spinoza comes to the conclusion that the Pentateuch was not written by Moses but perhaps by Ezra the scribe, who lived much later. Spinoza was expelled from the Synagogue because of his rationalism, and his works were put on the Index of Prohibited Books of the Catholic Church.

In England, the philosopher Thomas Hobbes (b. Westport, Malmesbury, 1588; d. Hardwick, 1679) came to the same conclusion in chap. 33 of his famous work *Leviathan* (1651).

Richard Simon (Dieppe, 1638–1712) was one of the pioneers of biblical criticism.[16] He was a member of the Congregation of the Oratory, a priest, a lawyer, and a specialist in Semitic languages. In his *Histoire critique du Vieux Testament* (1678), he maintains the Mosaic origin of the Pentateuch but suggests that the final form is due to the constant activity of scribes and judges from the beginning up to Ezra's time. On account of his ideas, Richard Simon was violently attacked by the Catholics, especially by Bossuet, expelled from the Oratory, and exiled to a small parish in Normandy.

---

14. I am citing only the most important authors. Others questioned the Mosaic origin of the Pentateuch as a whole or, at least, of certain parts, notably Deuteronomy 34, which tells of Moses' death. Among these critics were A. R. Bodenstein von Karlstadt (1486–1541), André Maes (Antwerp, 1516–1573), the English philosopher Thomas Hobbes (1588–1679), Tostatus bishop of Avila, and the Jesuit scholars Benedict Pereira and Jacques Bonfrère. The Talmud already attributed the redaction of the last chapter of the book of Deuteronomy to Joshua (*b. B. Bat.* 14b–15a). Many of these authors thought that Ezra was the final author of the Pentateuch. This position was also shared by Spinoza and Richard Simon.

15. See Cazelles, "Pentateuque," 731–33.

16. Ibid., 730–31; J. Steinmann, *Richard Simon et les origines de l'exégèse biblique* (Paris, 1959). For more details and a much larger bibliography, see Houtman, *Pentateuch*, 43–48.

His books also were put on the Index, and many of the 1,300 copies published were destroyed.[17] Some copies were saved, however, and his work was
translated into German by Johann Salomo Selmer and into English. However,
his influence was greater in Germany than in Great Britain.

C. The Classic Documentary Hypothesis

1. *The Inception of Critical Work:*
Witter, Astruc, and Eichhorn[18]

In 1711, a young Protestant pastor in Hildesheim, Henning Bernhard Witter (1683–1715), published a study of Genesis 1–3 in which he highlighted the
difference between the divine names Elohim (1:1–2, 4a) and YHWH Elohim
(2:4b–3:24). Witter conjectured that Moses used various "sources" to compose
the Pentateuch. His book was forgotten until 1925.[19]

Jean Astruc (1684–1766) is, in the eyes of many exegetes, the father of the
documentary hypothesis. He was one of the physicians of Louis XV, the son of
a Protestant pastor converted to Catholicism, and an amateur biblical scholar.
Like Witter, he constructed a theory of the Pentateuch's origin on the basis of
the different divine names, Elohim and YHWH. According to Astruc, Moses
most likely used at least three "sources" or "documents" (actually, he refers to
Mémoires) that he simply labeled A, B, and C. The first two "documents" are
characterized by their use of the divine names, and the third document contains texts that are independent from the first two. Moses merged these documents into a kind of synopsis, but, in the course of its transmission, the order
of the pages was changed. This explains the difficulties one now encounters
when reading the Pentateuch. Astruc limited his work to Genesis and Exodus
1–2 for a very simple reason: after the revelation of the divine name YHWH in
Exod 3:14 (cf. Exod 3:6), it becomes much more difficult to use the criterion
of the divine names.[20]

---

17. Richard Simon also published two other important works: *Histoire critique du texte du
Nouveau Testament* (1689) and *Histoire critique des versions du Nouveau Testament* (1690).

18. See A. de Pury and T. Römer (eds.), *Le Pentateuque en question: Les origines et la
composition des cinq premiers livres de la Bible à la lumière des recherches récentes* (Monde de la
Bible 19; Geneva, 1989; 2nd ed., 1992) 15–16.

19. See A. Lods, "Un précurseur allemand de Jean Astruc: Henning Bernhard Witter,"
ZAW 43 (1925) 134–35; cf. H. Bardtke, "Henning Bernhard Witter: Zur 250. Wiederkehr
seiner Promotion zum Philosophiae Doctor am 6. November 1704 zu Helmstedt," *ZAW* 66
(1954) 153–81.

20. See his work *Conjectures sur les mémoires originaux dont il paraît que Moyse s'est servi pour
composer le récit de la Genèse* (Brussels, 1753). This book was printed in Paris but published in
Brussels. Now see J. Astruc, *Conjectures sur la Genèse* (introduction and notes by Pierre Gibert; Paris, 1999).

In Germany, Johann Gottfried Eichhorn (1752–1825) took up Astruc's work and refined it. He became the first author of an *Introduction to the Old Testament* (1780–1783). At first, he continued to defend the Mosaic origin of the Pentateuch,[21] but he changed his opinion after the discoveries of de Wette.

From this time forward, the specialists can be separated into three groups that proposed three major theories of the origin of the Pentateuch: the hypothesis of documents, the hypothesis of fragments, and the hypothesis of complements.

According to the hypothesis of *documents*, which was based on the ideas of Astruc and Eichhorn, the Pentateuch as we know it today was formed by the compilation of several complete, independent, parallel documents.

The hypothesis of *fragments* is often wrongly linked with the name of a Catholic priest from Scotland, Alexander Geddes (1737–1802), who learned German in order to follow the development of exegesis in Germany.[22] Geddes encountered problems with ecclesiastical censorship because of his rationalism. The hypothesis of fragments, to come back to our topic, presumes that, at the outset, there were several sources—short narrative units or separate, incomplete texts—that were assembled long after Moses' death to form the current Pentateuch.[23] In Germany, two eminent scholars supported this position: Johann Severin Vater[24] and, with important alterations, Wilhelm de Wette.[25]

The third hypothesis, which involved *complements*, appeared a little later. I present it here in order to clarify the situation. Historians often attribute its introduction to Heinrich Ewald. To be more precise, Ewald suggested this idea but never defended it as such.[26] He advanced the hypothesis of a basic document (*Grundschrift*) combined with some older texts, such as the Decalogue (Exod 20:2–17) and the Covenant Code (Exodus 21–23), that an editor "completed" or supplemented with fragments from a Jehovist document (later called the Yahwist) during the last years of the monarchy of Judah.[27] The final work,

---

21. Eichhorn, *Einleitung in das Alten Testament*. On Eichhorn, see R. Smend, *Deutsche Alttestamentler in drei Jahrhunderten* (Göttingen, 1989) 25–37.

22. See R. C. Fuller, *Alexander Geddes, 1737–1802: Pioneer of Biblical Exegesis* (Sheffield, 1984); J. W. Rogerson, *Old Testament Criticism in the Nineteenth Century: England and Germany* (London, 1984) 154–57; W. Johnstone (ed.), *The Bible and Enlightenment—A Case Study: Dr. Alexander Geddes 1737–1802* (JSOTSup 377; London, 2004).

23. See A. Geddes, *The Holy Bible as the Books Accounted Sacred by the Jews and Christians* (London, 1792); idem, *Critical Remarks* (London, 1800).

24. J. S. Vater, *Commentar über den Pentateuch* (3 vols.; Halle, 1802–1805).

25. W. M. L. de Wette, *Beiträge zur Einleitung in das Alte Testament* (Halle, 1806–1807).

26. Houtman, *Pentateuch*, 93–94.

27. H. Ewald, review of J. J. Stähelin, *Kritische Untersuchung über die Genesis* (Basel, 1830) in *Theologische Studien und Kritiken* (1831) 595–606; earlier, Ewald had defended the unity of Genesis; see H. Ewald, *Die Komposition der Genesis kritisch untersucht* (Braunschweig, 1823). The theory of the complements was maintained by F. Bleek, *De libri Geneseos origine*

a product of redactional activity that took place over a period of several centuries, included the first six books of the Bible; for this reason, Ewald speaks of a Hexateuch.[28] Thus, the theory of complements, as it was to be developed subsequently, presupposed a "basic document" that was augmented at different periods by texts of diverse origins.

2. The Movement of Ideas in the 19th Century: Enlightenment, Liberal Theology, Romanticism, and an Interest in History[29]

Before discussing developments in the critical reading of the Pentateuch, we need to situate 19th-century exegesis in relation to the cultural movements of this same period to gain a better understanding of the new problems and new answers that were advanced. The exegetes of the 19th century lived in an intellectual world influenced by the philosophy of the Enlightenment (in German, *Aufklärung*), which fought for the independence of reason from all forms of authority. The Christian world tried to respond to this challenge by reconciling faith and reason, by reading the Bible critically and by interpreting its message religiously. This was done in both Protestant circles and Catholic circles. It was clear that the religious contents of the Bible needed to be separated from certain theories of its origin.

Slowly the idea developed that divine inspiration of the text does not exclude the historical, human origin of the biblical books. At this time, in Germany, "liberal theology" was dominant. This movement, in its most radical forms, wished to minimize as much as possible the supernatural facet of religion so that universal, rationalistic-humanist aspects might be enhanced.

Romanticism also greatly influenced the exegetes of the 19th century, especially in Germany. Its chief spokesman in the world of exegesis was Johann Gottfried Herder (1744–1803), who became famous for his book *Vom Geist der Ebräischen Poesie* (1783). Herder influenced many exegetes with his predilection for the idea that Hebrew culture had a spontaneous, natural origin. This was the beginning of attempts to rediscover moments in the past when thought was still "pure," unaffected by later deviations. Romanticism was also the reason

---

atque indole historica observationes (Bonn, 1836); idem, *Einleitung in das Alte Testament* (3rd ed.; Berlin, 1829); J. C. F. Tuch, *Commentar über die Genesis* (Halle, 1838; 2nd ed., 1871); also see de Wette, *Beiträge zur Einleitung* (5th ed., 1840; 6th ed., 1845). H. Ewald was to develop a very complex theory of the origins of the Hexateuch in his history of Israel (*Geschichte des Volkes Israels bis Christus* [2 vols.; Göttingen, 1843–1845; 3rd ed.; 1864]).

28. Ewald had many difficulties with the Prussian government because he refused to take the loyalty oath in 1867. He was forced to abandon teaching at the University of Göttingen.

29. See R. A. Ogden, "Intellectual History and the Study of the Bible," in *The Future of Biblical Studies* (ed. R. E. Friedman and H. G. M. Williamson; Semeia Studies; Atlanta, 1987) 1–18, especially pp. 1–16; Levinson, "Goethe's Analysis of Exodus 34 and Its Influence on Julius Wellhausen," 212–23.

for the growth of a negative attitude toward the later periods of biblical history, especially the Postexilic period, which according to some authors, was marked by legalism and a burgeoning pharisaic mentality. It lacked only the "new creation" to reverse this development—that is, the vitality that was to come from the New Testament.[30]

One last influence during this period arose in the German universities (at this time, the most influential in the field of biblical exegesis), where the categories of "history" were predominant. Influenced by the great historians,[31] philosophers such as Fichte, Schelling, and Hegel attempted to incorporate the categories of history into their own thinking. In the view of the historians and exegetes of the period, cultures go through phases of development comparable to the phases observable in the biological world: after birth comes the creative period of youth; then maturity, which corresponds to the first decline of vital energy; and, finally, the decay of old age that is a prelude to death. Just as in the case of Romanticism, evolution was not perceived as being positive, precisely because it did not lead to an apex. On the contrary, evolution brings on sclerosis, decline, and the loss of all forms of intellectual and religious life. De Wette's discoveries, Wellhausen's system, and Gunkel's research were all situated in this cultural context.[32]

3. De Wette

Scholars of the Pentateuch needed a historical "connection" in order to date the various sources, fragments, and supplements. Therefore, it was necessary to establish the date of at least one important text or to connect it to a historical event. This was the great accomplishment of Wilhelm Martin Leberecht de Wette (1780–1849).[33] De Wette began his research by studying the book of Chronicles. When he compared the work of the Chronicler to other books written about the period of the monarchy (i.e., the books of Samuel and Kings), he found himself faced with two quite dissimilar descriptions of Israel's religion. How could this difference be explained?

---

30. The Protestant theologian Friedrich Schleiermacher (1768–1834), a friend of de Wette, propounded similar ideas.

31. The chief historians were T. Mommsen, J. G. Droysen, and above all G. von Ranke.

32. See especially W. Vatke, *Die biblische Theologie wissenschaftlich dargestellt* (Berlin, 1835), who, following a Hegelian schema, divides the history of Israel into three periods: (1) the primitive, natural religion of the period of the Judges and the United Monarchy; (2) at the end of the Monarchy, the prophets purified Israel's history, which became more idealistic, moral, and spiritual; (3) finally, after the Exile, legalism became dominant. The last period was therefore the opposite of an apogee. Cf. L. Perlitt, *Vatke und Wellhausen* (BZAW 94; Berlin, 1965); de Pury and Römer, "Pentateuque," 28.

33. See J. W. Rogerson, *W. M. L. de Wette: Founder of Modern Biblical Criticism. An Intellectual Biography* (JSOTSup 126; Sheffield, 1992); also see, for a short biography, Smend, *Deutsche Alttestamentler,* 38–52.

De Wette solved the problem in a historical way by saying that the book of Chronicles must have been composed long after the events and probably dated to the Persian period or even as late as Hellenistic times. This conclusion had important consequences for the Pentateuch. For example, Chronicles states that Moses established the institution of the temple. According to de Wette, Chronicles has projected onto the Mosaic past the institutions of a much later period in order to grant them the stamp of antiquity.

Next, de Wette applied this same theory to the Pentateuch, contending that the legislative texts and narratives of the first five books of the Bible do not offer a faithful image of the past. Instead, these books represent the concerns of later periods, which were seeking to explain Israel's origins and destiny on the basis of the past. From this point on, the problem was clarified for de Wette and the exegetes of his time: a gap had been opened between "the world of the text" (the events recounted in the Pentateuch) and the "real world" (the world in which and for which the texts were written). It was now necessary to find a connection between the "world of the text" and the "real world." This was the next step in de Wette's studies.

In his thesis (1805), de Wette identified the book of Deuteronomy, at least its earliest version, with the "book" found in the temple during the reign of Josiah (2 Kings 22).[34] He came to this conclusion after having noted that the reforms carried out by Josiah (2 Kings 23) largely corresponded to the cultic requirements of the Deuteronomic laws. Their principal tenets concern the centralization and purification of the cult.

De Wette was not the originator of this idea; it had already been advanced by some of the Church Fathers. However, he was the first exegete to use it as a solid basis for dating the texts; that is, the laws and narratives that do not presuppose the centralization of the cult in Jerusalem must be earlier than the reform of Josiah, in 622 B.C.E.; conversely, the legislative texts or narratives that take it into account are logically later.

In the early modern exegesis of the Pentateuch, de Wette's discoveries constitute a decisive moment for two main reasons. First, his starting point was not, as it was for Witter, Astruc, Eichhorn, and their disciples, analysis of narratives. Like Richard Simon, de Wette preferred to focus his study on the laws and institutions of the Old Testament. Since de Wette, no one has found a more reliable basis, although there has been no lack of discussion on the matter.[35]

---

34. W. M. L. de Wette, *Dissertatio critica qua Deuteronomium diversum a prioribus Pentateuchi libris, alius cuiusdam recentioris autoris opus esse demonstratur* (Jena, 1805).

35. For a summary of recent discussions, see C. Conroy, "Reflexions on the Exegetical Task: A propos of Recent Studies on 2 Kgs 22–23," in *Pentateuchal and Deuteronomistic Studies: Papers Read at the XIIIth IOSOT Congress Leuven 1989* (ed. C. Brekelmans and J. Lust; BETL 94; Leuven, 1990); A. de Pury, T. Römer, and J.-D. Macchi (eds.), *Israel Constructs Its History:*

Second, the event that allows us to date the texts is not contained in the episodes depicted in the Pentateuch. Consequently, for most scholars from this point on, a great distance existed between the events described in the Pentateuch and the various periods during which the texts were written. It also became increasingly difficult to believe that Moses could have written the five books of the Torah.[36]

4. From de Wette to Wellhausen

Around 1800, many exegetes distinguished two main "sources" behind the Pentateuch: the Elohist and the Jehovist (later the Yahwist), based on the divine names used in the book of Genesis and in Exodus 1–2. The Elohist had presented a well-articulated narrative that structured the entire story. Furthermore, he appeared to have been more faithful to history, because the divine name YHWH was not revealed before Moses' lifetime (Exod 3:14; 6:3). Consequently, the Elohist was considered to be older and was referred to as a *Grundschrift*, "foundational document" (cf. Ewald). Three important works appeared that altered the academic picture before the arrival of Wellhausen.

1. In 1798, Karl David Ilgen differentiated between two "Elohists," notably in the Joseph story.[37] Ilgen was the one who coined the names "Elohist" and "Jehovist." Fifty years later, exegetes would again distinguish two Elohists: the "Priestly Writer" and the Preexilic Elohist who wrote in the Northern Kingdom; the delimitation of these sources, however, owed little to Ilgen's work. Nevertheless, we must admit that the critical reading of the book of Genesis by Ilgen is remarkable. Ilgen himself thought that the documents he identified were part of the archives of the temple of Jerusalem that had been scattered when the Babylonian army destroyed the city in 587/586 B.C.E. Ilgen's discovery was ignored until Hupfeld revived it in 1853.[38]

Deuteronomistic History in Recent Research (JSOTSup 306; Sheffield 2000); E. Eynikel, *The Reform of King Josiah and the Composition of the Deuteronomistic History* (OtSt 33; Leiden, 1996).

36. The exegetical world is not isolated. In de Wette's time, scholars of Classical literature were applying the same methods to Greek and Latin authors. For example, Friedrich August Wolf illustrated the composite character of Homer's works in his book *Prolegomena zu Homer*. See Blenkinsopp, *Pentateuch*, 6.

37. K.-D. Ilgen, *Die Urkunden des Jerusalemischen Tempelarchivs in ihrer Urgestalt, als Beytrag zur Berichtigung der Geschichte der Religion und Politik aus dem Hebräischen mit kritischen und erklärenden Anmerkungen, auch mancherley dazu gehörenden Abhandlungen*, vol. 1: *Die Urkunden der ersten Buchs von Moses* (Halle, 1798).

38. On this exegete, see B. Seidel, *Karl David Ilgen und die Pentateuchforschung im Umkreis der sogenannten Urkundenhypothese: Studien zur Geschichte der exegetischen Hermeneutik in der späten Aufklärung* (BZAW 213; Berlin, 1993).

2. Hermann Hupfeld (1796–1866), a professor first at Marburg and then at Halle, wrote an important work on the "sources of Genesis" in 1853.[39] He contributed to the scholarship of his time in two significant ways. First of all, he demonstrated the superiority of the documentary hypothesis over the hypothesis of fragments (Vater and de Wette in his early writings) and the hypothesis of complements or supplements (Ewald, Bleek, Tuch, and de Wette in his later writings). Second, like Ilgen, but without knowing of his work,[40] Hupfeld distinguished two Elohists, one earlier and one later. Consequently, according to Hupfeld, there are three sources on which Genesis is based, in the following chronological order: the first Elohist (who became known as the Priestly Writer), the second Elohist (the Elohist of the classic documentary hypothesis) and, finally, the Yahwist (Hupfeld coined the term *Yhwh-ist*). This sequence later would be altered.

3. One year later, in 1854, Rheim (1830–1888) definitively separated Deuteronomy from the rest of the Pentateuch and identified it as an independent source.[41] From then on, everything needed to delineate a complete hypothesis was available. Scholars had identified four sources: two Elohists (abbreviated E^1 and E^2), a Yahwist (abbreviated J, from the German *Jahwist*), and Deuteronomy (abbreviated D). They had a solid basis for a chronology: the connection between Deuteronomy and the reform of Josiah in 622 B.C.E. They only needed to complete one more task: to assign the correct passages to each of the writers.

5. Reuss, Graf, Kuenen, and Wellhausen: The Classic Documentary Hypothesis

In 1833, Edouard Reuss (1804–1891), a professor at Strasbourg, noticed that some of the Preexilic prophets ignored the prescriptions of the Mosaic Law, especially the ritual laws, which are in fact very close to other Postexilic texts such as Ezekiel. These laws must therefore be Postexilic. However, Reuss did not publish his findings.[42] It was his disciple and friend Karl Heinrich Graf (1815–1869) who demonstrated the validity of his insights, in 1866.[43]

Based on the conclusions of Reuss and Hupfeld, Graf argued that the Elohist must have been not the first but the last of the Pentateuchal sources and that he could not have written before the Exile. Independently, the renowned Dutch

---

39. H. Hupfeld, *Die Quellen der Genesis und die Art ihrer Zusammensetzung von neuem untersucht* (Berlin, 1853).

40. Houtman, *Pentateuch*, 95.

41. E. Riehm, *Die Gesetzgebung Mosis im Lande Moab* (Gotha, 1854).

42. See his late work: E. Reuss, *Die Geschichte der Heiligen Schriften des Alten Testaments* (Braunschweig, 1881).

43. K. H. Graf, *Die geschichtlichen Bücher des Alten Testaments: Zwei historisch-kritischen Untersuchungen* (Leipzig, 1866).

exegete Abraham Kuenen came to the same conclusions in 1869.[44] He was the first person to call this Elohist the *Priestercodex*, "Priestly Code," and to abbreviate the source with the letter P. He also introduced the term *Yahwist* (*Jahwist*) and the abbreviation J.

Julius Wellhausen, however, was the one who gave these studies their classic, final form. The success of his theories was largely due to the clarity of his presentation and the lucidity of his style.[45] The most important of Wellhausen's works is not, as is commonly thought, his *Composition des Hexateuchs und der historischen Bücher des Alten Testaments*.[46] In order to appreciate Wellhausen's genius and understand his objectives, one needs to read the *Prolegomena to the History of Israel*.[47]

Wellhausen was above all a historian who wanted to reconstruct a "history of Israel." From our later perspective, we can see how little interest the scholars of the 19th century had in the texts as such, for example, their literary qualities or their essential content. Commentaries were rare during that century. Influenced by the philosophy of Hegel and the Romanticism of Herder, exegetes primarily wanted to study "history"; for this reason, they put their energy into dating sources, because this is the indispensable starting point of such work. Moreover, they understood "history" as an evolutionary or a dialectic development according to the Hegelian scheme of thesis – antithesis – synthesis.[48]

However, as for the Romantics, the "ideal" period for historians was not the most recent but the oldest. Wellhausen, just as de Wette and many other authors of that time and as the writers who have followed them up to our day, had great esteem for the most ancient periods and appreciated later periods much less. These authors therefore saw evolution as a process of decay and degeneration. And ultimately, the Lutheran opposition of "Law" and "Gospel" (*Gesetz und Evangelium*) greatly influenced the reconstructions of the "Wellhausen

---

44. A. Kuenen, *Historisch-kritisch onderzoek naar het ontstaan en de verzameling van de boeken des Ouden Verbonds* (Leiden, 1861); idem, "Critische bijdragen tot de geschiedenis van den Israëlitischen godsdienst. V: De priestelijke bestanddeelen van Pentateuch en Josua," *Theologisch Tijdschrift* 4 (1870) 391–426, 487–526. also see J. F. L. George, *Die älteren jüdischen Feste in einer Kritik der Gesetzgebung des Pentateuchs* (Berlin, 1835).

45. On this author, see Smend, *Deutsche Alttestamentler*, 99–113. J. Wellhausen was successively professor at Greifswald, Halle, Marburg, and Göttingen.

46. Berlin, 1866; 3rd ed., 1899. In English the book's title would be "Composition of the Hexateuch and the Historical Books of the Old Testament."

47. With a reprint of the article "Israel," from the *Encyclopaedia Britannica*; Preface by W. Robertson Smith (Reprints and Translation Series; Atlanta, 1994). The first translation was made by W. Robertson Smith, who lost his position at Aberdeen University in 1881 because he shared Wellhausen's ideas. This also happened to John William Colenso, the Anglican bishop of what is now South Africa, who was removed from his office in 1869 because his books had spread German theories on the Pentateuch. See Blenkinsopp, *Pentateuch*, 12.

48. Vatke, *Biblische Theologie* (see n. 32 above).

school." As a disciple of liberal Protestantism, Wellhausen tended to identify the "Gospel" with a "natural," "rational," "humanistic" religion. Furthermore, he deeply admired the Prussian monarchy under which the unification of Germany was occurring.[49] For this reason he also had great esteem for David and the beginning of the United Monarchy, discovering many analogies between that epoch and his own country's contemporary history. In his eyes, the beginning of the Monarchy in Israel represented the Golden Age of the Israelite religion.

In the preface to the *Prolegomena*, Wellhausen openly expresses the feelings that the Old Testament inspired in him.[50] He began his reading with the books of Samuel, the story of Elijah, and the first prophets, Amos and Isaiah, whom he read with great pleasure. Then he said to himself that he should read the Law that preceded the prophets; but he quickly felt a strong aversion for this part of the Bible, especially when he came to the legal texts of Exodus, Leviticus, and Numbers. He did not think that Israel's religion was originally legalistic and ritual-based. When he discovered the works of Graf, he read them enthusiastically, and they comforted him because they showed the late character of the legal portions of the Bible.

Based on a careful study of the laws and narratives, Wellhausen consequently distinguished three major phases in Israel's religion: the beginnings of the Monarchy, the Deuteronomic reform, and the Postexilic period (the Second Temple). To these three phases corresponded three periods of literary activity. The Yahwistic and the Elohistic texts were written at the beginning of the Monarchy. Wellhausen rarely differentiated between these two sources, and he was satisfied with referring to a Jehovist. Deuteronomy was evidently begun at the time of the Deuteronomic reform of 622 B.C.E.

The Priestly writings go back to the Postexilic period.[51] The Law therefore did not mark the beginning of Israel; it marked the beginning of Judaism.[52] With regard to the documentary hypothesis, Wellhausen established the classic order of the sources: J (Yahwist), E (Elohist), D (Deuteronomy), and P (*Priestercodex* or Priestly Code, which Wellhausen called Q, from the Latin *quattuor*,

---

49. F. Crüsemann, *Der Widerstand gegen das Königtum* (WMANT 49; Neukirchen-Vluyn, 1978) 3–9.

50. Wellhausen, *Prolegomena*, 3–4.

51. In the first part of his *Prolegomena*, Wellhausen discusses: the liturgical centers, sacrifices, festivals, priests and Levites, and organization of the priesthood (taxes, tithes, and other duties). See a summary in H. Cazelles, "La Torah ou Pentateuque," in *Introduction à la Bible, II: Introduction Critique à l'Ancien Testament* (ed. H. Cazelles; Paris, 1973) 122–24; de Pury and Römer, "Pentateuque," 26–27.

52. See L. Perlitt, "Hebraismus—Deuteronomismus—Judaismus," *Biblische Theologie und gesellschaftlicher Wandel: Für Norbert Lohfink SJ* (ed. G. Braulik, W. Gross, and S. McEvenue; Freiburg-im-Breisgau, 1993) 279–95.

because this account contains four Covenants of God with humanity: the Covenants with Adam, Noah, Abraham, and with Israel at Sinai).[53]

The religion of the Yahwist was natural, spontaneous, free, and authentic. With Deuteronomy, a process of *Denaturierung* ("degeneration") began, during the course of which the religion was gradually centralized and ritualized. The rules replaced spontaneity. This process approached its apogee with the religion instituted by the Postexilic priesthood; legalism and ritualism began to overshadow freedom. The religion no longer developed on a foundation of concrete reality but was henceforth rooted in priestly abstractions.

A representative example of Wellhausen's thought is the way he presents the evolution of the sacrifices and Israel's festivals. According to Wellhausen, at the beginning of the Monarchy, the rhythm of the liturgy and sacrifices was dictated by seasonal labor. The dates were not fixed by a calendar, and families offered their sacrifices in local sanctuaries. With the Deuteronomic reform, the liturgical calendar became dissociated from life and nature. The festivals now became tied to the events of Israel's history, and mathematical calculation became more important than the change of the seasons. In its final phase (P), the liturgy lost all connection with life and nature. The priests introduced a precise calendar for each festival (Leviticus 23) and added a new event: the Day of Atonement (Leviticus 16; 23:26–32). Preoccupation with daily life gave way to abstraction and a sense of guilt, the cult was centered on sin, and the main purpose of the liturgy was atonement.

This negative vision of the Postexilic period and inability to grasp the significance of its unique historical context reveal the limits of the system advanced by Wellhausen and his disciples.[54] The evolutionary model adopted from the philosophy of Hegel and the romantic ideas of primitive, free, spontaneous religion are tools that historians and exegetes must handle with care. History is not obedient to philosophy, and primitive cultures are subject to more restrictions and constraints than Herder or Jean-Jacques Rousseau would have been willing to admit. Ultimately, Wellhausen was translating the Lutheran "creed" regarding the Law and the Gospel into historical categories. Thus, at the beginning of Israel's religion, an authentic "gospel" reigned, the religion of the Davidic Monarchy. Then the "Law" appeared with the Deuteronomic reform.

After the Exile, when the priests instituted the theocracy (or "hierocracy") of the Second Temple period, natural religion died, and legalism reigned. It was necessary to await the coming of the New Testament for the "Law of slavery" to be vanquished and replaced by the "Gospel of freedom." It is easy to criticize this perspective, simply by noting that Israel's history is much more complex

---

53. On this point, Wellhausen was mistaken. P only mentions two Covenants, the Noahic (Genesis 9) and the Abrahamic (Genesis 17).

54. See Blenkinsopp, *Pentateuch*, 9.

and that any attempt to summarize such a major movement of ideas on the basis of only two categories is very risky.

Despite their obvious limitations, Wellhausen's investigations are foundational for the study the Pentateuch today. A comparison of the various legal codes and the criteria for distinguishing the sources are two of the most convincing instruments of contemporary exegesis. Furthermore, Wellhausen demonstrated excellent intuition and good sense, and his prudence with regard to difficult cases is exemplary. From this point onward, the documentary hypothesis took on its classic form, which is familiar to all who read any introduction to the Pentateuch. Four sources are identifiable: the Yahwist (J), who wrote in the South during the 9th century; the Elohist (E), writing one century later in the Northern Kingdom, was influenced by the Former Prophets (8th century); Deuteronomy (D), the early core of which goes back to Josiah's reform in 622 B.C.E.; and finally, the Priestly Writer (P), who worked during the Exile or after the return from Exile.[55]

It is quite likely that the Pentateuch, as we know it today, was compiled during the Second Temple period; indeed, many scholars link this redactional work to Ezra's reform (cf. Nehemiah 8).

D. Gunkel, Noth, von Rad, and Form Criticism[56]

1. The Cultural Context of Form Criticism (Formgeschichte)

For about a century after Wellhausen, the documentary hypothesis commanded great respect. Although there continued to be some opposition, especially in Catholic and Jewish circles, most scholars supported Wellhausen's postulates.[57] Once the main sources had been identified, researchers endeavored chiefly to introduce new subdivisions. Sometimes these were so numerous that they actually provoked uneasiness and led to disaffection for a method that was no longer capable of setting its own limits.[58] Furthermore, the intel-

---

55. After Wellhausen, in the first half of the 20th century, some scholars proposed earlier dates for the various sources, especially for the Yahwist. G. von Rad, for example, dated him to the time of David and Solomon.

56. On this method, see the classic work of K. Koch, *The Growth of the Biblical Tradition* (trans. S. M. Cupitt; London, 1969).

57. Regarding French Catholicism, see J. Briend, "Lecture du Pentateuque et hypothèse documentaire," in *Le Pentateuque: Débats et recherches* (ed. P. Haudebert; LD 151; Paris, 1992) 9–32, especially pp. 10–20. Also see Blenkinsopp, *Pentateuch*, 12–13; de Pury and Römer, "Pentateuque," 44–48.

58. See ibid., 29–31; Blenkinsopp, *Pentateuch*, 13–14. For example, Bruno Baentsch identified seven "Priestly sources," each one with one, and sometimes two, redactions.

lectual climate began to change.[59] Two important factors began to influence the intellectual and academic climate of the second half of the 19th century: discoveries in the ancient Near East and a predilection for popular literature.

In Mesopotamia, the first important discoveries were made in the 1840s.[60] The investigations in Egypt had begun earlier. The task of deciphering the Egyptian language and Akkadian, especially, had considerable consequences for biblical exegesis.[61] Whereas Wellhausen had only been able to allude to ancient Arabic literature, publications now offered scholars abundant comparative material. The first work that had a great deal of impact on exegetical research was George Smith's *Chaldean Account of Genesis* (1876). This work is based on the eleventh tablet of the *Epic of Gilgamesh*, which contains an account of the Flood. Smith's publication had the effect of a bomb, for it transformed simplistic thinking regarding the unique character of biblical revelation. Gunkel, who grew up in this intellectual setting, was an enthusiastic follower of the *religionsgeschichtliche Schule*, "the history-of-religions school," which sanctioned a great deal of leeway in the comparison between similar phenomena in the various religions and cultures of Antiquity.[62]

The second factor was tied to the state of mind of a gradually more urbanized, technical, industrial society. In cities and universities, people reacted by demonstrating a new interest in folklore, popular psychology, and the rural society that was disappearing. Between 1815 and 1819, the Grimm brothers published their fairytale collections.[63] The same interest in folklore later influenced the world of biblical scholarship.

2. The Method Introduced by Gunkel (1862–1932)

In this new world of biblical scholarship, another method developed that would be associated with the documentary hypothesis until about 1970.

• While Wellhausen had primarily studied concepts and literature, the new generation wanted to rediscover textual origins in their prehistoric, primitive expression—the oral tradition. In both cases, however, the taste for origins remained predominant. The "Golden Age" of Israelite religion for Wellhausen was the period of the United Monarchy; for Gunkel and his followers, it was

---

59. See Ogden, "Intellectual History," 6–10.

60. Paul-Émile Botta at Khorsabad; Austen Henry Layard at Nineveh.

61. Jean-François Champollion deciphered the hieroglyphs (the Rosetta Stone and notably the obelisk from Philae) in 1821. He published his results the following year in his *Lettre à M. Dacier relative à l'alphabet des hiéroglyphes phonétiques* (1822). Major Henry Creswicke Rawlison deciphered the Besitun Trilingual Inscription (Darius I) in 1849.

62. An important representative of this school was Max Müller.

63. J. Grimm and W. Grimm, *Grimm's Fairy Tales* (Marburg, 1812–15).

necessary to go still further back in the past, to the period of the Judges, and further yet, to the time when Israel was still nomadic.

• This need to know the concrete setting in which the accounts originated found expression in the search for the *Sitz im Leben*, the existential context of literary texts: "Anyone who wants to understand an ancient literary genre must first ask where it was situated in the life of the people." The famous expression *Sitz im Leben* was coined by Gunkel precisely at this point in his work.[64] He sought to reconstruct the circumstances under which, for example, the lives of the patriarchs were recounted. He imagined that, on long winter nights, elders spent their time recalling the adventures of their forebears, with the family sitting around a fire. Everyone, especially the children, listened very attentively.[65] For the Psalms, the concrete setting was often a ritual institution.

• The scholars of this school insisted on a fundamental principle of romantic hermeneutics: an interpreter should have "sympathy" for the texts he reads. This principle was well known; de Wette had already referred to it in his writings.[66] Gunkel and his school went a step further by better integrating this principle into exegetical methodology. Gunkel maintained, for example, that exegesis is "more an art than a science."[67] Intuition, sensitivity, esthetics, and deep interest in literary form and style constituted the primary characteristics of this school. One simply cannot separate the form and the contents, the style and the message, esthetics and theology. Gunkel asserted that "proper form is essential to the expression of the contents."[68] More concretely, the task of the exegete is to define the "literary genre" of the text.[69] Literary genres are usu-

---

64. "Wer also eine antike Gattung verstehen will, hat zunächst zu fragen, wo sie ihren Sitz im Volksleben habe" (H. Gunkel, "Die Israelitische Literatur," in *Die Kultur der Gegenwart: Die orientalischen Literaturen* [ed. P. Hinneberg; Berlin, 1906] 53); also see "Die Grundprobleme der israelitischen Literaturgeschichte," *Deutsche Literaturzeitung* 27 (1906) = *Reden und Aufsätze* (Göttingen, 1913) 21–38, especially p. 33: "Each ancient literary genre is originally rooted in a particular place in the life of the people of Israel" ("Jede alte literarische Gattung hat ursprünglich ihren Sitz im Volksleben Israels an ganz bestimmter Stelle").

65. Idem, *Genesis*, xxvii; P. Gibert, *Une théorie de la légende: Hermann Gunkel (1862–1932) et les légendes de la Bible* (Paris, 1979) 289. Unfortunately, it must be said that on this specific point Gunkel's hypothesis is probably incorrect. We are not in 19th-century Germany but in the ancient Near East. In the Arab world today, there still are "professional storytellers" who, during festivals and sometimes in the marketplace, recount the legends and stories of bygone days. Other specialists refer to stories told in the "city gates."

66. Blenkinsopp, *Pentateuch*, 6.

67. Gunkel, "Grundprobleme," and *Reden und Aufsätze*, 14: "Exegese im höchsten Sinne ist mehr eine Kunst als eine Wissenschaft." Gunkel critized his colleagues for their lack of artistic sensitivity. Quoting Edouard Reuss, he called them "learned Philistines" (*gelehrtes Philistertum*); see H. Gunkel, "Ruth," *Reden und Aufsätze* (Göttingen, 1913) 65–92, especially p. 85.

68. "Die Rechte Form ist der notwendige Ausdruck des Inhalts" (Gunkel, "Grundprobleme," and *Reden und Aufsätze*, 23).

69. In German: *Gattung*.

ally defined according to three characteristics: a genre has a structure and a series of formulas; it has an atmosphere (*Stimmung*) and a perspective; and it has an existential context (*Sitz im Leben*).

3. Gunkel's Influence[70]

Hermann Gunkel (1862–1932) was the great genius of this period.[71] He was the author of several important works: a commentary on Genesis, an introduction to the Psalms, and various studies on the prophets. He is quite rightly considered the father of *Formgeschichte*, "form criticism."[72] The introduction to the third edition of his Genesis commentary has become a timeless classic of exegetical literature. As far as analytical "finesse" is concerned, no commentator has yet surpassed his section on the narrative style of Genesis.

The first sentence is particularly well known because it immediately expresses the spirit of the work: "Genesis is a collection of stories."[73] This statement reveals the extent of the gap between Wellhausen and Gunkel. According to Wellhausen, Genesis, like the rest of the Hexateuch, was a compilation of three or four written "sources." From Gunkel on, scholars isolated texts to study in their preliterary state; these were narratives that were subsequently put into "story cycles"[74] and then collected in "documents" such as the Yahwist's or the Elohist's.

For Gunkel, however, the "sources" were not literary compositions of great importance for exegesis. The oral stage of the narratives was much more interesting. Furthermore, Gunkel's followers explained many literary difficulties, such as the discrepancies between narratives, as vestiges of the oral origins of the texts. The "sources" were heterogeneous "materials" that had been assembled without attempting to harmonize them.

---

70. See Smend, *Deutsche Alttestamentler*, 160–81.

71. On H. Gunkel, see W. Klatt, *H. Gunkel: Zu seiner Theologie der Religionsgeschichte und zur Entstehung der formgeschichtliche Methode* (FRLANT 100; Göttingen, 1969); Gibert, *Une théorie de la légende* (see n. 65 above).

72. Other important works: H. Gunkel, *Schöpfung und Chaos in Urzeit und Endzeit: Eine religionsgeschichtliche Untersuchung über Gen. 1 und Ap. Joh. 12* (Göttingen, 1894; 2nd ed., 1921); idem, *Die Psalmen* (4th ed.; Göttingen, 1926); H. Gunkel and H. Begrich, *Einleitung in die Psalmen* (Göttingen, 1933). Other pioneers of the same school: Wolf Graf Baudissin (1874–1927); Albert Eichhorn (1856–1926); Hugo Gressmann (1877–1927), the author of *Mose und seine Zeit: Ein Kommentar zu den Mose-Sagen* (FRLANT 18; Göttingen, 1913).

73. "Die Genesis ist eine Sammlung von Sagen." Translating the German term *Sage* has presented many difficulties. I prefer the neutral translation "story" or "account." One could also translate "popular narrative." See P. Gibert, "Légende ou Saga," *VT* 24 (1974) 411–20; J. J. Scullion, "*Märchen, Sage, Legende*: Towards a Clarification of Some Literary Terms Used by Old Testament Scholars," *VT* 34 (1984) 321–36.

74. In German: *Sagenkränze*.

Today, Gunkel is still an essential reference point for exegesis of the Pentateuch, especially Genesis. Although some of his theses have been superseded,
his pioneer work in the field of stylistics and narrative analysis has not lost any
of its freshness. Anyone who reads his works will greatly benefit from them.[75]

Work continued after Gunkel, not only in Germany but also in Scandinavia
and in the English-speaking world. Certain scholars, such as Albrecht Alt, Gerhard von Rad, and Martin Noth still have considerable influence today, even
though their theses have been criticized and sometimes abandoned. However,
we cannot overlook these scholars in our presentation, because it is impossible
to understand present-day exegesis of the Pentateuch without referring to these
great masters.

4. Albrecht Alt (1883–1956), Gerhard von Rad (1901–1971), and Martin Noth (1902–1968)

Three famous scholars—Alt, von Rad, and Noth—illustrate, each in his
own way, the dominant trend in the first half of the 20th century, which con-
sisted of searching through the Pentateuch to find the original core of Israel's
faith. They discovered this core in the most ancient past of Israel, in premonarchic times. Israel's golden age was now thought to be the period of the Judges
or even earlier, the period when Israel was wandering in the semiwilderness
that borders the Promised Land.

In the academic world, the search for the "primitive core" of Israel's religion
reflected the efforts of the great theologians of this time to affirm the absolute
originality of Christianity in comparison with other religions. Behind much of
the research of this time stands the figure of Karl Barth, with his dialectic theology, especially in the context of the antithesis of "revealed religion" and
"natural religion" and the more traditional antithesis of "Law" and "Gospel"
(*Gesetz und Evangelium*). For scholars, certain "literary genres" or institutions
also proved the unique and absolutely original character of biblical revelation.
Here one may speak of a certain "religious positivism."[76] These theologians
and exegetes were fighting against the dominant secular ideologies of their
time, especially national-socialist ideology, and wanted to show that "faith" was

---

75. Some of Gunkel's works have been translated into English: H. Gunkel, *The Legends of
Genesis: The Biblical Saga and History* (New York, 1964); new translation: *The Stories of Genesis*
(Vallejo, CA, 1994); idem, *The Folktale in the Old Testament* (trans. M. D. Rutter; Historic
Texts and Interpreters in Biblical Scholarship 5; Sheffield, 1987); idem, *Genesis* (trans. M. E.
Biddle; Mercer Library of Biblical Studies; Macon, GA, 1997); idem, *An Introduction to the
Psalms* (Mercer Library of Biblical Studies; Macon, GA, 1998). In French, see Gibert, *Une
théorie de la légende.*

76. See H. J. Boecker, *Law and the Administration of Justice in the Old Testament and Ancient
Near East* (Minneapolis, 1980) 167. There is a similar trend in New Testament exegesis: the
quest for the *ipsissima verba* of Jesus Christ (cf. J. Jeremias).

not a natural phenomenon and had little to do with concepts such as "race" or "land." They were also defending the Old Testament against the anti-Semitism of several of their colleagues.

a. Albrecht Alt and Some Cornerstones of Israel's Faith:
The "God of the Fathers" and "Apodictic Law"[77]

• Two theses of Albrecht Alt deserve to be mentioned here. The first concerns the religion of the patriarchs. According to Alt, the biblical expression "God of the Fathers" stemmed from the religion of nomads, because the divinity was not tied to a place but to a person.[78] This divinity did not have a proper name; instead, he was identified by the ancestor's name—for example, the "God of Abraham" (Gen 26:23; cf. Gen 28:13; 32:10; 46:3; Exod 3:6). This primary element of Israel's religion harked back to the pre-Israelite nomadic period, and the patriarchs were the "religious founders" of Israel.[79] Thus, Israel's religion distinguished itself from the religion of Canaan, which was confined to sanctuaries.[80]

• The second thesis concerned the sphere of Israelite law. Once again, Alt set the biblical world in radical opposition to the culture of Canaan. To do this, Alt drew attention to biblical "apodictic laws" that have been juxtaposed with "casuistic laws."[81] The first type is found, for example, in the Decalogue. The formulas are generally concise and do not provide for exceptions. The second type, however, is introduced by formulas: "if . . ." or "when. . . ." Casuistic law appears to have originated in Canaan, while apodictic law was tied to Israel's nomadic past.[82] Like the "religion of the patriarchs," Alt thought that

---

77. On A. Alt, see Smend, *Deutsche Alttestamentler*, 182–207.

78. A. Alt, "The God of the Fathers," *Essays on Old Testament History and Religion* (trans. R. A. Wilson; Oxford, 1966) 3–86.

79. Ibid., 45. See H. Weidmann, *Die Patriarchen und ihre Religion im Licht der Forschung seit Julius Wellhausen* (FRLANT 94; Göttingen, 1968). This thesis has been thoroughly challenged by M. Köckert, *Vätergott und Väterverheissungen: Eine Auseinandersetzung mit Albrecht Alt und seinen Erben* (FRLANT 148; Göttingen, 1988). The texts examined by Alt are late, and their primary objective is the establishment of a theological connection between the narrative cycles of the various patriarchs.

80. Alt also studied the origins of Israelite settlement activity and introduced the idea of "progressive sedentarization" of seminomads. See Alt, "The Settlement of the Israelites in Palestine," *Essays on Old Testament History and Religion* (trans. R. A. Wilson; Oxford, 1966) 173–221; idem, "Erwägungen zur Landnahme der Israeliten in Palästina," *PJ* 53 (1939) 8–63 = *Kleine Schriften* 1.126–75; idem, "The Formation of the Israelite State in Palestine," in *Essays on Old Testament*, 223–309.

81. Idem, "The Monarchy in the Kingdoms of Israel and Judah," in *Essays on Old Testament*, 311–35.

82. It is difficult to verify Alt's assertions. To this point, archaeologists have not uncovered any trace of the "law of Canaan." There are also no written vestiges of Israel's nomadic past. Furthermore, apodictic law was present in the laws of other ancient Near Eastern peoples, although formulations of this sort appear less frequently there than in Israel.

"apodictic law" was characteristic of biblical law and had no equivalent in other religions, and this distinction confirmed for Alt the uniqueness of the biblical revelation.[83]

b. Gerhard von Rad and Israel's Kerygma [84]

Von Rad's most important theses concern the origin of the Hexateuch and the figure of the Yahwist. Like the other representatives of this same school, von Rad wanted to find the most authentic moments of a tradition, and he connected these with the origins. His investigations were also marked by the basic distinction between "Law" and "Gospel." Ultimately, his way of presenting the Yahwist was greatly influenced by the Romantic trend to look for "great personalities" behind important literary works.[85]

• *The "small historical creed."* G. von Rad observed that the study of sources had reached an impasse.[86] Consequently, he considered it more interesting to examine the "final form" of the Hexateuch.[87] With this purpose in mind, von Rad applied Gunkel's method to the Hexateuch as a whole—that is, the search for the "form" or "literary genre" and for the *Sitz im Leben*. With regard to "literary genre," he maintained that the Pentateuch in its present state is the amplification of a primitive core, the "small historical creed" that is found in ancient texts such as Deut 26:5b–9, 6:20–23, and Josh 24:2b–13.[88]

Two crucial moments stand out in these short confessions of faith that condense all of Israel's history into a few sentences: the Exodus and the gift of the land. The patriarchal history is only briefly mentioned at the beginning of the texts, while the history of origins (Genesis 1–11) and the gift of the law at Sinai are completely absent. Von Rad came to this significant conclusion: the "law"

---

83. For a critique, see Boecker, *Law and Administration of Justice*, 191–207 (with bibliography). For more on the syntax and literary history of casuistic law, see B. M. Levinson and M. M. Zahn, "Revelation Regained: The Hermeneutics of כי and אם in the Temple Scroll," *Dead Sea Discoveries* 9 (2002) 295–346.

84. On von Rad, see Smend, *Deutsche Alttestamentler*, 226–54; B. M. Levinson and D. Dance, "The Metamorphosis of Law into Gospel: Gerhard von Rad's Attempt to Reclaim the Old Testament for the Church," in *Recht und Ethik im Alten Testament* (ed. B. M. Levinson and E. Otto; Münster, 2004) 83–123; several essays in the volume *Das Alte Testament und die Kultur der Moderne* (ed. M. Oeming, K. Schmid, and M. Welker; Münster, 2004). Von Rad's main work is "The Form-Critical Problem of the Hexateuch," *The Problem of the Hexateuch and Other Essays* (New York, 1966) 1–78.

85. See Abrams, *The Mirror and the Lamp*.

86. What would von Rad say if he were to read certain recent monographs on the Pentateuch?

87. In German: *Leztgestalt* or *Endgestalt*; see von Rad, *Problem of the Hexateuch*, 1–2.

88. In the New Testament, the scholars of this period considered the "core" of the Gospels to be the *paschal kerygma*; cf. Acts 10:36–43; 1 Cor 15:3–8.

and "Israel's history" are two different "literary forms," each of which had its own *Sitz im Leben.*[89]

The "small historical creed" had its *Sitz im Leben* in the Festival of Weeks or of Harvest (Pentecost), and it was celebrated at Gilgal, not far from the Jordan. The Festival of Harvest was celebrated at Pentecost, because the earliest text (Deut 26:5b–9) was tied to the offering of firstfruits (Deut 26:2–3). It took place at Gilgal because this was where the entry into the Promised Land was celebrated—the highpoint of the "small historical creed" (Josh 4:19–24).

On the other hand, the gift of the Law was celebrated at Shechem in autumn, during the Festival of Booths, as prescribed in Deut 31:9–13. Shechem is where Joshua sealed the Covenant between YHWH and the people and established the Law (Joshua 24, especially 24:25–26). Shechem was therefore the proper place for this celebration. On the basis of these cultic "creeds" and the tradition of the gift of the law at Sinai, the Yahwist composed the framework of his Hexateuch's narrative during the Solomonic period.[90]

With the distinction between the "small historical creed" and the "gift of the Law," the dialectical opposition between "Gospel" and "Law," between a "religion of grace" and a "religion of works" reappeared. Moreover, the fact that von Rad placed the "small historical creed" at the beginning of Israel's history can only be understood in connection with affirmations that are important to dialectical theology. From the beginning, Israel's religion was structured around an affirmation of faith—"a creed"—and this implies the revelation of God in history. We are a long way from the "natural religion" of the Yahwist in Wellhausen's work ("natural religion" was part of Nazi ideology).[91]

• *The Yahwist.* In Gunkel's view, the Yahwist was only a compiler of stories (*Sagen*) who appeared at the end of a long redactional process. For von Rad, however, the Yahwist was a "great personality," a writer and a remarkable theologian of the Solomonic period. His contribution to the Hexateuch was essential. Without him, we would not have the grandiose edifice that exists today. Compared with him, the other "sources," the Elohist (E) and the Priestly (P) documents, were pale figures. Given this perspective, von Rad must still be

---

89. See H. H. Schmid, "Auf der Suche nach neuen Perspektiven für die Pentateuchforschung," in *Congress Volume: Vienna, 1980* (ed. J. A. Emerton; VTSup 32; Leiden, 1981) 375–94, especially pp. 387–88.

90. Von Rad's theory of "small historical creeds" did not hold up under critical attack. Von Rad's foundational texts actually turn out to be recent summaries of Deuteronomic and Deuteronomistic conception and therefore cannot be considered original in the process of literary formation.

91. For a thorough analysis, see B. M. Levinson and D. Dance, "The Metamorphosis of Law into Gospel: Gerhard von Rad's Attempt to Reclaim the Old Testament for the Church," in *Recht und Ethik im Alten Testament* (ed. B. M. Levinson and E. Otto; Münster: LIT Verlag, 2004) 83–110.

classified as a disciple of Herder and the Romantics because, for him, the "literary jewels" are always close to the source of the river [an allusion to the mythological jewels of the River Styx—editor].

In von Rad's perspective, what was the work of the Yahwist? Primarily, he completed a "creed" that was quite succinct; subsequently, he created links between the various elements of his composition. First of all, as we have seen, he combined the tradition of salvation history with the tradition of the gift of the Law on Mount Sinai. Then he enhanced this collection by adding other existing traditions, which he reformulated to correspond to his theological goals.

The "small historical creed" mentioned only Jacob (Deut 26:5). The Yahwist added to this the traditions about Abraham and Isaac. In order to connect the patriarchal stories to the Exodus, he inserted the Joseph story. The hero of this story represented, in von Rad's eyes, an ideal, wise administrator in harmony with the "enlightened" spirit prevalent in Solomon's court. Before this first section of the history of Israel as a people, J inserted a universalistic "prologue," a history of origins (Genesis 1–11), so that the history of Israel was placed within the frame of the history of humanity as a whole.[92]

From a theological point of view, von Rad was attempting to prove that the Davidic monarchy was, according to the Yahwist, the high point of Israel's history. The literary corpus reflects the spirit of an "enlightened" period. Von Rad went as far as to speak of a "Solomonic Enlightenment" (*Solomonische Aufklärung*).[93] This period fascinated this great exegete, as it had fascinated Wellhausen. The idea of a Solomonic Enlightenment was primarily based on the Joseph story, because the protagonist had to discover God's will without any supernatural assistance. God never spoke to him directly.

Certain "programmatic" passages clearly express the Yahwist's aim—for example, Gen 12:1–3. This oracle links the history of the universe (Genesis 1–11) to the history of the patriarchs, which is the beginning of Israel's history. According to von Rad, Genesis 1–11 describes a world in which sin and divine malediction increase daily. Gen 12:1–3 marks a watershed in the history of the universe: at this point, the history of curses becomes the history in which God promises, through Abraham, a "blessing for all the nations."[94] The divine

---

92. In reality, the Yahwist document does not begin until Gen 2:4b.

93. G. von Rad, "Josephsgeschichte und ältere Chokma," in *Congress Volume: Copenhagen, 1952* (VTSup 1; Leiden, 1953) 120–27 = *Gesammelte Studien zum Alten Testament* (2nd ed.; TBü 8; Munich, 1961) 272–80; cf. idem, *Problem of the Hexateuch*, 75–76; idem, *Holy War in Ancient Israel* (trans. M. J. Dawn; Grand Rapids, 1991) 81–84; idem, *Genesis: A Commentary* (trans. John H. Marks; Philadelphia, 1972) 28–30, 429–34; idem, *Theology of the Old Testament* (Edinburgh, 1962) 1.57 and 1.62. Cf. de Pury and Römer, "Pentateuque," 42.

94. Von Rad understands Gen 12:3b as follows: "In you all the families of the earth will be blessed." However, this interpretation is not obligatory. It is more plausible to understand it: "all the families of the earth will be blessed by your name"; in other words, "all the families

promise is fulfilled during David's and Solomon's time, when Israel becomes a "great nation" (Gen 12:2). The "great name" is the one given to David (Gen 12:2; cf. 2 Sam 7:9). The "families of the earth" are all the peoples assembled in David's kingdom ("the earth"), who are fortunate in that they are the recipients of divine blessing, thanks to the Davidic dynasty.[95] Gen 12:3 therefore actually contains the "Yahwist's kerygma" (cf. Rom 3:21–30).[96]

c. Martin Noth and Premonarchic Israel[97]

Martin Noth and Gerhard von Rad mutually influenced each other. However, while von Rad was more a theologian, Martin Noth was primarily a historian.[98] Three or four of Noth's insights have left deep marks on the history of exegesis.

• *Deuteronomy and the Deuteronomistic work.*[99]   According to Noth, with the exception of some even later passages, Deuteronomy in its present form did not become the fifth book of the Pentateuch until quite late. At an earlier stage, it was a preface to a large work extending from Joshua through 2 Kings. The Deuteronomist, who worked during the Exile, interpreted Israel's entire history in the light of "Moses' Law" and used it to assess each event and every reign. This Deuteronomist left his characteristic mark on many passages, such as 2 Kgs 17:7–23. Deuteronomy only became the fifth book of the Pentateuch when Deuteronomy 34 was added.

Furthermore, Noth observed that the sources of the Pentateuch—J, E, and P—are not present in the book of Joshua. This is difficult to explain because, just as for von Rad, in Noth's view "Israel's history" of necessity culminated with the entry into the Promised Land.

---

of the earth will bless one another, saying: Be blessed like Abraham." See Blum, *Komposition der vätergeschichte*, 349–52; and the parallel texts: Gen 48:20, Ps 72:17, Jer 29:22, Zech 8:13.

95. The analogy with the message of Romans 1 is striking. The nations are under "the wrath of God," and salvation comes from faith in Jesus Christ, the son of David.

96. This expression comes from H. W. Wolff, "Das Kerygma des Jahwisten," *EvT* 24 (1964) 73–98 = *Gesammelte Studien zum Alten Testament* (TBü 22; Munich, 1964) 345–73. In this case as well, there has been no lack of criticism. Gen 12:1–3 is probably a late, Postexilic text. In addition, the connection with David's reign is minimal.

97. On M. Noth, see Smend, *Deutsche Alttestamentler*, 255–75. Important works of M. Noth: *Überlieferungsgeschichtliche Studien: Die sammelnden und bearbeitenden Geschichtswerke im Alten Testament* (Tübingen, 1943; 2nd ed., 1957); idem, *A History of Pentateuchal Traditions* (Englewood Cliffs, NJ, 1972; repr. Chico, CA, 1981); idem, *History of Israel* (2nd ed.; New York, 1960).

98. See Blenkinsopp, *Pentateuch*, 17.

99. Noth, *The Deuteronomistic History* (2nd ed.; JSOTSup 15; Sheffield, 1991; translation of pp. 3–110 of *Überlieferungsgeschichtliche Studien*).

According to Noth, this hypothesis becomes obvious: when the Pentateuch was assembled, the story of the Conquest that was present in the earliest sources was eliminated in order to make way for what we now find in the book of Joshua. In his studies, consequently, Noth presupposed the existence of a Tetrateuch rather than a Pentateuch or a Hexateuch.

- *The major themes of the Pentateuch/Tetrateuch and "tradition history" (Überlieferungsgeschichte).*[100]   For Noth, the various themes that composed the actual Tetrateuch were transmitted separately before being compiled in a single work after a long redactional process. This is why he spoke of a "history of transmission." During the oral stage, there were five original themes: the departure from Egypt, the wanderings in the wilderness, the entry into the land, the promises made to the patriarchs, and the revelation at Sinai. The kinship with von Rad's theology is obvious. Furthermore, Noth maintained that these traditions were transmitted orally in local sanctuaries: their *Sitz im Leben* was therefore cultic. The substance of the traditions was fixed before they were put into writing. When the authors of the sources J, E, and P worked, they were content with putting into writing traditions that had already reached them in a fairly definitive form. This means that they actually added very little material: the history of the origins was considered to be the work of J, and the chronologies were attributed to P.[101]

- *Israelite amphictyony.*[102]   What was the institutional basis of these oral traditions? Given that, according to all the traditions, only one Israel existed, we must logically conclude that there was, already at the oral stage, "one" unique Israel. Because J was writing in David's time, "Israel" must be sought in the preceding era, that is, in the period of the Judges. The organized polity called Israel that formed and transmitted these common traditions consequently existed before the Monarchy.

---

100. Idem, *A History of Pentateuchal Traditions.*

101. Deep aversion to the National Socialism of his time motivated M. Noth in his research. This is why he, in the end, excluded Moses from the traditions of the Exodus, the wilderness, and the Sinai. The only reliable point of the Mosaic tradition was the reference to Moses' tomb. The Deuteronomist was the first author to give Moses a unique place in the traditions of Israel's origins. The earliest tradition, for example, attributed the mission of liberation to the "elders" and not to Moses. It is enough to use one German word to understand the allusion: Israel was not liberated by a *Führer* ("leader," "chief"). Likewise, Noth exalted the federation of tribes that preceded the Davidic Monarchy. The essential core of Israel's faith stemmed from this more "democratic" period, and subsequent periods did not add anything. Finally, the very pessimistic vision of his Deuteronomistic History, which described in general terms the collapse of the Monarchy, was developed while he was in Königsberg (today Kaliningrad) during the Second World War. Like Noth, the Deuteronomist is an independent personality who does not belong to any institution and judges the events of his time without any illusions. See de Pury, Römer, and Macchi, *Deuteronomistic History,* 52.

102. Noth, *Das System der zwölf Stämme Israels* (BWANT 52; Stuttgart, 1930).

Based on the model of Greek amphictyony, Noth developed the hypothesis of an analogous confederation of twelve tribes. These tribes had a common sanctuary where they celebrated their shared "tales." This is how a pan-Israelite tradition was gradually formed. The tribes were able to recruit an army to defend themselves against common enemies, and they had some form of basic political organization.[103]

- *The priestly narrative.*[104] M. Noth distinguished two strata within the Priestly Code: an earlier one, which he called the "Priestly narrative" (*P als Erzählung*), and a later one, the legislative "supplements" (Ps), such as Leviticus 1–7; 11–15; 17–26. We find the same distinction between "history" and "law" as in von Rad's works, but this time in relation to the Priestly Code. Noth's P document is quite similar to Graf's. For Noth, just as for Wellhausen before him, P provided the final editors and compilers of the Pentateuch (or Tetrateuch) with the basic frame or structure of their work.[105]

E. Other Schools of Research

Most new scholarly developments in Pentateuchal research originated in German-speaking universities. Moreover, other scholars showed some reserve toward ideas advanced in these liberal Protestant circles. In the Catholic world, especially, the reaction was very restrained. In 1906, a decree of the Pontifical Biblical Commission reaffirmed the Mosaic character of the Pentateuch but admitted that Moses may have used various sources and probably did not write everything himself. In addition, at the École biblique in Jerusalem, founded in 1894, Fr. Lagrange was already teaching the historical-critical method and the

---

103. This thesis was shaky because it found little support in the text, and it has now been abandoned. See S. Herrmann, "Das Werden Israels," *TLZ* 87 (1962) 561–74; idem, *A History of Israel in Old Testament Times* (trans. J. Bowden; 2nd ed.; Philadelphia, 1981); G. Fohrer, "'Amphictyonie' und 'Bund'?" *TLZ* 91 (1966) 801–16 and 893–904 = *Studien zur alttestamentlichen Theologie und Geschichte (1949–1966)* (BZAW 115; Berlin, 1969) 84–119; R. Smend, "Gehörte Judah zum vorstaatlichen Israel?" in *Fourth World Congress of Jewish Studies* (2 vols.; Jerusalem, 1967) 1.57–62; R. de Vaux, "The Twelve Tribes of Israel: The Theory of the 'Israelite Amphyctyony,'" in *Early History of Israel* (trans. D. Smith; Philadelphia, 1978) 695–715; C. H. G. de Geus, *The Tribes of Israel: An Investigation of the Presuppositions of Martin Noth's Amphictyony Hypothesis* (SSN 18; Assen, Amsterdam, 1976); Crüsemann, *Der Widerstand gegen das Königtum*, 194–222; N. K. Gottwald, *The Tribes of Yahweh: A Sociology of Liberated Israel, 1250–1050 b.c.e.* (Maryknoll, NY, 1979); C. Levin, "Das System der zwölf Stämme Israels," in *Congress Volume: Paris, 1992* (ed. J. A. Emerton; VTSup 61; Leiden, 1995) 163–78. For a summary of this question, see O. Bächli, *Amphictyonie im Alten Testament* (TZ Supplement 6; Basel, 1977); A. D. H. Mayes, "The Theory of the Twelve Tribe Israelite Amphictyony," in *Israelite and Judaean History* (ed. J. H. Hayes and J. M. Miller; OTL; Philadelphia, 1977) 297–308.

104. Noth, *History of Pentateuchal Traditions*, 8–9.

105. See de Pury and Römer, "Pentateuque," 38–39.

documentary hypothesis, despite all of the controversies and difficulties that sprang up along the way.[106]

In Scandinavia, Gunkel's writings were largely echoed by scholars.[107] In 1927, the Norwegian scholar S. Mowinckel defended a thesis on the cultic origin of the Decalogue. According to him, the Ten Commandments were part of a New Year celebration during the premonarchic period.[108] The Danish scholar J. Pedersen argued that Exodus 1–15 was a "cultic legend" that was recited during Passover.[109]

Later on, studies on oral tradition had great success in Sweden, especially in Uppsala.[110] I. Engnell, one of the foremost representatives of the Swedish school, adopted a radical position that called into question the documentary hypothesis. According to his investigations, which were unfortunately brought to a halt by his untimely death, the ancient traditions were transmitted orally until the Postexilic period. These traditions were not put into writing until after the Exile, and then in two phases. A school inspired by Deuteronomistic ideology accomplished the first compilation, which more or less corresponds to Deuteronomy plus Noth's Deuteronomistic History (Joshua–2 Kings). A Tetrateuch produced by a Priestly type of editor was then added to this work.[111] E. Nielsen (Denmark) likewise stressed the essential role of oral tradition in the formation of the Pentateuch.[112]

In the United States, study of the texts progressed concurrently with archaeological and epigraphic discoveries. The documents coming from Mesopotamia and especially from Ras Shamra (Ugarit) generated nonstop investigation into the historical foundation of the events described in Old Testament texts.

W. F. Albright is often considered to be the founder of the North American school, and F. M. Cross is, together with G. E. Mendenhall, one of its chief

---

106. M.-J. Lagrange, *Historical Criticism and the Old Testament* (trans. E. Myers; ATLA Monograph; London, 1905); for other details on this great figure, see idem, *L'Écriture dans l'Église: Choix de portraits et d'exégèse spirituelle, 1890–1937* (LD 142; Paris, 1990).

107. On the Scandinavian school, see the article by E. Nielsen, "The Tradition-Historical Study of the Pentateuch since 1945, with Special Emphasis on Scandinavia," in *The Production of Time: Tradition History in Old Testament Scholarship* (ed. K. Jeppesen and B. Otzen; Sheffield, 1984) 11–28.

108. S. Mowinckel, *Le décalogue* (Paris, 1927).

109. J. Pedersen, "Passahfest und Passahlegende," *ZAW* 52 (1934) 161–75. "Legend" is a technical term that signifies an "edifying narrative concerning a holy person or place." The term comes from the Latin *legenda*, lit., "things to be read," from the verb *legere*, "to read." The term refers to accounts that monks were to read on specific occasions.

110. This is also the case for the New Testament even up to our day. See, for example, the works of Gerhardsson and Riesenfeld.

111. Engnell, *Gamla Testamentet*, vol. 1; idem, "Methodological Aspects of Old Testament Study," *VT* 7 (1960) 13–30; idem, *A Rigid Scrutiny: Critical Essays on the Old Testament* (trans. J. T. Willis; Nashville, 1969).

112. E. Nielsen, *Oral Tradition* (London, 1954).

representatives. One characteristic of their research is the practice of relating the Bible to the ancient Near East. Albright established a connection between certain patriarchal customs and the legal documents discovered at Nuzi (in Mesopotamia). The migrations of Israel's ancestors must be seen in the context of the migrations of caravans of merchants who used donkeys for transporting goods. They are depicted in paintings on the tombs at Beni-Hasan in Egypt.[113] Mendenhall traced the Covenant at Sinai back to the 12th century B.C.E. based on analogies between the structure of the Sinai Covenant and Hittite vassal treaties.[114] Cross advanced the hypothesis of an oral epic poem of Israel's origins that was similar to Ugaritic texts and that preceded the prose text that we now possess.[115]

The most important works in French originated from the *École biblique* in Jerusalem. I mentioned above the pioneer work of its founder, Fr. Lagrange. He was unfortunately not able to publish his commentary on Genesis. After his passing, his students Abel,[116] Vincent, and, above all, R. de Vaux continued his work. R. de Vaux's method closely resembles the American school in some ways, although it puts more emphasis on the study of the text and the traditions.[117]

Let us not forget that, within the Catholic Church, the first edition of the *Jerusalem Bible* was published in 1956; it was the first Bible and the first scholarly work that was able to speak openly and with the *imprimatur* about the documentary hypothesis. Gradually, the idea emerged that critical interpretation of the Bible does not threaten faith. On the contrary, critical interpretation promotes a mature, responsible comprehension of the texts on which the faith of the Church community is based. The most important documents on this issue are the encyclical letters *Providentissimus Deus* (Leon XIII, 1893); *Divino afflante spiritu* (Pius XII, 1943); *Dei Verbum* (Vatican II); and the document of the Pontifical Biblical Commission, *The Interpretation of the Bible in the Church* (1993).[118]

---

113. W. F. Albright, "Abram the Hebrew: A New Archaeological Interpretation," *BASOR* 163 (1961) 36–54.

114. G. E. Mendenhall, "Covenant Forms in Israelite Tradition," *BA* 17 (1954) 50–76 = *Law and Covenant in the Ancient Near East* (Pittsburgh, 1955).

115. Cross, *Canaanite Myth and Hebrew Epic*.

116. See above all F. M. Abel, *Géographie de la Palestine* (2 vols.; EB; Paris, 1933; 3rd ed., 1967); idem, *Histoire de la Palestine depuis la conquête d'Alexandre jusqu'à l'invasion arabe* (2 vols.; EB; Paris, 1952).

117. R. de Vaux, *The Bible and the Ancient Near East* (trans. D. McHugh; Garden City, NY, 1971); idem, *Early History of Israel* (trans. D. Smith; Philadelphia, 1978).

118. On these documents, see P. Laghi, M. Gilbert, and A. Vanhoye, *Chiesa e Sacra Scrittura: Un secolo di magistero ecclesiastico e di studi biblici* (SubBi 17; Rome, 1994); Joseph A. Fitzmyer, *The Biblical Commission's Document "The Interpretation of the Bible in the Church": Text and Commentary* (SubBi 18; Rome, 1995); D. P. Béchard (ed.), *The Scripture Documents: An Anthology of Official Catholic Teachings* (Collegeville, MN, 2002).

In these documents, the Catholic Church grants the right of citizenship to the critical reading of the Bible. *Divino afflante spiritu* and *Dei Verbum* dealt primarily with the legitimacy of a reading based on "literary genres." The Pontifical Biblical Commission document enumerated a series of methods and approaches that foster a better understanding of the biblical texts[119] and firmly criticized only one type of reading: fundamentalist interpretation.

The world of Jewish scholarship was, at first, predominantly suspicious of the historical-critical method and the documentary hypothesis. Too many of Wellhausen's and Gunkel's assertions were anti-Semitic. More than one religious soul considered their theories profane. Nevertheless, some scholars did use the method developed in the German-speaking universities but arrived at their own conclusions. This was the case with Y. Kaufmann and his followers, who defended an early, Preexilic date for the Priestly document.[120] On the other hand, U. Cassuto, an Italian Jew, battled all his life against the documentary hypothesis.[121] Likewise, B. Jacob's commentary on Genesis was, to a large extent, a refutation of Gunkel's commentary on the same book.[122]

This lengthy overview shows that each age and each culture asked new questions of the Pentateuch, and each found new answers in it. By the 1970s, the scholarly landscape was therefore quite diversified, even though everyone essentially agreed on a working basis, which for the large majority of exegetes was and still is the documentary hypothesis.[123] Nonetheless, this agreement was not to last for long.

---

119. *Interpretation of the Bible in the Church* (Vatican City, 1993). The text exists in several languages.

120. Y. Kaufmann, "Probleme der israelitisch-jüdischen Religionsgeschichte," *ZAW* 48 (1930) 23–43; idem, *The Religion of Israel: From Its Beginning until the Babylonian Exile* (Chicago, 1960). Also see, along the same lines, M. Haran, *Temple and Temple-Service in Ancient Israel* (Oxford, 1979; repr. Winona Lake, IN, 1985). On this school of thought, see T. M. Krapf, *Die Priesterschrift und die vorexilische Zeit: Yehezkel Kaufmanns vernachlässigter Beitrag zur Geschichte der biblischen Religion* (OBO 119; Fribourg and Göttingen, 1992).

121. U. Cassuto, *The Documentary Hypothesis and the Composition of the Pentateuch* (London, 1961).

122. B. Jacob, *Das erste Buch der Tora*; also see idem, *The Second Book of the Bible: Exodus* (New York, 1992).

123. See the Introductions to the Old Testament of this time in German: O. Eissfeldt, *The Old Testament: An Introduction* (trans. P. R. Ackroyd; New York, 1965); E. Sellin and G. Fohrer, *Einleitung in das Alte Testament* (9th ed.; Heidelberg, 1965); O. Kaiser, *Einleitung in das Alte Testament = Introduction to the Old Testament* (trans. J. Sturdy; Minneapolis, 1975); in French: Cazelles, "La Torah ou Pentateuque," 95–244; in English: H. H. Rowley, *The Growth of the Old Testament* (London, 1950); C. R. North, "Pentateuchal Criticism," in *The Old Testament and Modern Study* (ed. H. H. Rowley; Oxford, 1951) 48–83; R. E. Clements, "Pentateuchal Problems," in *Tradition and Interpretation* (ed. G. W. Anderson; Oxford, 1979) 96–124; in Italian: J. A. Soggin, *Introduzione all'Antico Testamento = Introduction to the Old Testament* (2nd ed.; OTL; London, 1980).

Chapter 7

Recent Developments in
the Study of the Pentateuch

For some years, confusion has reigned in academic study of the Pentateuch, and this situation may continue for a long time. In my view, except to state this fact, it is useless to enumerate the various opinions or to present a long list of the authors of different schools of thought. As in the preceding chapter, my primary aim instead is to try to grasp the reasons for such a variety of methodologies and results. Each problem is rooted in a cultural context, and knowing the cultural context helps us to understand it better. Even scholars are sons or daughters of their time, and the reading of their works on the Pentateuch largely confirms this.

A. Criticisms of the Documentary Hypothesis

1. The Cultural and Intellectual Background of the 1970s[1]

The academic climate reached a watershed around the 1970s. Several factors contributed to this development. The Second World War had left deep wounds in Europe. A world had been destroyed, and the world rising up out of the ruins was ideologically divided. In 1968, student revolts exploded practically everywhere in the world, expressing the feelings of the postwar generation.[2] New themes appeared in theology, such as the "theology of the death of God," "secularization," "liberation theology," and the "theology of hope." Psychology

---

1. For more details concerning the debates between 1970 and 1980, see, among others, N. E. Wagner, "Pentateuchal Criticism: No Clear Future," *Canadian Journal of Theology* 13 (1967) 225–32; E. Otto, "Stehen wir vor einem Umbruch in der Pentateuchkritik?" *Virkündigung und Forschung* 22 (1977) 82–97; B. J. Diebner, "Neue Ansätze in der Pentateuchforschung," *Dielheimer Blätter zum Alten Testament und seiner Rezeption in der Alten Kirche* 13 (1978) 2–13; J. Van Seters, "Recent Studies on the Pentateuch: A Crisis in Method?" *JAOS* 99 (1979) 663–73; J. Vermeylen, "La formation du Pentateuque à la lumière de l'exégèse historico-critique," *RTL* 12 (1981) 324–46; E. Zenger, "Auf der Suche nach einem Weg aus der Pentateuchkrise," *TRev* 78 (1982) 353–62; A. H. J. Gunneweg, "Anmerkungen und Anfragen zur neueren Pentateuchforschung," *TRu* 48 (1983) 227–53; *TRu* 50 (1985) 107–31.
2. Rolf Rendtorff, for example, was the rector of the University of Heidelberg in 1968.

and sociology had progressively greater influence in the intellectual world. A new scientific field, linguistics, also began to attract exegetes.

Pentateuchal studies at this time have become the scene of a kind of "death of the father." The great masters of the past have been unmasked, and even the foundations of research have begun to crumble. Scholars are no longer satisfied to discuss particular aspects of this or that theory. They go further, even questioning the presuppositions of research.[3] Thus, the documentary hypothesis finds itself on trial.[4] Some scholars have even gone as far as attacking historical-critical exegesis itself.[5]

In the Anglo-American world, the "new criticism" of literature also has had a major influence. This method insists on the autonomy of the literary text and of the science that studies it. Understanding a text does not necessarily mean explaining its origin, which was the intent of "literary criticism" and "source criticism" from Wellhausen's time on. Searching for the origins and genesis of a text is the historian's task. Literary studies set aside the history of the text and its author(s) in order to explain it as it appears—*prout iacet* ("in its current state)—in its final version or, as Childs put it, in its "canonical" form.[6] The important term in this phrase is the adjective "final." Whereas, during the entire period dominated by the ideas of German Romanticism, scholars sought the authentic meaning of Israel's religion and history in the "origins"—that is, a "Golden Age" situated in the past—scholars now are more interested in the "end" of history.

For Wellhausen, the Postexilic period was the time that had witnessed the birth of "Judaism," the decline of Israel's authentic religion. At the beginning of the 1970s, however, it was generally thought that all of the important texts were born during the exile or shortly thereafter. As a result, the Yahwist left the

---

3. See in particular H. H. Schmid, "Auf der Suche nach neuen Perspektiven."

4. See, among the very first, F. V. Winnett, "Re-examining the Foundations," *JBL* 84 (1965) 1–19.

5. See especially R. Rendtorff, "Between Historical Criticism and Holistic Interpretation: New Trends in Old Testament Exegesis," in *Congress Volume: Jerusalem, 1986* (VTSup 40; Leiden, 1988) 298–303; idem, "The Paradigm Is Changing: Hopes and Fears," *BibInt* 1 (1993) 34–53.

6. See, for example, Childs, *Exodus,* who clearly explains his thesis in the preface: "The purpose of this commentary is unabashedly theological. . . . Its purpose is to understand Exodus as scripture of the church. . . . It will be immediately clear from this perspective that a different understanding of the role of biblical interpretation is being offered from that currently held by the majority of scholars within the field" (p. ix). Also see Clines, *Theme of the Pentateuch,* 5: "I am here arguing that the Pentateuch is a unity—not in origin, but in its final shape. Two centuries of Biblical criticism have trained us to look for unity, if at all, in the Pentateuch's sources rather than in the final product. I have thought it worthwhile to suggest that it is time that we ignored the sources—hypothetical as they are—for a little, and ask what the Pentateuch as a whole is about; that it to say, what is its theme."

comfortable court of David or Solomon to live in exile in Babylon,[7] or perhaps (in the opinion of some) he even participated in the reconstruction of Jerusalem.[8] Others prefer to eliminate all historical considerations (or "diachronic" study) from research and just approach the text in its "final" or "canonical" form ("synchronic study").

More specifically, three factors characterize this period: the experience of crisis, the experience of complexity, and a suspicion of ideology. The growing interest in the crisis of the Exilic/Postexilic period is deeply rooted in the more or less clear consciousness of the fact that the northern Western world is going through a comparable crisis: one world is drawing to an end and another, very different world is being born.[9] Experiencing crisis also implies experiencing the complexity of historical events. The contemporary world is fragmented and pluralistic; consequently, it is difficult to distinguish linear developments leading to the progress or decline of historical events. Reality may no longer be reduced to such simple representations as was possible in Wellhausen's time. For the same reason, deep suspicion of ideology rules in the world of biblical studies, as well as in the intellectual world in general. Presuppositions are analyzed with great care, and absolute affirmations seem impossible. A text never has "only one meaning"; it always has many meanings, based on the perspective of each interpreter.[10]

These three factors are not all equally present in all areas of research. However, the general situation has changed. From now on, no one can begin to study the Pentateuch without first taking into consideration what his or her methodological presuppositions are, because there is no longer a consensus.

2. Contesting Basic Theses about Premonarchic Israel

As the years went by, the documentary hypothesis was identified with a specific picture of Israel's origins and specifically with premonarchic Israel. A tight connection therefore existed between the hypotheses of Israel's origins and the composition of the Yahwist document. Today's debate is primarily about whether the Yahwist's prehistory existed in the form of an oral tradition.

The first attacks were launched against the idea that a premonarchic "patriarchal period" could be reconstructed. The world of the patriarchs may have

---

7. See, recently, Levin, *Der Jahwist*.

8. M. Rose, *Deuteronomist und Yahwist: Untersuchungen zu den Berührungspunkten beider Literaturwerke* (ATANT 67; Zurich, 1981): the Yahwist follows the Deuteronomist.

9. H. H. Schmid, "Auf der Suche nach neuen Perspektiven," 390: "[Is this interest in late periods] not due to the fact that we too are living in a late period?" ("Hängt dies damit zusammen, daß wir selbst in gewissem Sinne in einer Spätzeit leben?").

10. See, among others, McKnight, *Postmodern Use of the Bible*. Note also the deconstructionism of A. Derrida, who considers the texts fundamentally unstable.

belonged to literature but not to Israel's history or prehistory. Two North American scholars—one from Canada, J. Van Seters;[11] and the other from the United States, T. L. Thompson—are the chief representatives of this trend.[12]

Israel's "nomadic period," with its characteristic vocabulary, such as the "God of the fathers" (A. Alt, V. Maag), is another thesis that does not stand up under examination. The "God of the fathers" is not tied to an ancient, proto-Israelite era. It is instead a late literary construction binding together the various patriarchal traditions.[13] The thesis of A. Alt on the gradual settling of Israel and his seminomadic family has also been severely criticized.[14] Israel did not actually come from the wilderness. Instead, the people always had lived in the land of Canaan, and the settlement, or Conquest, was in reality an internal phenomenon, a kind of evolution or revolution during which power passed from the hands of the Canaanites to another people, subsequently called "Israel."[15]

M. Noth's thesis of an amphictyony also turns out to be weak and collapses under critical analysis.[16] The parallel with the Greek amphictyony lacks a solid

---

11. J. Van Seters, *Abraham in History and Tradition* (New Haven, CT, 1975).

12. T. L. Thompson, *The Historicity of the Patriarchal Narratives: The Quest for the Historical Abraham* (BZAW 133; Berlin, 1974).

13. See B. J. Diebner, "Die Götter des Vaters: Eine Kritik der 'Vätergott'-Hypothese Albrecht Alts," *Dielheimer Blätter zum Alten Testament und seiner Rezeption in der Alten Kirche* 9 (1975) 21–51; H. Vorländer, *Mein Gott: Die Vorstellung vom persönlichen Gott im Alten Orient und im Alten Testament* (AOAT 23; Kevelaer and Neukirchen-Vluyn, 1975); E. Ruprecht, "Die Religion der Väter: Hauptlinien der Forschungsgeschichte," *Dielheimer Blätter zum Alten Testament und seiner Rezeption in der Alten Kirche* 11 (1976) 2–29; more recently, also see Blum, *Komposition der Vätergeschichte*, 495–97; Köckert, *Vätergott*; cf. T. N. D. Mettinger, "The God of the Fathers: Divine Designations in the Patriarchal Narratives," *In Search of God: The Meaning and Message of the Everlasting Names* (Philadelphia, 1987) 50–74. On this whole question, see Weidmann, *Die Patriarchen und ihre Religion*.

14. G. E. Mendenhall, "The Hebrew Conquest of Palestine," *BA* 25 (1962) 66–87 = *The Biblical Archeologist Reader* (vol. 3; Garden City, NY, 1970) 100–120; idem, *The Tenth Generation: The Origins of the Biblical Tradition* (Baltimore, 1973); idem, "Change and Decay in All Around I See: Conquest, Covenant and *The Tenth Generation*," *BA* 39 (1976) 152–57; Gottwald, *The Tribes of Yahweh*; B. Zuber, *Vier Studien zu den Ursprüngen Israels* (OBO 9; Fribourg and Göttingen, 1976). On Israel's "nomadic ideal," see the criticism of S. Talmon, "The 'Desert Motif' in the Bible and in Qumran Literature," in *Biblical Motifs: Origins and Transformations* (ed. A. Altmann; Cambridge, MA, 1966) 31–63.

15. More recently, see I. Finkelstein, *The Archaeology of the Israelite Settlement* (Jerusalem, 1988); W. Thiel, "Vom revolutionären zum evolutionären Israel? Zu einem neuen Modell der Entstehung Israels," *TLZ* 113 (1988) 401–10; R. Neu, *Von der Anarchie zum Staat: Entwicklungsgeschichte Israels vom Nomadentum zur Monarchie im Spiegel der Ethnosoziologie* (Neukirchen-Vluyn, 1992); A. J. Frendo, "Five Recent Books on the Emergence of Ancient Israel: Review Article," *PEQ* 124 (1992) 144–55; T. L. Thompson, *Early History of the Israelite People: From the Written and Archaeological Sources* (Studies in the History of the Ancient Near East 4; Leiden, 1992); P. Kaswalder, "L'archeologia e le origini d'Israele," *RivB* 41 (1993) 171–88.

16. See chap. 6, n. 102.

foundation because it is impossible to prove the existence of an Israelite organization of twelve tribes or the existence of common institutions, such as a central sanctuary.[17]

Von Rad's theories are no exception. The basis of his theory of the formation of the Pentateuch cracks under a rigorous scrutiny of texts such as Deut
26:5b–9, 6:20–23; Josh 24:2b–13. These texts are not ancient; they are, on the
contrary, recent Deuteronomistic creations that presuppose an earlier compilation of ancient traditions.[18]

After the disintegration of the major hypotheses regarding premonarchic Israel, it became difficult to situate the Yahwist's composition in that period. As
the face of the Yahwist changed, the face of the documentary hypothesis also
evolved.

B. The Problem of the Various Sources

1. The Elohist[19]

After its separation from the Priestly Code or Priestly Writer, the Elohist
source was the "poor stepchild" of the documentary hypothesis. Scholars generally attributed to the Elohist the texts or fragments that they could not attribute to J or to P,[20] thus gathering into the Elohist's "basket" the "crumbs" left
on the table after the other sources had been served. We might say that, like a
phantom, E only appeared in the dark corners of the Pentateuch. Scholars used
E to solve problems in difficult texts such as Genesis 15; 20–22; 28:10–22; parts
of the Joseph Story; Moses' call (Exodus 3–4); the Sinai pericope (Exodus 19–
24); and the story of Balaam (Numbers 22–24).

---

17. See R. Smend, *Jahwekrieg und Stämmebund: Erwägungen zur ältesten Geschichte Israels*
(FRLANT 84; Göttingen, 1963) 56–70; W. H. Irvin, "Le sanctuaire central israélite avant
l'établissement de la monarchie," *RB* 72 (1965) 161–84.

18. C. W. H. Brekelmans, "Het 'Historische Credo' van Israel," *Tijdschrift voor Theologie* 3
(1963) 1–11; L. Rost, "Das kleine geschichtliche Credo," *Das kleine geschichtliche Credo und
andere Studien zum Alten Testament* (Heidelberg, 1964) 1–25; W. Richter, "Beobachtungen
zur theologischen Systembildung in der alttestamentlichen Literatur anhand des 'kleinen geschichtlichen Credo,'" in *Wahrheit und Verkündigung* (FS W. Schmaus; Munich, 1967) 175–
212; J. P. Hyatt, "Were There an Ancient Historical Credo and an Independent Sinai Tradition?" in *Essays in Honor of H. G. May* (Nashville, 1970) 152–70; N. Lohfink, "Zum 'kleinen
geschichtlichen Credo' Dtn 26,5–9," *Theologie und Philosophie* 46 (1971) 19–39; S. Kreutzer,
Die Frühgeschichte Israels in Bekenntnis und Verkündigung des Alten Testaments (BZAW 178; Berlin, 1989).

19. For the texts, see Campbell and O'Brien, *Sources of the Pentateuch,* 166–93; for an
overview of the history of the research, see de Pury and T. Römer, "Pentateuque," 45–46;
for the characteristics of source E, see Zenger (ed.), *Einleitung,* 111–12.

20. See the study of O. Procksch, *Das nordhebräische Sagenbuch: Die Elohimquelle* (Leipzig,
1906).

The source attributed to E does indeed raise many difficulties. For example, certain texts considered Elohistic do not use the divine name Elohim (Genesis 15; the Decalogue, Exod 20:2–17) or they contain the divine name YHWH (cf. Gen 22:11, 14). This is surprising, to say the least, and drives the critical enterprise to acrobatics that are more perilous than convincing. Only the narratives in Genesis 20–22 have common characteristics and provide enough solid support for the hypothesis of a "source" or, at least, a compilation of narratives coming from the same milieu.[21]

Already in 1933, P. Volz and W. Rudolph[22] questioned the existence of an Elohistic source containing a complete, independent account of Israel's origins. According to them, the Elohist never existed. The texts attributed to the Elohist actually belong to J, or they may have been additions of Deuteronomistic origin. Their thesis enjoyed almost no success at the time. Only Mowinckel was to adopt a similar position: E seemed to him to be a "variant of J," that is, a series of texts that were parallel to J's and were transmitted orally for a long time before being integrated into the Yahwist's work.[23] Recently, many authors have agreed with these scholars *a posteriori*. Today, only a few scholars continue to speak about an "E source."[24] Objections to the existence of such a "source" have been summed up by Zenger in his Introduction.[25]

In the Pentateuch that we have, E may appear, if at all, only in fragmentary form. There is no agreement concerning the beginning of E. Often, authors seek it in Genesis 15, a problematic text in which the divine name Elohim does not appear (see above). The narratives attributed to this source have few common elements. Furthermore, it is difficult to determine what connects them. This is why only a few scholars have succeeded in discovering a "plot" or "theological purpose" behind the Elohistic narrative.

Some of the texts previously attributed to E are now considered to be late. This is the case, for example, with Genesis 22 ("the testing of Abraham").[26] In the classic documentary theory, E was situated in the Northern Kingdom, so it

---

21. S. E. McEvenue bases his defense of the Elohist on precisely these texts; see "The Elohist at Work," *ZAW* 96 (1984) 315–32.

22. P. Volz and W. Rudolph, *Der Elohist als Erzähler: Ein Irrweg der Pentateuchkritik?* (BZAW 63; Giessen, 1933); W. Rudolph, *Der "Elohist" von Exodus bis Josua* (BZAW 68; Berlin, 1938).

23. S. Mowinckel, *Erwägungen zur Pentateuchquellenfrage* (Oslo, 1964).

24. However, see Campbell and O'Brien, *Sources of the Pentateuch*, 161–93 (with some skepticism); W. Jenks, *The Elohist and North Israelite Traditions* (SBLMS 22; Missoula, 1977); R. B. Coote, *In Defense of Revolution: The Elohist History* (Minneapolis, 1991).

25. See Zenger (ed.), *Einleitung*, 111–12.

26. Furthermore, at the crucial moment of the story, the angel of YHWH appears—not the angel of Elohim (Gen 22:11; compare with 21:17). For the date of Genesis 22, see T. Veijola, "Das Opfer des Abraham: Paradigma des Glaubens aus dem nachexilischen Zeitalter," *ZTK* 85 (1988) 129–64.

was common to look for or to identify a connection between E and the prophets Elijah and Hosea. This is perplexing,[27] because, in 1 Kings 17–21, Elijah is the hero of a religious demonstration against the worship of Baal and in favor of the worship of Yhwh, not of Elohim. The same argument is applicable, *mutatis mutandis*, to Hosea, who only rarely uses the divine name Elohim. A more useful theory would be the Elohistic redaction of the Psalter, although it is seldom considered Preexilic. Other models are also applied to explain the existence of the texts usually attributed to E. For example, they may be considered a series of selective "complements," the artifacts of a redaction that did not want to lose any of the ancient traditions.

2. The Yahwist[28]

In recent research, the discussion mainly revolves around two topics regarding the Yahwistic source: its existence as a "source" and its date.

a. Is There a Yahwistic Source (J)?

R. Rendtorff, G. von Rad's successor at the University of Heidelberg, directly attacked the Yahwist hypothesis.[29] His starting point was M. Noth's research. From a methodological angle, Rendtorff noticed a contradiction between Noth's *Traditionsgeschichte* or *Überlieferungsgeschichte* ("tradition history," a method close to the *Formgeschichte* ["form criticism"] of H. Gunkel and his disciples) and Wellhausen's *Literarkritik* ("source criticism"). For the former, research begins with the "small units," or short narratives. These narratives were introduced into a composition of "major units," Noth's great themes. The "narrative blocks" had internal coherence and were relatively independent from one another. However, "source criticism" presupposes the existence of long, independent, complete, written units at the beginning of the process of the Pentateuch's formation.

---

27. We will develop Zenger's argument on this point.

28. For the texts, see Campbell and O'Brien, *Sources of the Pentateuch*, 91–160; for an overview of current positions, see de Pury and Römer, "Pentateuque," 55–66; for a discussion of J's date, see Zenger (ed.), *Einleitung*, 109–11.

29. R. Rendtorff, "Literarkritik und Traditionsgeschichte," *EvT* 27 (1967) 138–53; idem, "Traditio-Historical Method and the Documentary Hypothesis," in *Proceedings of the Fifth World Congress of Jewish Studies*, vol. 1: *Ancient Near-East as Related to the Bible and the Holy Land* (Jerusalem, 1969) 5–11; "The 'Yahwist' as Theologian? The Dilemma of Pentateuchal Criticism," *JSOT* 3 (1977) 2–9; idem, *Das überlieferungsgeschichtliche Problem des Pentateuch* (BZAW 147; Berlin, 1976); idem, "The Future of Pentateuchal Criticism," *Henoch* 6 (1984) 1–15; on his work, see L. Zaman, *R. Rendtorff en zijn "Das überlieferungsgeschichtliche Problem des Pentateuch": Schets van een Maccabeër binnen de hedendaagse Pentateuchexegese* (Brussels, 1984). Rendtorff's positions are recapitulated in his *Das Alte Testament*, 1983, which has been translated into Italian, French, and English: *The Old Testament: An Introduction*.

From Gunkel's time on, scholars had been using these methods simultaneously, unaware of the difficulties. According to Rendtorff, these two methods are incompatible. How could "small units" fit into the "documents"—for example, Wellhausen's J? Either the original unit lost its characteristics in the process and can no longer be identified, or it did not lose its distinctiveness, and the "documents" cannot be unified because they are only compilations of disparate texts. In other words, J cannot be, simultaneously, a *Sammler von Sagen* ("story-collector"), as H. Gunkel saw him, and a great theologian who designed a vast literary composition according to a preestablished plan, as G. von Rad maintained.

In addition, Rendtorff emphasized the essential differences between the patriarchal stories and the Exodus. The stories of Israel's ancestors are unified by the theme of the promises, especially promises about the land. When the narrative of the Exodus begins, however, this promise is no longer in view. Israel leaves Egypt and wanders through the wilderness toward a land "flowing with milk and honey" (Exod 3:8), but there is no mention of the land promised to the fathers, except in a few isolated (and late) texts such as Exod 13:4, 11; 32:13; 33:1; cf. Num 14:16.

However, the idea of walking toward the "land promised to the fathers" appears frequently in Deuteronomy.[30] If the promises made to the patriarchs, the texts concerning the Exodus, and the wanderings in the wilderness belong to the same Yahwistic source, then this phenomenon is hard to explain. According to Rendtorff, it is simpler to think that these two narrative blocks developed independently before being brought together in the Pentateuch. Thus Rendtorff adopts a model that is close to the "hypothesis of fragments."[31] He prefers to start with the small units (*Einzelsagen*) of literary "blocks" (*grössere Einheiten*, "major units"). In other words, he opts for M. Noth's method instead of "source criticism." Without saying so explicitly, he is not interested in the oral tradition but only deals with *written* texts.

He also rejects the idea that continuous sources can be found throughout the Pentateuch, contending that a division into sources sometimes destroys the structure of the texts and hampers our understanding of their theological intent. Rendtorff enumerates six "major units" in the Pentateuch/Hexateuch: the story of origins (Genesis 1–11); the stories of the patriarchs (Genesis 12–50); the departure from Egypt (Exodus 1–15); the wandering in the wilderness (Exodus 16–18, Numbers 11–20); the Sinai pericope (Exodus 19–24); and the Conquest (Joshua).

---

30. See Deut 1:8, 21, 35; 6:10, 23; 8:1, etc. For a complete list, see T. Römer, *Israels Väter*, 12–14.

31. On this subject, scholars also refer to the model of "narrative cycles" (*Erzählkränze*). See Zenger (ed.), *Einleitung*, 72.

Rendtorff distinguishes two redactional enterprises in the formation of the actual Pentateuch, one that bears the mark of the Deuteronomistic school and the other the characteristics of the Priestly school. Added to this are some later redactional insertions.[32] This redactional work is already apparent in the "major units." Thus, the theme of the promises, which links the narratives concerning the three patriarchs, is, according to Rendtorff, of Deuteronomistic origin.

Rendtorff's hypotheses have been taken up and developed by his student Erhard Blum in two voluminous studies, the first on the patriarchal traditions and the second on Moses.[33] The figure of Moses integrates the themes of the Exodus, Sinai, and the wandering in the wilderness, and this reduces the number of "major units" initially proposed by Rendtorff. In Blum's view, the Pentateuch in its present form is the product of a compromise that was reached during the Persian era. There were, at that time, two important currents; one was a "lay" movement and the other was priestly. The first movement essentially brought together aristocratic landowners of Judea, and its representative organization was the institution of the "elders." The second movement defended the theology and the prerogatives of the priestly families attached to the Second Temple of Jerusalem. Both movements had composed their own "history of the origins of Israel," and the two works existed side by side. The first was created by the "laymen"—that is, the "elders"—and is called "composition D" or the "Deuteronomistic composition" (*D-Komposition* or *KD*). The second work is called "composition P" or the "Priestly composition" (*P-Komposition* or *KP*). When the Persian government decided to grant some authority to the province of Judea, it was necessary to establish a single constitutional document to define this new political entity. In addition, Postexilic Israel had to be unified in order to survive as a people.

For these internal and external reasons, the two "compositions" were combined into a single work that formed the actual Pentateuch, which thus became the official document representing "Persian imperial authorization." In other words, the Pentateuch was, in the eyes of the Persian authorities, the official law of the empire for Jews, especially for Jews in the province of Judea ("Yehud").[34]

---

32. Here again we find an idea analogous to the ideas of I. Engnell in *Gamla Testamentet*, vol. 1.

33. Blum, *Die Komposition der Vätergeschichte*; idem, *Studien zur Komposition des Pentateuch*; on the latter work, see J.-L. Ska, "Un nouveau Wellhausen?" *Bib* 72 (1991) 253–63; E. Cortese, "Pentateuco: La strada vecchia e la nuova," *Liber Annuus* 43 (1993) 71–87.

34. See P. Frei's thesis, "Zentralgewalt und Achämenidenreich," in *Reichsidee und Reichsorganisation im Perserreich* (ed. P. Frei and K. Koch; OBO 55; Fribourg and Göttingen, 1984; 2nd ed., 1996) 7–43. Blenkinsopp (*Pentateuch*, 229–43) adopts a position comparable with Rendtorff's and, especially, Blum's. He also thinks that the Pentateuch is composed of two "strata," one of a Deuteronomic type, composed in continuity with the Deuteronomistic

Thus, in the eyes of the "Heidelberg school," the Yahwist no longer exists. It has also become quite difficult in many cases to separate the most ancient elements from later redactional elements in the Postexilic "compositions." Frequently, Blum abandons this enterprise with regard to the Exodus–Numbers unit. In his first work on Genesis, however, it was easier to rediscover the ancient, Preexilic substrate of the accounts, because of the very character of the narratives.

We cannot present a complete evaluation of this immense work, perhaps the most impressive, together with the books by J. Van Seters, in recent years.[35] Nevertheless, in my view, four points of debate deserve a closer examination:

1. The relationship of Deuteronomy, the Deuteronomistic History (Joshua–2 Kings), and the texts of the Pentateuch: Deuteronomy and the Deuteronomistic work are not unified.[36] It would also be useful to study the redactional techniques in these works and to compare them with the redactional techniques in Genesis–Numbers.

2. The question of the legislative codes and their connection with the narrative texts merit closer study.[37]

3. If we maintain that the two "compositions" (*KD* and *KP*) have combined and organized older materials, would it not be possible to recognize them?

4. The problem of a postdeuteronomic and postpriestly redaction: certain later texts cannot be classified as either Deuteronomistic or Priestly, because their style and theology bear the mark of both schools.

History, and the other of Priestly origin. He also explains the origin of the Pentateuch itself with reference to the work of P. Frei and in light of Persian imperial authorization.

35. For criticism, see, among others, E. Otto, "Kritik der Pentateuchkomposition," *TRu* 60 (1995) 163–91, especially pp. 164–81; Zenger (ed.), *Einleitung*, 73; S. McEvenue, "The Speaker(s) in Ex 1–15," in *Biblische Theologie und gesellschaftlicher Wandel: Für Norbert Lohfink SJ* (ed. G. Braulik, W. Gross, and S. McEvenue; Freiburg-im-Breisgau, 1993) 220–36.

36. See N. Lohfink, "Deutéronome et Pentateuque: État de la recherche," in *Le Pentateuque: Débats et recherches* (ed. P. Haudebert; LD 151; Paris, 1992) 35–64 = "Deuteronomium und Pentateuch: Zum Stand der Forschung," *Studien zum Deuteronomium und zur deuteronomistischen Literatur*, vol. 3 (Stuttgarter biblische Aufsatzbände; Altes Testament 20; Stuttgart, 1995) 13–38, especially pp. 14–15.

37. Neither Rendtorff nor Blum deals with this question. However, two other representatives of the "Heidelberg school" have shown an interest in the legislative codes. See R. Albertz, *A History of Israelite Religion in the Old Testament Period* (2 vols.; trans. J. Bowden; London, 1994); F. Crüsemann, *Bewahrung der Freiheit: Das Thema des Dekalogs in solzialgeschichtlicher Perspektive* (Kaiser Traktate 78; Munich, 1983); idem, "Das Bundesbuch: Historischer Ort und institutioneller Hintergrund," in *Congress Volume: Jerusalem, 1986* (VTSup 40; Leiden, 1988) 27–41; idem, "Der Exodus als Heiligung: Zur rechtsgeschichtlichen Bedeutung des Heiligkeitsgesetzes," in *Die hebräische Bibel und ihre zweifache Nachgeschichte: Festschrift für Rolf Rendtorff zum 65. Geburtstag* (ed. E. Blum, C. Macholz, and E. W. Stegemann; Neukirchen-Vluyn, 1990) 117–29; idem, *The Torah: Theology and Social History of Old Testament Law* (trans. A. W. Mahnke; Edinburgh, 1996).

b. A Postdeuteronomic Yahwist

In two different places, Canada and Switzerland, the idea has developed that the Yahwist was not the most ancient source. In fact, its relationship to Deuteronomy and the Deuteronomistic work is suggestive of a much later date. At present, a good number of scholars support the idea that the Yahwist is more recent than Deuteronomy and the Deuteronomistic work. Their arguments are based on literary, historical, and archaeological considerations.

• From an archaeological point of view, there is no support for the existence of a premonarchic "patriarchal period." This is also the case for the Exodus and the wanderings in the wilderness: there is no formal archaeological evidence to support the historicity of the biblical narratives of these events. This conclusion is obviously in contradiction with the theses of the Albright school.

• Van Seters expresses doubt with regard to the work of Gunkel, Noth, and von Rad on the oral tradition. It is impossible, according to Van Seters, to rediscover an ancient oral tradition behind the patriarchal or Mosaic traditions.

• There are many linguistic, thematic, and theological connections between the so-called Yahwist and the writings that date to the Exile or shortly after the Exile. Some extrabiblical parallels confirm these connections between the Yahwist and the later periods of Israel's history.

• For Van Seters and Rose, the Yahwist chronologically follows the Deuteronomist and corrects him. The Yahwist is opposed to the Deuteronomist's legalism and nationalism and reveals himself as more liberal, more humanistic and universalistic. The work of the Yahwist actually constitutes a "foreword" added to the work of the Deuteronomist *a posteriori*.

• The Yahwist is a historian comparable to the Greek historians of the same era, such as Herodotus and Hellanicus. His purpose is analogous: he wants to create a consciousness and identity for the people of Israel based on their past, just as the Greek historians did for their own nation.

• The most renowned representatives of this stream of thought are the Canadians F. V. Winnett, N. E. Wagner, and above all J. Van Seters;[38] in

---

38. F. V. Winnett, *The Mosaic Tradition* (Toronto, 1949); idem, "Re-examining the Foundations." N. E. Wagner, "Pentateuchal Criticism: No Clear Future"; idem, "Abraham and David?" in *Studies in the Ancient Palestinian World Presented to Professor F. V. Winnett* (ed. J. W. Wevers and D. B. Redford; Toronto Semitic Texts and Studies; Toronto, 1972) 117–40. See, above all, J. Van Seters, *Abraham in History and Tradition*; idem, *In Search of History: Historiography in the Ancient World and the Origins of Biblical History* (New Haven, CT, 1983; repr. Winona Lake, IN, 1997); idem, *Der Jahwist als Historiker* (ed. H. H. Schmid; Theologische Studien 134; Zurich, 1987); idem, *Prologue to History: The Yahwist as Historian in Genesis* (Louisville, 1992); idem, *The Life of Moses*; idem, "Cultic Laws in the Covenant Code (Exodus 20,22–23,33) and Their Relationship to Deuteronomy and the Holiness Code," in *Studies in the Book of Exodus* (ed. M. Vervenne; Leuven, 1996) 319–45.

Switzerland and Germany, H. H. Schmid, M. Rose, H. Vorländer, and H.-C. Schmitt.[39]

Recently, C. Levin published a monograph on the Yahwist in which he presented a position similar in some respects to the views of Van Seters and Rose.[40] Levin's Yahwist is an editor or a redactor who, during the Babylonian Exile, collected and reinterpreted ancient fragmentary sources. He wanted to give new hope to the exiles, and for this reason he was critical of the Deuteronomist, especially with regard to the centralization of the cult. In the eyes of J, Yнwн is present everywhere, not just in the temple of Jerusalem. He accompanies and blesses his people in their land as well as in Exile, just as he accompanied and blessed the patriarchs and then his people in Egypt and in the wilderness. For Levin, J is an Exilic redaction, posterior to the Deuteronomist.

His hypothesis reproduces elements from several models proposed earlier. In the beginning, there were only isolated narratives, as in the hypothesis of "fragments." The Exilic Yahwist collected these texts and compiled them into a single account. This redactional activity has some points in common with the model proposed by the hypothesis of "complements." Ultimately, Levin revises the documentary hypothesis. According to him, the Pentateuch is composed of three "documents" or "sources": the Yahwist, the Priestly source, and Deuteronomy.[41]

After this survey, it becomes difficult to argue for the existence of an ancient work (perhaps going back to the beginnings of the monarchy) that recounts

---

39. H. H. Schmid, *Der sogenannte Jahwist: Beobachtungen und Fragen zur Pentateuchforschung* (Zurich, 1976); idem, "In Search of New Approaches in Pentateuchal Research," *JSOT* 3 (1977) 33–42; idem, "Vers une théologie du Pentateuque," in *Le Pentateuque en question: Les origines et la composition des cinq premiers livres de la Bible à la lumière des recherches récentes* (ed. A. de Pury; Le monde de la Bible; Geneva, 1989) 361–86. M. Rose, *Deuteronomist und Jahwist*; idem, "La croissance du corpus historiographique de la Bible: Une proposition," *RTP* 118 (1986) 217–326; idem, "Empoigner le Pentateuque par sa fin! L'investiture de Josué et la mort de Moïse," *Le Pentateuque en question* (ed. A. de Pury; Geneva, 1989) 129–47. H. Vorländer, *Die Entstehungszeit des jehowistischen Geschichtswerkes* (Europäische Hochschulschriften 23; Theologie 109; Frankfurt, 1978). See H.-C. Schmitt, *Die nichtpriesterliche Josephsgeschichte* (BZAW 154; Berlin, 1980); idem, "'Priesterliches' und 'prophetisches' Geschichtsverständnis in der Meerwundererzählung Ex 13,17–14,31: Beobachtungen zur Endredaktion des Pentateuch," in *Textgemäß: Aufsätze und Beiträge zur Hermeneutik des Alten Testaments* (FS E. Würthwein; ed. W. Zimmerli; Göttingen, 1979) 138–55; idem, "Redaktion des Pentateuch im Geiste der Prophetie: Beobachtungen zur Bedeutung des 'Glauben'-Thematik innerhalb der Theologie des Pentateuch," *VT* 32 (1982) 170–89; idem, "Die Hintergründe der 'neuesten Pentateuchkritik' und der literarische Befund der Josefsgeschichte," *ZAW* 97 (1985) 161–79.

40. See Levin, *Der Jahwist.*

41. For an evaluation of Levin, see the reviews by E. Blum, *TLZ* 120 (1995) 786–90; D. Carr, *CBQ* 57 (1995) 354–55; E. Otto, "Kritik der Pentateuchkomposition," especially pp. 182–90; J.-L. Ska, "Le Pentateuque: État de la recherche à partir de quelques nouvelles 'Introductions,'" *Bib* 77 (1996) 425–28.

Israel's origins. Furthermore, I prefer to leave open the question about a relationship between the Exilic or Postexilic Yahwist and the Deuteronomic/Deuteronomistic work, as some scholars have proposed. These studies have another weak point: they only concentrate on the narrative sections of the Pentateuch. With the exception of an article by Van Seters, there are no exhaustive studies of the legal texts.[42]

As for the posited affinity between the Yahwist and the Greek historians, some major difficulties prevent us from pushing the comparison any further than a few superficial analogies. The Pentateuch is a religious work; it contains laws that give it an undeniably legal character; and it does not present itself explicitly as the work of a single author. Finally, the purpose of the Pentateuch is neither to inform nor to entertain the reader, unlike the works of the Greek authors. The Pentateuch presents itself as a normative text for Israel's life.[43]

c. A Limited Yahwist

In order to respond to the difficulties advanced by the authors presented above, some scholars have returned to a version of the hypothesis of complements. They presuppose the existence of a primitive, very limited Yahwistic source that was completed in various periods. Therefore, these scholars postulate that the Yahwistic work was formed by a series of successive redactional additions (*Fortschreibung*). It is sometimes possible to distinguish seven levels or more in a single pericope. The best-known representatives of this trend are P. Weimar, E. Zenger (at first), and J. Vermeylen.[44]

E. Zenger has proposed a slightly different hypothesis.[45] His model reproduces elements of the hypothesis of fragments or "narrative cycles" (*Erzählkränze*) as well as of the documentary hypothesis. At the first stage of the redactional process, only the "narrative cycles" existed independently:[46] a series

---

42. Van Seters, "Cultic Laws in the Covenant Code" (see n. 38).

43. See Blenkinsopp, *Pentateuch*, 37–42.

44. Some significant works: P. Weimar, *Untersuchungen zur priesterschriftlichen Exodusgeschichte* (Forschung zur Bibel 9; Würzburg, 1973); idem, *Untersuchungen zur Redaktionsgeschichte des Pentateuch* (BZAW 146; Berlin, 1977); idem, *Die Berufung des Mose*; idem, *Die Meerwundererzählung*; E. Zenger, *Die Sinaitheophanie* (Forschung zur Bibel 3; Würzburg, 1971); idem, *Israel am Sinai: Analysen und Interpretation zu Exodus 17–34* (Altenberge, 1982); Weimar and Zenger, *Exodus*; E. Zenger, "Le thème de la 'sortie d'Égypte' et la naissance du Pentateuque," in *Le Pentateuque en question* (ed. A. de Pury; Geneva, 1989) 301–31; J. Vermeylen, "La formation du Pentateuque à la lumière de l'exégèse historico-critique"; idem, "Les premières étapes de la formation du Pentateuque," in *Le Pentateuque en question*, 149–97; idem, "Le vol de la bénédiction paternelle: Une lecture de Gen 27," in *Pentateuchal and Deuteronomistic Studies* (ed. C. Brekelman and J. Lust; BETL 94; Leuven, 1990) 23–40. For a short evaluation, see Zenger (ed.), *Einleitung*, 72.

45. Ibid., 73 and 108–23.

46. Summary in ibid., 119.

of narratives about Abraham and Sarah as well as about Abraham and Lot (Genesis 12–19*), coming from the kingdom of Judah; a narrative cycle about Jacob and Laban, produced in the Northern Kingdom and later elaborated on in the kingdom of Judah; the Joseph story, which perhaps originated in the North or, more likely, in the South; the ancient story of the Exodus (Exodus 1–14*), written in the Northern Kingdom.

The first redactional work of any size to advance a panoramic view of Israel's history was composed in Jerusalem after 700 B.C.E.—that is, after the fall of Samaria in 722 and Sennacherib's campaign in 701 and under the influence of the prophets Amos, Hosea, and Isaiah. Zenger calls this work the *Jerusalemer Geschichtswerk*, "Jerusalemite historical work." Its authors probably came from priestly and prophetic circles. They created, among other texts, the Sinai pericope. During the Exile, this work was again revised and expanded; this is how the old "Covenant Code" (Exod 20:22–23:33) was incorporated. Zenger entitles this "revised" work the *Exilisches Geschichtswerk*, "Exilic historical work."[47] This is the most characteristic, most original aspect of Zenger's hypothesis. Finally, first the "Priestly narrative," written during the Exile ca. 520 B.C.E., and then the Exilic/Postexilic version of Deuteronomy were added to the "Exilic history."

These proposals are not easy to evaluate. Nevertheless, they are hardly credible, because they increase the number of levels and redactional insertions to the point of exceptional complexity. As Ockham put it, *Frustra fit per plura quod fieri potest per pauciora*,[48] a statement that can be restated "Why complicate what can be simplified?" We could also borrow another of Ockham's expressions: *Redactiones non sunt multiplicandae praeter necessitatem*.[49] The best hypothesis is the one that explains the largest number of facts with the greatest simplicity. Zenger's hypothesis itself is not uninteresting, but genuine correspondences with other sections of the Bible—for example, the prophetic books—are lacking. Zenger speaks of the influence of Amos, Hosea, and Isaiah on the "Jerusalemite historical work," but he does not discuss the nature of this influence. Finally, he does not sufficiently take into account the fact that Postexilic redactional work must have taken place when the various "sources" were compiled.

Zenger maintains a "high" (early) date with regard to the "Jerusalemite historical work" because the theology of this history is different from the Deuteronomistic work. In other words, the scheme "unfaithfulness/punishment/

---

47. Ibid., 73.

48. Literally, "In vain one augments what may be reduced."

49. "Redactions should not be multiplied needlessly." The original expression in Latin is: *Entia non sunt multiplicanda praeter necessitatem* ("Beings should not be multiplied without necessity"). We can also quote Noth, who writes: *Eine literarkritische Möglichkeit ist jedoch noch keine literarkritische Notwendigkeit* ("The possibility of discovering sources does not imply the necessity of discovering them"; M. Noth, *1 Könige* [BKAT 9/1; Neukirchen-Vluyn, 1969] 246).

conversion/salvation," which is typical of the Deuteronomist, does not appear in Genesis–Numbers. The promises made to the patriarchs in Genesis do not use the Deuteronomistic scheme of "promise/fulfillment." The themes of conversion and peace, characteristic of the Deuteronomist, are not found in Genesis–Numbers. To conclude, according to Zenger, the theology of sin in Genesis–Numbers is not the theology of the Deuteronomist.[50]

Be this as it may, the difference can easily be explained if we postulate a Postexilic (postdeuteronomistic) date for several problematic texts in Genesis–Numbers. We should not underestimate Postexilic literary activity either, an activity that is evident in the books of Chronicles, Ezra–Nehemiah, the last sections added to the book of Isaiah, not to speak of a large part of Leviticus. The reconstruction of the temple and the restoration of the faith community within the Persian Empire created a new situation that undoubtedly called for the revision and reinterpretation of the "data" presented by the sources and the most ancient traditions. This was particularly necessary with regard to the Sinai pericope, which constitutes the core of today's Pentateuch.

d. The Classic Position: W. H. Schmidt, F. Kohata, H. Seebass, L. Ruppert, and L. Schmidt

A small number of influential scholars continue to defend the documentary hypothesis in its classic form. They persistently postulate the existence of a Yahwist at the beginning of the United Monarchy. In this context, they like to refer to the reign of Solomon. The best-known representative of this stream of thought is W. H. Schmidt.[51] His colleague in Bonn, H. Seebass, follows the same path.[52] One of W. H. Schmidt's students, F. Kohata, has presented her views in a study of Exodus 3–14.[53]

---

50. Zenger, "Le thème de la 'sortie d'Égypte,'" 328–29.

51. See, above all, his Introduction: W. H. Schmidt, *Einführung in das Alte Testament*; idem, *Exodus 1,1–6,30*; idem, "Ein Theologe in salomonischer Zeit? Plädoyer für den Jahwisten," *BZ* 25 (1981) 82–102; idem, "Plädoyer für die Quellenscheidung," *BZ* 32 (1988) 1–14; idem, "Elementäre Erwägungen zur Quellenscheidung im Pentateuch," in *Congress Volume: Leuven, 1989* (ed. J. A. Emerton; VTSup 43; Leiden, 1991) 22–45; idem, "Die Intention der beiden Plagenerzählungen (Exodus 7–10) in ihrem Kontext," in *Studies in the Book of Exodus* (ed. M. Vervenne; Leuven, 1996) 225–43.

52. See, among others, H. Seebass, "Gehörten Verheißungen zur ältesten Bestand der Vätererzählungen?" *Bib* 64 (1983) 189–210; idem, "Que reste-t-il du Yahwiste et de l'Élohiste?" in *Le Pentateuque en question* (ed. A. de Pury; Geneva, 1989) 199–214; idem, "À titre d'exemple: Réflexions sur Gen 16//21,8–21//26,1–33," in *Le Pentateuque en question*, 215–30; idem, *Genesis I: Urgeschichte (1,1–11,26)* (Neukirchen-Vluyn, 1996). H. Seebass is presently writing a commentary on the book of Numbers for the series Biblischer Kommentar [editor's note: this has now appeared: *Numeri* (BKAT 4; Neukirchen-Vluyn, 1993)].

53. F. Kohata, *Jahwist und Priesterschrift in Exodus 3–14*; idem, "Die Endredaktion (Rp) der Meerwundererzählung," *AJBI* 14 (1988) 10–37.

Other scholars follow the "beaten path" of the documentary hypothesis, although they often correct the map (as is the case, for example, with L. Ruppert[54] and L. Schmidt[55]). Recently, these scholars have influenced scholars outside Germany as well.[56] The validity of these scholars' positions essentially depends on their ability to respond to the objections raised by the authors mentioned above. The question is therefore: How shall we solve the new problems now under discussion? Can new wine be put into old wineskins? Can we propose old solutions to solve new problems?

e. Conclusion: What Remains of the Yahwist?

After this overview of the recent discussion on the Yahwist, it seems clear that there is no lack of problems. The tranquil consensus that reigned in the 1970s has receded in the face of confused dissent. Nowadays, everyone proposes different dates, other explanatory models and, frequently, different boundaries of the texts. The number of theories is increasing, but not one of them is truly convincing. Despite these uncertainties, we may draw some conclusions. Three points stand out clearly.

1. It seems increasingly difficult to agree that an ancient Yahwist source ever existed. At the origin of the tradition, there was not one single complete document; instead there were "narrative cycles" (*Erzählkränze*).[57] This model, which is close to the hypothesis of "fragments," provides a better explanation

---

54. L. Ruppert, "Die Aporien der gegenwärtigen Pentateuchdiskussion und die Josef-erzählung der Genesis," *BZ* 29 (1985) 31–48 = *Studien* (see below), 89–109; idem, *Genesis: Ein kritischer und theologischer Kommentar*, vol. 1: *Gn 1,1–11,26* (Forschung zur Bibel 70; Würzburg, 1992); also see his collection of articles *Studien zur Literaturgeschichte des Alten Testaments* (Stuttgarter Biblische Aufsatzbände 18; Stuttgart, 1994). Sometimes L. Ruppert comes close to the propositions of P. Weimar. Cf. Zenger (ed.), *Einleitung*, 72.

55. Above all, see: L. Schmidt, *Literarische Studien zur Josephsgeschichte* (BZAW 167; Berlin, 1986); idem, "Jakob erschleicht sich den väterlichen Segen: Literarkritik und Redaktion in Genesis 27,1–45," *ZAW* 100 (1988) 159–83; idem, *Beobachtungen und Fragen zu der Plagener-zählung in Exodus 7,14–11,10* (StudBibl; Leiden, 1990); idem, "Väterverheißungen und Pentateuchfrage," *ZAW* 104 (1992) 1–27; idem, *Studien zur Priesterschrift*; idem, "Weisheit und Geschichte beim Elohisten," in *"Jedes Ding hat seine Zeit": Studien zur israelitischen und altorientalischen Weisheit. Diethelm Michel zum 65. Geburtstag* (BZAW 241; Berlin, 1996) 209–25.

56. This is basically the position of the Introduction by Campbell and O'Brien, *Sources of the Pentateuch*; also see S. Boorer (student of A. F. Campbell), *The Promise of Land as Oath: A Key to the Formation of the Pentateuch* (BZAW 205; Berlin, 1992); K. Berge, *Die Zeit des Jah-wisten: Ein Beitrag zur Datierung jahwistischer Vätertexte* (BZAW 186; Berlin, 1990); E. Cortese, "Pentateuco: La strada vecchia e la nuova," *Liber Annuus* 43 (1993) 71–87; cf. E. W. Nicholson, "The Pentateuch in Recent Research: A Time for Caution," *Congress Volume: Leuven, 1989* (ed. J. A. Emerton; VTSup 43; Leuven, 1991) 10–21.

57. Compare with the models of R. Rendtorff, E. Blum (for Genesis), and E. Zenger.

for certain facts that have never received enough consideration. I am going to illustrate this by presenting some of these facts.

There are, for example, few connections between the story of the origins (Genesis 2–11) and the stories of the patriarchs.[58] In Genesis 2–11, the "earth" (*'ădāmâ*) is the cultivated land; but in the patriarchal traditions, this word designates the entire earth (Gen 12:3; 28:14) or the Promised Land (28:15). Another term signifying the "earth" (*'ereṣ*) designates the world in Genesis 1–11 and the Promised Land in Genesis 12–50. The patriarchs are nomads, while the first inhabitants of the land are farmers. The language in Genesis 1–11 is colored by later wisdom teachings.[59]

Differences also exist within the patriarchal cycles. The first patriarch, Abraham, lived in the southern part of the territory of Canaan, in Hebron (Gen 13:18) or Beer-sheba (21:33; 22:19). He moved around in the Negeb (12:9), went down to Egypt (12:10–20), and settled for a while at Gerar, near the Philistines (20:1; 21:34). Jacob, on the other hand, is in contact with the north (Shechem, Bethel; Gen 35:1–7)[60] or Haran in northern Mesopotamia (chaps. 29–33). Many factors distinguish the story of Joseph from the other traditions: here neither the promises nor the blessing are mentioned.

When we come to the Exodus, the texts no longer deal with the "land promised to the patriarchs" (Rendtorff). The Sinai theophany also remains isolated. Is it ever mentioned during the wanderings in the wilderness? It is therefore more reasonable to imagine that, in the beginning, there were only small groups of isolated narratives, with their specific topics. These groups were only assembled into one vast unit at a second stage in order to create a "history of the origins of Israel."

2. The redactional work took some time, and it was probably completed in several steps. We should ask ourselves, however, whether the attempt to create links between the various "blocks" occurred long before the Deuteronomic/Deuteronomistic work (Dt/Dtr) and the Priestly narrative (P). The "small historical creeds" (Deut 6:21–23; 26:3–9) and the Priestly text of Exod 6:2–8 are the first texts to connect the patriarchs to the Exodus. Another text of the same kind is Num 20:14–16.[61]

---

58. See F. Crüsemann, "Die Eigenständigkeit der Urgeschichte: Ein Beitrag zur Diskussion um den 'Jahwisten,'" in *Die Botschaft und die Boten: Festschrift für Hans Walter Wolff zum 70. Geburtstag* (ed. J. Jeremias and L. Perlitt; Neukirchen-Vluyn, 1981) 9–29; Blenkinsopp, *Pentateuch*, 64–66, 69–70, and 77–78; Zenger (ed.), *Einleitung*, 114–15; cf. my "Pentateuque," 251.

59. See Alonso Schökel, "Motivos sapienciales y de alianza en Gn 2–3."

60. Beer-sheba is mentioned, however, in Gen 28:10.

61. Kreutzer, *Die Frühgeschichte Israels in Bekenntnis und Verkündigung des Alten Testaments.*

We must not reject too quickly the idea that this redactional work followed Dt/Dtr and P, rather than preceding them. The theological syntheses of Dt/Dtr and P created an indispensable framework for the organization of the earliest narrative material.[62] Despite the opposition of some renowned scholars, it seems increasingly more difficult to speak of a Yahwist going back to Solomon's time, and there are good reasons for this.[63] In fact, the universal and mono-theistic (or monolatristic) theology of the texts traditionally attributed to J could hardly have preceded the preaching of the first prophets and the first syn-theses of the Deuteronomic work. The studies of Israel's religion do not en-courage us to situate this theology at the beginning of the history of the chosen people. The "sense of history" and the techniques of literary composition that we encounter in the classic J could hardly have preceded the appearance of the first literary works of the prophets or similar "historical" works produced in the ancient Near East. There is nothing comparable from the time of David and Solomon. If J had written before the prophets, they would have taken his work into consideration when talking about Israel's past. According to recent studies, some of the fundamental texts of the traditional J, such as Gen 12:1–4a or the story of the origins (Gen 2:4b–8:22), are late texts. Critical investigation of the "promises made to the patriarchs" is going in the same direction.

The often-evoked parallelism between the narratives of 1–2 Samuel (con-cerning David's ascension to the throne and his succession) and the classic J does not stand up under criticism either. If J had to provide a base for the com-position of 1–2 Samuel, as is sometimes maintained, why then are the connec-tions between the two not more obvious? In addition, the theologies of J and 1–2 Samuel have few points in common.

I have demonstrated that there are many reasons to think that J, if it ever ex-isted, was not a very early work. Moreover, J should be considered the product of redactional work that elaborated on older narrative cycles. The question whether J was composed before the Exile (Zenger), during the Exile (Levin), or after the Exile (Rose, Van Seters) remains for the moment unanswered. I personally think that it is necessary to give more consideration to postdeuter-onomistic and postpriestly literary activity.[64]

---

62. P provides a good portion of the Pentateuch's plotline. See Wellhausen, *Prolegomena to the History of Israel*, 332: "It is as if Q[P] were the scarlet thread on which the pearls of JE are hung"; Noth, *History of Pentateuchal Traditions*, 11.

63. See the objections of Blenkinsopp, *Pentateuch*, 124–25; Whybray, *Introduction*, 25–27; Zenger (ed.), *Einleitung*, 108–10; Carr, *Reading the Fractures of Genesis*, 220–32; cf. Ska, "Pen-tateuque," 251.

64. See E. Otto, "Die nachpriesterschriftliche Pentateuchredaktion im Buch Exodus," in *Studies in the Book of Exodus* (ed. M. Vervenne; Leuven, 1996) 61–111.

3. My last observation relates to methodology. It should be noted that more and more scholars tend to agree on the starting point of their research. The number of those who presuppose the existence of sources such as J without any further justification is constantly decreasing. The analysis begins "upstream"— that is, it starts with the text in its current form. In this way, synchrony (the study of the text in its final form) precedes diachrony (the study of the text's origin). This means that, before establishing the existence of sources, an exegete examines the structure and coherence of the text. Only after this, and on the basis of solid evidence—for example, tension, "fracture," or "incoherency"— does he or she go on to the next stage and speak of "sources" or of "redactions."

It has become more difficult to "carve up" or to "atomize" a well-wrought narrative in order to discover two or three sources in it because—whether we like it or not—the episode must be present in all these sources. Even when discussing the question of "sources" or "redactions," scholars prefer to verify the solidity of their conclusions. The time when it was possible to distribute all the verses of the Pentateuch with great assurance into four big "baskets," J, E, D, or P, now belongs to the past, at least for the majority of specialists.

Scholars want to verify the links connecting the various texts before affirming any kind of kinship between them. They begin their study by establishing a provisional relative chronology; then they try to establish a connection between the texts and certain periods of Israel's history. We must admit that Rendtorff and Blum were right on this point: the study of the form of the text must precede "source criticism" (*Literaturkritik*).[65]

To conclude: along with the Elohist, the Yahwist has also lost credit. The features of his face have become ever blurrier. This is why certain scholars prefer to speak about "nonpriestly texts" (Blum, Carr); and it is possible that, one day, Pentateuchal scholars will even abandon the abbreviation J.

Whatever the Yahwist's future may be, one thing is certain: anyone who reads the nonpriestly texts in a critical way today needs more than ever to distinguish clearly the narrative units and the legal codes, on the one hand, and the more recent redactional layers, on the other. At present, regarding the beginnings of the traditions, the model that increasingly stands out is the model of "fragments" or "narrative cycles."

---

65. See my "Récit et récit métadiexégétique en Ex 1–15: Remarques critiques et essai d'interprétation de Ex 3,16–22," in *Le Pentateuque: Débats et recherches* (ed. P. Haudebert; LD 151; Paris, 1992) 135–71, especially 144–46; Carr (*Reading the Fractures of Genesis*) applies this method to the book of Genesis with good results.

3. The Problem of the Priestly Narrative [66]

The Priestly narrative (P) never found itself in the path of the cyclone that ravaged research on the Pentateuch. Because of the especially recognizable style and theology of the texts belonging to this "source," they have always been relatively easy to identify: for example, Gen 1:1–2:4a; 17; 23; 28:1–9; 35:11–15; Exod 6:2–8; 25–32; 35–40*; Leviticus 9; Num 20:1–13*; and the Priestly layer in Genesis 6–9; Exodus 7–11; 14; 16; Numbers 13–14.[67]

With the exception of a few discussions on the demarcation of the Priestly narrative, there are five main problems: the nature of the Priestly narrative, its conclusion, its relationship to the "Holiness Code" (Leviticus 17–26), its theology, and its date.

a. The Nature of the Priestly Narratives [68]

Recently, various authors have affirmed that the Priestly Writer (P) did not compose a complete, independent "source" of the Pentateuch.[69] Instead, his work seems to constitute a redactional layer, a kind of commentary and complement to the ancient sources. The main argument in favor of this opinion is the fact that P is incomplete. It does not contain a detailed account of everything that we find in the other sources of the Pentateuch. It does not mention Cain and Abel; it leaves out many episodes in the lives of Abraham and Sarah as well as Jacob and Esau; it says almost nothing about Joseph; it avoids speaking about the Covenant at Sinai and contains very little about the wanderings in the wilderness. Of course, no one asked P to furnish a parallel for each text present in the earlier sources. The real problem is situated elsewhere; it is related to certain gaps that appear in the Priestly Writer's own framework.

---

66. On this point, see Zenger (ed.), *Einleitung*, 92–108; J.-L. Ska, "De la relative indépendance de l'écrit sacerdotal," *Bib* 76 (1995) 396–415. For an English translation of P, with a short commentary, see Campbell and O'Brien, *Sources of the Pentateuch*, 21–90.

67. For a delineation of this text, see Zenger (ed.), *Einleitung*, 94–95. Also see the important contribution of K. Elliger, "Sinn und Ursprung der priesterlichen Geschichtserzählung," *ZTK* 49 (1952) 121–42 = *Kleine Schriften zum Alten Testament* (TBü 32; Munich, 1966) 174–98. Delimitation of the texts: pp. 121–22 = pp. 174–75.

68. See my "Relative indépendance," 397–402. For the bibliography, see p. 402 n. 24.

69. See, above all, Cross, *Canaanite Myth and Hebrew Epic,* 293–325; Rendtorff, *Überlieferungsgeschichtliche Problem*, 130–46; Blum, *Komposition der Vätergeschichte*, 130–46; idem, *Studien zur Komposition des Pentateuch*, 219–332 (with important nuances); Van Seters, *Abraham in History and Tradition*, 279–95; idem, *Life of Moses*, 103–12. This opinion is also shared by P. Volz, "P ist kein Erzähler," in Volz and Rudolph, *Elohist als Erzähler*, 135–42. For a discussion of these theses, see Lohfink, "Priesterschrift," 189–225, especially pp. 196–201 (bibliography p. 197 n. 28) = *Studien zum Pentateuch*, 213–53, especially pp. 221–25 (with bibliography p. 221 n. 28).

In the P narrative, several episodes or passages are missing, even though they should appear, because they are necessary for the coherence of the text. For example, P does not mention the birth of Jacob and Esau (Gen 25:26b). In Gen 27:46–28:9, Isaac sends Jacob to his Uncle Laban so that he can get married. But, after that, the reader looks in vain for a reference to this marriage in P. The beginning of the Joseph story is very fragmentary and needs elaboration that is not found in the Priestly narrative.[70] Moses appears in Exod 6:2 without having been introduced. The departure from Egypt in Exod 12:40–42 is not explained. There are still other analogous cases. For example, Gen 2:4b, "These are the generations of the heavens and the earth," seems to be the title of the following passage (Gen 2:4b–25, a nonpriestly text), rather than the conclusion to the preceding one (P-text). In Exod 7:1–5, YHWH sends Moses on a mission to Pharaoh. But when Moses and Aaron meet the king, they do not transmit the message entrusted to them. In Exod 14:15 YHWH asks Moses: "Why do you cry out to me?" In the preceding narrative, however, Moses did not cry out!

In order to solve these problems, it is necessary to study the entire Priestly narrative. Two facts emerge from this study: first, as we have just seen, the Priestly Writer is incomplete; second, the theology, the vocabulary, and the way of presenting the events are so distinct from the other sources that P cannot be considered a "complement." His work has a certain independence; this explains why we prefer to talk about the "relative independence" of P. The Priestly Writer knows the ancient sources and presupposes that his reader knows them. He dialogues with these traditions, corrects and reinterprets them, and proposes a new vision of Israel's history. Throughout all of this, P develops his own theology, which is both *independent* of and *related* to the ancient traditions.

Let us make a comparison: P builds a house, but uses the traditions that have preceded him as a foundation. But he is not satisfied with completing, decorating, embellishing, and adding to a work begun by others before him. P builds a new residence on these ancient foundations.[71]

b. The Conclusion of the Priestly Narrative[72]

It is possible to enumerate at least five different positions that hope to solve the problem of the conclusion: the narrative of the Priestly Writer ends in Josh

---

70. These different elements have been enumerated by Noth, *History of Pentateuchal Traditions*, 14–15.

71. See N. Lohfink, "Priesterschrift," 197 and 200 = *Studien zum Pentateuch*, 221–22, 224–25; J.-L. Ska, "Relative indépendance," 404–5.

72. See ibid., 413–15; idem, "Le Pentateuque," 263–65; cf. Zenger (ed.), *Einleitung*, 94–96. For bibliography, see Lohfink, "Priesterschrift," 198 n. 30 = *Studien zum Pentateuch*, 223–24 n. 30.

18:1, 19:51 (Lohfink, Blenkinsopp[73]). The traditional position, since Well-hausen and especially since Noth, is that P concludes in Deut 34:1, 7–9. L. Perlitt attacks this position and contends that P ends earlier, in Numbers 27.[74] Zenger and Otto go back as far as Leviticus 9; according to them, P ends his account with the solemn inauguration of the cult.[75] Finally, T. Pola is even more radical: in his view, P ends in Exodus 40.[76]

This problem is complex because it touches on the very nature of the Priestly narrative. In order to know where it ends, it is necessary to know P's purpose. If we say, for example, that P's only aim was the establishment of the cult, he may very well have concluded in Leviticus or even in Exodus 40. If P was interested in the "land," he would have given his opinion on this subject,[77] in which case it becomes difficult not to attribute certain texts to P that explain why Israel, or some of its leaders, did not enter into the land of Israel—for example, Numbers 13–14* and Num 20:1–13*. Furthermore, the condemnation of Moses and Aaron raises the question of their succession; this question is not answered until Num 20:22–29* and chap. 27*.

How can this question be solved? The argumentation often runs the risk of being circular: research proceeds from a "concept" that determines the nature of P in order to identify the corresponding texts and, at the same time, it defines the nature of P on the basis of these same texts. In order to avoid this risk, it seems preferable to begin with the texts that are incontestably attributed to P. This is the case with Genesis 17 and Exod 6:2–8. The vocabulary and the theology of these two pericopes are clearly Priestly. The first text contains the Priestly "program" regarding the patriarchs; Exod 6:2–8 is a summary of Israel's history reaching from Abraham to the entry into the Promised Land.

Now, both texts speak at length about the "land." There are only a few doubts regarding P's authorship of Exod 6:8: "I will bring you into the land that I swore to give to Abraham, Isaac, and Jacob; I will give it to you for a possession. I am YHWH."[78] Some scholars want to see the verse as a Deuteronomis-

---

73. See J. Blenkinsopp, "The Structure of P," *CBQ* 38 (1976) 275–92, especially pp. 287–91; idem, *Pentateuch*, 185; for N. Lohfink, see the preceding note and my "Relative indépendance," 413 n. 70.

74. L. Perlitt, "Priesterschrift im Deuteronomium?" *ZAW* 100 Supplement (1988), 65–88 = *Deuteronomium-Studien* (FAT 8; Tübingen, 1994) 123–43. Cf. my "Pentateuque," 263 n. 67.

75. Zenger (ed.), *Einleitung*, 94–96; see Otto, "Die nachpriesterschriftliche Pentateuchredaktion," 83 n. 100.

76. T. Pola, *Die ursprüngliche Priesterschrift: Beobachtungen zur Literarkritik und Traditionsgeschichte von P^g* (WMANT 70; Neukirchen-Vluyn, 1995).

77. Cf. E. Cortese, *La terra di Canaan nella storia sacerdotale del Pentateuco* (RivBSup 5; Brescia, 1972).

78. Kohata (*Jahwist und Priesterschrift*, 29–34) attributes this verse to a Deuteronomic editor because P is not interested in the land. But the vocabulary of Exod 6:8 is not Deuteronomic, because it uses the verb "swear" (*šbʿ, Niphal*), whereas the text has the expression

tic or late addition. However, the weakness of this position is easily exposed. Genesis 17, the text of the Covenant between God and Abraham and the institution of circumcision, explicitly speaks about the promise of land (Gen 17:8). Exod 6:2–8 refers to this promise at the beginning of the passage and at the end (Exod 6:4, 8) in order to show that the Exodus and the entry into the land fulfill the promise made to the fathers (cf. 6:5). We cannot (as some scholars would like) eliminate v. 8 without destroying the structure and meaning of the entire passage:[79]

> [2]God also spoke to Moses and said to him: "I am the LORD. [3]I appeared to Abraham, Isaac, and Jacob by my name '*'ēl šadday*'; I did not make myself known to them under my name, YHWH. [4]I also established my covenant with them, to give them the land of Canaan, the land in which they resided as aliens. [5]I have also heard the groaning of the Israelites whom the Egyptians are holding as slaves, and I have remembered my covenant. [6]Say therefore to the Israelites, 'I am YHWH, your God, and I will free you from the burdens of the Egyptians and deliver you from slavery to them. I will redeem you with an outstretched arm and with mighty acts of judgment. [7]I will take you as my people, and I will be your God. You shall know that I am YHWH your God, who has freed you from the burdens of the Egyptians. [8]I will bring you into the land that I swore to give to Abraham, Isaac, and Jacob; I will give it to you for a possession. I am YHWH.'"

I do not intend at this point to go into the details of this text, which has an especially rich meaning. The important point that needs to be underlined is the promise of the land. God connects his name "YHWH" to the fulfillment of this promise made to the patriarchs, and God's faithfulness to his promises is the impetus for the Exodus. In other words, God brings Israel out of Egypt and leads them to the Promised Land because he remembers the Covenant made with the patriarchs (cf. Genesis 17).

Let us now return to our question: Is it possible to eliminate v. 8 from this oracle without also leaving out v. 4—that is, the God who promised to give the land? If we eliminate v. 4, we will also have to eliminate v. 5, which mentions the Covenant and recalls its motivation. Actually, by doing this, nothing will be left of the oracle. Eventually, the topic of "land" reappears several times in P (Gen 17:8; 28:4; 35:12; 48:4; Exod 6:4, 8).

If the promise of the land is a part of the divine plan, then P is not just interested in the cult. The organization of the cult is an important stage, but it is

---

"raise one's hand" (*nś' 'et-yād*), which also appears in Ezek 20:28, 42, a text that is close to P and not to Dt (also see Num 14:30). In addition, the expression "hereditary possession" (*môrāšâ*) is found in Ezekiel but not in Dt. See Ezek 11:15; 25:4, 10; 33:24; 36:2, 3, 5.

79. See the preceding note. On this key text of P, see my "Place d'Ex 6,2–8 dans la narration de l'exode," *ZAW* 94 (1982) 530–48; idem, "Quelques remarques sur Pg et la dernière rédaction du Pentateuque," in *Le Pentateuque en question* (ed. A. de Pury; Geneva, 1989; 2nd ed., 1992) 95–125, especially pp. 97–107. See also J. Lust, "Exodus 6,2–8 and Ezechiel," in *Studies in the Book of Exodus* (ed. M. Vervenne; Leuven, 1996) 209–24.

not the final phase of the Israelites' journey with their God. Consequently, P must still explain why Moses, Aaron, and the entire generation of the Exodus did not enter into the "land." Texts that have traditionally been attributed to P (for example, Numbers 13–14*; 20:1–13*; 20:22–29*; chap. 27*) provide the requested explanation.

Deut 34:1, 7–9 raises another complex question. The vocabulary is not that of P; it is difficult to separate vv. 7–9 from their context. And there is a problem that is even more serious: P does not report Moses' death because 34:5 is not attributed to him! There are good reasons to believe that this is a late, postdeuteronomic or postpriestly, text.[80] However, if P's ultimate objective is the entry into the Promised Land, why should we not read Josh 18:1, 19:51 as the conclusion of P? It seems as though P would extend to the installation of the tabernacle at Shiloh, which marked the moment when God and his people took possession of the land. Henceforth, God resided in the midst of his people, in the Promised Land.

Exod 6:8 definitely leads in this direction. However, for the supporters of this thesis, the heart of the argument lies elsewhere—in the intentional parallelism between Gen 1:28 and Josh 18:1b. For these authors, the two texts enclose the entire Priestly narrative like a vast inclusio:

Gen 1:28: [. . .] and subdue [the whole earth].

Josh 18:1b: The land lay subdued before them.

According to some authors, the promise in Gen 1:28 is fulfilled only in Josh 18:1b and nowhere else in the Pentateuch. However, this thesis faces the following strong objections.[81]

• Why privilege Gen 1:28 in this argument? Why not refer to one of the other incidents alluded to in Joshua 18–19, such as the promise of the land (*běrît*) made to the fathers (Genesis 17); or the "glory" (*kabôd*; Exod 40:34–36); or Israel's recognition of YHWH (Exod 6:7, 29:46)?

• Joshua 18–19 only contains one of P's characteristic themes—the "tent of meeting" (*'ōhel mô'ēd*). How can we explain the absence of the other topics tied to the cult, such as the "glory" (Exod 29:43–46, 40:34–36; Lev 9:24; cf. 1 Kgs 8:11)?

• The Priestly Writer clearly distinguished the history of origins (Genesis 1–9*) from the history of Israel, which begins with Abraham. The program of Israel's history is found in Genesis 17. However, Joshua 18–19 does not make

---

80. See above, n. 73. Cf. Zenger (ed.), *Einleitung*, 95.

81. See E. Zenger, *Gottes Bogen in den Wolken: Untersuchungen zu Komposition und Theologie der priesterschriftlichen Urgeschichte* (Stuttgarter Bibelstudien 112; Stuttgart, 1983) 100; idem, *Einleitung*, 95–96; Ska, "Pentateuque," 263–64.

any allusion to Genesis 17, not even to what the matter of the land (cf. Gen 17:8). According to P, Israel's history is divided into two phases: first, the period of the promises made to the patriarchs and, second, the history of the people, understood to be the fulfillment of those promises (see Exod 6:2–8). Moses constitutes the hinge or turning point permitting the transition from the first phase to the second phase. However, Joshua 18–19 does not mention Moses at all, and there is no connection between it and Exod 6:8, which announces the entry into the land promised to the fathers. At first glance, Josh 18:1b, "The land lay subdued before them," seems to be related to Gen 1:28, "subdue the earth." However, Josh 18:1b is closer to later, postpriestly texts such as Num 32:22, 29 and 1 Chr 22:18.

For all of these reasons, it seems preferable to look for P's conclusion in Numbers 27.

c. The Priestly Writer and the "Holiness Code" (Leviticus 17–26)[82]

The Holiness Code (abbrev. H), first identified by A. Klostermann in 1877, owes its name to a formula frequently repeated in Leviticus 17–26: "You shall be holy, for I am holy."[83] Many authors think that this code has a priestly origin, although this does not mean that it belongs to the Priestly Writer as such. Recently the independence of the Holiness Code has been questioned once again.[84] For example, Blum has argued that there is a logical and thematic continuity between the "Priestly narrative" and the Holiness Code: after the installation of the sanctuary in the midst of the people (Exodus 40), Israel had to conform itself to the holiness of the one who was dwelling within it (Leviticus 17–26).[85] Is this argument sufficient for asserting that P and H form a single literary entity that is the product of a single author or of a single editorial group during the same period?

Despite the logical coherence underscored by Blum, other indications, principally literary features, preclude accepting this line of thought. The logical bond that Blum pointed out actually has a redactional origin. In other words, it was created by the editors of the Pentateuch. One might even conjecture that

---

82. For a summary, see Blenkinsopp, *Pentateuch*, 223–24; Zenger (ed.), *Einleitung*, 103–5.

83. A. Klostermann, "Ezechiel und das Heiligkeitsgesetz," *Zeitschrift für lutherische Theologie* 38 (1877) 401–45 = idem, *Der Pentateuch I* (Leipzig, 1893) 368–418. The abbreviation H comes from the German word *Heiligkeitsgesetz*, "Law of Holiness/Holiness Code."

84. See V. Wagner, "Zur Existenz des sogenannten 'Heiligkeitsgesetzes,'" *ZAW* 86 (1974) 307–16; Blum, *Studien zur Komposition des Pentateuch*, 318–28.

85. Ibid., 318–19: "*After* the foundation of the sanctuary and the cult, it is a question [in the 'Holiness Code'] of the logical requirement of *corresponding behavior* on the part of (all) Israel." ("Nach *den* Stiftungen von Heiligtum und Kult geht es hier also folgerichtig um das geforderte Korrespondenzverhalten (*ganzen*) Israels.")

the authors of the Holiness Code composed it in order to complete the Priestly writing. In fact, there are plenty of reasons to think that H is later than P.[86]

• H corrects P with regard to the "land." According to P, YHWH grants possession of the land to Abraham's descendants (see Gen 17:8; 28:4; 35:12; 48:4; Exod 6:4, 8; the latter text uses the Hebrew word *môrāšâ*, "hereditary possession"). However, in H's view, the land remains exclusively the property of YHWH (Lev 25:23–24, 38). The Israelites are not the owners of the land but only "aliens and tenants" (Lev 25:23).

• The conceptions of the relations between YHWH and his people differ in H and in P. According to Exod 6:7 (P), YHWH frees Israel in order to make them into "his people" and his family.[87] In Lev 25:42, 26:13, Israel remains the "servant of YHWH," a term that emphasizes obedience to God.

• H modifies the Priestly theology of the Covenant. In P's view, there is only one true Covenant (*běrît*) for Israel: the unilateral and irrevocable oath God made to Abraham (Genesis 17; cf. Exod 6:2–8). For H, on the contrary, the promises are conditional (Lev 26:3–39) because there are blessings and maledictions tied to the observance (and nonobservance) of the Law. In addition, YHWH remembers the Covenant with the patriarchs if the people repent after having sinned (Lev 26:40–45).[88]

• H's vocabulary is often closer to Deuteronomy's than to P's.[89]

---

86. See, above all, A. Cholewinski, *Heiligkeitsgesetz und Deuteronomium: Eine vergleichende Studie* (AnBib 66; Rome, 1976) 334–38; I. Knohl, "The Priestly Torah versus the Holiness School: Sabbath and the Festivals," *HUCA* 58 (1987) 65–117; J. Milgrom, *Leviticus 1–16* (AB 3; Garden City, NY, 1991) 3–35; E. Otto, "Das 'Heiligkeitsgesetz': Leviticus 17–26 in der Pentateuchredaktion," in *Altes Testament: Forschung und Wirkung. Festschrift für Henning Graf Reventlow* (ed. P. Mommer and W. Thiel; Frankfurt am Main, 1994) 65–80; idem, "Del Libro de la Alianza a la Ley de Santidad: La reformulación del derecho israelita y la formación del Pentateuco," *EstBib* 52 (1994) 195–217, especially pp. 215–16; idem, *Theologische Ethik des Alten Testaments* (Theologische Wissenschaft 3/2; Stuttgart, 1994) 237; I. Knohl, *The Sanctuary of Silence: The Priestly Torah and the Priestly School* (Minneapolis, 1995).

87. This formula is the one used for a wedding or the adoption of a new member by a family. See Gen 12:19; 25:20; 28:9; 34:4, 21 (wife); Esth 2:7, 15 (daughter); 2 Kgs 4:1 (servant). See A. Tosato, *Il matrimonio israelitico: Una teoria generale* (AnBib 100; Rome, 1982) 73–74, 77.

88. See N. Lohfink, "Die Abänderung der Theologie des priesterlichen Geschichtswerks im Segen des Heiligkeitsgesetzes: Zu Lev. 26,9, 11–13," in *Wort und Geschichte: Festschrift für Karl Elliger zum 70. Geburtstag* (ed. H. Gese and H. P. Rüger; AOAT 18; Kevelaer and Neukirchen-Vluyn, 1973) 129–36 = idem, *Studien zum Pentateuch* (Stuttgart, 1988) 157–68. See the criticism of Blum, *Studien zur Komposition des Pentateuch*, 326–27. Leviticus 26 foresees two situations: in the land or in Exile. In the land, Israel is obliged to observe the Law. If they do not observe it, they fall under God's curse. But when the Israelites are exiled and confess their sins, God remembers his Covenant with the patriarchs and does not completely reject his people (26:40–45).

89. See C. Feucht, *Untersuchungen zum Heiligkeitsgesetz* (Berlin, 1964) 112–33; W. Thiel, "Erwägungen zum Alter des Heiligkeitsgesetzes," *ZAW* 81 (1969) 40–72, especially. pp. 69–73.

• There are differences between the instructions for Passover in Exodus 12 (P) and Leviticus 23 (H). The latter attempts to reconcile the ritual in Exodus 12 with the ritual in Deut 16:1–8.[90] Furthermore, it is difficult to explain why a single work contains *two* different laws regarding Passover.

• The notion of "holiness" is not identical for P and H. In the Priestly narrative, "holiness" is exclusively a quality of the altar, the sanctuary, and the priesthood (Exod 29:42–46[91]). In H, holiness is required of all the people (Lev 19:2; 20:7, 24–26; 21:8; 22:31–33; cf. 11:44–45[92]).

• The problem of the "nations" from which Israel must separate themselves does not yet appear in P (cf. Lev 20:22–26).

d. The Theology and the Structure of P[93]

The study of P's theology largely coincides with the study of its structure. Various proposals about the structure of P have been made because it shows much evidence of this kind of work. For example, scholars have listed more or less ten "*tôledôt* formulas" ("generation formulas") in Genesis and ten "formulas of Israel's wandering in the wilderness" in Exodus and Numbers.[94]

The revelation of God occurs in three phases, and each one of these phases corresponds to a different divine name: the Creation, which is the work of "God" (*'ĕlōhîm*); the time of the promises, when God reveals himself as El Shaddai (*'ēl šadday*, "the all-powerful God"[?]; cf. Gen 17:1, Exod 6:3); finally, YHWH, the God of the Exodus, the people of Israel, and the fulfillment of the promises, reveals his name to Moses (Exod 6:3).

P presents two covenants, one with Noah and the entire creation (Gen 9:1–17) and the other with Abraham and his offspring, the people of Israel (Genesis 17). There are four "sins" in P: the "violence" of the generation of the Flood (*ḥāmās*—Gen 6:11, 13); the "brutality" of the Egyptians (*perek*—Exod 1:13–14); the generation of the wilderness "slanders the land" (*dibbat hā'āreṣ*—Num 13:32, 14:36–37); finally, Moses and Aaron do not believe in God and do not sanctify his name (Num 20:12). Each sin is followed by a corresponding punishment. Water is the instrument used for punishment in the Flood (Genesis 1–8*) and in the miracle of the sea (Exodus 14*). These two accounts are connected to the creation of the sea in Gen 1:9–10. The other two punishments

---

90. See E. Otto, "פֶּסַח *pāsaḥ*; פֶּסַח *pesaḥ*," *TDOT* 12:1–24, esp. 17–19.

91. Ska, "Exode 19,3–6," 307–8.

92. On the other hand, for H, just as for P, YHWH sanctifies the priesthood (Lev 21:12–15; 22:9, 16).

93. For an overview of the discussions, see Zenger (ed.), *Einleitung*, 98–103; cf. Blum, *Studien zur Komposition des Pentateuch*, 287–332.

94. Lohfink, "Priesterschrift," 189–225 = *Studien zum Pentateuch*, 213–54; French translation: "L'Écrit sacerdotal et l'histoire," *Les traditions du Pentateuque autour de l'exil* (Cahiers Évangile 97; Paris, 1996) 9–25.

take place in the wilderness, which is where the rebels and then Aaron and Moses die without being allowed to enter into the Promised Land.[95]

The account of the construction of the tent of meeting contains many allusions to Creation. For example, the cloud covers the mountain for six days, and YHWH calls Moses on the seventh day to give him instructions regarding the cult (Exod 24:16; cf. Gen 1:1–2:3). The concluding formulas in Exod 39:32, 43 repeat those of Gen 1:31, 2:1–3: "In this way all the work . . . was finished"; "Moses saw that they had done all the work"; "Moses blessed. . . ."[96]

Scholars have used P's markers in various ways. For some, P divides history into two great periods, the first period of the ten *tôledôt* ("generations") in Genesis, which is followed by the ten stages of Israel in the wilderness (Exodus–Numbers). The Exodus forms the link between these two halves of the diptych (N. Lohfink).[97] In the footsteps of Wellhausen, W. H. Schmidt proposes dividing P into four periods: the Creation, the Flood, Abraham's time, and Moses' time.[98] P. Weimar and E. Zenger prefer a two-part division: Gen 1:1–Exod 1:7 and Exod 1:13–Deut 34:9. The first section concentrates on the growth of the people (cf. Gen 1:28 and Exod 1:7), and the second section deals with the journey to the land (cf. Lohfink). O. H. Steck prefers another bipartite division and distinguishes the "history of the origins of the world and of humanity" (Genesis 1–11), from Adam to Abraham; and the "history of Israel's origins," from Abraham to Moses. In this case, Abraham is the key figure, not Moses.[99]

It is not really possible to fit all of these elements into one structure. Furthermore, P undoubtedly never intended to give his readers a clear account

---

95. See N. Lohfink, "Ursünden," 38–57 = *Studien zum Pentateuch*, 169–89; Ska, "Séparation des eaux et de la terre ferme."

96. See, among others, Kearney, "Creation and Liturgy"; N. Lohfink, "Der Schöpfergott und der Bestand von Himmel und Erde: Das Alte Testament zum Zusammenhang von Schöpfung und Heil," in *Sind wir noch zu retten? Schöpfungsglaube und Verantwortung für unsere Erde* (ed. G. Altner et al.; Regensburg, 1978) 15–39, especially pp. 33–34 = *Studien zum Pentateuch*, (Stuttgarter biblische Aufsatzbände: Altes Testament 4; Stuttgart, 1988) 191–211, especially pp. 205–7; N. Negretti, *Il settimo giorno: Indagine critico-teologica delle tradizioni presacerdotali e sacerdotali circa il sabato biblico* (AnBib 55; Rome, 1973) 162–64; M. Oliva, "Interpretación teológica del culto en la perícopa del Sinai de la Historia Sacerdotal," *Bib* 49 (1968) 348–51; Weimar, "Sinai und Schöpfung"; B. Janowski, "Tempel und Schöpfung: Schöpfungstheologische Aspekte der priesterschriftlichen Heiligtumskonzeption," *Gottes Gegenwart in Israel: Beiträge zur Theologie des Alten Testaments* (Neukirchen-Vluyn, 1993) 214–46, especially pp. 238–39, 244.

97. See above, n. 94.

98. W. H. Schmidt, *Einführung*, 104–12.

99. O. H. Steck, "Aufbauprobleme in der Priesterschrift," in *Ernten was man sät: Festschrift für Klaus Koch zu seinem 65. Geburtstag* (ed. D. R. Daniels, U. Glessmer, and M. Rösel; Neukirchen-Vluyn, 1991) 287–308. The structure proposed by Blum (*Studien zur Komposition des Pentateuch*, 287–332) is analogous: "the creation of the world and its decline" ("die Schöpfungswelt und ihre Minderung"); "the partial restoration in Israel" ("die partielle Restitution in Israel").

that was composed in accord with the canons of modern structuralism. Many scholars try to subdivide the Priestly *narrative*, but P was attempting to organize *the history of Israel*. Given this fact, it is necessary, as in many other cases, to distinguish the text clearly from the world to which it refers.

In more technical terms, we need to distinguish *story* from *discourse*. The "story" is the reality the reader reconstructs as he or she reads the text, and the "discourse" is the concrete text.[100] The Priestly Writer constantly plays on these two levels. More concretely, on the basis of the data and the schemas provided by P, the reader must reconstruct a "story" of the world in which Israel's history is inscribed. Therefore, it is more important to determine the stages of this "story" precisely than to know how the text or the discourse is structured. In the following paragraphs, I will speak only about the "story," without attempting to recover a perfectly geometrical structure in the texts.[101]

In order to achieve the most reliable results, it seems appropriate to begin with theological assertions made by P, because the Priestly text sees history as the fulfillment of a divine plan. One of the major differences between P and the other "sources" is precisely the outspoken theological tone that he gives to his account.

Indeed, many scholars have noted that divine discourses are relatively more frequent in P than in the older texts. These discourses are most often "narrative programs," in the technical language of narrative analysis.[102] In P, God rewrites and "programs" a story that is divided into two great periods: universal history and Israelite history. The history of the world is subdivided into the Creation (Genesis 1–5*) and the renewal of Creation by means of the Flood (Genesis 6–9).

Likewise, the history of Israel is divided into two periods: the history of the ancestors (the patriarchs) and the history of Israel as a people. The most important texts are Gen 1:1–2:4a; 9:1–17; 17; and Exod 6:2–8. The God of the universe is Elohim; the God of Israel's ancestors is El Shaddai; YHWH is the God of the people of Israel. God reveals himself explicitly only to Israel, first to the patriarchs and then to the entire people. Before going into the heart of "this theology," we need to verify our first impressions by comparing some key texts.

The history of origins constitutes the foundation on which God constructs the history of Israel. This explains why there are many correspondences between these two parts of the narrative. For example, the Noahic Covenant

---

100. On the origin and the function of this distinction received from the Russian formalists, see my *"Our Fathers Have Told Us": Introduction to the Analysis of Hebrew Narratives* (SubBib 13; Rome, 1990) 5–6.

101. With regard to the style of P, the important study is McEvenue, *Narrative Style*. He defines it as follows: "Its essence is variety within system" (p. 51). This is why excessive attempts at structuralizing are certain to fail.

102. See my "Sincronia," 157 and 230.

(Genesis 9) corresponds to the Abrahamic Covenant (Genesis 17). The "sign" of the first covenant is the rainbow (Gen 9:12), and the "sign" of the second is circumcision (Gen 17:11).

The Egyptians who oppressed the Israelites disappeared in the waters of the sea (Exodus 14*), just as the violent generation of the Flood disappeared in its waters (Genesis 7*). In both cases, God acts as the world's Creator because he commands the waters and makes the "dry land" (*yabbāšâ*) appear or reappear (Gen 1:9–10; 8:14; Exod 14:16, 22, 29). The blessing that God grants to humanity in Gen 1:28, "Be fruitful, multiply, fill the earth," is repeated in 9:1 for Noah and his descendants. It is then echoed in the blessing given to Abraham (Gen 17:2, 16; cf. 17:20), and again in the blessing of Jacob (28:3; 35:11; 48:4). This patriarchal blessing becomes a reality in Gen 47:27 and Exod 1:7.

The God who feeds the living creatures that dwell in the world (Gen 1:29–30; cf. 6:21) also nourishes his people in the wilderness by giving them manna (Exod 16:15). The Israelites discover, in Exodus 16, the rest on the seventh day that God inaugurated on the seventh day of Creation (Gen 2:1–3). We have already noted the connections between the accounts of Creation and the construction of the tabernacle. The creator of the universe comes and lives in the midst of his creation when Israel has become his people (Exod 6:7, 29:43–46, 40:34–36). The tent of meeting is the "palace" of the "sovereign of the universe," at the heart of his kingdom.[103] This evidence is sufficient to prove that P wanted to construct a history in the form of a diptych to stress the continuity between and progression of the history of the world and the history of Israel.

In addition, the two phases of the first part have some essential points in common. God created the world from primeval chaos—a universe of darkness covered by water (Gen 1:2, 9–10). With the Flood, Creation partially returned to this primeval chaos because the earth was again entirely covered by water, which destroyed a corrupt, violent generation. When dry land reappeared (Gen 8:14; cf. 1:9–10), Noah and his family left the Ark to repopulate the world (cf. 8:16–17). In 9:1, God renews the blessing of 1:28, and in 9:2–3 he changes the regulation with regard to food that had been given in 1:29–30.

The two phases of Israel's history have fewer elements in common. The rhetoric is different and highlights the passage from promise to fulfillment. Texts such as Exod 2:23–25 and 6:2–8 focus on the second phase of the Priestly story. When Israel finds itself in Egypt, God "remembers" the promise he made to Abraham, Isaac, and Jacob (Exod 2:24, 6:5). God promised three things to Abraham: that he would give him numerous offspring (Gen 17:2–6) and land (17:8) and that he would be his God (17:7–8). The promise of numerous offspring is fulfilled in Gen 47:27 and Exod 1:7. A second promise is

---

103. See, above all, Weinfeld, "Sabbath, Temple, and the Enthronement of the Lord"; compare with the studies referred to in n. 96.

fulfilled when YHWH comes to reside among his people (Exod 40:34–35; cf. Exod 6:7, 29:45–46). Only one promise still awaits fulfillment: the land. However, according to P, the nonfulfillment of this promise is due to Israel's sin. God is not responsible for this failure, as Numbers 13–14* clearly states. The generation of the Exodus did not want to conquer the land, and this is why they were condemned to die in the wilderness. It is the second wilderness generation that will enter the land promised to the patriarchs (Num 14:26–38*).

P's aim is to rediscover, in the past, the solid foundations on which the community of Israel can rebuild itself. For P, these foundations are religious. The existence of the postdiluvian world entirely depends on God's unilateral Covenant with Noah (G 9:1–17). In other words, this foundation is indestructible because it rests on God alone. The violence of living beings cannot destroy the world. Similarly, Israel's existence has its basis in God alone—the unilateral covenant of El Shaddai with Abraham and his descendants (Genesis 17). On this point, P modifies the Deuteronomic theology of the Covenant. For Dt, blessing depended on the people's observance of the Law. Because the people were not faithful, the curse of Exile struck them. It was therefore necessary to find in the past a more solid foundation, a foundation that was not bound to humanity's very fragile faithfulness. P discovers this foundation in God's unilateral and unconditional Covenant with Abraham (Genesis 17).

On this basis, P develops his theology of the "glory."[104] YHWH reveals this "glory" for the first time in Exodus 14 (vv. 4, 17–18), when he "glorifies himself" by means of victory over Egypt. His glory reappears in the wilderness when God gives the manna to the people (Exod 16:10). Then, it covers Mount Sinai (Exod 24:16–17) and takes possession of the tent of meeting (Exod 40:34–35; cf. 29:43). Finally, it manifests itself again during the inauguration of the cult (Lev 9:23). After this, the "glory" appears two more times: first (Num 14:10), in order to punish the rebellious generation that has "given an unfavorable report about the Promised Land," and second, when he gives the thirsty people water that springs from the rock (Num 20:6). Thus, the "glory" unites two important aspects of divine revelation: YHWH's actions in Israel's history and his presence in the cult. In the tent of meeting, Israel venerates the "glory" of YHWH, the Lord of their history.[105]

YHWH is also the creator of the universe. He uses his creative power to free Israel (Exodus 14*)[106] and to nourish them (Exodus 16*).[107] The striking

---

104. Westermann, "Die Herrlichkeit Gottes in der Priesterschrift"; Struppe, *Die Herrlichkeit Jahwes in der Priesterschrift.*

105. See my *Passage de la mer,* 101–7.

106. See, above all, the allusions to the "dry land" in Exod 14:16, 22, 29; cf. Gen 1:9–10 (8:14). Ska, *Passage de la mer,* 95–96; idem, "Séparation des eaux," 517–19.

107. See Gen 1:29, 6:21, Exod 16:15, with the same terminology (*ntn l . . . lĕʾoklâ,* "to give to . . . for food").

similarities between Exodus 24, 39–40, and Genesis 1 also underline the fact that Israel's God is the creator of the universe.[108] This is why the basis of Israel's faith is the foundation of the universe itself.

Finally, the "glory" moves with the tabernacle to guide and accompany Israel on the people's way through the wilderness toward the Promised Land. The wilderness is not the last stage of the journey. Moreover, if YHWH's "glory" is present in the midst of the people, this means that the undertaking cannot fail. The double nature of the "glory" as the concrete, effective presence of YHWH both in Israel's history and in Israel's cult permits us to solve some problems having to do with the nature of P. The first of these concerns the ultimate goal of the Priestly Writer. Many scholars maintain that P is primarily interested in the cult. The narrative must therefore conclude in the Sinai pericope, after the inauguration of the tent of meeting (Exodus 40; see T. Pola) or after the first sacrifices (Leviticus 9; Zenger, Otto).[109]

Another, smaller group of scholars thinks that P's true agenda is the return to the land.[110] Actually, in P's view, the cult is inseparable from history: consequently, the inauguration of the cult is not an end in itself. If the "glory" of God guides history, the promise of the land made in Exod 6:8 cannot fail. Thus, the "glory" unites both dynamic and static aspects of P's theology—the tension with regard to the future (the possession of the land) and God's presence near his people in the sanctuary.[111]

In the same way, the Priestly narrative moves in two opposite directions. On the one hand, it attempts to anchor Israel's existence in the past, in God's work of Creation and in the unconditional covenants with Noah and Abraham.[112] On the other hand, texts such as Genesis 17, 28:1–9, 35:9–15, and Exod 6:2–8 contain "strategies" for a future that go well beyond the narrative's conclusion. P finds in the past the strength to live in the present and the hope with which to build a better future. After all is said and done, it is impossible to re-

---

108. This aspect of P's theology resembles Second Isaiah, for whom YHWH is the creator and redeemer. See the use of the verbs *bārā'* ("to create") and *gā'al* ("to redeem") in Isa 43:1; cf. 54:5.

109. Also see Noth, *History of Pentateuchal Traditions*, 8.

110. See, above all, K. Elliger, "Sinn und Ursprung," 129; R. Kilian, "Die Hoffnung auf Heimkehr in der Priesterschrift," *Bibel und Leben* 7 (1966) 39–51; E. Cortese, *La terra di Canaan nella storia sacerdotale del Pentateuco*; idem, "La teologia del documento sacerdotale."

111. See the discussion in Blum, *Studien zur Komposition des Pentateuch*, 287–332. In my opinion, the concept of *Gottesnähe* ("nearness of God"), chosen by Blum and then adopted by Janowski and Zenger, has two aspects: YHWH is close to Israel because he "resides" in the midst of his people (Exod 6:7; 29:45–46) and because he acts in history (Exodus 14*; 16*; Numbers 13–14*; 20*). Cf. my "Relative indépendance," 406–7.

112. For Lohfink ("Priesterschrift," 202–15, 215–25 = *Studien zum Pentateuch*, 227–42, 242–53), P wants to "go back to a mythical world" and "refuses a dynamic world." See the reaction of Blum, *Studien zur Komposition des Pentateuch*, 330–31.

duce the dialectical tension flowing through Priestly theology without the risk of impoverishing it.

e. The Date of P [113]

Scholars have proposed three dates for the composition of P: before the Exile (Y. Kaufmann and his school), the end of the Exile or the beginning of the return (K. Elliger), and the period that immediately followed the reconstruction of the Second Temple (a growing number of scholars). The first group of scholars, largely consisting of Jewish exegetes, defends a Preexilic date and bases this hypothesis on two main arguments: the language[114] and the fact that the First Temple must have had ritual laws. Actually, these authors mainly refer to the laws contained in P and in the book of Leviticus and are much less concerned with narratives.[115]

The second and third groups disagree because of their different interpretations of the Priestly narrative.[116] According to the second group, P contains a "plan for the future" because Israel is going through a period of transition. The "wilderness," where the people are at the end of the narrative, corresponds to the Exile or the time of the first return. Israel still has to enter into the land and rebuild the temple. The Priestly narrative, especially the Sinai pericope and the description of the cult, should therefore be read as a "utopia."[117]

The third group argues that P was written to justify and to legitimize the "hierocracy" of the Second Temple. Consequently, P's redaction comes after the reconstruction of the temple and provides its "etiology."[118] If we consider the Priestly narrative in its current form rather than the earlier materials that the Priestly Writer might have incorporated, we find good reason to assert that it

---

113. See the summary in Zenger (ed.), *Einleitung*, 97–98. Cf. J. Hughes, *Secrets of the Times: Myth and History in Biblical Chronology* (JSOTSup 66; Sheffield, 1990) 43–54.

114. See, for example, A. Hurvitz, *A Linguistic Study of the Relationship between the Priestly Source and the Book of Ezekiel: A New Approach to the Problem* (CahRB 20; Paris, 1982); idem, "Dating the Priestly Source in Light of the Historical Study of Biblical Hebrew: A Century after Wellhausen," *ZAW* 100 Sup. (1988) 88–100; cf. M. F. Rooker, *Biblical Hebrew in Transition: The Language of the Book of Ezekiel* (JSOTSup 90; Sheffield, 1990). Criticism can be found in J. Blenkinsopp, "An Assessment on the Alleged Preexilic Date of the Priestly Material in the Pentateuch," *ZAW* 108 (1996) 495–518.

115. See Krapf, *Die Priesterschrift und die vorexilische Zeit.*

116. See W. H. Schmidt, *Einführung*, 104.

117. Zenger (ed.), *Einleitung*, 97, 102. Compare the authors cited in n. 110. Also see V. Fritz, *Tempel und Zelt: Studien zum Tempelbau und zu dem Zeltheiligtum der Priesterschrift* (WMANT 47; Neukirchen-Vluyn, 1977) 149 n. 162.

118. See, above all, L. Schmidt, *Studien zur Priesterschrift*, 259. Cf. Blum, *Studien zur Komposition des Pentateuch*, 304–6, especially p. 305 n. 68. However, Blum talks about KP, a much vaster work than the traditional "Priestly narrative" because it also comprises all of Leviticus.

dates to at least the period of the Exile. The centralization of the cult is an accepted fact and no longer calls for explanation or polemic, as Wellhausen had
shown. P is therefore chronologically situated *after* Josiah's reform and the first
Deuteronomy.

We should add that P has many factors in common with the two great
prophets at the end of the Exile or the beginning of the Postexilic period,
Ezekiel and Second Isaiah. Ezekiel and P share a theology of "glory" and a
"recognition of YHWH" as well as a global vision of Israel's history (Ezekiel 20
and Exod 6:2–8).[119] The Second Isaiah insists, like P, on the relationship
between "Creation" and "redemption" and on monotheism.[120] Finally, P dialogues with the Deuteronomic/Deuteronomistic literature with regard to the
Covenant. All of this leads us to posit a date around the end of the Exile.[121]

Now, in order to know whether P wrote before or after the construction of
the temple, we need a specific indication. Up to now, the hypotheses have
generally been based only on probabilities. In my opinion, P did provide evidence that may help to solve this problem. This requires that we first accept
that Numbers 14 is a part of P, as I have already suggested above. The evidence
in question is given in Num 14:9, where Joshua exhorts the Israelites, "Do not
fear the people of the land"—that is, the Canaanites. This expression, "the
people of the land," has an interesting history. In the book of Kings it refers to
the land-owning aristocracy of Judah who are faithful to David (2 Kgs 11:20,
14:21, 21:24, 23:30) and it has a positive meaning. However, in the books of
Ezra and Nehemiah, the expression has negative connotations. The "people of
the land" represent the portion of the population that was not exiled and that,
later on, opposed the returning exiles. These "people of the land" mainly
wanted to prevent the reconstruction of the temple (cf. Ezra 3:3; 4:4; 9:1, 2,
11; 10:2, 11; Neh 9:24, 30; 10:29, 31, 32).

Num 14:9 also speaks negatively about the "people of the land."[122] On the
one hand, Israel finds itself in the wilderness and wants to enter the Promised
Land. On the other hand, hostile people occupy the land and frighten Israel. Israel goes as far as refusing to enter into the territory because of the "people of
the land." How should this kind of text be interpreted? Who actually are these
"people of the land"? Two verses in Ezra may help to solve the puzzle: Ezra 3:3
and 4:4. In the first verse, Jeshua the priest and his brothers, with Zerubbabel
and his brothers rebuilt the altar on its foundation, although "they were in

---

119. See Lohfink, "Priesterschrift," 195 = *Studien zum Pentateuch*, 219–20; Houtman,
Pentateuch, 327–28; for Ezekiel 20 and Exod 6:2–8, see Lust, "Exodus 6:2–8 and Ezekiel."
120. See Houtman, *Pentateuch*, 375 n. 55.
121. See Zenger (ed.), *Einleitung*, 97.
122. See, above all, A. H. J. Gunneweg, "ʿm hʾrṣ: A Semantic Revolution," *ZAW* 95
(1983) 437–40; E. Lipiński, "עם ʿam." *TDOT* 11.163–77, esp. pp. 172–73.

dread of the people of the land."[123] Ezra 4:4–5 indicates the cause of the conflict between the two groups. The people that had remained in the land wanted to take part in the reconstruction of the temple, but Zerubbabel and the exiles who had come back with him were opposed to this. The inhabitants retaliated by preventing the exiles from rebuilding the temple throughout the entire reign of Cyrus, who died in 529 B.C.E., and up to the beginning of the reign of Darius (522–546 B.C.E.).

What was the reason for this refusal? Was it a power struggle or a disagreement over land? The text does not say. Whatever the reason was, it is certain that the inhabitants who had remained in the land opposed the returnees in this very bitter conflict for a long time.[124] Furthermore, the books of Ezra and Nehemiah assimilate these "people of the land" into Israel's traditional enemies, the Canaanite populations subjugated by Joshua (Ezra 9:1; cf. Neh 9:8, 24). Consequently, these people are disqualified because they are "pagan" and do not observe the Mosaic Law (cf. Neh 10:29), especially the law of the Sabbath (Neh 10:32). Thus, they cannot inherit the land. In fact, they are destined to be destroyed.

There are good reasons for situating P in this context, during the reign of Cyrus and before 520 B.C.E. P describes the great project of the return, its partial failure caused by the opposition of the "people of the land," and the discouragement of the Israelites who malign the land (Num 13:32, 14:36–37). The entry into the land is consequently deferred to the next generation. This corresponds to the lapse of time between the reign of Cyrus (d. 529 B.C.E.) and the reign of Darius (522–486 B.C.E.).

C. The "Synchronic" Study of the Pentateuch [125]

We must note the clear contribution of various new methods of research to the study of the Pentateuch. However, there are so many schools of thought that it is impossible to present them all in the scope of this Introduction.[126] The most important methods are the "canonical reading" of Scripture, structuralism, semiotics, and narratology.

---

123. For the translation of the expression ʿammê hāʾărāṣôt, "peoples of the land" and not "of the lands," see Joüon-Muraoka, §136o.

124. It is plausible that the "people of the land" referred to here were the Judahites who were not exiled. Other scholars refer to foreign invaders such as, for example, the Edomites. The first solution seems preferable. See the study of B. Schramm, *The Opponents of Third Isaiah: Reconstructing the Cultic History of the Restoration* (JSOTSup 193; Sheffield, 1994) 53–61.

125. See Houtman, *Pentateuch*, 249–78, for a detailed presentation of the different schools.

126. For bibliography, see M. Minor, *Literary-Critical Approaches to the Bible* (West Cornwall, CT, 1992); M. A. Powell, *The Bible and Modern Literary Criticism: A Critical Assessment*

The canonical reading of the Bible is primarily connected with B. S. Childs and J. A. Sanders.[127] Structuralism originated in France, in the world of ethnology and anthropology. The most famous name in the field is C. Lévi-Strauss;[128] The specialists in this field also speak of "rhetorical criticism."[129] Semiotics is the child of Russian formalism, and it has found a second home in France and Quebec.[130] Narratology applies to biblical texts a method, called "new criticism" or "close reading," that originated in the English-speaking world.[131]

Each of these methods provides an interesting analysis of the Pentateuch. However, each also has its limits. Synchronic reading is mostly interested in the reading of specific texts. Few studies deal with entire books or the Pentateuch

---

and *Annotated Bibliography* (New York, 1992); D. F. Watson and A. J. Hauser, *Rhetorical Criticism of the Bible: A Comprehensive Bibliography. With Notes on History and Method* (Biblical Interpretation Series 4; Leiden, 1994).

127. See, among others, Noble, *The Canonical Approach*; R. Rendtorff, *Canon and Theology* (OBT 30; Minneapolis, 1994).

128. See, among others, P. Beauchamp, *Création et séparation: Étude exégétique du premier chapitre de la Genèse* (Paris, 1969; 2nd ed., 2005); R. Barthes (ed.), *Structural Analysis and Biblical Exegesis: Interpretational Essays* (trans. A. M. Johnson Jr.; Pittsburgh, 1975); R. C. Culley, "Some Comments on Structural Analysis and Biblical Studies," in *Congress Volume: Uppsala, 1971* (VTSup 22; Leiden, 1972) 129–42; D. Patte, *What Is Structural Exegesis?* (Philadelphia, 1976).

129. Concerning the "program" of this school, see J. Muilenburg, "Form Criticism and Beyond," *JBL* 88 (1969) 1–18; J. J. Jackson and M. Kessler (eds.), *Rhetorical Criticism: Essays in Honor of J. Muilenburg* (Pittsburgh, 1974); J. Wuellner, "Where Is Rhetorical Criticism Taking Us?" *CBQ* 49 (1987) 448–63. Also see R. Meynet, *L'analyse rhétorique: Une nouvelle méthode pour comprendre la Bible* (Initiations; Paris, 1989).

130. A. J. Greimas is the literary critic who has had the greatest influence on scholars. For some examples of the application of this method, see E. J. van Wolde, *A Semiotic Analysis of Genesis 2–3: A Semiotic Theory and Method of Analysis Applied to the Story of the Garden of Eden* (SSN 25; Assen, 1989); Groupe d'Entrevernes, *Analyse sémiotique des textes. Introduction—Théorie—Pratique* (5th ed.; Lyon, 1985); G. Savoca, *Iniziazione all'analisi biblica strutturalista: Teoria e applicazioni* (Messina, 1989). Determining the distinction between *structural* ("structural"), *structurel* ("structuralism"), and *sémiotique* ("semiotic") is difficult. For an evaluation, see J.-N. Aletti, "Exégèse biblique et sémiotique," *RSR* 80 (1992) 9–28.

131. See my "'Nouvelle critique' et l'exégèse anglo-saxonne," *RSR* 80 (1992) 29–53. Some important works: J. P. Fokkelman, *Narrative Art in Genesis: Specimens of Stylistic and Structural Analysis* (SSN 17; Assen, 1975 = Biblical Seminar 12; Sheffield, 1991); R. Alter, *The Art of Biblical Narrative* (New York, 1981); M. Weiss, *The Bible from Within: The Method of Total Interpretation* (Jerusalem, 1984); S. Bar-Efrat, *Narrative Art in the Bible* (JSOTSup 70; Bible and Literature Series 17; Sheffield, 1989); A. Berlin, *Poetics and Interpretation of Biblical Narrative* (Bible and Literature Series; Sheffield, 1983 = Winona Lake, IN, 1994); D. M. Gunn and D. N. Fewell, *Narrative in the Hebrew Bible* (Oxford Bible Series; Oxford, 1993); J. Licht, *Storytelling in the Bible* (Jerusalem, 1978); M. A. Powell, *What Is Narrative Criticism?* (Minneapolis, 1992; London, 1993); Ska, *"Our Fathers Have Told Us"*; idem, "Sincronia"; M. Sternberg, *The Poetics of Biblical Narrative: Ideological Literature and the Drama of Reading* (Indiana Literary Biblical Studies; Bloomington, IN, 1985); and J.-P. Sonnet, *The Book within the Book: Writing in Deuteronomy* (Biblical Interpretation 14; Leiden: Brill, 1997).

as a whole.[132]

Other problems have arisen. Some structuralist studies tend to privilege recurring terms or expressions in strategic locations in the text such as, for example, chiasms and inclusios, or expressions that appear at the center of concentric structures. This, however, often is a matter of moving from structure to semantics, and we are not always certain that the structural clues are sufficient for discerning that one part of a text is more important than the others. The geometric center of a text is not necessarily its semantic center. For example, the most important statement may come in a conclusion that follows a lengthy introduction. Furthermore, not all the terms have the same value. In a sentence, verbs are primary while other words often play only secondary roles.

In many of these analyses, interpreters run the risk of falling into a trap of "obsession" or "absolutization of terms." When the meaning of a term or a sentence needs to be determined, the movement of the text must have priority over more static aspects, and each assertion must be interpreted within its context.[133] Synchronic research does not always give enough consideration to the distinction between "form" and "content." Or, to use the language of linguistics, it does not always clearly distinguish between the "signifier," the "signified," and the "referent."[134] For these scholars, the text often refers only to itself.

Many synchronic analyses ignore textual problems. Let us look at an example. It would be useless to search synchronic analyses of Genesis 12–25 for a satisfying explanation to one well-known problem of chronology: why does Genesis 21 present Ishmael as a newborn child carried by his mother when, according to information provided by other texts, he must already be close to 17 years old? He is 13 in Gen 17:25; Isaac, who is born a year later (Gen 17:21; 18:14), is weaned when he is about 3 years old (Gen 21:8; cf. 2 Macc 7:27b), and this is when Hagar and Ishmael are sent away permanently (Gen 21:9–21).

---

132. There have been attempts at structural analysis of important passages such as the story of Abraham; see D. Sutherland, "The Organisation of the Abraham Promise Narratives," *ZAW* 95 (1983) 337–43; A. Abela, *The Themes of the Abraham Narrative: Thematic Coherence within the Abraham Literary Unit of Genesis 11,27–25,18* (Malta, 1989); for the Jacob cycle, see Fokkelman, *Narrative Art*, 237–41; M. Fishbane, *Text and Texture: Close Readings of Selected Biblical Texts* (New York, 1979); for the book of Genesis, see G. A. Rendsburg, *The Redaction of Genesis* (Winona Lake, IN, 1986); R. L. Cohn, "Narrative Structure and Canonical Perspective in Genesis," *JSOT* 25 (1983) 3–16 = *The Pentateuch: A Sheffield Reader* (ed. J. W. Rogerson; Biblical Seminar 39; Sheffield, 1996) 89–102. For the Pentateuch as a whole, see Clines, *The Theme of the Pentateuch*; Knierim, "The Composition of the Pentateuch." For a criticism of Rendsburg, see M. Brettler, "Rendsburg's *The Redaction of Genesis*," *JQR* 78 (1987) 113–19; for a criticism of Knierim, see Blum, *Studien zur Komposition des Pentateuch*, 381–82 n. 77.

133. Cf. J. Dupont, "Le Magnificat comme discours sur Dieu," *La nouvelle revue théologique* 102 (1980) 321–43, especially p. 330 n. 18.

134. The signifier is the concrete discourse, consisting of words and sentences. The signified is the expressed idea or concept. The referent is the concrete reality to which the discourse refers.

In certain circles, it is common to talk about the "autonomy" of the text, which should be interpreted independently from its author and from the study of the circumstances of its composition. This is perhaps possible in the case of modern literature, because we have the same culture as the authors and the works do not have a long redactional history behind them. But even in the field of modern literary criticism, there are contradictory opinions on the subject.[135]

It is not possible to speak about the "autonomy of a literary work" in the case of ancient texts, which were written according to criteria and conventions of a different culture. Neither is it possible to use modern *fiction* as a basis for the study of the Bible without considering the distance separating the two.[136] Synchronic study itself should lead scholars to examine the historical context of the texts, because the texts must be read and interpreted according to their inherent norms. These norms derive from a culture that was different from ours. Consequently, historical-critical research often succeeds in solving more simply the questions that any honest interpreter cannot help asking when reading.[137] There is undoubtedly nothing to be gained by provoking a "war of methods" or fighting to defend one type of analysis over another. Methods are only instruments that an interpreter uses, based on the nature of the subject he or she intends to study. In this field, as in many others, dialogue is more profitable than controversy and presents more opportunities.

The best method is the one that succeeds in explaining the text of the Pentateuch with the greatest clarity and without ignoring the complexity that the preceding chapters have attempted to underline.[138] "Losing" time by walking down the paths that have been opened by research during the past centuries is actually to gain time; one does not need to do the work that has already been done and may be able to avoid repeating past mistakes. At least this is the hope.

---

135. See, for example, the reactions of authors such as Hirsch, *Validity in Interpretation*; idem, *The Aims of Interpretation*; L. M. Poland, *Literary Criticism and Biblical Hermeneutics: A Critique of Formalist Approaches* (American Academy of Religion Academy Series 48; Atlanta, 1985); B. Polka, *The Dialectic of Biblical Critique: Interpretation and Existence* (New York, 1986); U. Eco, *The Limits of Interpretation* (Bloomington, IN, 1990).

136. See Blum, *Studien zur Komposition des Pentateuch*, 381.

137. See ibid., 380–82. Even enthusiatic advocates of synchronic study such as Alter and Sternberg willingly admit the need for historical study of the OT. See Alter (*Art of Biblical Narrative*, 32–33), who stigmatizes the "lack of method" of those who "tend to treat the biblical narrative as if it were the product of a single effort, like a modern novel. . . . They show no interest in this case for the historical research that tells us about the conditions of the formation of biblical texts and about their often composite nature." Also see Sternberg, *Poetics of Biblical Narrative*, 10: "the hard antihistorical line in hermeneutics is too condescending and inconsistent . . . to make a viable theory." Saint Augustine (in his *Doctr. chr.* 1.2.42) presents an analogous principle. In simple terms, he affirms that everything that history teaches us about ancient times is very useful for understanding the Scriptures, even if this teaching takes place outside the Church.

138. See Levinson, "The Right Chorale."

Chapter 8

Basic Characteristics of Ancient Literature

After a survey of the difficulties that arise in reading the Pentateuch and a presentation of the theories proposed from Patristic times up to our day, we are now able to make an evaluation. However, before going into the heart of the matter, it seems useful to me to propose several axioms for a critical reading of ancient literature. These axioms are simple, well-known principles, but presenting them together in a single chapter is helpful because manuals and specialists speak about them only occasionally and sporadically while dealing with other topics.

The principles presented here first explain how and why the biblical authors were able to conceive a work such as the Pentateuch, a work of mediocre literary quality, as judged by taste, because of the large numbers of repetitions, tensions, and contradictions that clash with our modern sensibility. Second, in the last two sections, I will reflect on the conditions necessary for the development of writing in antiquity and on a parallel extrabiblical text, the *Gilgamesh Epic*.

A. The Law of Antiquity or Precedence

Antiquity was a fundamental value in the milieu in which the Bible was written. This assertion seems more than obvious, but it is very important for an understanding of Scripture. Let us take an example in the New Testament. When Saint Paul, in his letter to the Galatians, wants to show the superiority of justification by faith over justification by keeping the Law, he states that faith *comes before* the Law, because Abraham came before Moses. This chronological priority gives greater importance to faith in the eyes of both Paul and his addressees (Gal 3:17–19): "My point is this: the law, which came *four hundred thirty years later*, does not annul a covenant previously ratified by God, so as to nullify the promise" (3:17).

In the letter to the Romans, Paul presents an analogous argument regarding circumcision. He wants to show that, based on his faith, Abraham is the father of those who are circumcised and of those who are uncircumcised. In other words, faith opens the door to salvation even if the pagans are uncircumcised, and the Law cannot be an impediment. Paul presents the following argument: when Abraham believed in the divine promise and his faith was reckoned to him as righteousness (Gen 15:6), he had not yet been circumcised. The circumcision took place later, in Genesis 17. Hence, for Paul, Abraham is the father of all those who are uncircumcised and who, like him, are justified by faith alone, without circumcision (Rom 4:9–12).

This kind of argumentation may surprise modern readers, but it was perfectly normal for readers in antiquity. When Jesus states in John 8:58, "Very truly, I tell you, before Abraham was, I am," he evokes the same principle: he existed before Abraham, and he is therefore superior to Abraham.

Applications of this "law of antiquity" or "precedence" frequently appear in the Old Testament. The genealogies in the Bible are all intended to prove the ancient origin of families and institutions. In another passage, when Jeremiah says that God chose him before he was conceived (Jer 1:5), he asserts that his vocation comes from God, not from personal ambition or human motivation. His consecration therefore came before his conception, and so it is not of human origin.

Similarly, the dignity of the sanctuaries depends on their antiquity. The temple and the cult of Bethel are tied to Jacob (Gen 28:10–22), whereas Jerusalem is implicitly connected to Abraham (Gen 22:1–19; cf. 22:14; 2 Chr 3:1).[1] This is why the cult of Jerusalem is superior to the cult of Bethel. A short note in Num 13:22 reveals a bit of chauvinism: "Hebron was built seven years before Zoan in Egypt"; this gloss is intending to prove the superiority of Hebron over the great Egyptian city. Obviously, the law of primogeniture also fits into this category. This law is behind Wisdom's claim of superiority over all other creatures, because it was "engendered" at the beginning (Prov 8:22). Even YHWH's assertion in Second Isaiah, "I, YHWH, am first, and will be with the last," echoes this law (Isa 41:4; 44:6).

The situation in the Pentateuch is no different. For example, the construction of the tent of meeting and the cultic institutions go back to the period of the wanderings in the wilderness—that is, to a time long before the temple of Solomon. It was indeed necessary to establish the permanent value of these institutions. The temple that Solomon built was destroyed by the Babylonian armies in 586 B.C.E. However, according to the texts of the Pentateuch, the cult was much older than the Monarchy, and therefore it could not be eradicated by the catastrophe of the Exile.

The same principle also applies to other civil or religious institutions in Israel. According to the Bible, the essential part of Israel's legal "constitution" was developed during the Mosaic period, not during the Davidic monarchy. After the failure of the Monarchy, it was a critical necessity to find a foundation

---

1. Actually Abraham passed by Bethel and Shechem *before* Jacob and built altars there (Gen 12:6, 7, 8). According to these texts, Abraham was the true founder of these cults, not Jacob.

for Israel's reconstruction. This foundation, of course, had to be ancient. Israel therefore went from David to Moses. Furthermore, if Moses preceded the Monarchy in time, the Monarchy was logically subject to the Mosaic Law and was judged by it. This is the reasoning of the authors of the "Deuteronomistic History."

For the Priestly Writer, it is essential to underscore the connection between Israel's history and the Creation of the world. According to this same Priestly Writer, the Noahic and Abrahamic Covenants are superior to the Sinai Covenant because they are older. What is true for the cult is even truer for the narratives of Genesis that speak of the world's Creation and the patriarchs. What was the reason for tracing Israel's faith back to the Creation of the world and to the first ancestors of the people? Why did it not begin with Moses? The Post-exilic period, during which the Pentateuch received its final form, once again gives us the answer. At this time, Israel is living among nations that dominate it and is in contact with other cultures that it cannot ignore. In this context, the narratives of Genesis 1–11, especially the first account of the Creation, intend to show that Israel's God has no reason to be envious of the divinities of other nations.

This seems to be obvious to anyone who reads the Bible today, particularly in a Christian or monotheistic world, but it was much less evident in the midst of the upheavals of the Exilic and Postexilic periods, when Israel was going through the most dramatic period of its existence and was in danger of being wiped off the map of the world. Israel's religious leaders and intelligentsia had to respond to terrible challenges forced on them by the nations that had succeeded in conquering the land and destroying the most sacred symbols of their life—their religious and political institutions, the temple and the monarchy. It was crucial to be able to show that Israel's God was not at all inferior to the powerful divinities of the conquerors. Because superiority largely depended on antiquity, it was necessary to prove that the God of Israel was very ancient. In this context, it is easier to understand why it was fitting to have narratives about the Creation of the world in which the sole architect of the universe was Israel's God.

One might easily misunderstand what I am writing about faith in a Creator God. A question inevitably arises: did Israel actually "invent" a Creator God in order to "save face" in the eyes of the Mesopotamian peoples who had similar accounts such as, for example, the story of *Enuma Elish*?

Two aspects need to be distinguished. On the one hand, there is Israel's faith, with all of its potentialities. On the other hand, we have history, with its questions and requirements. Israel's faith was not expressed in an abstract world sheltered from the traumatic experiences of history. On the contrary, it was always expressed in response to challenging events. It is an established fact, for example, that faith in a unique God, the world's Creator, is expressed univocally and unambiguously for the first time in Second Isaiah (Isaiah 40–55). Some elements of this faith were already present in older texts. However, before the Postexilic period, it was not necessary to affirm as clearly faith in a unique God, the Creator of the universe. This implies a deepening of faith rather than an "invention." Israel recognized its God as being the unique Creator of the universe; it did not invent a new "god."

Moreover, it was crucial to be able to maintain that Israel's God is the Creator of the universe and not simply a local divinity. YHWH indeed failed as a local divinity precisely because he had not been able to save his people from their enemies. But Israel's God is also the God of the universe, with dominion over all the nations. The prophet Jeremiah states, for example, that YHWH himself has declared war on his people. He himself will lead the Babylonian army against his own city, Jerusalem.[2] But if God leads the enemies' armies, he is also the one who, according to Second Isaiah,[3] decrees their defeat and puts Cyrus on the international scene in order to allow his people to return to their land. The Second Isaiah also adds that Israel's God is the God of the universe because he is the first and the last.[4] It is essential for YHWH to be the first—to have existed before all things—in order to assert his transcendence.

The narratives in Genesis 1–11 relating to the origin of the world and the nations are situated in this same milieu. They defend, in narrative form, theological theses of primary importance. The universe is not in the hands of anonymous powers, nor do worldly potentates govern it. Furthermore, it is not the work of foreign divinities. The world was created by Israel's God, and he alone has power over all creation.

The argument concerning the patriarchs is analogous, but it is situated in a purely Israelite context. The patriarchal narratives are intending to instill a basic conviction: the God of the Exodus and the God of the patriarchs is the same unique God. When God appeared to Moses for the first time, he revealed his identity in the following way: "I am the God of your father, the God of Abraham, the God of Isaac, and the God of Jacob" (Exod 3:6). This assertion leaves no doubt about the connection between the religion of the patriarchs and the religion of the Exodus. The God of Moses is not different from the God of the patriarchs. Consequently, Moses' God was not invented by the man of God. This is not a more "recent" religion than the religion of the patriarchs, which—because of its antiquity—could have claimed true superiority. Why is the identity of the God of the Exodus and the God of the patriarchs so strongly maintained?

---

2. See, for example, Jer 4:5–8.
3. See Isa 41:2–3, 25–29; 45:1–6.
4. Isa 44:6, 48:12.

The answer is once again revealed in data from the Postexilic period. When the community of Israel reconstructed itself, one group rather quickly became dominant: the returnees from Babylon. They were economically, culturally, and politically the strongest. A conflict arose between the "people of the land" (those who stayed in the country during the Exile) and those who were coming home from the Exile. It is even possible that the roots of the conflict went farther back in time. During the Exile, those who remained in Israel claimed to be the sole heirs of the land and based their claim on the figure of Abraham: "the inhabitants of these waste places [the ruins of Jerusalem and Judah after the deportation] in the land of Israel keep saying, 'Abraham was only one man, yet he got possession of the land; but we are many; the land is surely given us to possess'" (Ezek 33:24).

However, those who had been deported referred mainly to the figure of Moses and the experience of the Exodus (or the new exodus) to support their rights. Without going into detail on the discussions between the different factions, we can affirm that the book of Genesis was intended as a reply to the criticism and an end to the controversy. Israel has only one God because the God of the patriarchs is the God of the Exodus, and the God of the Exodus fulfills the promises made to the patriarchs (cf. Gen 15:13–16; Genesis 17; and Exod 6:2–8). There can be no conflict between the two. This also means that the "true" God is the God of the patriarchs *and* the God of the Exodus and that "true" Israel descended from the patriarchs *and* lived through the Exodus. "True" Israel is therefore first and foremost made up of the exiles' group.

Thus, it is clear, getting back to our topic, that the texts of the Pentateuch want to show the antiquity of Israel's traditions: Israel is older than the Monarchy and older than the Conquest of the land. The God of the Exodus is the God of the patriarchs. Israel's God is the Creator of the universe. Antiquity is needed to prove the worth of Israel's traditions to the nations. Among the people, however, the purpose is to reconcile and unite the various factions of Postexilic Israel.

B. The Law of Conservation:
Nothing Is Eliminated

The second law results from the first: if what is ancient has such great value, then nothing can be eliminated. If a tradition is ancient, it must be maintained even if it has been superceded. A law cannot be abolished, even if it is no longer applicable. Ancient society is fundamentally conservative. Indeed, nothing is eliminated; everything is preserved and interpreted.[5] There are many examples

---

5. See Fishbane, *Biblical Interpretation*, 1–19.

of this procedure in the Old Testament, especially in the Pentateuch. The most remarkable is the case of the three legislative codes. The Deuteronomic Code (Deuteronomy 12–26) presents itself on the whole as a revision of the Covenant Code (Exodus 21–23). The Holiness Code (Leviticus 17–26) reproduces and extends this judicial work of interpretation and updating in several areas.

Most scholars support this theory, which is reasonable enough. However, even we do not admit the theory that biblical Law evolved, it is still surprising to encounter in the Pentateuch three different codes that deal with similar questions in different ways.[6] The Bible wanted to preserve these three codes although they disagree on various points. In addition, the same Lord proclaimed all of these laws on the same Mount Sinai (or Horeb) to the same Moses. From a formal and judicial point of view, no essential difference exists between the three codes: they all have the same authority. In order to know which law is to be applied in a specific case, it is necessary to perform an exegetical exercise.

The same phenomenon exists in the narrative texts. Different versions of an event are juxtaposed but not harmonized. For example, the Bible has kept two versions of Yhwh's covenant with Abraham, one in Genesis 15 and the other in Genesis 17. There are three versions of the wife/sister episode, as we saw above. Many interpreters contend, with good reason, that the second episode, in Genesis 20, is a "revised" version of the first one (Gen 12:10–20). We still find the first version in Genesis, even though the second version could very well have replaced the first one. In the few cases in which we have two versions of the same event combined into a single account, as in Genesis 6–9, Exodus 14, and Numbers 13–14, the earlier version has not been suppressed.

In Genesis 1–3, there are two consecutive accounts of Creation. It would have been easier to eliminate one of these in favor of the other. In this case as well, the redactors and editors of the Bible preferred to leave their readers with an obvious "doublet," even if this meant upsetting the coherence of the section as a whole.

In the case of the Pentateuch, the desire to collect everything that tradition had handed down became particularly strong during the time of the Second Temple. In the first stages of composition, however, the redactors and editors felt freer to rewrite an ancient text in accord with their own style and criteria. The following section explains this fact.

---

6. For the recent tendency to disqualify all attempts at diachronic reading of the different legislative codes in the Bible, see R. Westbrook, "What Is the Covenant Code?" *Theory and Method in Biblical and Cuneiform Law: Revision, Interpolation and Development* (ed. B. M. Levinson; JSOTSup 181; Sheffield, 1994) 15–36; and the criticism of B. M. Levinson, "The Case for Revision and Interpolation within the Biblical Legal Corpora," in *Theory and Method in Biblical and Cuneiform Law: Revision, Interpolation and Development* (ed. B. M. Levinson; JSOTSup 181; Sheffield, 1994) 37–59.

C. The Law of Continuity and Updating

Although the ancient world was conservative, it also preserved only the things that had value for the present time. The Pentateuch (and this holds true *mutatis mutandis* for the rest of the Bible) aimed at two complementary goals. It attempted both to reconnect with the past and to prove the permanent value of the ancient traditions for the present time.

Furthermore, Israel did not hold onto its traditions merely to admire them in a display case. Interest in the past was always tied to current concerns. Deuteronomy is the book of the Pentateuch that illustrates this best. Chapter 5 is typical of this dual concern, in the introduction to the theophany at Mount Horeb: "Not with our ancestors did YHWH make this covenant, but with us, who are all of us here alive today" (Deut 5:3). Despite the difficulties of interpretation, especially in identifying the "fathers" and those who are speaking in first-person plural ("us"), the text's intent is clear enough: the Covenant does not belong to the past but to the present.[7] Deuteronomy's fondness for the term "today" is one of the many signs of its desire to update older traditions.

The same preoccupation appears in various passages in Second Isaiah. One text is famous: "Do not remember the former things, or consider the things of old. I am about to do a new thing; now it springs forth, do you not perceive it?" (Isa 43:18–19). The idea presented in this oracle seems to clash with what we have just asserted. How could YHWH ask his people to forget the things of the past if they are so important? The problem, in the present context, is different. After the Exile, Israel was tempted to reminisce on a past that had no impact on the present. In the past, YHWH had acted but now he has forgotten his people: "Zion said, 'YHWH has forsaken me, my Lord has forgotten me'" (Isa 49:14). Some people actually thought that Israel's faith had reached its end. Now, after the Exile, Israel's God was no longer acting. This implied a need to find other ways of salvation. However, the Pentateuch seeks to prove the continuing validity of the ancient traditions for the Postexilic community. The signs of this agenda are obvious.

Many additions by late or not-so-late authors aimed at "updating" the ancient texts. The reinterpretation of ancient laws in later codes clearly shows the need for adapting the legislation to new situations. This is true for the laws on slavery as well as for laws concerning loans or the celebration of festivals. Examples abound, and it is not necessary to dwell on this point.

---

7. On this problem, see T. Römer (*Israels Väter*, 45–53), who proposes the following interpretation: the Covenant is made with the generation present at Horeb, not with a different generation of the past. Therefore, the text insists on the topicality of the event in the "narrative world." Of course, this text is indirectly addressed to its recipients and aims at convincing them that the Covenant is actually for them as well.

The desire to update can sometimes be discerned in small details; at other times, there are longer additions; and, finally, we find new versions of events juxtaposed with older accounts. In Gen 18:6, one word was added to give the text a slightly different turn. Abraham asks Sarah to prepare cakes for their three guests and tells her to take three measures of "flour" (*qemah*). A later editor simply added another, more precise word: "choice flour" (*sōlet*). The Hebrew text is overloaded; at least one of these terms is redundant. The second one, "choice flour," is quite likely secondary. The word appears chiefly in cultic laws.[8] An editor wanted to specify that the flour used to prepare the cakes was the same as the flour used in the cult.[9] For this editor, YHWH was one of the guests, and this is why the meal had to correspond to the law on ritual offerings. The redactional addition updates the narrative so that Abraham becomes, for the readers of this later time, a faithful observer of the Law and a model to be imitated (see Gen 18:19; 22:18; 26:5).

What can be verified in the case of a simple detail applies *a fortiori* to more important passages. We have seen the function of later additions such as Gen 12:1–4a and Exod 19:3b–8. Gen 12:1–4a makes Abraham the ancestor of all those who left Mesopotamia to settle in the Promised Land. Texts such as Gen 28:13–15 and 31:3 present Jacob as the model for the exiles who are returning home. Deuteronomy "updates" the ancient traditions on various levels and reinterprets them in order to answer adequately the questions that arose after the Assyrian invasions, after the fall of Jerusalem, and at the time of reconstruction.[10]

The Priestly Writer, in turn, endeavors to convince his addressees of the validity of the ancient traditions. P rereads, reinterprets, and updates the history of the origins, the promises made to the patriarchs, the history of the Exodus, the Sinai legislation, and Israel's wanderings in the wilderness in order to build a bridge from the past to the present over the crevasse of the Exile. This way of seeing things requires a bit of nuancing, and we should note that not all interpreters share these convictions concerning Deuteronomy and the Priestly Writer. However, very few are unwilling to concede that a certain amount of reinterpretation and updating exists in these texts.

---

8. See, for example, Exod 29:2, 40; Lev 2:1, 4, 5, 7, etc. (13 times); Num 6:15; 7:13, 19, etc. (27 times).

9. See Wellhausen, *Prolegomena*, 62; Gunkel, *Genesis*, 195.

10. Cf. E. Otto, "Von der Programmschrift einer Rechtsreform zum Verfassungsentwurf des Neuen Israel: Die Stellung des Deuteronomiums in der Rechtsgeschichte Israels," in *Bundesdokument und Gesetz: Studien zum Deuteronomium* (ed. G. Braulik; Herders biblische Studien 4; Fribourg, 1995) 93–105. See further B. M. Levinson, "Textual Criticism, Assyriology, and the History of Interpretation: Deuteronomy 13:7a as a Test Case in Method," *JBL* 120 (2001) 211–43.

The Pentateuch as a whole complies with the same requirement. Out of the various elements that compose it, the Pentateuch established a foundation on which Postexilic Israel could reconstruct itself. The two pillars supporting this construction were the Law and the temple. Insistence on the Law as such appears primarily in Deuteronomy and in the tradition from which it derives. The cult of the temple is undeniably one of the major provisions of the Priestly Writer.[11] The Pentateuch as a whole provides the historical and legal authentication and legitimation for these two institutions. Israel became a people when, through the mediation of Moses, Yhwh gave them a Law and founded their cult. If these institutions were valid before the Monarchy, they ought still to be valid after its disappearance. A resort to the Mosaic past is called for by the needs of the present.

After the Exile, one of the biggest problems concerned the land. Was it really worth leaving Babylon or Egypt to return to Israel? Genesis answers these questions by asserting that the promises made to the patriarchs are still of current interest. They are unilateral, unconditional promises tied to a divine oath (cf. Genesis 15 and 17) that nothing can abolish.

Even though the text of Genesis ends with Jacob going down to Egypt with his entire family, it insists (twice) that the stay in Egypt is temporary: God appears to Jacob and promises that he will "go up" again to the Promised Land (Gen 46:1–5a); and, before dying, Joseph states that God will visit his people and lead them back to the land promised to Abraham, Isaac, and Jacob (50:24).

The Pentateuch ends in the same way: from the summit of Mount Nebo, Moses can see the whole country that God swore to give to the three patriarchs. Moses does not enter this land, but everything has been prepared for the people, led by Joshua, to cross the Jordan.

The major concern of these texts is to show the realization of the promises made to the patriarchs. It is indeed difficult to find a strictly "archaeological" interest in the past in the Pentateuch. Israel recalls the past because it is "foundational" to the present.

D. The Law of Economy:
Only What Is Necessary Should Be Written

After the above presentation of abstract principles with regard to redaction of the Pentateuch, it is important to ask some questions about the material

---

11. Anyone wishing to follow the development of Israel's religious ideas and institutions up to the New Testament will find these two "pillars": on the one hand the Law, defended by the Pharisees, and on the other hand, the temple, which was the preoccupation of the Sadducees. Paul was arrested because he was conspiring against the people, the Law, and the "place"—the temple (Acts 21:28). The Law and the temple were sacred for Israel because the life of the people depended on them.

problems encountered by those responsible for the final redaction of the work. A modern reader can hardly imagine the concrete problems involved in writing in the ancient world.[12] Few persons were able to write. The materials were very expensive, and all the work was done by hand. Today, for example, it takes a scribe approximately one year to copy the entire Torah; and it requires 62 animals' skins sewn together. The price of a manuscript of this kind can vary between $18,000 and $40,000.[13] In antiquity, the price would have been even higher.

Writing on a scroll was time-consuming and very expensive. Space had to be conserved for quite obvious economic reasons. Anyone who looks closely at the most ancient manuscripts, from Qumran, or at the most recent manuscripts notices that the margins and the spaces between lines are quite small. It was important to make the best possible use of space in order to avoid wasting precious material.[14]

However, in comparison with manuscripts from other cultural regions—for example, Greece—biblical manuscripts have larger margins, more space between lines, and the scribes generally use a space to separate words. We do not know if these practices in Israel are very ancient. The first important manuscripts in our possession are in fact the scrolls from Qumran. Is it possible that manuscripts were created in earlier periods? Because we have no information, our answers can only be hypothetical.

The production of manuscripts required special economic conditions. Although the alphabetic system was simpler than the cuneiform signs of Mesopotamia or the hieroglyphs of Egypt, scribes still had a difficult task because they had to learn not only the alphabet but also the formulas and procedures for preparing the materials they were to write on. Furthermore, during the Pre-exilic period a "scribe" was more of a civil servant at court rather than just a simple "secretary" (see 2 Sam 8:17, 20:25; 1 Kgs 4:3; 2 Kgs 22:3; Jer 36:12).

Spending time writing was a luxury that only a wealthy society could afford; that is to say, a few people in the society—the scribes—were able to live with-

---

12. See D. W. Jamieson-Drake, *Scribes and Schools in Monarchic Judah: A Socio-Archaeological Approach* (JSOTSup 109; Sheffield, 1991) 222–37; among the most important works, we must mention A. Lemaire, *Les écoles et la formation de la Bible dans l'ancien Israël* (OBO 39; Fribourg and Göttingen, 1981); M. Haran, "On the Diffusion of Literacy and Schools in Ancient Israel," in *Congress Volume: Jerusalem, 1986* (VTSup 40; Leiden, 1988) 81–95.

13. Data furnished by L. Avrin, *Scribes, Script and Books: The Book Art from Antiquity to the Renaissance* (Chicago, 1991) 115–17.

14. The "law of economy" may support a recent theory proposed by the Australian scholar A. F. Campbell, who argues that many texts were in fact "summaries" that served as "outlines" for the narrators and all who had to proclaim the sacred texts in public. The economic conditions of the time may explain this. See A. F. Campbell, "The Reported Story: Midway between Oral Performance and Literary Art," *Semeia* 46 (1989) 77–85.

out participating in the production of the basic necessities for themselves and their families. According to recent research, the economic conditions for literary development in Israel, especially in Jerusalem, did not develop until between the 8th and the 7th centuries B.C.E.[15] This thesis forces us to abandon the widespread notion that there was a royal court in David's and Solomon's time in which highly developed literary activity took place.[16]

Archaeological and epigraphic data and recent research on writing in the kingdom of Judah support neither the hypothesis of a Yahwist theologian in the court of Solomon[17] nor von Rad's thesis of an Enlightenment that occurred in his court around the 10th century B.C.E.[18] At that time, Jerusalem did not have the means to support a class of professional scribes.[19] The economic and cultural growth only reached a level high enough for the birth and development of literary activity of this sort two centuries later, first in Samaria and then in Jerusalem. Furthermore, this was the period when the first writing prophets appeared—for example, Amos and Hosea in the North and then Isaiah and Micah in the South.

There is another case of writing that we need to consider in this context. The oldest biblical text discovered up to now in Israel is inscribed on two small silver cylinders unearthed in 1989 in the Valley of Gehennah in Jerusalem (Keteph Hinnom, close to St. Andrews Scottish Church). These scrolls contain the priestly blessing of Num 6:24–26. According to the specialists, these scrolls go back to the 7th century or to the beginning of the 6th century B.C.E.[20] Based on this information, it is hard to imagine that the written sources of the Pentateuch, or of the Bible, go back beyond the 8th century B.C.E.[21] Of course, we cannot exclude *a priori* the possibility that there were some written documents before that time. However, the specialists in this field do not encourage us to search in that direction.

Can this information help us to do a better job of evaluating the theories on the Pentateuch? It is not easy to give a univocal answer to this question.[22]

---

15. Jamieson-Drake, *Scribes*, 74–80 and passim.

16. See above all ibid., 138–44.

17. Cf. W. H. Schmidt, "Ein Theologe in salomonischer Zeit?"

18. Von Rad, "Josephsgeschichte und ältere Chokma."

19. On this period, see H. M. Niemann, *Herrschaft, Königtum und Staat: Skizzen zur soziokulturellen Entwicklung im monarchischen Israel* (FAT 6; Tübingen, 1993).

20. See G. Barkay, "The Priestly Benediction on Silver from Keteph Hinnom in Jerusalem," *Cathedra* 52 (1989) 37–76 (Hebrew; proposed date: end of the 7th century B.C.E.); A. Yardeni, "Remarks on the Priestly Blessing on Two Ancient Amulets from Jerusalem," *VT* 41 (1991) 176–85 (proposed date: 6th century B.C.E.).

21. Cf. A. de Pury, "Osée 12 et ses implications pour le débat actuel sur le Pentateuque," in *Le Pentateuque: Débats et recherches* (ed. P. Haudebert; LD 151; Paris, 1992) 175–207, especially p. 176.

22. See the discussion in N. Lohfink, "Gab es eine deuteronomistische Bewegung?" in

Recent studies in the field of writing that we have cited above lead us to think that scribes began by writing short texts. A guild of scribes who had just learned to master literary techniques was not really prepared to produce a long document immediately. In any case, it is not possible to develop a comprehensive theory of the Pentateuch on the basis of fragmentary information.

At first, the scribes wrote on stones (cf. Deut 27:2–3), metal cylinders, sherds (potsherds, *ostraca*), clay tablets, or papyrus imported from Egypt. After the Exile, parchment was commonly used.[23] Once parchment came into use, it became easier to write longer documents. All these considerations provide grist for the mill of the scholars who think that the Pentateuch began with small units and that larger units came later. In other words, first came "fragments" and then "documents."

Other theories have become problematic because of research on writing. For example, it is hard to imagine, mainly for economic and technical reasons, that scribes or editors could make many additions to extant texts. Scrolls were very precious objects, and they were kept until they could no longer be used— until the writing began to disappear because the material had degraded or for some other reason. This implies that there were few opportunities for modifying the text, making corrections, or inserting supplements.

Furthermore, in the ancient manuscripts, small margins limited the potential for insertions. Another consideration must be added to this first observation: because the Pentateuch was a sacred text, special authority and serious reasons were necessary to permit modifications to be made. Nevertheless, some authors go as far as positing the existence of seven or eight (or even more) redactional levels in a single text. This hardly seems plausible, because one would have had to rewrite the entire scroll in order to insert a lengthy addition. Finally, the manuscripts of Qumran, despite their differences, do not bear the mark of multiple redactional additions.

One more remark needs to be made: there were probably not many manuscripts or scrolls in circulation. With the exception of official institutions, such as the temple, who would have had the financial means to buy them or to commission the writing of such expensive scrolls? The multiplication of scrolls is a recent phenomenon. The destruction of the temple in 70 C.E. certainly influenced the distribution of the Scriptures throughout the Hebrew communities of the diaspora. Because the temple had been destroyed, the Law alone was left to nourish Israel's religious life.

Jeremia und die "deuteronomistische Bewegung" (ed. W. Gross; BBB 98; Weinheim, 1995) 91–113, especially pp. 335–47.

23. See M. Haran, "Book-Scrolls in Israel in Preexilic Times," *JJS* 33 (1982) 161–73; idem, "Book-Scrolls at the Beginning of the Second Temple Period: The Transition from Papyrus to Skins," *HUCA* 54 (1983) 111–22.

According to the Talmud, there were three manuscripts of the Torah in the temple of Jerusalem when it was sacked by Titus's armies.[24] We do not know how many existed elsewhere. The communities in Alexandria, Egypt (where the Greek Bible [LXX] was translated) and in Babylon, as well as the small community at Qumran, had sacred books. How many copies of the Law were in circulation during the Persian period? Probably only large urban communities possessed expensive scrolls of the Law. The economic and cultural conditions necessary for the purchase and use of the Scriptures undoubtedly developed initially only in rather important cities. Furthermore, public use of the scrolls implied the kind of religious organization that was more commonly found in large centers than in small isolated villages.

E. Extrabiblical Parallels

Recently, the various theories on the formation of the Pentateuch have been strongly criticized by the advocates of synchronic reading. Although some of the criticism is justified, the study of extrabiblical parallels nevertheless confirms the diachronic view of the Pentateuch's origin. In short, the extrabiblical parallels show that the texts not only have a long history behind them but they also make it possible to retrace the major lines of this history. Scholars have at their disposal a great deal of material justifying comparisons with the Pentateuch: legal codes, religious and profane narratives, historical records, chronicles of military campaigns, and even travel journals.

Many studies compare biblical legislation with the laws of Mesopotamia or the Hittite Empire.[25] Various Mesopotamian legal codes, which can be dated with some certainty, show that Law can and must evolve in accordance with important political, economic, and social changes.[26] One example will suffice. The Hittite laws occasionally use the following expressions: "before"/"now." Grammatically speaking, the text goes from forms of past tense to present tense. This transition appears in a law on belligerence:

---

24. See *y. Taʿan.* 4.68a; cf. S. Talmon, "The Three Scrolls of the Law that Were Found in the Temple Court," *Textus* 2 (1962) 14–27 = *The Canon and Masorah of the Hebrew Bible: An Introductory Reader* (ed. S. Z. Leiman; Library of Biblical Studies; New York, 1974) 455–68.

25. For bibliography, see B. M. Levinson (ed.), *Theory and Method in Biblical and Cuneiform Law*; E. Otto, "Biblische Rechtsgeschichte: Ergebnisse und Perspektiven der Forschung," *TRev* 91 (1994) 283–92.

26. See the contributions collected by B. M. Levinson (ed.), in *Theory and Method in Biblical and Cuneiform Law*. For example, the essays by Levinson, "The Case for Revision and Interpolation within the Biblical Legal Corpora," 37–59; E. Otto, "Aspects of Legal Reforms and Reformulations in Ancient Cuneiform and Israelite Law," 160–96. Also see idem, "Town and Rural Countryside in Ancient Israelite Law: Reception and Redaction in Cuneiform and Israelite Law," *JSOT* 57 (1993) 3–22.

If someone blinded a person or broke his teeth *before*, he had to pay one mina of silver, but *now* he must pay twenty shekels of silver.[27]

However, biblical examples of this are rare. Ruth 4:7 is the only text that explicitly refers to a former legal procedure:

> Now this was the custom *in former times* in Israel concerning redeeming and exchanging: to confirm a transaction, the one [seller] took off a sandal and gave it to the other [buyer]; this was the manner of attesting in Israel.[28]

This explanation, or intrusion, of the narrator implies that the addressees no longer know this custom; this is why the author of Ruth 4:7 feels it necessary to give some information about it. We do not, however, find anything comparable in the Pentateuch. It is not easy to discover the reason for this state of things. Correcting a law was undoubtedly delicate when this law was marked with the seal of divine authority. Biblical authors used more subtle means to indicate what law was in force. This short investigation shows clearly enough that the development of law was a well-known phenomenon in the ancient Near East. Hence, we should not be surprised to find signs of this in the Bible.

Concerning narratives, the literature of the ancient Near East provides several examples of redaction similar to the redaction identified by critics in the Pentateuch. J. H. Tigay, for example, compares the way the *Gilgamesh Epic* evolved with some of the results of biblical exegesis.[29] This comparison is very instructive. The textual history of the *Gilgamesh Epic* covers 1,500 years, and archaeologists have found many copies or fragments of copies from various periods. The specialists in the field therefore have abundant material at their disposal to allow them to reconstruct the various phases of the text's formation. It is worthwhile considering this development more closely; there are lessons to be drawn that help us to understand better the formation of the Pentateuch.

Tigay distinguishes four main phases in the development of the *Gilgamesh Epic*: first, isolated narratives, written in Sumerian (2100 B.C.E.); then, the first complete narrative in Akkadian, from the Old Babylonian period (2000–1600 B.C.E.); revisions in the Middle Babylonian period (1600–1000 B.C.E.); and finally, the Standard Babylonian version, known to us thanks to the copy preserved in the library of Assurbanipal (668–627 B.C.E.).[30]

---

27. (Hittite Laws §7.) Example given by B. M. Levinson, "The Human Voice in Divine Revelation: The Problem of Authority in Biblical Law," in *Innovation in Religious Traditions* (ed. M. A. Williams, C. Cox, and M. S. Jaffee; Religion and Society; Berlin, 1992) 35–71, especially p. 42.

28. See the explanation given by Levinson, ibid., 44.

29. See above all J. H. Tigay, "An Empirical Model for the Documentary Hypothesis," *JBL* 94 (1975) 329–42; idem, *The Evolution of the Gilgamesh Epic* (Philadelphia, 1982); idem (ed.), *Empirical Models for Biblical Criticism* (Philadelphia, 1985).

30. See, above all, idem, "The Evolution of the Pentateuchal Narratives in the Light of the Evolution of the *Gilgamesh Epic*," in ibid., 21–52.

The first two narratives relate episodes associated with the life of the hero of Uruk, Gilgamesh; there is no connection between these episodes.[31] The first version in Akkadian assembles the isolated accounts into the first large narrative unit. Up to now, it has been impossible to establish whether there were intermediate stages between the isolated Sumerian narratives and the first large, unified work written in Akkadian.

There is a clearly observable evolution between the first and the second stage.[32] First, the independent episodes were placed in a unified plot line organized around a single topic—the quest for immortality. This theme was already present in some of the Sumerian narratives, but not in all of them. The element permitting the connection of the various parts is Enkidu, the character who becomes Gilgamesh's friend in the Akkadian epic.

Second, the author of the Akkadian text made a choice. He decided to eliminate a few earlier episodes—for example, the narrative about Gilgamesh and Agga. The reasons for these choices often remain obscure. Third, the Akkadian epic introduced its own elements of diverse origins. Fourth, the author largely restructured and rewrote the texts available to him. There are many substantial differences between the Sumerian episodes and their Akkadian counterparts, to such an extent that it would be impossible to reconstruct a Sumerian episode on the basis of the form it was given in the Akkadian text.[33]

The third phase corresponds to the versions of the epic in the Middle Babylonian period. At that time, according to Tigay, the great freedom that the author of the preceding period had enjoyed, when he dealt with the preexisting material of the narrative, disappeared. Of course, the editors still added some sentences, even entire sections, or reformulated poetic passages in more modern language. However, it is clear that they did not "create" a new work. They handed on a "revised" version of the work that had been composed at an earlier period. To put it more simply, they acted like editors and no longer like original authors.[34]

The final stage covers the period from the 9th or the 8th century all the way down to the 2nd or 1st century B.C.E. The best-known version of the epic is the one found in the library of Assurbanipal (668–627 B.C.E.), the text of which was composed between 1200 and 1000 B.C.E. The changes seem to be of little

---

31. Eight extant Sumerian episodes mention Gilgamesh: (1) Gilgamesh and the land of the living; (2) Gilgamesh and the bull from heaven; (3) the death of Gilgamesh; (4) the flood, a theme that is only indirectly related to Gilgamesh; (5) Gilgamesh, Enkidu, and the underworld; (6) Gilgamesh and Agga; (7) a fragment that is particularly difficult to decipher, UET 6, no. 60; (8) a hymn to Shulgi, the king of Ur, contains two small fragments of hymns addressed to Gilgamesh by Shulgi. Cf. Tigay, "Evolution of the Pentateuchal Narratives," 30.

32. Ibid., 32–35.

33. Ibid., 35–38.

34. Ibid., 38–39.

importance. Because the texts from the Babylonian period were all fragmentary, it is important to be prudent in doing this comparative study. Nevertheless, it seems that some basic modifications were made at this time. Three passages were added: a prologue that emphasizes the wisdom acquired by Gilgamesh during the course of his adventures; this prologue precedes the hymn that most likely introduced the ancient epic in the Old Babylonian period. The other two additions are the famous story of the flood, on tablets XI and XII, with the mention of the underworld, where Enkidu, who had died earlier (tablet VIII), reappears.[35]

At this stage, the process of development comes to an end. Only minor differences exist between the various versions. These differences mainly have to do with spelling, grammar, and formatting. We now have a relatively stable *textus receptus*.

A brief comparison with studies of the Pentateuch reveals some similarities in the development of the *Gilgamesh Epic* and certain models proposed by specialists in the formation of the Pentateuch. Four of these similarities are especially important:

1. The theory of the evolution of the *Gilgamesh Epic*, as the assyriologists have reconstructed it, has many points in common with the model H. Gunkel presented for Genesis at the beginning of the 20th century. Gunkel said that Genesis is *eine Sammlung von Sagen* (a "collection of popular stories"). According to this great German scholar, the book of Genesis was composed of small, independent narrative units, just like the *Gilgamesh Epic*, which first existed as a collection of independent stories about the same hero.

We now have a further argument in favor of the model preferred by the Heidelberg school (Rendtorff, Blum, Albertz). The introductions published recently by Blenkinsopp and by Zenger, as well as Levin's study of the Yahwist, also go in this direction.[36] The "hypothesis of fragments," to put it in classical terms, is to be preferred over the other hypotheses about the first stage of the Pentateuch's formation. But how do we explain the transition from small units to the first large work?

In the case of the *Gilgamesh Epic*, the transition was not gradual. There were no intermediary stages like the stage Gunkel had proposed with regard to Genesis. It should be noted, however, that the *Gilgamesh Epic* is in itself a "narrative cycle" with a single hero.

Let us imagine the existence of several collections of episodes or "narrative cycles" in the Bible. In Genesis and elsewhere in the Pentateuch, many cycles

---

35. Ibid., 41–42.
36. See Blenkinsopp, *Pentateuch*, 124–25; Zenger (ed.), *Einleitung*, 108–19; Levin, *Jahwist*, 34–35 and 436–41.

are juxtaposed, and each of the cycles has its own theme and characteristics. The situation is therefore different, and we must avoid pushing the comparison too far. In any case, Tigay's research backs the hypothesis that "fragments" existed before "documents."

2. The author of the longest narrative enjoyed great freedom, freedom to such an extent that it is not possible to reconstitute the original version of any episode on the basis of the form it was given at the following stage. In this case also, some scholars apply an analogous principle in their interpretation of the Pentateuch. According to Blum, for example, it is not always possible to distinguish clearly between the "tradition" and the "redaction," that is, to separate the earlier elements from the redactional work that elaborated on and organized them into the large narrative units of the Pentateuch.[37] The example of the *Gilgamesh Epic* should therefore encourage scholars to be prudent when reconstituting the previous stages of given texts. Furthermore, many exegetes today think it risky, or even impossible, to rediscover the oral tradition behind a written text.[38]

3. The great freedom that characterized the work of the Old Babylonian period gradually evaporated. In later times, it practically disappeared. Tigay notes that, during the earliest periods, the additions were well integrated and, in many cases, we could not identify them if we did not have various versions for comparison. Toward the end of the process, the additions were not as well integrated and, consequently, it becomes easier to recognize them. In this context, Tigay mentions a principle advanced by M. Greenberg that I paraphrase as follows: "Adaptability and integration are characteristic of the first stages of transmission; rigidity and a lack of assimilation are characteristic of semicanonical material at the redactional stage."[39] In other words, whereas an editor has no trouble modifying a text during the first stages of transmission, toward the end of the development he can only insert additions into the preexisting text, not transform it. Finally, the easier it is to recognize an addition, the greater the chance that it is a late alteration.

4. A series of phenomena well known to biblical scholars also appears in the *Gilgamesh Epic*. Consequently, despite criticism voiced by various schools from the fundamentalists to representatives of the "New Criticism," scholars may feel confident in continuing to use the classic tools of source criticism. For example,

---

37. Blum, *Studien zur Komposition des Pentateuch*, 208–18 ("Zum Verhältnis von Tradition und Komposition in Exodus und Numeri").

38. P. S. Kirkpatrick, *The Old Testament and Folklore Studies* (JSOTSup 62; Sheffield, 1988).

39. M. Greenberg, "The Redaction of the Plague Narrative in Exodus," in *Near Eastern Studies in Honor of William Foxwell Albright* (ed. H. Goedicke; Baltimore, 1971) 243–52, especially p. 245: "The less integrated the disturbance is into its context, the later it may be assumed to have been combined." Cf. Tigay, "Evolution of the Pentateuchal Narratives," 43.

"resumptive repetitions" found in the *Gilgamesh Epic* are evidence of relatively long redactional additions.[40] Furthermore, in the *Gilgamesh Epic* as in the Pentateuch, it is possible to identify several "sources" because their styles and vocabularies differ.[41] Thus, the account of the flood uses a special formula to introduce the discourses. There is another indication: the wife of Utnapishtim, the hero of the flood, is called "woman" in this narrative, but in other parts of the section in which she appears, the word "wife" is used. Finally, the style of the flood narrative is less homogenous and more repetitive.

Elsewhere, the various versions of the same episode in the *Gilgamesh Epic* use different names for a single character. This immediately makes us think of Jacob/Israel, Reuel/Jethro/Hobab, and YHWH/Elohim. In the *Gilgamesh Epic*, the hero of the flood is called Utnapishtim. However, in one passage, the name Atrahasis appears—the name of a hero in another epic probably used by the author of the *Gilgamesh Epic* (*Gilgamesh* XI 187). This is quite likely an error overlooked by the editor. In any case, it clearly indicates the presence of the "source" that was largely used for the flood narrative that was added to the *Gilgamesh Epic*.

Inconsistencies in the content may also indicate that an addition has been inserted. As we saw above, tablet XII of the Neo-Babylonian epic introduced Enkidu, Gilgamesh's friend, who had died much earlier (tablet VIII). Finally, grammatical inconsistencies may also signify a redactional intervention. The author who introduced the story of the flood used the first-person singular form when he rewrote the older narrative about Atrahasis. The narrative setting requires this change because Utnapishtim tells his own story to Gilgamesh. However, in XI 37, a part of the narrative that used third-person singular remains: "[The god Ea] said to his servant, to me." The editor added "to me," but he did not correct the text. The reason for this decision is not clear. But this phenomenon is instructive, and it reveals another redactional intervention.

One phenomenon or one criterion is generally not enough to establish the presence of an addition or redactional intervention or the use of a source. Decisions should be based on converging indications, and the standards in this kind of work should be high. Comparison with the study of the *Gilgamesh Epic* confirms—if this is necessary—the value of the critical work that has been done during the past two centuries on the pentateuchal "sources." Although a few conclusions may appear fragile and debatable, the work as a whole is hardly in doubt.

On the other hand, we must not forget that there are fundamental differences between the *Gilgamesh Epic* and the Pentateuch. The biblical text is sacred, and it had normative value for the people of Israel. It was a founding text,

---

40. Ibid., 48.
41. Ibid., 42, 45, and 47.

the "constitution" of Postexilic Israel, which is why it contains both laws and narratives.

The *Gilgamesh Epic* certainly occupied an important and perhaps unique place in Mesopotamian culture, but it may hardly be said to have had normative value. This difference is significant for the rules presented above. On the one hand, it was absolutely necessary to update the contents of the Pentateuch and to adapt them to contemporary circumstances. On the other hand, the potential for revising and modifying texts that were considered to be sacred was more strictly limited, especially in later periods.

The differences cannot be denied. But all things considered, they are differences of degree and not of nature. The necessary nuances taken into account, the comparison is still very instructive, and the value of Tigay's research remains indisputable.[42]

---

42. Scholars have also used the *Diatessaron* of Tatian to verify some of their hypotheses regarding the formation of the Pentateuch. See G. F. Moore, "Tatian's *Diatessaron* and the Analysis of the Pentateuch," *JBL* 9 (1890) 201–15 = *Empirical Models* (ed. J. Tigay; Philadelphia, 1985) 243–56; H. Donner, "Der Redaktor: Überlegungen zum vorkritischen Umgang mit der Heiligen Schrift," *Henoch* 2 (1980) 1–30; for a summary, see Carr, *Reading the Fractures of Genesis*, 19–20, 24–25.

For a response to recent challenges to the theories advocated in this chapter, see the Postscript, p. 233.

Chapter 9

Reference Points for
Reading the Pentateuch

Within the limited scope of this introduction, I will not be able to propose a complete theory of the origins and formation of the Pentateuch. Moreover, at this time, we may not yet be capable of such an undertaking. Instead, I will present some points of reference for orienting a critical reading of the Pentateuch. In addition, I will attempt to indicate the most valuable elements of contemporary theories. This chapter will undoubtedly be the most problematic of the entire book. It will not be possible to present a complete argument on each point. Even the bibliography cannot be exhaustive, for this would be both impossible and almost useless. Anyone with knowledge of the subject will easily find the books to consult, and other readers should not have to read through long lists of unfamiliar names.

This chapter presents three main theses:

1. The Pentateuch in its final form is a Postexilic work. The present composition and disposition of the various sections go back to the Persian period. In order to grasp the intent of the work as such, it is necessary to study the period in question.

2. The work as it appears today is complex and thus contains earlier sections. The first important question that arises in this context concerns the existence of a Preexilic document. I do not believe there was one, and I will attempt to justify my conclusion.

3. This does not mean that we should rule out the existence of Preexilic material such as short narratives, well-developed narrative cycles, or collections of laws. On the contrary, it is still possible to recognize ancient material within the Pentateuch as we know it. We cannot always precisely indicate the extent or date of this material, but it was reused and thus it comes from a preceding period. This is an important point I wish to make.

What basic insight can lead to a plausible theory about the Pentateuch? As we saw in the chapter devoted to the history of research, de Wette's discovery offers a solid basis for several hypotheses that have followed one after the other over the course of the past two centuries. Because no other equivalent discovery has been made, scholars must content themselves with going back through the same data. Theories may be honed, qualified, and corrected, and it may even be possible to reach different conclusions, but they cannot really add anything new: the same elements reappear in another form and a different order. Without a new de Wette, it will be difficult to elaborate a "new documentary theory."[1]

There is, however, no lack of new factors. They come primarily from two areas of research. First, archaeological discoveries have provided interpreters with material of great importance: written and iconographic documents, narrative and legislative texts, as well as diplomatic and administrative records. Of course, their comparison with the Pentateuch involves special consideration, because everything needs to be interpreted, including the archaeological record. Nevertheless, Tigay's comparison with the *Gilgamesh Epic* opens the way to other comparisons of the same type, comparisons that should be rewarding. Second, discussion of methodology in the various fields has provided new tools for research. Moreover, the use of diverse methods is sometimes productive. For example, the dialogue between synchronic and diachronic readings has proved constructive in several cases.[2] Consequently, we may be able to construct a theory, without too much speculation, that truly will further a better understanding of the Pentateuch.

A. The Pentateuch and the
Reconstruction of Israel after the Exile

Let us use a simple analogy. The Pentateuch is like a city rebuilt after two earthquakes. The first occurred in 721 B.C.E., when the Assyrian army conquered Samaria and put an end to all of the country's political and religious institutions. Which traditions of the Northern Kingdom survived this disaster? This is difficult to ascertain. We can only be sure about traditions that came from the South, and these were influenced by the polemics between the two rival kingdoms. Nonetheless, we may speculate that some of these traditions were transferred to Jerusalem after the fall of Samaria.

Then, another earthquake destroyed Jerusalem in 586 B.C.E., after a premonitory tremor in 596 B.C.E. In 586, after a long siege, Nebuchadnezzar's Babylonian army captured the city, burned it, and devastated it. We will always have trouble imagining what the population of the city lived through at that time. All of their precious possessions disappeared simultaneously: the

---

1. F. García López ("De la antigua a la nueva crítica del Pentateuco," *EstBib* 52 [1994] 7–35, especially p. 17 n. 27) adopts an idea advanced by E. Otto.

2. For example, the work of E. Blum on Genesis and on Exodus–Numbers borrows many ideas from synchronic studies. Also see D. Carr, who follows the same route in his study of Genesis.

monarchy, which had guaranteed their independence, and the temple, which had been one of the most important symbols of the religious life of the Southern Kingdom.

After the exile, when Cyrus, who had conquered the Babylonians, allowed the exiles to return home to their land, the situation became very complex.[3] The relationship between those who were coming back from Mesopotamia and those who had stayed in the country was far from peaceful.[4]

After many trials and tribulations, the exiles gained the upper hand and began rebuilding the temple of Jerusalem: the *gôlâ* (Hebrew for "exile") group took charge of this undertaking. Not only were the city and the temple reconstructed, but also the community itself was reestablished in accordance with the principles and exigencies of the *gôlâ*. This reconstruction had to meet two needs. First of all, the community needed to rediscover its roots in the past. This first point does not require a long explanation. Jerusalem was reconstructed—that is, the old city, not a new one (Isaiah 54)—for continuity with the past. The same people were being reborn in the same land, under the guidance of the same God. The work of the Postexilic community of Jerusalem was fundamentally a work of restoration: "Israel," as such, was reborn. In other words, this was not the birth of a new people with other ideals and completely different institutions. It was necessary to reconnect with the ancient traditions and rebuild the bridge to the Preexilic past.

Second, it was just as necessary to demonstrate the contemporary value of the ancient traditions and to convince the people that it was possible to rebuild on the old foundations. The two needs at first appear contradictory, but this was the dilemma that the people and their leaders had to solve.

Now, returning to our comparison, we can identify three types of edifices in the reconstruction. Some structures have survived, partially or entirely, the two earthquakes; some are better preserved than others. Next to the rubble and the ruins, a few buildings are almost entirely intact. Elsewhere, there are entirely new buildings that have replaced those that disappeared. Finally, a whole series of composite structures has appeared in which we can recognize ancient elements that have been used in the remodeling, with new sections being added at different periods. In some cases, it is very difficult to distinguish the ancient parts from the new sections. The proportion of old and modern materials is never identical. As a result, it takes trained eyes to read the history of the city and its various quarters. Having said this, we need to remember that all of the edifices, whether ancient or modern, have the same purpose: they have been

3. For a short description of this period, see H. M. Barstad, *The Myth of the Empty Land* (Symbolae Osloenses Fasc. Suppl. 28; Oslo, 1996).

4. Cf. P. Sacchi, *Storia del Secondo Tempio: Israele tra VI secolo a.C. e I secolo d.C.* (Turin, 1994) 92–104; Schramm, *The Opponents of Third Isaiah*, 53–80.

built to accommodate and respond to the needs of their inhabitants. The city is not merely a museum preserving the past; it is attempting to create the conditions indispensable for the survival of people who have recently come through a painful experience.

Just like this city, the Pentateuch contains ancient material meant to establish a connection with the past and new material that responds to current questions. Some sections have been retouched or restored several times. However, the heart of the Postexilic community throbs in every part of the city. Each section, whether ancient or modern, offers refuge, faith, and hope. All of it must therefore be interpreted in the context of the Postexilic period, along with this period's interests and preoccupations.

Even ancient texts, composed during the earliest periods, in a very different milieu and in response to other needs, are found in the Pentateuch simply because they were of particular value to the Postexilic community. They belonged to its heritage and were "useful" for its life and faith.

In what follows, I intend to provide a "map" or "guidebook" to today's visitors of this reconstructed "city" of the Pentateuch so that they may recognize as clearly as possible the different edifices encountered and distinguish various ancient and more-recent styles.

B. Anchor Points for Interpretation: Three Codes, Three Theologies, and the Final Redaction

1. The Three Codes of the Pentateuch

What anchor points do we have after the storm that shook exegesis during the 1970s? To get one's bearings in the Pentateuch as it appears today, it is necessary to begin once again with the intuitions of de Wette, Reuss, Graf, Kuenen, and Wellhausen.

Despite all the controversies, the three codes are still the surest starting point for a critical reading of the Pentateuch.[5] The Covenant Code (Exodus 21–23) precedes the Deuteronomic Code (Deuteronomy 12–26), which in turn comes before the Holiness Code (Leviticus 17–26).[6] The Covenant Code presupposes

---

5. E. Otto ("Die nachpriesterschriftliche Pentateuchredaktion im Buch Exodus," 64) suggests adding a fourth element to these three codes—the Decalogue, which is an Exilic and Deuteronomic composition. He places the Decalogue between Deuteronomy (Preexilic) and the Holiness Code.

6. Van Seters ("Cultic Laws"; idem, "The Law of the Hebrew Slave," *ZAW* 108 [1996] 534–46) tries to show that the Covenant Code is more recent than Deuteronomy. For example, the law in Exodus 21 appears to be more recent than the law in Deuteronomy 15. In my opinion, this is not completely convincing. Van Seters must, among other things, correct the text of Exod 20:24 concerning the "law of the altar" so that it corresponds to his thesis. He

a society at the heart of which were leaders of "extended families" who settled the most important conflicts on the local level—that is, in small towns or villages.

In the Deuteronomic Code, the centralization of the cult was accompanied by judicial centralization. The extended family had to relinquish a large part of

gives the following translation: "In every place where you invoke my name, I will come to you and bless you" ("Cultic Laws," 325–26). The Hebrew text says: "in every place where I cause my name to be remembered I will come to you and bless you" (first-person singular). J. Van Seters prefers the reading of the Syriac version, which is more intelligible, and concludes that the text does not allude to different altars but to various places where pious Israelites invoked the name of YHWH. So, there is no contradiction between the law and the centralization of the cult commanded in Deuteronomy 12. Consequently, Exodus 20 may be posterior to Deuteronomy 12. There are at least five important objections to this interpretation: (1) Why would one chose the Syriac text rather than the *lectio difficilior* of the MT? If we agree with Van Seters that the original text was in the second-person singular, how can we explain the change from second person to first person? (2) It is not true that, "since the clear and usual meaning of the verb *hzkyr* is 'to invoke', it makes no sense for the deity to say: 'I will invoke my name' and scholars have been ingenious in trying to invent other suitable meanings" ("Cultic Laws," 325). A quick look in a dictionary suffices to show that this is not the case. 2 Sam 18:18 offers an excellent parallel. Absalom has a monument built because, as he says, "I do not have a son to recall my name [*baʿabûr hazkîr šĕmî*]." Absalom wants his name to be remembered, and so he has a monument built that "commemorates him." The meaning of Exod 20:24b is analogous: just as the remembrance of Absalom's name is tied to a monument, the remembrance of YHWH's name is tied to the altar or altars, thus marking the place where the legitimate cult is instituted. See J. J. Stamm, "Zum Altargesetz im Bundesbuch," *TZ* 1 (1945) 304–6. It is not justifiable to assert in an imperious manner that "it is certain that the verb should be second person singular" (ibid.). (3) The invocation of the name in Exod 20:24–26 occurs in a ritual context. Each verse mentions the altar. Consequently, even the translation: "you will invoke my name" presupposes that the invocation takes place in a sanctuary, close to an altar. This verse then does not exclude the possibility of several places of worship, and the question of the connection with Deuteronomy 12 remains. (4) Deut 12:13–14 clearly alludes to Exod 20:24b: "Take care that you do not offer your burnt offerings at any place you happen to see [*bĕkol-māqôm*]. But only at the place [*kî ʾim-bammāqôm*] that YHWH will choose in one of your tribes—there you shall offer your burnt offerings." The expression *bĕkol-māqôm* in Deut 12:13 echoes the formula *bĕkol-hammāqôm* in Exod 20:24b and corrects it. Certain manuscripts, such as the Samaritan and some of the targums, also have *bĕkol-hammāqôm* in Deut 12:13 in order to stress the connection with Exod 20:24b. See Levinson, *Deuteronomy and the Hermeneutics of Legal Innovation*, 23–36. (5) Furthermore, Van Seters does not really take into account the general context of the two codes. The world of the Covenant Code is almost exclusively agricultural and pastoral; it is the world of extended families and small villages. The Deuteronomic Code presupposes a world that is more centralized and urbanized, where the family loses its importance while the importance of the centralized institutions increases. A study of the legal, social, and historical background of these two codes does not corroborate Van Seters's thesis, which is based on a series of selective observations. See further B. M. Levinson, "Is the Covenant Code an Exilic Composition? A Response to John Van Seters," in *In Search of Pre-exilic Israel: Proceedings of the Oxford Old Testament Seminar* (ed. J. Day; JSOTSup 406; London: T. & T. Clark, 2004) 272–325.

its power to the central authority in Jerusalem. Deuteronomy "unifies" by asserting that Israel constitutes one people with one God and one temple. This centralization was the result of the Assyrian invasions that ravaged and destroyed the Northern Kingdom in 721 B.C.E. and the Southern Kingdom in 701 B.C.E. Only Jerusalem was not conquered in 701, although it had to pay a very high price in order to survive. Administrative and legal reforms became necessary because the invasions had shattered, if not totally destroyed, local and family structures. King Josiah (640–609 B.C.E.) and his court took advantage of the weakening Assyrian Empire to give the reform a progressively greater religious and political dimension. The desire for religious, political, and administrative centralization took advantage of a favorable situation and translated it into legal terms. Behind the Deuteronomic Code, we can recognize the promoters who contributed to the reform: the court officers (Jerusalem's aristocracy), the influential landowners of Judah, the priesthood, and the monarchy.

After the Exile, the Holiness Code insisted on the idea of a "holy" people, "separated" from other nations. Because Israel was no longer an independent nation, the identity of the people now had to be rooted primarily in its religious institutions—that is, the Law and the temple. The primary concerns of this code are easier to understand in this context. The cult has an important place in the Holiness Code. In addition, the insistence on laws of purity, separation from other nations, and specific rules in the area of sexuality aims above all at preserving the identity of people who feel that their very existence is in danger. It is necessary to establish new boundaries, even in everyday behavior.

The comparison of these three codes provides a set of criteria for the reading of the narrative texts as well as a framework that helps to situate them. In short: the narratives that do not presuppose the centralization of the cult should, theoretically, come before the Deuteronomic reform; the texts that call for it are contemporary; and the texts that presuppose it follow its establishment. Like all other criteria, this standard should be used with requisite prudence.

2. Three Theologies of the Pentateuch

Next to the realm of law, the field of theology offers the most solid bases for the interpretation of the Pentateuch. The theological principles we encounter appear in Deuteronomy, the Priestly Writer, and the Holiness Code (Leviticus 17–26). Deuteronomy, the Priestly Writer, and the Holiness Code contain three theologies, three visions of history, and three programs for Israel's society. Deuteronomy develops a theology of the Covenant with YHWH, which interprets the bond between God and his people as similar to the vassal treaties of the ancient Near East. The Covenant is bilateral and has conditions. The blessings—and hence the existence of Israel—are tied to the people's obedience to the Law. The Deuteronomistic History therefore interprets the fall of Jerusalem and the Exile as consequent upon Israel's unfaithfulness. This is a well-known fact.

Now a crucial question arises: Is there still hope for Israel? On what theological basis could the future of the people be reconstructed? The Priestly narrative largely answers this question. If the Sinai/Horeb Covenant is no longer valid, it must be replaced by another that will remain valid. According to P, YHWH made a "Covenant" with Abraham (Genesis 17) *before* concluding the Covenant at Sinai with the entire people.[7] Following a principle well known today, this older covenant is superior to the one made at Sinai. Furthermore, the Abrahamic Covenant is unilateral and unconditional. The promises therefore do not depend on the faithfulness of the people.

For the Priestly Writer, "Israel," which has been deprived of its political independence and monarchs, becomes a religious "assembly" united around the divine presence, the "glory." "Holiness," a quality that defines places and individuals maintaining a privileged relationship with the divine presence (the "glory"), is bestowed on the priesthood, tent, and altar (Exod 29:44).

Finally, the Holiness Code (H) corrects certain points in P in order to present a synthesis of Deuteronomic theology and of the Priestly theology.

a. The covenant is once again bilateral and conditional (Lev 26:3–4, 14–16), as in Deuteronomy; but the unilateral "Covenant" or the promise made to the patriarchs remains valid (Lev 26:41–42, 44), just as for P: if the Israelites are faithful, "I will bring them into the land of their enemies; if then their uncircumcised heart is humbled and they make amends for their iniquity, then will I remember my covenant with Jacob; I will remember also my covenant with Isaac and also my covenant with Abraham, and I will remember the land."

b. The holiness of the entire people is required ("You shall be holy, for I am holy"; Lev 11:44–45; 19:2; 20:7, 26; 21:8; 22:31–33), just as in Dt, where the entire people is holy because of its election (Deut 7:6; 14:2; 26:19). But holiness is also a special quality of the priesthood (Leviticus 21), as in P's theology (Exod 29:44). For H, Israel is holy because of the experience of the Exodus: at that moment, God separated his people from the nations (Lev 11:45; 18:1–5; 22:33). Furthermore, the people remain holy if they observe the laws of purity and faithfully perform the ritual prescriptions (22:31–33). In this way H unites "grace" and the "Law," because the holiness freely bestowed at the moment of the Exodus from then on depends on the people's faithfulness to the divine Law.

c. The liturgy of expiation (Leviticus 16) is another strong point of the theology proposed by the Holiness Code. This liturgy gives the people the possibility, on regular occasions, to reconcile themselves with YHWH and to go beyond the crises caused by their unfaithfulness.[8]

---

7. See W. Zimmerli, "Sinaibund und Abrahambund: Ein Beitrag zum Verständnis der Priesterschrift," *TZ* 16 (1960) 268–80 = *Gottesoffenbarung: Gesammelte Aufsätze zum Alten Testament* (TBü 19; Munich, 1969) 205–16.

8. See B. Janowski, *Sühne und Heilsgeschehen: Studien zur Sühnetheologie der Priesterschrift und der Wurzel KPR im Alten Orient und im Alten Testament* (WMANT 55; Neukirchen-Vluyn, 1982).

On this point as well, H attempts to break deadlocks in which the former theologies had gotten stuck. Dt had foreseen nothing concrete to deal with the case of unfaithfulness. On this same point, P is rather laconic. H continually reflects on "sin" and "expiation," concepts rooted in the bitter experience of Exile and disappointments after the return.

Quite often, academic research underestimates the importance of Leviticus's theology. The shadow of Wellhausen and his generation still looms over the scholarly world, which considers the Postexilic period to be a moment of spiritual decadence and religious sclerosis.[9] A large part of the final compilation of the Pentateuch does, however, go back to this period and comes from the theological school that wrote the Holiness Code.[10] This period in Israel's history must also be studied according to the needs of its time and not according to absolute, timeless criteria, or even worse, in reference to the tastes of our time.

These three theologies, Dt, P, and H, with the three different legal codes constitute the key elements of the Pentateuch's structure. If we situate things in their chronological order, the result is as follows: the Covenant Code (Preexilic), the Deuteronomic Code (end of the Monarchy), Deuteronomistic theology (end of the Monarchy and Exile); the Priestly narrative (first generation after the return); the Holiness Code with the post-Priestly and post-Deuteronomistic theology (Second Temple).

C. Did a Preexilic Source on Israel's Origins Exist?

The most plausible model today seems to be the one that combines theories proposed during the past century—that is, the hypothesis of fragments, the hypothesis of supplements, and the hypothesis of documents. At the beginning of the redaction of the Pentateuch, these were only isolated narratives or short

---

9. See Blum, *Studien zur Komposition des Pentateuch*, 356 n. 85: "The picture of the transformation of the 'People of Israel' into the 'Jewish community/church/confession' after the exile is one of the most tenacious and cherished misconceptions of Old Testament exegesis." ["Das Bild von der Transformation des 'Volkes Israel' zu der 'Gemeinde/Kirche/Konfession Judentum' nach dem Exil ist eines der hartnäckigsten und beliebtesten Fehlkonzepte der alttestamentlichen Exegese."]

10. See Lohfink, "Die Abänderung der Theologie der priesterlichen Geschichtswerks im Segen des Heiligkeitsgesetzes"; idem, "'Ich bin Jahwe, dein Arzt' (Ex 15,26): Gott, Gesellschaft und menschliche Gesundheit in der Theologie einer nachexilischer Pentateuchbearbeitung (Ex 15,25b.26)," in *"Ich will euer Gott werden": Beispiele biblischen Redens von Gott* (ed. H. Merklein and E. Zenger; SBS 100; Stuttgart, 1981) 11–73 = *Studien zum Pentateuch* (Stuttgartbiblische Aufsatzbände 4; Stuttgart, 1988) 91–155. Also see E. Otto, especially his essays "Die Paradieserzählung Genesis 2–3: Eine nachpriesterschriftliche Lehrerzählung" and "Die nachpriesterschriftliche Pentateuchredaktion im Buch Exodus." Along the same line, see the introduction by J. Blenkinsopp, the commentary by G. J. Wenham on Genesis, and my studies of Genesis 6–9, Gen 12:1–4a, and Exod 19:3–6.

narrative cycles, as the hypothesis of fragments originally suggested.[11] The "sources" appeared later, after the Deuteronomic theology and, primarily, with the Priestly Writer. Finally, after the Exile, the actual Pentateuch came into being, resulting from the compilation and revision of existing sources. A certain number of texts were added at strategic points, as posited by the hypothesis of supplements.[12]

In the following section, I will deal only with the first stages of this evolution—the earliest texts, which were prior to P.

1. A "Preexilic Source"?

One of the problems often discussed today concerns the existence of a Preexilic and complete "source." Like many recent scholars, I do not think that an authentic "source" ever existed before the Exile or even before the Priestly document. There are, however, good reasons to think that "narrative cycles" and "legal codes" existed before the Exile, though they did not yet form an organic unit.

There are four reasons for this conclusion, which may seem drastic, at least at first.

To begin with, the first texts that convince us of the existence of a "history of the people's origins" in Israel—or at least an account covering the various periods of this history of origins—and that structure these periods with a specific design are rather late. These texts are the famous "small historical creeds" of von Rad (Deut 6:20–23; 26:5b–9) and a Priestly text (Exod 6:2–8). The latter, more clearly than the others, connects the patriarchal history to the Exodus. In Exod 6:2–8, the Exodus is the fulfillment of the promise (*běrît*) that YHWH made to the patriarchs (Exod 6:4, 5, 8). Deut 6:20, for its part, begins with the Exodus, and Deut 26:5 refers to Jacob (the Aramean nomad), but the only connection among the successive events is chronological. One brief "summary" or "small creed" may be older: Num 20:14–16, a text that is difficult to date precisely but that, for some scholars, goes back to the period of Hezekiah.[13] Other more recent studies have preferred later, Exilic or Postexilic, dates for this text

---

11. We once again encounter H. Gunkel, his study of Genesis, R. Rendtorff, E. Blum, and even, to a certain extent, C. Levin, J. Blenkinsopp, and R. N. Whybray.

12. This model was also preferred in a recent study by Carr, *Reading the Fractures of Genesis.* See especially the summary on pp. 290–93. In my opinion, Carr does not leave enough room for a post-Deuteronomic and post-Priestly redaction.

13. See Kreutzer, *Die Frühgeschichte Israels in Bekenntnis und Verkündigung des Alten Testaments,* 119–40, especially p. 138; cf. S. Mittmann, "Num 20,14–21: Eine redaktionelle Kompilation," in *Wort und Geschichte: Festschrift Karl Elliger* (ed. H. Gese and H. P. Rüger; AOAT 18; Kevelaer and Neukirchen-Vluyn, 1973) 143–49. These two authors work from the perspective of the classic documentary hypothesis.

because they consider Numbers 20 to be later than Deut 26:3–8.[14] The second solution should be preferred for several reasons. Numbers 20 explains and interprets Deut 26:3, 7: the "father" in Deut 26:3 (in the singular) is "the fathers" (plural) in Num 20:15. The "cry" in Deut 26:7 is less developed than in Num 20:15–16, which also mentions "bad treatment." A comparison with other texts—for example, Judg 11:16–18—leads in the same direction.[15]

The strongest argument in favor of an Exilic/Postexilic date is, in my view, the presence of the "angel" (Num 26:16), who only appears in later additions or later texts, such as Exod 14:19a, 23:20–23, 32:34, 33:2–3; Judg 2:1–5 (cf. Gen 24:7).[16] This angel, who takes the place of YHWH and no longer identifies himself with YHWH, reflects a theology that is more conscious of transcendence and hesitates to use anthropomorphisms.[17] In any case, to indicate the "fathers," the text uses generic terms and is satisfied with describing a simple chronological sequence. It does not establish a logical connection between the "promises made to the fathers" and the "Exodus."

Second, the texts that tie together the small units in the Pentateuch are late. The redactional additions are not perfectly integrated into their context and this is, according to the rule advanced by Greenberg, a sign of their late origin. The phenomenon is more evident in the book of Genesis, but it also clearly appears in Exodus–Numbers.[18] This is especially true of the connections between the patriarchal traditions and the Exodus. If the Exodus and the patriarchal traditions had been joined at an early period, why does the account of Moses' call (Exodus 3–4) (a rather late text) not mention the "promises to the fathers"? This text contains the "narrative program" of the entire Exodus–Numbers section, and it is strange that its bond with the book of Genesis is not stronger (cf. Rendtorff).

Third, we need to explain the silence of the Preexilic prophets. Of course, an argument from silence is not always conclusive, and at times it is even weak. We can only use it if we can prove that the Preexilic prophets should have spoken about the traditions of the Pentateuch, if they knew them.[19] From my standpoint, the following points should be considered closely. The Preexilic prophets mention isolated traditions more or less explicitly, but none of their oracles formally connects the Exodus to the patriarchs. In the eyes of the Preexilic

---

14. See Blum, *Studien*, 118–20; Römer, *Israels Väter*, 551–52; Van Seters, *Life of Moses*, 386–93.

15. See ibid., 389–90.

16. See Blum, *Studien*, 365–66.

17. This "angel" is different from the angel in Gen 16:7–14; Exod 3:2; Judg 6:11–12, 21–22; 13:3–18, who is identified with YHWH in the course of the account.

18. Compare with Carr's argumentation, in *Reading the Fractures of Genesis*, passim (summary, pp. 290–93), along the same lines as Rendtorff and Blum.

19. See Blum, *Studien*, 218.

prophets, the Exodus does not yet constitute the fulfillment of the promises made to the patriarchs, as later would be the case for P (E 6:2–8). Hosea sets Jacob in opposition to Moses but does not unite them in the same history of salvation (Hos 12:3–5, 13 and 12:10, 14). The same Hosea also refers to the departure from Egypt (2:17, 11:1, 12:14, 13:4; cf. Amos 9:7) and certain episodes of life in the wilderness (2:16–17, 9:10, 13:5).[20] These texts do not mention the patriarchs.

Going on to Second Isaiah and Ezekiel, we encounter the same situation. For the past 20 years, these prophets, especially Second Isaiah, have often been cited to corroborate a late, Postexilic dating of many traditions in the Pentateuch. Because Second Isaiah is the first, or one of the first, writers to mention Noah (Isa 54:9; cf. Ezek 14:14), Abraham and Sarah (Isa 41:8, 51:2; cf. Ezek 33:24 and Isa 29:22), and the Exodus (Isa 43:16–21 and passim; cf. Ezekiel 20), some authors have concluded that these traditions are Postexilic.[21]

However, Second Isaiah refers to well-known traditions; he does not invent them. In Antiquity, creating a tradition was not really recommended if one wanted to be convincing. One could only argue on the basis of traditions that had been a part of a people's collective memory for a long time.[22] Second Isaiah is explicit on this point when referring to the Exodus (43:18): "Do not remember the former things, / or consider the things of old." When the prophets invite people "not to remember the former things," they are implying that the people were remembering them. The text undeniably calls on the "collective memory" of its addressees. Second Isaiah does not introduce unknown elements into this discussion because the tradition of the Exodus is older than Second Isaiah and his time. In addition, it must be noted that even in Second Isaiah the traditions are juxtaposed and do not form a unified whole.

The construction of a theory postulating the existence of a "history of Israel" on the basis of the limited information provided by Second Isaiah would therefore be risky. The glue capable of unifying the various elements of this construction is still missing. Ezekiel does not help us get much further. Ezekiel 20, which deals mainly with the Exodus and Israel's wanderings in the wilderness, does not mention the promises made to the patriarchs.[23] Then, when it mentions Abraham, it says nothing about the Exodus (Ezek 33:24).[24]

---

20. For Hosea, see H.-D. Neef, *Die Heilstraditionen Israels in der Verkündigung des Propheten Hosea* (BZAW 169; Berlin, 1987). See, for example, the table on pp. 248–49. According to Neef, Hosea knows the tradition of Jacob, as well as the traditions of the Exodus, Sinai, and the wanderings in the wilderness.

21. See especially Van Seters, *Abraham in History and Tradition*, 275–76; idem, "The Religion of the Patriarchs in Genesis," *Bib* 61 (1980) 220–33.

22. See Blum, *Studien*, p. 218 n. 44.

23. The oracle mentions the "house of Jacob." This is not enough to reveal a close tie between the patriarchal traditions and the Exodus.

24. Cf. Römer, *Israels Väter*, 513–17.

Third Isaiah also mentions Abraham, Israel/Jacob, and Moses, but these figures are once again only juxtaposed. Some scholars suggest that they are part of one and the same history because the prophet knows all three of them. Other scholars respond to this objection by asserting that the prophet alludes to distinct traditions in Israel's past and thus creates a "narrative parataxis" with possible, but not explicit, connections. In short, Third Isaiah seems instead to place Moses opposite Abraham and Jacob in the same way that Hosea places Moses opposite Jacob.[25]

Fourth, current research in the fields of religious history and historiography in the ancient Near East does not encourage us to think that Israel was capable in ancient times of working out a vast "history" and a well-articulated theology in which YHWH was the unique, true God of the universe. This kind of history presupposes a collective consciousness of the people's own unity and common destiny. In addition, it presupposes a theology sufficiently developed to affirm YHWH's uniqueness and universality.[26] A clear affirmation of "monotheism" is found in Second Isaiah, and some hints of it can be seen in Jeremiah. Moreover, the comprehensive historiographical syntheses of the ancient Near East, such as the Greek and Mesopotamian histories, did not appear much before the 6th century B.C.E. Finally, it is problematic to speak of an authentic "nation" called "Israel" at the time of the Davidic Monarchy.[27]

In conclusion, a "history of Israel's origins" is hard to imagine prior to later times. The Deuteronomic reform was accompanied by the idea of "one unique God, one unique people, one unique temple." This was the period when the conditions were right for conceiving the first historical and theological synthesis of Israel. In fact, a new perspective had to be created after the fall of the Northern Kingdom in 721 B.C.E.

Josiah's reform in 622 B.C.E. also needed the solid theological foundation that we find in the primitive version of Deuteronomy. Here we must ask if the necessity of writing a "history of Israel" or at least fragments of such a history was felt before or after the redaction of Deuteronomy. Some authors, such as J. Van Seters and C. Levin, prefer to talk about an Exilic or Postexilic Yahwist, who certainly was postdeuteronomic. E. Zenger, on the other hand, proposes the existence of a "Jerusalemite history" at the time of Manasseh (after 700/690 B.C.E.).[28] In my view, however it is difficult to prove the existence of this "Jerusalemite history." Its profile is not clear. Likewise, Zenger concedes that

---

25. See ibid., 537.

26. Concerning the development of Israel's religion, see O. Keel and C. Uehlinger, *Gods, Goddesses, and Images of God in Ancient Israel* (trans. A. W. Mahnke; Minneapolis, 1996; original German, 1992).

27. See J. W. Flanagan, *David's Social Drama: A Hologram of Israel's Early Iron Age* (JSOTSup 73; SWBA 7; Sheffield, 1988); Niemann, *Herrschaft, Königtum und Staat*.

28. Zenger (ed.), *Einleitung*, 73 and 112–19.

the "Jerusalemite history" was not really unified.[29] The arguments that have been presented therefore need to be reexamined.

2. Was There a Literary Connection between the Patriarchs and the Exodus before Deuteronomy?

After the fall of Samaria, the situation became especially difficult. According to Zenger, this was the context in which the "Jerusalemite history" was developed in order to answer questions about the future of Israel, the existence of which was threatened by the Assyrian forces. All of this is plausible but still does not prove the existence of such a document. The strongest argument comes from Deuteronomy. If, as Zenger maintains, the primitive core and the Preexilic sections of Deuteronomy presuppose the existence not only of narrative cycles but also of a history integrating the patriarchs and the Exodus, I would support the thesis of a Preexilic "Jerusalemite history." However, in my view, this has not been satisfactorily demonstrated.

a. Deuteronomy

One of the central ideas of Deuteronomy is the Covenant, and this is why the primitive version of Deuteronomy is based almost exclusively on the Covenant at Horeb. As Lohfink puts it, the Israel of Deuteronomy is the *Israel of Horeb*.[30] Israel was born at Horeb and cannot survive unless it remains faithful to Horeb—that is, to the Covenant with the unique YHWH. Lohfink adds: all the rest is only the "portico and the vestibule."[31] However, "the rest" also comprises the promises made to the ancestors and the Exodus. In order to establish more precisely the nature of this "portico and vestibule," we need to answer several complex questions. Does Deuteronomy create or presuppose a connection between the promises to the ancestors and the Exodus? Who are the "fathers" ("ancestors") that Deuteronomy talks about? Recently, Römer argued that the "fathers" are not the patriarchs (Abraham, Isaac, Jacob) but the ancestors in Egypt. According to him, the "fathers" only came to be identified with the great figures of Genesis at a later period.[32]

Answering the first question is not simple. Of course, Deuteronomy often evokes the promises made to the "fathers" (root *ʾbʿ*).[33] The real problem is to know whether these Deuteronomic texts actually refer to the traditions or to

---

29. Ibid., 119.

30. N. Lohfink, *Die Väter Israels im Deuteronomium: Mit einer Stellungnahme von Thomas Römer* (OBO 111; Fribourg and Göttingen, 1991) 104–5.

31. Ibid., 105.

32. Römer, *Israels Väter.*

33. See ibid., 11: Deut 1:8, 35; 4:31; 6:10, 18, 23; 7:8, 12–13; 8:1, 18; 9:5; 10:11; 11:9, 21; 13:18; 19:8; 26:3, 15; 28:11; 29:12; 30:20; 31:7, 20–21; 34:4.

older texts—to put it more concretely, to certain passages of Genesis. The theory of "fragments" or "narrative units" would largely be adequate for explaining this phenomenon. In order to prove the existence of a "document" such as Zenger's "Jerusalemite history," it would be necessary to prove, on the one hand, that Deuteronomy presupposes an organic work, not just isolated narrative cycles; and, on the other hand, that the ancient texts really were integrated into this unified work. The most sensitive point is the connection between the promises made to the patriarchs and the traditions concerning the Exodus.[34]

We must therefore ask the following question: Did Deuteronomy create the ties between the "fathers" and Moses—between the promises made to the ancestors and the experience of the Exodus? Or, conversely, did Deuteronomy find this idea in an older document that considered the Exodus to be the fulfillment of the promises made to the fathers, a document that we might discover among the texts of the Pentateuch? For the moment, I am setting aside the recent discussion of the identity of the "fathers."[35] Zenger adopts the position of Lohfink, who identified the "fathers" with the patriarchs (see Deut 1:8; 6:10; 9:5, 27; 29:12; 30:20; 34:4), and this is the thesis I want to examine here. Actually, it would be much easier to say that the "fathers" of Deuteronomy are not the patriarchs, because then there would be no connection between Genesis and Deuteronomy, and the discussion would immediately be over.

I am also setting aside delicate questions about the various levels of Deuteronomy. According to this hypothesis, Deuteronomy with all of its redaction history was later than the Preexilic, predeuteronomic document that some scholars call "Yahwistic" and also later than Zenger's "Jerusalemite history."

b. The Sinai Pericope (Exodus 19–Numbers 10)[36]

Because the central tradition of Deuteronomy is the tradition of Horeb, it is useful to see which traditions Deuteronomy relates to it. Many texts do indeed make a connection between the promise to the fathers and the Covenant at Horeb or the Law. The most explicit text is Deut 29:9–12:

---

34. Zenger (ed.), *Einleitung*, 116–17.

35. See the discussion between Römer, *Israels Väter*; and Lohfink, *Väter Israels im Deuteronomium*. In my opinion, it is difficult to support such extreme positions: "the fathers of Deuteronomy are never assimilated to the patriarchs" or "the fathers of Deuteronomy are always the patriarchs mentioned in Genesis." In Deuteronomy, the term "fathers" has more than one meaning; it is therefore necessary to study it within the different contexts in order to determine its meaning in each specific case. Nonetheless, recent research in the field, especially K. Schmid's work, has confirmed T. Römer's opinion. I have also observed that Exod 6:2–8, a Priestly text, creates for the first time a real and explicit theological and narrative link between the promises to the patriarchs and the Exodus.

36. For these texts, see Blum (*Studien zur Komposition des Pentateuch*, 81–82), who attributes them to his KD (Deuteronomic composition).

¹⁰You stand assembled today, all of you, before Y<small>HWH</small>, your God . . . ¹¹to enter into the covenant of Y<small>HWH</small> your God, sworn by an oath, which Y<small>HWH</small> your God is making with you today; ¹²in order that he may establish you today as his people, and that he may be your God, as he promised you and as he swore to your ancestors, to Abraham, to Isaac, and to Jacob.

The Covenant concluded in Deuteronomy 29 (which repeats the Covenant at Horeb)[37] is the fulfillment of the promise Y<small>HWH</small> made to the patriarchs. However, other texts base possession of the land that Y<small>HWH</small> promised to the fathers on observance of the Law proclaimed at Horeb (Deut 6:10–13, 17–19; 8:1, 17–18; 11:8–9, 18–21; 19:8–9; 30:19–20; cf. 28:11). Deut 7:8 is the only text that indicates that the Exodus is a fulfillment of the promises made to the fathers:

⁸It was because Y<small>HWH</small> loved you and kept the oath that he swore to your ancestors, that Y<small>HWH</small> has brought you out with a mighty hand, and redeemed you from the house of slavery, from the hand of Pharaoh king of Egypt.

There is a strict correlation between these texts in Deuteronomy, which probably belong to different levels, and the oath sworn to the fathers and the two central events of the Mosaic traditions: the Exodus and Horeb.

Second, we need to see if it is possible to make the same connection within older, predeuteronomic traditions. This investigation leads to a negative conclusion: the oldest non-Priestly texts present no connection between the patriarchs and the Exodus or between the patriarchs and Sinai. This connection was therefore created by (either ancient or recent) Deuteronomic texts. A short investigation will be convincing enough.

The pericope concerning Sinai (Exodus 19–Numbers 10), with all its complexity, contains very few references to the patriarchs. The Decalogue, today considered to be a work of late origin, mentions the land in the context of the respect due to parents, but it does not mention the promises made to the patriarchs:

Exod 20:12: Honor your father and your mother, so that your days may be long in the land that Y<small>HWH</small> your God is giving you.

Exod 23:20–33 refers to the conquest of the land but says nothing of the promise made to the fathers. This would have been the best place to insert the classical phrase "the land I swore to give to your fathers." But there is not the slightest trace of this.

The only verses that allude to the patriarchs in the Sinai passage are Exod 32:13 and 33:1. These texts are generally considered to be late. This is clear in the case of Exod 32:13, which is part of Moses' intercession, a text with a strong Deuteronomistic coloration (32:11–14). However, these two texts im-

---

37. See Lohfink, "Bund als Vertrag im Deuteronomium."

ply an idea that is not exactly Deuteronomistic. Moses asks YHWH not to destroy his people after the episode of the golden calf so as not to invalidate the
promises made to the patriarchs. But he does not say that YHWH acted up to
this point because of the ancient promises and that he should thus continue to
act in favor of his people. Exod 33:1 is perhaps clearer because it implies a
tighter connection between the Exodus, the wanderings in the wilderness, and
the promises made to the patriarchs:

> YHWH said to Moses, "Go, leave this place, you and the people whom you have
> brought up out of the land of Egypt, and go to the land of which I swore to Abra-
> ham, Isaac, and Jacob, saying, 'To your descendants I will give it.'"

However, this text cannot be very old. It contains phrases, formulas, and
themes that come from Exodus 32 and other texts, some of which are Deuteronomic.[38] It is therefore probably more recent than the texts it has gathered.
This text was very likely created to connect Exodus 32 and the rest of the narrative, in which new relations between YHWH and his people are established
after the episode of the golden calf. The crucial question here is to know
whether YHWH will continue to guide his people toward the Promised Land
and how he will do this.

In conclusion, let us note that no ancient text of the Sinai pericope mentions the patriarchs. Certainly, nowhere is it said, as in Deut 29:12, that YHWH
concluded a Covenant with Israel out of faithfulness to the promise made to
the patriarchs.

c. The Departure from Egypt (Exodus 1–15*)

A similar investigation of the texts that relate the departure from Egypt leads
to the same conclusions. No pre-Priestly (and pre-Deuteronomic) text presents
the Exodus from Egypt as the fulfillment of a former promise. Only the Priestly
text in Exod 6:2–8 suggests this. There are also two allusions to a promise
made to the patriarchs in Exod 13:5 and 11. However, these two verses do not
connect the departure from Egypt to this "promise." They merely indicate the
moment when the laws of Exodus 13 should come into effect.

Furthermore, the majority of interpreters classify Exodus 13 with the later
texts of Exodus 1–15. On the other hand, it is surprising that we do not find a

---

38. "Your people, whom you brought up out of the land of Egypt," Exod 32:7, 33:1;
"the land that I swore to Abraham, to Isaac, and to Jacob," Gen 50:25, Exod 33:1, Num
32:11, Deut 34:4; "I am going to send an angel in front of you . . . ," Exod 23:20, 32:34; the
list of the peoples in Exod 33:2 reappears with some minor differences in 23:23 (in 33:2, the
Canaanites are at the top); "a land flowing with milk and honey," Exod 3:8, 17; 13:5; Lev
20:24; Num 16:13, 14; Deut 6:3; 11:9; 26:9, 15; 27:3; Josh 5:6; Jer 11:5; 32:22; the formula
is accompanied by a list of the peoples in Exod 3:8, 17; 13:5; and 33:2–3; "stiff-necked
people," Exod 32:9; 33:3, 5; 34:9; Deut 9:6, 13.

connection between the Exodus and the patriarchs in the account about Moses' call (Exodus 3–4). The text identifies the God who appears to Moses as the God of the patriarchs (3:5), but it does not go much further. It does not suggest in any way that the land to which Yнwн is leading his people is the land he promised to the fathers (Exod 3:8, 17). Although Exod 3:1–4, 18 is later than the context in which it has been inserted (Exod 2:23a and 4:19), a link between the fathers and Moses' mission does not appear here.

d. The Wanderings in the Wilderness

One of the few texts that mention the other traditions is Num 11:12. Here Moses says to Yнwн:

> Did I conceive all this people? Did I give birth to them, that you should say to me, "Carry them in your bosom, as a nurse carries a sucking child, to the land that you promised on oath to their ancestors?"

This verse evokes the "fathers" and the Promised Land. But the vocabulary is clearly Deuteronomic, and the passage is therefore late. The verb "promise on oath" is typical of Deuteronomy and related literature. The syntax of this sentence is problematic. It would have been more natural to say: "Carry it . . . to the land *I* promised on oath to give to their fathers," as some Samaritan and LXX manuscripts propose.[39] These are the main reasons that lead me to think that this is a later addition.

e. The Book of Genesis

The same thing holds true for the book of Genesis. A few texts explicitly mention the Exodus, and all of them are late. The first one is Gen 15:13–16. Genesis 15 is a much-discussed text and, today, very few interpreters consider it to be very early, at least in its present form.[40] Moreover, vv. 13–16 are additions and therefore belong to the latest levels of the text. The "resumptive repetition" of v. 12, "as the sun was going down," in v. 17, "when the sun had gone down," is the first indication. Verses 13–16 interrupt the action that begins in 15:7–12 and ends in 15:17–18 with the conclusion of the Covenant. Gen 15:13–16 is a late redactional text that cannot be used to prove an original connection between Abraham and the Exodus.

Some interpreters think that Gen 15:7–12, 17–18 probably alludes to the theophany at Sinai. This would be a good "bridge" between Abraham and

---

39. See Noth, *Numbers*, 86–87; Römer, *Israels Väter*, 558; Blum, *Studien zur Komposition des Pentateuch*, 81 (bibliography, n. 160), 103.

40. See Blum, *Komposition der Vätergeschichte*, 367–72; Köckert, *Vätergott*, 198–247; Carr, *Reading the Fractures of Genesis*, 165; see especially M. Anbar, "Genesis 15: A Conflation of Two Deuteronomic Narratives," *JBL* 101 (1982) 39–55.

Exod 19:24. The vocabulary in Gen 15:17 actually contains some elements that might evoke the theophany in Exod 19:10–19—for example, the "fire pot" (*tannûr*: Gen 15:17; *kibšan*: Exod 19:18), the "smoke" (*ʿšn*: Exod 19:18; Gen 15:17), and the "flaming torch" (*lappîd*: Gen 15:17; Exod 20:18). Other elements are missing, such as the thunder. However, the covenant vocabulary ("to cut" a covenant—*krt běrît*) is not found in Exodus 19 but in Exod 24:8, a late text. Furthermore, the Abrahamic Covenant is an isolated passage that corresponds to part of Genesis 17, a Priestly text. These possible allusions to the Sinai theophany do not imply that an ancient Abraham cycle and an ancient account of the Sinai theophany ever belonged to the same narrative unit. The allusions only allow us to conclude that the author of one of these texts knew the other text. Nothing in Genesis 15 suggests that another covenant is to be expected. It is not excluded, but there is insufficient proof. Other elements and more explicit indications are necessary.

Only Gen 46:1–5a alludes to the return of Jacob's family from Egypt to the land of Canaan, but this text too is secondary and differs from its context.[41] In various respects, it stands out from the rest of Joseph's story. Above all, this passage contains the only divine discourse, the only vision, and the only ritual act in Genesis 37–50. It is moreover an "insertion." In 45:27, the sons show their father the carts Joseph has sent to make his journey to Egypt easier. In the next verse, Jacob/Israel, finally convinced by this argument, decides to leave. The reader finds the continuation of the story in 46:5b, when the sons of Jacob/Israel put their father and the entire family in the carts that will take them to Egypt.[42] This last action is surprising because there has already been one departure and one stop at Beer-sheba (46:1).

Finally, God's order in 46:3–4 comes when the patriarch, on his own initiative, has already decided to leave (45:28). Normally, the oracle should have preceded the decision. Now, let us note that in the primitive account, as in the addition of 46:1–5a, the names of Jacob and Israel alternate in a chiasm:

> Jacob: 45:25
> > Israel: 45:28; 46:1, 2
> Jacob: 46:5a and 5b

Gen 50:24 is the second non-Priestly text of Genesis that connects the history of the patriarchs to the Exodus. Here, Jacob promises that YHWH will visit his people and "bring them up" to the land promised to Abraham, Isaac, and

---

41. For discussion and bibliography, see Blum, *Komposition der Vätergeschichte*, 246–49 and 297–301; Carr, *Reading the Fractures of Genesis*, 211 n. 70.

42. Note the similarity of vocabulary: "[Jacob] saw the wagons that Joseph had sent to carry him" (45:27b); "they carried Jacob, their father . . . in the wagons that Pharaoh sent to carry him."

Jacob. This is a late addition to the conclusion of the Joseph story. The traces left by the editor can still be seen: Gen 50:22–23, 26 contains a short account of Joseph's death, but between the two sections of this passage, his "will" was inserted (vv. 24–25). The reference to Joseph's age of 110 years in 50:22 is repeated in 50:26a. The hinge uniting these two verses is the verb *mwt* "to die" (50:24a, 26a).

The vocabulary and themes of 50:24–25 appear again in Exod 13:19 and Josh 24:32. According to Exod 13:19, Moses took Joseph's bones with him, in accordance with the wish he had expressed in Gen 50:24–25, and in Josh 24:32 they are finally buried at Shechem. The strongest argument in favor of the secondary character of Gen 50:24–25, however, is the strange fact that the "promise" made to the three patriarchs is never mentioned in the Joseph story. The theme appears unexpectedly and without preparation. Notably, Joseph does not speak of it when he invites his brothers to come settle in Egypt with their father (Gen 45:9–11). Nor does Jacob mention it when his sons come back and invite him to go down to Egypt with them (45:28); he might have objected that God had promised the land of Canaan to his ancestors.[43]

The result of the above study is that it seems most plausible that the connection between the patriarchal traditions and the Exodus traditions is a late creation and does not go back to an earlier period. There was no complete "document" before Deuteronomy and the Priestly Writer—none that could have already united the two narrative "units." The traditions were juxtaposed and sometimes even opposed. For example, Hosea 12 sets Jacob in opposition to Moses; in Ezek 33:23–29, Abraham is set in opposition to the Law; and in Isa 63:11, 16, Abraham is set in opposition to Moses. The first text that creates a clear narrative and theological link between the patriarchs and the Exodus is a Priestly text, Exod 6:2–8 (cf. K. Schmid).

D. The Preexilic Materials of the Pentateuch

In the following section I will attempt to identify the oldest materials in each of the books of the Pentateuch. It will not be possible to offer thorough argumentation for each claim. From the hypotheses elaborated in recent times, I have chosen those that seem most plausible, easiest to verify, and most helpful for understanding the text of the Pentateuch in all its complexity.

1. The Book of Genesis

The various traditions of the book of Genesis existed separately before being compiled. In the context of a pre-Deuteronomic Pentateuch, we need to dis-

---

43. For discussion and bibliography, see Carr, *Reading the Fractures of Genesis*, 166–67.

tinguish a history of origins (Genesis 2–11), the Abraham cycle (12–25), some traditions concerning Isaac (Genesis 26), the Jacob cycle (25–35), and the Joseph story (37–50).

a. A History of Origins

The history of origins presents special problems.[44] Many passages appear to be post-Deuteronomistic or post-Priestly. Distinguishing the earliest elements from later elaborations is not easy. In the case of the account of the Flood, I think it is possible to show in a convincing way that the narrative attributed to the Yahwist was actually composed of a series of post-Priestly additions.[45] In any case, Genesis 2–11 has its own history, and connections with the rest of the Pentateuch are almost completely absent.[46]

The world of Genesis 2–11 is a world of sedentary groups, essentially composed of farmers, shepherds, and city dwellers. The problems dealt with concern the relations between YHWH, humanity as a whole, and the soil (*ʾadāmâ*); today we would say, "nature." Nowhere in Genesis 2–11 is there preparation for what follows. The narrative unit is self-contained. Furthermore, the problems that appear after Genesis 11 are quite different: they are the problems of a family seeking a land (or a home), their migrations, the problems tied to lineage, then oppression and freedom, and the legal constitution of a landless people.

Genesis 2–11 was conceived at a late period as a universalistic prologue to the entire history of salvation. In other summaries of this history, only late texts such as the prayer of Nehemiah (Nehemiah 9) begin with an allusion to Creation (9:6) before mentioning the patriarchs (9:7). This is also the case in Psalm 136. For a long time, interpreters considered Gen 12:1–3 to be the "hinge" that united the history of origins to Israel's history. The universal blessing promised to Abraham comes as grace to a world placed under "divine wrath" (cf. Rom 1:8). The text may even have reused some of the elements of Gen 11:1–9, such as the phrase "great name" (11:4; cf. 12:2). A close study of Gen 12:1–3 does not confirm this thesis, however. Gen 12:1–3 is a late, Postexilic insertion containing Israel's birth certificate, not a promise of universal salvation. The text says nothing of a universal blessing, but it mentions the universal renown that Abraham will acquire.[47]

---

44. Ibid., 234–48.

45. J.-L. Ska, "El relato del diluvio." This opinion is also shared by B. D. Eerdmans, J. Blenkinsopp, G. J. Wenham, and B. Gosse.

46. See especially Crüsemann, "Die Eigenständigkeit der Urgeschichte"; Köckert, *Vätergott*, 264–65; Carr, *Reading the Fractures of Genesis*, 241.

47. J.-L. Ska, "L'appel d'Abraham et l'acte de naissance d'Israël (Gn 12,1–4a)," 367–89. For a detailed analysis of the text and its interpretation, see Blum, *Komposition der Vätergeschichte*, 349–59; Köckert, *Vätergott*, 276–97; Carr, *Reading the Fractures of Genesis*, 179–94.

b. The Stories of the Ancestors (Genesis 12–50)

We can easily distinguish some narrative units among the stories of the patri-archs. These narrative units have their own characteristics: the Abraham cycle (12–25), some traditions concerning Isaac (26), the Jacob cycle (25, 27–35), and the story of Joseph (37–50). A short description of these texts will lead us to see that the connections between the various units are late constructions.

Abraham.   Abraham lived in a region near southern Canaan; he was in con-tact with Egypt (Genesis 12:10–20) and the Philistines (Genesis 20–21); he lived in Hebron and Beer-sheba, not far from the desert. On the other hand, Jacob was in contact with the Arameans in the region of Haran and lived near Shechem and Bethel. There are great differences between the Abraham and Jacob cycles: the plot, the atmosphere, the geographical setting, and many other details distinguish the narratives devoted to these two patriarchs.

Isaac also remains isolated, in Genesis 26. And, in the case of the Joseph story, it is hardly necessary to point out its unique characteristics. Many of the important themes that appear in the preceding cycles are missing. This story differs from the rest of the Pentateuch primarily in style.[48] The narrative is much more unified, it is more directly centered around the destiny of the main figure, and God intervenes only indirectly in the adventures of its hero. The "Egyptian" imprint on many episodes of Genesis 37–50 is another factor. The literary and artistic qualities of this narrative oblige us to put it in a separate category.[49]

The Abraham cycle was constituted from some isolated accounts and short narrative cycles.[50] We can say with some certainty that some of the oldest texts are the Abraham–Lot cycle (Genesis 13* and 18*–19*); perhaps the stay in Egypt (12:10–20) and the two versions of Hagar's expulsion (16:1–14* and 21:8–20*); as well as some traditions concerning the stay of Abraham in Gerar (21:22–34).[51] Other episodes are more recent, just as are the various texts—promises and itineraries—that tie Abraham's story to the rest of the patriarchal traditions.[52] Gen 20:1–18 is probably a later piece that presupposes knowledge of similar episodes and tries to justify the behavior of the actors—namely, God,

---

48. On the literary characteristics of the various parts of Genesis, see the excellent article by Cohn, "Narrative Structure and Canonical Perspective in Genesis."

49. For more details, see Humphreys, *Joseph and His Family*, 135–214, especially pp. 194–214; Carr, *Reading the Fractures of Genesis*, 271–89.

50. Blum, *Komposition der Vätergeschichte*, 273–89 (cf. pp. 289–97); I. Fischer, *Erzeltern Is-raels*, 333–43.

51. There are good reasons for affirming that Genesis 20 is more recent than Gen 12:10–20. See ibid., 223–28.

52. See Zenger (ed.), *Einleitung*, 119, who was influenced by I. Fischer, *Erzeltern Israels*, 333–43; Carr, *Reading the Fractures of Genesis*, 202.

Abraham, and Abimelech. Gen 22:1–19, Abraham's trial, and Genesis 24, Isaac's marriage, are considered late—that is, Postexilic—compositions today.[53] Some problematic texts remain, such as Genesis 14 and 15. Although they may contain a few ancient elements, a long redactional process is evident in their present texture. This means that these are very late texts.[54]

Isaac. The only chapter devoted to Isaac, Genesis 26, is isolated in context.[55] It is placed between the two major episodes of the rivalry between Jacob and Esau: Gen 25:27–34, the episode of the lentil stew; and Genesis 27, the "stolen blessing." It constitutes an "interpolation" or a "digression."

Both sons, Esau and Jacob, are strangely absent from Genesis 26.[56] The chapter describes a series of conflicts that take place in the region of Gerar, and King Abimelech steps in. These unique features set this chapter apart from those surrounding it. The function of Isaac in the book of Genesis is to authenticate his descendants' rights to the land: Isaac is the only patriarch who is born in the land, lives his whole life in the land, and dies in the land. This is also the reason why God explicitly forbids him to go to Egypt in Gen 26:2.

Jacob. The Jacob cycle has its own characteristics. It also existed independently before becoming part of the book of Genesis.[57] This hypothesis is based on solid arguments. The primitive core of Jacob's story is unrelated to Abraham's. Furthermore, when the story ends, in Genesis 33 and 35, there has been no preparation for the Joseph story. The narrative as such does not require a continuation.

Jacob's story is more unified than Abraham's. It is possible to identify, without too much hesitation, a narrative unit that describes Jacob's conflicts with Esau and Laban.[58] This unit contains two episodes concerning the rivalry between Esau and Jacob (Gen 25:27–34, perhaps a later composition, and 27:1–45); the vision at Bethel, (28:10–12, 16–19*); the conflicts between Jacob and his uncle and father-in-law, Laban (29:1–32:1); the return to the land of Canaan (32–33*; 35:1–8, 16–20).[59]

---

53. See Veijola, "Das Opfer des Abraham"; A. Rofé, "An Inquiry into the Betrothal of Rebekah," in *Die Hebräische Bibel und ihre zweifache Nachgeschichte: Festschrift für Rolf Rendtorff* (ed. E. Blum, C. Macholz, and E. W. Stegemann; Neukirchen-Vluyn, 1990) 27–40.

54. See Carr, *Reading the Fractures of Genesis*, 163–66, with bibliography.

55. Blum, *Komposition der Vätergeschichte*, 301–7.

56. For more details, see Carr, *Reading the Fractures of Genesis*, 205.

57. Blum, *Komposition der Vätergeschichte*, 66–203 (conclusion: pp. 202–3).

58. See the analysis of Carr, *Reading the Fractures of Genesis*, 258–61, who uses the works of Blum and Kessler.

59. See Zenger (ed.), *Einleitung*, 119; Carr, *Reading the Fractures of Genesis*, 256–57, who bases his research on the work of Blum.

In these passages, we can detect separate narratives that were connected to specific places or sanctuaries; they may have been older and may have existed independently before being integrated into the "Jacob cycle." These texts include the "sacred legend" of Bethel (28:10–12, 16–19*); the episode of Peniel (32:23–33*); the move from Shechem to Bethel (35:1–5*, 16–20*).[60]

Genesis 34, the episode with Dina and Shechem, constitutes a "digression" that has its own history. It was inserted here because of the mention of Shechem and Hamor in Gen 33:19. The narrative theme of Gen 33:19–20 reappears in 35:1–5. In the final composition (Genesis 33–35), Genesis 34 may explain why God ordered Jacob to leave Shechem and to move to Bethel (Gen 35:1).

Jacob's story originated in the North. It is connected with places that characterize this region—for example, Bethel, Shechem, and Peniel (cf. 1 Kgs 12:25, 29).

Joseph.   The literary and theological characteristics of the Joseph story are well known,[61] and the commentaries provide good summaries. This story, more than all the others in the book of Genesis, is internally coherent.[62] At the beginning of the narrative, the reader only needs to know about the existence of Jacob's family in order to understand the plot. The Jacob of Genesis 37–50 is different in every way from the devious, audacious patriarch of Genesis 25–35. He has become a weak, old man, imprisoned by his emotional preferences.

At the heart of this story we find Joseph's conflict with his brothers and the "sale" (chap. 37), Joseph's ascent to power in Egypt (40–41), and the famine, the brothers' journeys to Egypt and their reconciliation (42–45).[63] The story of Judah and Tamar, in Genesis 38, is not part of the Joseph cycle. This narrative piece interrupts the plot line and introduces themes and motifs that have nothing to do with the events of Genesis 37–50. Genesis 38 is probably an addition or an "intermezzo" between Genesis 37 and Genesis 40.

Genesis 39 also differs from the rest of Joseph's story in many ways. Yhwh appears only in this chapter. Here, Joseph ends up in prison, where he gains a prestigious position; but then in chap. 40, he serves two prisoners, and his "master" (the same captain of the guard as in 37:36 and 39:1, we presume) has forgotten what happened in the preceding chapter. Moreover, the conclusion of this chapter is not completely satisfying from a narrative point of view, because the misdeed of Potiphar's wife remains undiscovered and unpunished. Chapter 39 is also the only section with a known Egyptian parallel—the "story of the two brothers." All of this leads us to think that an editor inserted this

---

60. Carr, ibid., 268.

61. Blum, *Komposition der Vätergeschichte,* 229–57.

62. See, among others, Westermann, *Genesis 37–50,* 18–24; Humphreys, *Joseph,* 131 and 195–96; Carr, *Reading the Fractures of Genesis,* 271–89.

63. For this paragraph, see Humphreys, *Joseph,* 194–207.

chapter, with some minor changes, into another, existing chapter. In fact, at the end of the account, Joseph finds himself in exactly the same situation as at the beginning, precisely in the service of an Egyptian officer (37:36, 39:1, 40:3–4).

Genesis 37 requires special explanation. The oldest part of the narrative describes how Joseph was "stolen" by the Midianites, while Reuben tried to save him. The Judah version, which relates how Joseph was sold to the Ishmaelites, is later and was added to the preceding account. However, in Genesis 42–45 the figure of Judah is not secondary. On the contrary, he is the central character, and it is impossible to overlook his intervention without distorting or destroying the story's plot.

Although we cannot be absolutely certain about this, I think that the solution should be looked for in the transfer of Joseph's story from the North to the South. Judah can have a key role in this story centered on Joseph, a personage who quite certainly originated in the North, only if the narrative was "transferred" to and revised in the Kingdom of Judah. Genesis 37, in its first version written in the North, seems to contain the oldest core of the story.

The Southern author/editor transformed the story by adding Judah's involvement in chap. 37 and by rewriting, almost entirely, chaps. 42–45, in which Judah is a part of the connective tissue of the present narrative: Judah convinces his brothers to sell Joseph (37:26–27); Judah convinces Jacob to let Benjamin leave for Egypt (43:3–14); Judah, by his speech in favor of Benjamin, turns the situation around when he (unknowingly) influences Joseph to let himself be recognized by his brothers and to reconcile with them (44:18–34).

In the course of these three actions, Judah's position and character evolve. In chap. 44, in the episode with the cup, Joseph provokes a situation similar to the situation in chap. 37. He gives the brothers an opportunity to get rid of another of their father's favorite sons, Benjamin, and Judah himself offers to replace the potential victim. However, he was the one who had suggested that they sell Joseph in chap. 37. Judah's "transformation" is easier to understand if we consider it to be the result of a "Southern" revision of the earliest account. Judah becomes the instrument of reconciliation in a family wounded by discord. This attitude certainly corresponds to the role played by the region of Judah after the fall of Samaria. Thus, the Joseph story probably originated in the North and was later transferred to the South.[64] At a later stage, it was used to prolong the Jacob story, and then this compilation was added to the Abraham cycle to form one account about Israel's ancestors.

I think that the work of the final redaction was carried out during the Postexilic period, just as was the work of compiling the the principal texts of this

---

64. See Zenger (ed.), *Einleitung*, 119, in the same direction as W. Dietrich, H. Donner, H.-C. Schmitt, and H. Schweizer. Also see Carr, *Reading the Fractures of Genesis*, 277–83.

layer (mainly Gen 12:1–4a; 13:14–17; 26:2–5; 28:13–14, 15; 31:3; 46:1–5a; 50:24–25; cf. Blum).

2. Exodus, Sinai, and the Wanderings in the Wilderness

The vast narrative unit uniting the Exodus and the wanderings in the wilderness is fraught with problems. I can only propose a plausible hypothesis based on the most viable recent research. First of all, critical research has been able, allowing for a sufficient safety margin, to distinguish the story of the departure from Egypt (Exod 1–2*, 4*, 5*, 7–12*, 14–15*), the Sinai pericope (19, 24, 32–34), the Decalogue (20:1–19*), the "Covenant Code" (Exodus 21–23*), the traditions concerning Israel's wanderings in the wilderness (Exodus 15*, 17–18*; Numbers 11*, 12*, 13–14*, 20–21*, 25*), and the story of Balaam (Numbers 22–24*). These traditions are relatively independent. Even within certain units, "flaws" can be noted that allow us, with a high degree of probability, to formulate a hypothesis of independent sources for certain "narrative sequences."

a. The Oppression in Egypt and Moses' Early Years

Exodus 1 describes, in a few scenes, Pharaoh's first vexatious measures against Israel. Exodus 2 introduces Moses, the future savior. In recent years, many authors have studied the style of these chapters.[65] It is very similar to the style of the popular stories (*Sagen*) of Genesis 12–35 that Gunkel examined very closely. These accounts in their present form constitute a narrative cycle that precedes and prepares for the call of Moses (Exod 3:1–4:18). A close reading reveals that these two chapters are not entirely in harmony with their present context. Tensions and unintelligible elements remain that can only be explained if these accounts existed separately before being integrated into a larger narrative regarding the oppression suffered by Israel in Egypt and its happy ending. On the other hand, these may actually be late accounts.

At the very beginning of the narrative, we observe a certain tension in regard to the larger context.[66] The theme of the rapid growth of the people is limited to Exodus 1, as is the construction of the supply cities. After Exodus 1–2 there is no further mention of Pharaoh's desire to eliminate the male children in order to keep the people from multiplying. There is also a unique tension between the cause of the oppression and the measures adopted. Will forced labor really diminish the number of the population? This is not certain. Furthermore, if Pharaoh wants to use the Hebrews as a servile work force, why does he try to eliminate precisely the male children? Finally, the fact that the Egyp-

---

65. For bibliography, see, among others, G. F. Davies, *Israel in Egypt*.
66. For a detailed discussion, see W. H. Schmidt, *Exodus 1, 1–6, 30*, 16–26.

tians cannot tolerate the Hebrews is not really compatible with their fear when they see them leaving the land (1:10).

The next section (1:15–22) also presents a problem. If the people have greatly multiplied, how can two midwives alone assist all the women in child-birth? Only the orders given to the midwives to eliminate the male children seem to align with the theme of the extraordinary growth of the Hebrew people. This section also constitutes an excellent introduction to Moses' birth and the dangers surrounding the event. The current account seems to contain various themes, such as the growth of the population and their slavery, as well as popular motifs, such as the involvement of the midwives.

The episodes that inaugurate Moses' career belong to the same narrative genre.[67] A parallel to the story of Moses' birth (Exod 2:1–10) exists in the story of Sargon of Agade. The theme of the child preserved against the odds and raised secretly belongs to the folklore of all times. However, this account presupposes the preceding narrative—specifically, Pharaoh's order to throw all the Hebrew male children into the Nile. At least two parallels to the meeting at the well (of Moses and the Midianite women, Exod 2:15–22), another motif or "typical scene" in folklore, are also found in Genesis (Genesis 24 and Gen 29:1–14).

Afterward, this part of Moses' life will hardly even be developed. In the scenes that follow, only Exod 3:1, 4:18, and 18:1–3 (cf. Num 10:29; Judg 1:16, 4:11) allude to Moses' stay in the house of his father-in-law in Midian, and no narrative directly mentions his stay in Pharaoh's palace. Two short episodes are placed between his birth and his marriage: Moses kills an Egyptian in order to defend one of his Hebrew brothers; and Moses is rebuked by one Hebrew who is quarreling with another Hebrew, and he must flee because Pharaoh has learned about the assassination of the Egyptian. The origin of this passage is perhaps secondary. Its main aim is to connect the scenes of Moses' birth and marriage in the land of Midian.

The "call of Moses" (Exod 3:1–4:18) is a later narrative that was inserted be-tween Exod 2:23a and 4:19, as B. D. Eerdmans and M. Noth have observed.[68] There are clear indications that Exod 3:1–4:18 is a unit that once existed sepa-rate from its immediate context. After the announcement of Pharaoh's death (2:23a), Yʜᴡʜ tells Moses to go back to Egypt because his persecutors are dead (4:19). However, in 4:18, Moses has already talked with his father-in-law Jethro about returning to Egypt. In the command that Yʜᴡʜ gives in Exod 4:19, he does not mention any of the elements that appear in the narrative of Exod 3:1–

---

67. See ibid., 51–62 and 79–88.

68. See B. D. Eerdmans, *Alttestamentliche Studien III: Das Buch Exodus* (Giessen, 1910) 16; Noth, *History of Pentateuchal Traditions*, 31–32 n. 103. For a more complete demonstration, see Blum, *Studien zur Komposition des Pentateuch*, 20–22; Ska, "Récit et récit métadiexégé-tique en Ex 1–15," 156.

4:18—for example, Moses' objections and the mission that he had previously received. Furthermore, the account of his call does not allude to Pharaoh's intention of killing Moses. The man of God could have used this fact to object to God's request, but this is not what happens. This is hard to understand because it is not until 4:19 that he learns that Pharaoh is dead. We could skip from 2:23a to 4:19 without any difficulty, however. The death of Pharaoh (2:23a) is the reason invoked to convince Moses to go back to Egypt. In 4:20 Moses' wife and son, who were present in 2:21–22 but absent from 3:1 to 4:18, reappear.

The name of Moses' father-in-law is Jethro (*yitrô*) in 3:1 or Jether (*yeter*) 4:18, but he calls himself Reuel in 2:18. The thread connecting Exod 2:23a to 4:19 clearly was broken in order to insert a detailed report about Moses' call (3:1–4:18). This account may have used older materials, especially in the scene of the burning bush (3:1–6).

Exodus 5 also presents some peculiarities that dissociate it from its context. This passage is related to Exod 1:8–12, where the beginning of the oppression and forced labor is described, although the reason for this oppression (i.e., the Egyptians' fear in face of the Hebrew population growth) is not mentioned at any point. The bricks made by the Hebrews may very well have been used in the construction of the cities named in 1:11, but Exodus 5 does not refer to these cites explicitly. The narrative has been revised and amplified in order to introduce the figure of Aaron (5:1, 20).[69]

b. The Egyptian Plagues

"Fractures" also appear in the account of the Egyptian plagues (Exodus 7–11*).[70] For example, the plague narrative never clearly refers to the oppression in Egypt. The Israelites live in the land of Goshen, separate from the Egyptians (8:18; 9:4–7, 26; 10:23), and do not seem to have to work at constructing supply cities (cf. Exod 1:11). The theme of slavery, especially the making of bricks, disappears after chap. 5 and does not reappear clearly until Exod 14:5 (cf. 14:11–12). This may be a case of narrative economy, because the account of the plagues centers on the contest between YHWH and Pharaoh and therefore does not deal with the fate of the Hebrews. We should also note that the verb "let go" (*šlḥ*, Piel) also means "to liberate," "to set free" (slaves). The narrative does presuppose a context in which the situation of the Hebrews in Egypt is not enviable. Be that as it may, Moses never explicitly asks Pharaoh to put an

---

69. For more details, see W. H. Schmidt, *Exodus 1,1–6,30*, 247–50.

70. For Exodus 1–15*, see especially Weimar and Zenger, *Exodus*; W. H. Schmidt, "Die Intention der beiden Plagenerzählungen (Exodus 7–10) in ihrem Kontext." The analysis proposed here does not exclude considering the final text to be a literary masterwork, as some authors claim; for example, W. H. Schmidt, in various works; or, to cite a representative of another school, G. Fischer, "Exodus 1–15."

end to the forced labor of the Hebrews. Instead, he solicits permission to go into the wilderness in order to celebrate a festival there (3:18; 5:1; 7:16, 26; 8:16, 21–24; 9:1, 13; 10:3, 7, 8–11, 24–26). Although one request does not exclude the other, the emphasis is different.

The beginning of the plague narrative in Exod 7:14 is not easily connected to the preceding chapters. In this verse, YHWH tells Moses of Pharaoh's refusal, while in 5:22–23, Moses informs YHWH of this. Moreover, Exod 7:14 introduces another theme, the hardening of Pharaoh's heart, that does not figure in Exodus 5.[71] The origin of the plague narrative may therefore be different from the origin of the surrounding narratives.

Exodus 7–11* contains some analogies with prophetic literature,[72] such as, for example, the presence of the "messenger formula," "thus says YHWH" (Exod 7:17, 26; 8:16; 9:1, 13; 10:3; 11:4), and the "recognition formula," "you shall know that I am YHWH" (Exod 7:17; 8:18; 9:14, 29; 10:2; 11:7). Even the effectiveness of Moses' intercession may constitute a prophetic motif (Exod 8:4–9, 25–27; 9:27–33; 10:16–19). The hardening of the heart is a theme that appears in the writings of several prophets (Isa 6:10; Jer 5:21; Ezek 2:4, 3:7).

There is a partial analogy between the plague narrative and Amos's visions (Amos 7–9): the progression and the results are similar because a judgment is imminent in both cases. Amos 7–9 also mentions the prophet's intercession (Amos 7:2, 5; cf. 7:8). Amos 4:6–12 is another text that can be compared with the account of the plagues. YHWH sends a series of punishments, but the people do not return to him, just as Pharaoh is not convinced by the plagues. The textual contacts between Amos and the plague narrative nonetheless remain limited. The "prophetic" characteristics of the plague narrative, however, set these chapters apart and distinguish them clearly from the other sections of Exodus 1–15.[73] With regard to dating the narrative, there is an important text, 1 Sam 6:6, which evokes the plagues in the context of the war between Israel and the Philistines.[74] It seems quite plausible that this text in 1 Samuel is Preexilic and originated in the North. In all probability, then, a tradition concerning the plagues existed in the Northern Kingdom. However, the present narrative was not necessarily written in the Northern Kingdom. We lack solid clues that would permit us to propose a more precise solution. We could envision, at the very most, an implicit connection between the Isaianic anti-Egyptian propaganda (Isa 18:1–7, 19:11–15, 20:1–6, 30:1–7, 31:1–3; cf.

---

71. Ska, "Récit et récit métadiexégétique," 158.

72. Childs, *Exodus*, 144–49.

73. For other, less convincing, propositions, see ibid., 142–44; Van Seters (*Life of Moses*, 80–86), who writes about Exilic/Postexilic prophecy.

74. In this narrative, the tenth plague (i.e., the death of the firstborn) stands out. Its structure and vocabulary are different.

36:9) and the plague narrative. This would once again situate us in prophetic circles.

The current account of the plagues is structured in two different ways. For the Priestly narrative, the plagues constitute a series of "signs and wonders" that prepare, announce, and prefigure the final judgment. The texts that structure this Priestly narrative are Exod 7:1–5 and 11:9–10. The final judgment is evoked in Exod 12:12 and in the account of the crossing of the sea (Exodus 14*).[75] The second way of structuring Exodus 7–11 appears in Exod 3:16–22, 6:1, and 11:1–3. In these passages, the divine plan has two contrasting stages: the failure of the first stage leads to the success of the second. The plagues are "wonders" worked by YHWH (3:20), but they do not convince Pharaoh. He will only allow Israel to leave after the last intervention—the death of the first-born (3:20–21, 6:1, 11:1).[76] Certain elements of these chapters are late insertions, such as, for example, the presence of Aaron and his staff.

c. The Miracle of the Sea (Exodus 14*)

The non-Priestly narrative of Exodus 14 does not seem to know the episode of the plagues. Neither Pharaoh nor his ministers mention them at the beginning of the account. Israel has "fled" (Exod 14:5), and no one seems to remember the tragic events of Exodus 12* when, in the middle of the night, Pharaoh implored Moses to leave Egypt with his people. Important elements of the plague narrative disappear, notably the festival that was to be celebrated after three days in the wilderness. On the other hand, the theme of slavery unexpectedly reappears (14:5).[77] The prophetic vocabulary found in the account of the plagues is missing in Exodus 14*, however. There are strong indications that lead us to think that Exodus 14* came from a relatively autonomous tradition. On the basis of Hos 2:17; 11:1; 12:10, 14; and a few texts in Amos (2:10, 3:1, 9:7), which are perhaps less certain, many scholars suggest that Exodus 14 also originated in the North.

d. The Sinai Pericope

The explicit connection between Sinai and the departure from Egypt is found in Exod 19:4–6, a Postexilic text that links these two events logically and chronologically:

---

75. See my "Plaies d'Égypte dans le récit sacerdotal (Pg)," *Bib* 60 (1979) 23–35; idem, "La sortie d'Égypte (Ex 7–14) dans le récit sacerdotal (Pg) et la tradition prophétique," *Bib* 60 (1979) 191–215; Blum, *Studien zur Komposition des Pentateuch*, 242–56; L. Schmidt, *Beobachtungen zu der Plagenerzählung*. For Exodus 14, see my *Passage de la mer*, 97–99.

76. Blum, *Studien zur Komposition des Pentateuch*, 20–22; Ska, "Récit et récit métadiexégétique," 150–65.

77. Also see the allusion to the slavery in Egypt in 14:11–12, which is a late addition.

⁴You have seen what I did to the Egyptians, and how I bore you on eagles' wings and brought you to myself. ⁵Now therefore, if you obey my voice and keep my covenant, you shall be my treasured possession out of all the peoples. Indeed, the whole earth is mine, ⁶but you shall be for me a priestly kingdom and a holy nation. These are the words that you shall speak to the Israelites.

With the exception of this text, there are very few allusions to the departure from Egypt in Exodus 19–34, and the few allusions that exist are probably late additions. The best known of these allusions is situated at the beginning of the Decalogue and in all likelihood is of recent origin (Exod 20:2).⁷⁸ Other allusions to the Exodus are scattered throughout the Covenant Code, in passages that belong to the second part of the code and that are often considered to be later (Exod 22:20; 23:9, 15). Even if these were ancient texts, they have no direct connection to the Exodus and Sinai pericope as such but simply refer to a well-known tradition.

The Sinai pericope is one of the most complicated passages in the entire Pentateuch. E. Otto limits the primitive core of this text to Exod 19:2b, 3a, 10–20*; 34:(11a), 18–23, 25–27.⁷⁹ According to E. Zenger, the core is larger: 19:3a, 10–12aα, 14–18; 20:18–20; 24:4aγ, b, 5; 32*; 34:6–7, 14, 18–23, 25–26.⁸⁰ Many other opinions have been voiced on this subject; be that as it may, the most ancient sections are probably in the theophany of Exod 19:10–19 and in the legislation of Exodus 34.⁸¹

In addition to the delimitation of the primitive core, which is vigorously debated, the origin of the passage presents special problems. Many scholars today maintain that it had a cultic origin deriving from either the holy war liturgies⁸² or the cult at Jerusalem.⁸³ It is impossible to answer these questions with certainty.⁸⁴ It seems to me that the Sinai theophany is a text that has been revised

---

78. See Hossfeld, *Der Dekalog*; C. Dohmen, "Der Dekaloganfang und sein Ursprung," *Bib* 74 (1993) 175–95.

79. Otto, "Die nachpriesterschriftliche Pentateuchredaktion," 99.

80. E. Zenger, "Wie und Wozu die Tora zum Sinai kam: Literarische und theologische Beobachtungen zu Exodus 19–34," in *Studies in the Book of Exodus* (ed. M. Vervenne; Leuven, 1996) 265–88.

81. For the connection between the theophany and the Law, see Levin, "Der Dekalog am Sinai." Challenging the antiquity of Exod 34:11–26, see Levinson, *Deuteronomy and the Hermeneutics of Legal Innovation*, 69–70; and S. Bar-On, "The Festival Calendars in Exodus XXIII 14-19 and XXXIV 18-26," *VT* 48 (1998) 161-95.

82. Based on the study of J. Jeremias, *Theophanie: Die Geschichte einer alttestamentlichen Gattung* (WMANT 10; Neukirchen-Vluyn, 1965). See Van Seters, *Life of Moses*, 254–70.

83. Cross, *Canaanite Myth*, 163–69; R. J. Clifford, *The Cosmic Mountain in Canaan and the Old Testament* (HSM 4; Cambridge, MA, 1972) 155; J. Levenson, *Sinai and Zion: An Entry into the Jewish Bible* (San Francisco, 1985).

84. See, among recent studies, Dozeman, *God on the Mountain*; Renaud, *La théophanie du Sinaï*.

primarily because it contains the experience on which Israel based its existence as a people; as a result, it bears the marks of this people's complex history. The text, in its present form, is certainly Postexilic, post-Priestly, and post-Deuteronomistic. It will always be extremely difficult to find a suitable method for identifying with substantial certainty the oldest elements and—even more difficult—for determining their origin.

e. The Covenant Code

With regard to the Covenant Code, two problems must be distinguished: (1) the origin of the various laws or small collections of laws and (2) the redaction of the code as such. The first redaction of the code could hardly have occurred before the 7th or 8th century B.C.E., because it requires a sufficiently developed legal and literary culture, which according to recent research could not have existed any earlier.

Some scholars suggest dating it approximately to Hezekiah's time.[85] Why such a late period? The reasons presented by Crüsemann, in particular, result from historical and sociological reflections. The Covenant Code gives special attention to slaves, foreigners, and financial transactions, and this presumes a society in which these activities created great social disparities. According to the prophets Amos, Hosea, Isaiah, and Micah, this was precisely the situation in the 8th and 7th centuries B.C.E. Recent research on the history and culture of Israel confirms this opinion.

f. Israel's Wandering in the Wilderness

Israel's wandering in the wilderness needs to be studied independently. The figure of Moses permits the connection and unification of narratives and traditions of different origins. Nevertheless, the traditions about the wilderness wanderings contain only a few allusions to the Egyptian oppression (Exodus 1, 5), the plagues (Exodus 7–12*), or the miracle of the sea (Exodus 14*). All of the texts refer to the sojourn in Egypt (Exod 14:11–12, 16:3; Num 11:4–6, 14:1–4, 16:13–14, 20:2–5, 21:5) and, more rarely and without details, to the departure from Egypt (Exod 18:1, 8–11; Num 20:15–16).[86] Num 20:15–16 is the text that most clearly combines the two moments of Israel's history into one

---

85. Crüsemann, "Das Bundesbuch" (on pp. 28–35, 41, Crüsemann speaks generally about the monarchy of the 7th and 8th centuries B.C.E.); Albertz (*History of Israelite Religion*, 1.180–86) mentions Hezekiah's time explicitly. For a discussion of recent theories on this subject, see G. Lasserre, "Quelques études récentes sur le Code de l'alliance," *RTP* 125 (1993) 267–76 (above all F. Crüsemann, L. Schwienhorst-Schönberger, Y. Osumi, and E. Otto). D. P. Wright provides additional arguments for this dating, in "The Laws of Hammurabi as a Source for the Covenant Collection (Exodus 20:23–23:19)," *MAARAV* 10 (2003) 11–87; also Levinson, "Is the Covenant Code an Exilic Composition?"

86. On these texts, see primarily the study by Schart, *Mose und Israel im Konflikt*.

narrative sequence: YHWH leads the Israelites out of Egypt and into the wilderness of Kadesh *because* the Egyptians mistreated them.

As we saw above, this text belongs to a late period; that is, it is more recent than Deuteronomic texts such as Deut 26:3–6. Together with the Priestly text of Exod 6:2–8 and the more-recent Gen 15:13–16, this is one of the few documents of the Tetrateuch that combine the "fathers," the stay in Egypt, and the wanderings in the wilderness into one narrative summary. It is an example of the theological and literary activity of the Postexilic period. So, we may very well have here one of the "cornerstones" of today's Pentateuch.

Similarly, there are few references to the theophany and the Sinai legislation. As in other cases, this argument from silence should not be stressed too strongly. Because the narratives depict a rebellious people who want to return to Egypt, they cannot simultaneously refer to a time when Israel was enslaved in Egypt. However, Moses never uses past oppression as an argument for discouraging those who want to return to Pharaoh's land. There are also several other unique features, such as the structure, style, and reference to specific sites in the wilderness that give these narratives a distinctive character.

Reminiscences about the desert wanderings are quite noticeable in the prophetic books, especially in Hos 2:16–17, 12:10; Amos 2:10; Jer 2:2–3; and Ezekiel 20. There is no unanimously accepted opinion on the dating and interpretation of these texts.[87] Many of the accounts in Exodus–Numbers are local traditions that have been reused in new contexts, such as the conflicts between the people and Moses.

Can we perceive in the wilderness wandering narratives an echo of opposition to the reforms of Hezekiah or Josiah? Or is there a note of opposition to the prophets? Or were these episodes reread in the light of conflicts that arose after the return from Exile? Whatever the case may be, the tone in these texts is often tense and presupposes a context marked by bitter controversies with political and religious connotations.

The desert traditions first appeared in the North (Hosea) and only later in the South (Jeremiah). However, during and after the Exile, the theme of the wanderings in the desert manifested negative connotations for the first time, and the period was seen as a time of rebellion (Ezekiel 20, Neh 9:16–18; cf. Ps 78:17–42, 95:7–11, 106:13–33). As Noth already pointed out, the theme of the "murmuring" and rebellion in the wilderness is often an addition to earlier narratives and is, in our opinion, of Postexilic origin.

The traditions concerning Balaam (Numbers 22–24) have their own history, as attested by the extrabiblical documents from Deir ʿAlla.[88]

---

87. Cf. Talmon, "The 'Desert Motif' in the Bible and in Qumran Literature."
88. See J. A. Hackett, *The Balaam Text from Deir ʿAlla* (HSM 31; Chico, CA, 1984).

To conclude, there is material in the Pentateuch that can reasonably be considered Postexilic. However, it is still difficult, if not impossible, to prove the existence of large narrative units prior to the Exile. The oldest texts that we can identify are stories or short, isolated, independent "narrative cycles" deriving from the collective memory of the people and their civil and religious leaders. The explicit literary connections between the various traditions and cycles, or larger narrative units, are essentially late—that is, Postexilic.

Chapter 10

The Pentateuch and Postexilic Israel

When was the Pentateuch in its present form composed? What factors impelled the Postexilic community of "Israel" to assemble and organize all the legislative and narrative elements in a single work? Why was this work not more strongly unified, and why have so many marks of its literary creation been preserved? In this chapter, I will attempt to answer questions about the historical background—religious, civil, political, and social—of the formation of the Pentateuch. Many theories have already been proposed. However, I will only discuss two hypotheses—the most important and the most interesting: the theory of Persian imperial authorization and the theory of the community of citizens assembled and organized around the temple.

A. Persian Imperial Authorization[1]

When the Postexilic community was reconstituted and began to organize itself, it felt that a legal foundation was needed. Because Jerusalem was a part of the Persian Empire, it was surely necessary for the Postexilic community to obtain some kind of official permission that provided a specific, concrete, legal basis and context for them to function. The undertaking had a political dimension that could not be overlooked by Persia. Recently, some scholars have proposed an idea that has resonated with many others: Persian imperial authorization.[2] This theory has many advocates but also many opponents. Here, as in other areas of scholarship, no consensus has been reached. In the following section, I will present a short synthesis of the discussion.

---

1. P. Frei and K. Koch (eds.), *Reichsidee und Reichsorganisation im Perserreich* (OBO 55; Fribourg and Göttingen, 1984; 2nd ed., 1996; I am quoting the second edition); R. G. Kratz, *Translatio imperii* (WMANT 63; Neukirchen-Vluyn, 1987); Lohfink, "Gab es eine deuteronomistische Bewegung?" 313–83, especially pp. 369–71 = *Studien*, 3.64–142, especially pp. 129–30; P. Frei, "Die Persische Reichsautorisation: Ein Überblick," *ZABR* 1 (1995) 1–35; U. Rüterswörden, "Die Persische Reichsautorisation der Tora: Fact or Fiction?" *ZABR* 1 (1995) 47–61; J. Wiesehöfer, "'Reichsgesetz' oder 'Einzelfallgerechtigkeit'? Bemerkungen zu P. Freis These von der Achämenidischen 'Reichsautorisation,'" *ZABR* 1 (1995) 36–46.
2. See Frei, "Zentralgewalt und Lokalautonomie im Achämenidenreich," 6–36.

1. P. Frei's Hypothesis

According to the theory advanced by P. Frei in 1985, the Persian Empire developed a unique political attitude toward many nations under its authority. Rather than trying to unify the areas under their dominion or centralize their control, the Persians took a tolerant stance and proved that they were much more intelligent than their predecessors. They left subjected peoples some room for political, cultic, religious, and economic autonomy, but in return the people had to respect the central authority and—what is most important—pay taxes. This structure was sanctioned by means of legal documents that P. Frei calls "imperial authorizations." He illustrates his theory with examples. According to this hypothesis, the central government of Persia (that is, the king and the imperial court) approved and sealed certain laws or local regulations with its own authority, and this might be termed imperial "sanction" or "ratification." Frei prefers to speak of *authorization* because *sanction* is an expression used in the context of penal law, and the word *ratification* belongs to the vocabulary of international law.[3]

F. Crüsemann, E. Blum, and R. Albertz, among others, have adopted this theory.[4] According to these three representatives of the "Heidelberg school," there was a close tie between Persian imperial authorization and the formation of the Pentateuch. Because it was necessary to present the Persian authorities with a single law accepted by the entire population in order to obtain this "authorization," the various groups that constituted the Postexilic community had to come to an agreement.

The two major groups were, on the one hand, the priestly families of Jerusalem and, on the other hand, the major landowners of Judah. Each of these groups had its own "history of the origins" of Israel that legitimated its prerogatives. In Blum's terminology, these were Composition P (KP) or Priestly composition, and Composition D (KD) or Deuteronomistic composition.[5]

---

3. Ibid., p. 15 n. 17.

4. F. Crüsemann, "Le Pentateuque, une Tora: Prolégomènes et interprétation de sa forme finale," in *Le Pentateuque en question* (ed. A. de Pury and T. Römer; Le monde de la Bible 19; Geneva, 1989), 339–60, especially pp. 347–48; Blum, *Studien*, 345–60; Albertz, *History of Israelite Religion*, 2.466–80; for a critical position, see Lohfink, "Gab es eine deuteronomistische Bewegung?" 313–82, especially pp. 369–70 = *Studien zum Deuteronomium*, 3.65–142, especially pp. 128–30.

5. According to Blum, Composition D (KD) chronologically preceded Composition P (KP). The two groups, each of which was responsible for one of the two "compositions," later harmonized the two into a single document for presentation to the Persian authorities. The unique character of KP becomes clearer if, as Blum thinks, it was composed to correct and complete KD and to constitute, together with the latter, the one fundamental text required by the king of Persia. Consequently, although KP has its own individuality, it is constantly in dialogue with other traditions. See Blum, *Studien*, 345–60. For his part, Albertz

These two compositions were combined into one document that became, essentially, our Pentateuch or a quite similar document. In the final shape of the text, we find a few additions introduced after the blending of the two massive "compositions." The authors of the "Heidelberg school" assert that the Pentateuch was the document that the community of Jerusalem presented for approbation as the Persian law for the Province of Judah and for all the Jews of the Empire. In other words, the Pentateuch was the document submitted for Persian imperial authorization. This theory is very interesting, and it has appealed to many scholars; we find it in the introductions by Blenkinsopp and Zenger (first edition).[6] But, of course, as might be expected, there has been no lack of opposition to the theory.

2. Evaluation of the Hypothesis

Many questions are left unanswered, but three points should be considered carefully. (1) Some authors express doubt about the very existence of "Persian imperial authorizations." The documentation concerning this phenomenon appears ambiguous to them. (2) Was the Pentateuch this official document, or was there some other legal text? (3) What motivated the formation of the present Pentateuch: was it Persian politics or was it the judicial/political and spiritual needs of the community that gathered around the temple of Jerusalem?

a. The Question of Documentation

P. Frei bases his study of documentation on texts of various origins. The fundamental text is the Trilingual Inscription of Letoon (Xanthus, in Lycia); he then mentions the collection of Egyptian laws compiled by Darius I; the letter from the Jewish community on Elephantine concerning the Passover celebration; three biblical texts—the "decree" of Artaxerxes on behalf of Ezra (Ezra 7:11–26), the story of Daniel 6 (Daniel in the lion's den), and the decree in Esther 8; the inscription of Sardis;[7] a document concerning a boundary dispute

---

thinks that two commissions of theologians worked successively. The first was composed of laymen who worked on "Composition D," and then the priests interacted with it and expanded it, creating a counterproposal that we call Composition P. Finally, the two groups appointed a committee of experts who, in a "symposium," came to a compromise. The text of this compromise was then given to the Persian authorities for their "authorization." See Albertz, *History of Israelite Religion*, 2.466–80.

6. Blenkinsopp, *Pentateuch*, 239–42; Zenger (ed.), *Einleitung*, 39–44; Zenger adopts some of the reflections of O. H. Steck, *Der Abschluß der Prophetie im Alten Testament: Ein Versuch zur Frage der Vorgeschichte des Kanons* (Biblische Studien 17; Neukirchen-Vluyn, 1991) 13–21.

7. Frei abandons the example in the 2nd edition of his book (1996); see the chapter entitled "Zentralgewalt," 90–96.

between Miletus and Myus; and some other possible examples.[8] The discussion is long and complicated. The texts are often laconic, and the argumentation is sometimes based on the conjectured content of missing sections. The interpretation of the biblical texts is also complex, especially in the case of Daniel 6 and Esther 8, which are not historical documents. More than once, Frei himself recognizes that he can only posit the existence of an "authorization" as one of the possible explanations of the texts, because the documents are not univocal.

After having gone through the documents and considered the opinion of the experts in this field, I find that doubts persist.[9] The information is not always congruent, and there are differences among the proposed examples. We can assert, at the most, that the Persian Empire recognized the specified rights of some cities or regions in the Empire. It is more difficult to prove the existence of a generalized, unified policy. There were unique cases, and each of these must be analyzed independently.[10]

On the other hand, it is certain that the reconstruction of the walls and the temple of Jerusalem was not possible without the explicit approval of the central government of Persia. Quite possibly, the Pentateuch in its present shape came into being in these circumstances. Consequently, we should investigate the possibility of situating the Pentateuch in this context. More concretely, we must inquire about the connection between the composition of the Pentateuch and the mission of Ezra.

• *The interpretation of Ezra 7:12–26.*   To move forward in our discussion, we need to read Ezra 7, which contains the most important document on the rights of the Postexilic community of Jerusalem. The essential verses are as follows:

> [12]Artaxerxes, king of kings, to the priest Ezra, the scribe of the law of the God of heaven. . . . [13]I decree that any of the people of Israel or their priests or Levites in my kingdom who freely offers to go to Jerusalem may go with you. [14]For you are sent by the king and his seven counselors to make inquiries about Judah and Jerusalem according to the law of your God, which is in your hand. . . . [25]And you, Ezra, according to the God-given wisdom you possess, appoint magistrates and judges who may judge all the people in the province Beyond the River who know the laws of your God; and you shall teach those who do not know them. [26]All who will not obey the law of your God and the law of the king, let judgment be strictly executed on them, whether for death or for banishment or for confiscation of their goods or for imprisonment.

---

8. See the complementary discussion in ibid., 37–113.

9. Also see the negative evaluation of Otto, "Die nachpriesterschriftliche Pentateuchredaktion im Buch Exodus," especially pp. 66–70, where he expresses doubts about the "imperial authorization." None of the documents presented by P. Frei is truly "imperial law."

10. See Wiesehöfer, " 'Reichsgesetz' oder 'Einzelfallgerechtigkeit'?"

Certain aspects of this "decree" of the king of Persia should be noted: the permission given to each Israelite to settle in Judah; the law of God becomes the state law; the text establishes the rights of the temple in Jerusalem; the legal organization of Judah is in the hands of Ezra.

The document in Ezra 7 talks about a "law" that it calls "the law of the God of heaven" (7:12) and "the law of your God" (the God of Ezra; 7:14, 25, 26). Verse 26 adds the expression "law of the king." According to some authors, we have here one of the strongest arguments in favor of imperial authorization, because the phrase should be interpreted as identification: "the law of God," that is, "the law of the king." If this is true, the law of God that Ezra brings with him becomes the royal law, with all of its legal obligations. Frei supports this interpretation.[11] His main argument is that the text mentions only one law prior to v. 26, the "law of God." Consequently, when the expression "law of the king" appears, a reader would usually consider the two terms to be identical. If the text had wanted to introduce a distinction, it would have done so much more explicitly.

However, other scholars think that the "law of God" should be distinguished from the "law of the king." Generally, these scholars assert that, in addition to the "law of God" that contains legislation on religious matters, the text mentions a "law of the king" that primarily deals with civil rights.[12] In simpler terms, the two "laws" represent two different series of laws, and according to the decree of the king, the province Beyond the River (Transeuphrates) is subject to both. There is support for this interpretation in, for example, 2 Chr 19:11, which distinguishes between the legal matters that pertain to YHWH (the religious tribunals) and the legal matters that are under the jurisdiction of the king (the civil tribunals).[13]

This second hypothesis, however, does not fit the context very well. Indeed, what is the meaning of the term "law" or "decree of the king" (in Aramaic, *dātāʾ dî malkāʾ*) in Ezra 7:11–26? The simplest solution is to say that it designates the decree that the king gave to Ezra, which is summarized in Ezra 7:11–26. The king "gives orders" to Ezra (7:13) and to the treasurers of Transeuphrates (7:21). Ezra also receives an order to organize the legal administration (7:26). Finally, the king provides for punishment to be imposed on those who do not obey the law (7:26). There are, therefore, enough elements for defining this text as a "royal decree," in which the king orders submission to the

---

11. Frei, "Zentralgewalt," 20–21 and 51–54.

12. See the interpretation of H. G. M. Williamson, *Ezra, Nehemiah* (WBC 16; Waco, TX, 1985) 85, 104–5; cf. Frei, "Zentralgewalt," 53; J. Blenkinsopp, "The Mission of Udjahorresnet and Those of Ezra and Nehemiah," *JBL* 106 (1987) 409–21, especially pp. 412, 418–19.

13. Ibid., 419.

"law of God." My interpretation is, then, not very different from the imperial-authorization interpretation. However, I do think that the judicial extension of Ezra's mission and of the decree of Artaxerxes was limited in terms of geographical space. These measures only applied to Jerusalem and its dependent territory.

• *The Pentateuch and the "law of the God of heaven."* One question remains: is it possible to identify our Pentateuch or a similar text with this "law of God"? As I indicated above, some scholars without hesitation identify the document of the supposed "imperial authorization" or, more simply, the law of Israel during the Persian period with the Pentateuch or its immediate predecessor. However, this hypothesis presents difficulties.

The first objection is judicial. The Pentateuch contains many laws: there are three main codes and others of lesser importance, such as the "cultic Decalogue" in Exodus 34 and the laws of the Priestly Code in Exodus 25–31 or in the book of Numbers. Which law should be applied? To be able to settle conflicts, the Persian government had to know which standard was in effect.

A second objection stems from the fact that the Pentateuch contains a great deal of narrative material that, in itself, has no judicial importance. Why would anyone burden an official document with so many items that are external to its central purpose? Frei provides no example of this kind of material (narrative, etc.) in his documentation illustrating imperial authorization. Furthermore, these narratives contain material that might have caused consternation in the Persian court. For example, the promise of land reaching from the River of Egypt to the great river (Euphrates; Gen 15:18) and the accounts of the Transjordanian conquest (Numbers 21, 25, 31) were not innocent texts. Of course, not all of the promises made to the patriarchs gave the land such generous dimensions as Genesis 15, but these texts certainly could cause uneasiness in a power that claimed this territory as its own.

How would the officials of Persia's royal court (or the Persian governor in Jerusalem) have reacted to reading chapters such as Deuteronomy 7 (Israel must completely annihilate the peoples occupying the land), Deuteronomy 20 (the rules of war), or Deut 17:14–20 (the "right of the king")? What reactions would have been provoked by verses such as Deut 26:19 or 28:1, in which Yhwh calls Israel to place itself above all other nations? It is really not hard to imagine; and these facts explain why these texts probably were not part of Ezra's "law" that was known and approved by the Persian government. The Persian administration probably did not peruse or monitor all of the documents written in the Empire. But an "imperial authorization" was an official document with important political implications, and therefore it is difficult to conclude that it could have contained anything threatening to the security or stability of the Empire. Another example: were the oracles of Balaam (Numbers 22–24) texts that could be read by a king concerned with keeping the peace in his Empire, texts that would reassure him regarding the submission of his subjects? All in all, we have good reason to think that the document was much shorter and more unified than the Pentateuch in its present shape.

There is yet another objection: why do we not possess a copy of the Pentateuch in Aramaic for the use of the Persian authorities? We have only an Aramaic version of Artaxerxes' letter in Ezra 7:11–26.[14] Several official documents mentioned by Frei are bilingual or even trilingual, one of the languages being Aramaic. But the Pentateuch is written in Hebrew, which means that its editors preferred to use the language of the past rather than to adapt to the contemporary political situation.

Finally, according to Frei's hypothesis, the Pentateuch became the official document of imperial authorization and thus the "law" for all Jews in the Persian Empire. How can we, if this is the case, explain the Jewish community in Elephantine, in Egypt, which clearly did not observe several essential points of the Torah? The Egyptian community had its own temple and its own cult. Furthermore, the Persian governor of Judah was the person who promoted the reconstruction of the Elephantine altar after its destruction—a measure that is not easy to reconcile with the regulations in Deuteronomy 12 regarding the centralization of the cult.[15]

b. Which Law Did the Persian Authorities Approve?

The text of Ezra, which is not necessarily complete, only mentions in passing the silver and gold offerings brought to the temple (7:15–16), sacrifices (7:17), the financing of the temple (7:20–22), exemptions from duties and taxes for the employees of the sanctuary (7:24), and the judicial organization of the territory of the Transeuphrates province (7:25). The temple occupies most of the space in this decree. So, it is natural to think that this law is mainly concerned with the organization of the cult. Only the judicial administration (7:25–26) was not directly tied to the cult. Why not posit that the law approved by the Persians primarily regulated the cult, as did the Priestly legislation? This legislation would largely have met the requirements of the Persian court.

---

14. This objection is raised by H.-C. Schmitt, "Die Suche nach der Identität des Jahweglaubens im nachexilischen Israel: Bemerkungen zur theologischen Intention des Pentateuch," in *Pluralismus und Identität* (ed. J. Mehlhausen; Munich, 1995) 259–78, especially pp. 264–65. Compare the response of Carr (*Reading the Fractures in Genesis*, 327–33), who tends to minimize the strength of the objections. All the same, none of the parallels proposed by Frei corresponds to the Pentateuch in volume and complexity of compiled material. His parallels are all purely judicial documents. None of them contains narratives concerning either conquest or war, as does the Pentateuch.

15. Rüterswörden, "Die Persische Reichsautorisation," 59–61; Otto, "Nachpriesterschriftliche Pentateuchredaktion," 69.

This is K. Koch's thesis, and I find good reason to agree with him, although a few corrections need to be made.[16] Koch introduces a useful distinction between the actual unit Ezra–Nehemiah and the significance of Ezra 7:11–26 as such—that is, the decree of Artaxerxes. In the canonical book of Ezra–Nehemiah, the allusions to divine orders all refer to the Law contained in the Pentateuch. However, if we limit our discussion to the decree of Artaxerxes, the situation is different. This decree mainly refers to Priestly texts.

Thus, the distinction between priests, Levites, and laymen (Ezra 7:13) is also found in Numbers 1–10. Another list of offices, in Ezra 7:24—priests, Levites, singers, doorkeepers, temple servants, and other servants—is not found in the Pentateuch but is found in Chronicles. "Freewill offerings" (Ezra 7:15–16) is an expression that frequently appears in Priestly texts, as well as in the cultic laws of Deuteronomy (12:6, 7; 16:10; 23:24).[17]

The animals to be offered—bulls, rams, and lambs (Ezra 7:17)—are those mentioned in the legislation of Leviticus 1–7. Wine, oil, and salt (7:22) also are a part of the offerings in Leviticus 2. Wine, oil, and salt (7:22) for libations reappear in the same context in Exod 29:40; Num 15:4–5, 6–7, 9–10; 28:4–7, 12–14; and 1 Chr 9:29 and are missing in the Deuteronomic laws. The judicial organization of Ezra 7:25 corresponds to Deut 16:18.[18]

To conclude, the document that takes shape as a result of this discussion is composed of a series of cultic rules, mainly (but not exclusively) of Priestly origin. This does not correspond exactly to the Holiness Code (Leviticus 17–26) or to a specific document of Priestly legislation. The texts mentioned are found in various parts of the Pentateuch (Exodus, Leviticus, Numbers, and Deuteronomy). The decree of Artaxerxes was perhaps simply a "compendium" or collection of the laws that were essential for the implementation of Ezra's mission and for defining the rights and obligations of the province of Transeuphrates.[19] The collection contained only what was necessary, and therefore it could not have been the Pentateuch in its present arrangement or in a similar form. Nevertheless, the redaction of this "compendium" presupposes the exist-

---

16. K. Koch, "Weltordnung und Reichsidee im alten Iran und ihre Auswirkungen auf die Provinz Jehud," in *Reichsidee und Reichsorganisation im Perserreich* (ed. P. Frei and K. Koch; 2nd ed.; OBO 55; Fribourg and Göttingen, 1996) 134–337, especially pp. 274–78.

17. See Exod 35:29; 36:3; Lev 7:16; 22:18, 21, 23; 23:38; Num 15:3; 29:39; Deut 12:6, 7; 16:10; 23:24; Ezek 46:12; Hos 14:5; Amos 4:5; Ps 54:8; 68:10; 110:3; 119:108; Ezra 1:4; 3:5; 8:28; 2 Chr 31:14; 35:8.

18. Koch thinks that this verse is a late addition.

19. Blum's argument (*Studien zur Komposition des Pentateuch*, 352–55) is based on allusions to the Law in the work of the Chronicler (that is, Ezra–Nehemiah and 1–2 Chronicles). In this view, as Koch has noted, there is no doubt that the Law to which these books refer is in fact the Pentateuch. In any case, these books are late.

ence of laws or collections of laws that were later inserted into the composition of the Pentateuch.

I cannot deal here with the very complex questions of the historicity of the Ezra 7 narrative and its related problems. Even if we were to adopt a minimalist position and consider the text of Ezra to be entirely or partly fiction, it must nevertheless have corresponded to some sort of reality. For example, the reconstruction of the walls and temple of Jerusalem in a province of the Persian Empire, which from a distance controlled the strategic passageway leading to Egypt, would have had to have the king's agreement.[20] This does not mean, however, that Ezra 7 must be taken literally.

c. How Did the Pentateuch Come to Be?

If the Pentateuch in its current shape was not the text of a Persian imperial authorization, how can we explain its formation? I think that the internal needs of the Postexilic community best justify this phenomenon. When Judah acquired relative autonomy, mainly in the religious sphere, it became possible and even necessary to reinforce the unity of the community by means of its new institutions. The Persian authorities created a favorable situation for the composition of a document that became the "identity card" of the Postexilic community. However, the Persian Empire was not trying to obtain a unique document that was the product of a compromise between two groups, the priests and the elders. The real motives leading to the redaction of the Pentateuch are to be looked for within Israel—more precisely, in Jerusalem and in the province of Judah (Yehud), at the time of the reforms introduced by Ezra and Nehemiah (or Nehemiah and Ezra).[21]

One fundamental argument confirms this view. The primary purpose of the Pentateuch, for whoever reads it as a whole, is not to regulate life within a province of the Persian Empire but to define the conditions of membership in a specific community called "Israel." There are two primary conditions: blood ties and a "social contract."[22] The blood ties are established by genealogies and,

---

20. For bibliography and a discussion of the question, see Frei, "Zentralgewalt," 54–61; Koch, "Weltordung," 213–16. For the strategic importance of the province of Judah within the Persian Empire, see ibid., 308; Koch mentions other religious and ethnic motivations that explain why Judah might have enjoyed privileged position in the Persian Empire (pp. 308–14).

21. The chronological problems of Ezra–Nehemiah are well known, but they do not really have any implications for my work here. For a recent summary, see H. G. M. Williamson, *Ezra and Nehemiah* (OTG; Sheffield, 1987); G. Steins, "Die Bücher Esra und Nehemia," in *Einleitung in das Alte Testament* (ed. E. Zenger; StB 1/1; Stuttgart, 1995) 175–83; Sacchi, *Storia del Secondo Tempio*, 105–26.

22. A. de Pury, "Dos leyendas sobre el origen de Israel (Jacob y Moisés) y la elaboración del Pentateuco," *Estbib* 52 (1994) 95–131.

thus, by the book of Genesis. The members of Israel are descendents of Abraham, Isaac, and Jacob. The "social contract" is the Covenant, with all the rights
and duties, both religious and civil, that it entails.

The internal justifications are therefore dominant. The purpose of the texts,
as we saw above, is to present the importance of ties to the past. This is why
three codes are used to demonstrate the judicial continuity between Preexilic
Israel and Postexilic Israel. For the same reason, the cultic and civil legislation is
situated in the past, at the time of the wanderings in the wilderness, long before
the Conquest of the land or the Monarchy. Instead of letting itself be assimilated or become just another province in the vast Empire, Postexilic Israel
wanted to safeguard its identity. Persian politics gave it the opportunity to do
this.

Israel survived as a faith community united above all by its religious traditions and institutions, not as an independent nation. The origin of the Pentateuch is to be explained in this context.

B. The Theory of Citizens Connected with the Temple
(*Bürger-Tempel-Gemeinde*)

1. The Hypothesis of J. P. Weinberg

In the 1970s, a Latvian scholar, J. P. Weinberg, advanced a new theory concerning the organization of the Postexilic community of Jerusalem.[23] According to his theory, the community was organized around the temple. At this
time, especially in Babylonia, temples were like today's banks and commercial
centers. They had official status, recognized by the Persian Empire, and this
gave them a relatively autonomous position, notably in the financial area.

Weinberg illustrates his theory with examples from Asia Minor, Babylonia,
and Egypt.[24] J. Blenkinsopp has adopted these ideas and added other examples.[25] This hypothesis can also be supported with biblical data. Indeed, the
temple played a primary role in Ezra's reform. The decree of Artarxerxes, according to the version in Ezra 7, contains financial instructions that fit well

---

23. J. P. Weinberg, "Die Agrarverhältnisse in der Bürger-Tempel-Gemeinde der Achämenidenzeit," in *Wirtschaft und Gesellschaft im Alten Vorderasien* (ed. J. Harmatta and G. Komoróczy; Budapest, 1976; 2nd ed., 1990) 443–46; idem, *The Citizen-Temple Community*
(JSOTSup 151; Sheffield, 1992). For a summary, see Koch, "Weltordung," 203–4.

24. In his study, Frei mentions examples of similar financial regulations regarding the
sanctuaries, especially the Letoon inscription.

25. J. Blenkinsopp, "Temple and Society in Achaemenid Judah," in *Second Temple Studies,
I: Persian Period* (ed. P. R. Davies; JSOTSup 117; Sheffield, 1991) 22–53. Also see D. L. Pe-
tersen, "Israelite Prophecy: Change versus Continuity," in *Congress Volume: Leuven, 1989* (ed.
J. A. Emerton; VTSup 43; Leuven, 1991) 191–203, especially pp. 197–203.

with Weinberg's theory: the temple is to receive donations of gold and silver (7:15–16) that will serve for cultic expenditures and especially for sacrifices; Ezra may freely dispose of the rest (7:18). Tribute is not to be imposed on the priests and the employees of the sanctuary (7:24). Whoever does not respect the rules of the community is to be "banned," such as, for example, those involved in a mixed marriage (Ezra 10:8).[26]

The privileged situation of Jerusalem in comparison with the province of Judah may also explain the conflicts that arose at that time and that are evoked in some passages.[27] The disagreement between the returnees and the "people of the land" that is often mentioned in the books of Ezra and of Nehemiah may stem from the opposition by the "people of the land" to the reconstruction of the temple. This construction clearly implied that the region would be under the economic and political dominion of the temple, and the temple was under the control of priests who had returned from Babylon.

These arguments support Weinberg's thesis that the Postexilic community of Jerusalem benefited from special status, with financial advantages for all citizens connected with the temple. This does not mean, however, that we must endorse every detail of Weinberg's theory, such as the numerical projections that he proposes for the province of Judah (Yehud; see C. E. Carter).

2. The Citizen-Temple Community and the Pentateuch

The theory of the Citizen-Temple Community, a community of citizens united around the temple, is better documented than the theory of imperial authorization and proves to be more convincing. The Persian government recognized the rights and privileges of the temple and of the community whose life was connected to it. This was, in fact, the content of the supposed "authorization" that gave relative local autonomy to the province of Judah. The decree in Ezra 7 also confirms this view, because it largely deals with the restoration and organization of the cult in the temple of Jerusalem. Furthermore, the two versions of Cyrus's edict agree regarding the reconstruction of the temple (Ezra 1:1–4; 2 Chr 26:22–23). Even if this text is not "historical," it is still emblematic of the mentality of this time. The interpretation of the events reflected in these texts is evidence of a key factor in the thinking of the writers: after the Exile, the community of Israel organized itself around the sanctuary at Jerusalem.

Therefore, we need to seek the origin of the present form of the Pentateuch within the community gathered around the temple. This community had its "Law," the "Law of God," which had been officially approved by the Persian

---

26. Koch, "Weltordung," 203.
27. See Sacchi, *Storia*, 92–104.

authorities according to the decree of Artarxerxes. The temple and the Law were the two institutional pillars of Postexilic Israel. According to this hypothesis, the community is defined in Exod 19:6 as a "holy nation," a "priestly people," and "God's treasured possession." This same community is consecrated by the sprinkling of blood in Exod 24:3–8, when they promise to observe and listen to the Law. In Exod 24:9–11, the "vision of God" and the "meal" in the presence of the divinity confirm and legitimate the authority of the priests and the elders, the two groups who are responsible for the community.[28] In Deut 31:9, Moses entrusts the Law to the priests and the elders. These two institutions are those that survived the Exile and took the lead during and after the return.[29]

The central position occupied by the "tent" and the cult is easy to explain in this context. The Pentateuch develops a narrative arc that links Creation to the tent (Genesis 1 and Exodus 40). According to this canonical organization of the books or scrolls, a first vast stage of the history of the universe comes to a close in Exodus 40: the Creator has found a dwelling within creation. The books of Genesis and Exodus describe the various stages leading to this result. YHWH, the Creator of the universe, chooses a people for himself, he liberates them, and comes to live in their midst (Exod 40:34–35). Later, YHWH himself speaks from this place (Lev 1:1, Num 1:1) and accompanies the people during their wanderings to the Promised Land (Exod 40:36–38, Num 9:15–23; cf. Deut 31:14–15). This "thread" unifies a large part of the Pentateuch and highlights one of the most important factors for the Postexilic community, precisely because the "tent" was the prototype for the temple.

The Pentateuch had two functions within the Postexilic community. First, it provided criteria for membership in the community. Second, it established with clarity the power structure and the respective positions of the various groups that coexisted at that time. The narratives and the genealogies of Genesis define the qualifications for membership in the community. The "legislative books" (Exodus–Deuteronomy) furnish the community's judicial foundation. Thus, an Israelite is a descendent of Abraham, Isaac, and Jacob, who listens to and puts into practice the Mosaic Law entrusted to the priests and to the elders.[30] Only those who fit this definition are members of the "community of

---

28. Ska, "Le repas de Exod 24,11."

29. J. Buchholz, *Die Ältesten Israels im Deuteronomium* (Göttinger theologische Arbeiten 36; Göttingen, 1986); Ska, "Récit et récit métadiexégétique," especially pp. 165–70; Blum, *Studien zur Komposition des Pentateuch*, 339–45; cf. N. Lohfink, "Die Ältesten Israels und der Bund: Zum Zusammenhang von Dtn 5,23; 26,17–19; 27,1.9f und 31,9," *BN* 67 (1993) 26–41.

30. In this context, it is easier to understand the significance of laws that specify when someone is excluded from the community. These are, essentially, laws of a cultic type and laws concerning purity and impurity (Lev 7:27; 17:3–4, 8–9, 10; 19:8; 20:18). Many of the

the temple" and are able to benefit from the privileges granted by the king of Persia to the temple of Jerusalem and the province of Judah (Yehud).

We find the same concerns in the books of Ezra and Nehemiah. There are many genealogies in these books, just as in Chronicles.[31] The insistence on the community's purity is another characteristic of the Postexilic community: in addition to ethnic origin, one's observance of certain cultic rules may determine membership in the community—such as, for example, the acts of rejecting the impurity of the people of the land and celebrating Passover (Ezra 6:20–21). Conversely, not observing the rules on mixed marriage is cause for exclusion from the community (Ezra 10:8). Again, finally, the two institutional pillars of the community are the temple and the Law (Ezra 3:1–13, 4:24–6:18; Nehemiah 8).

The convergence between the later strata of the Pentateuch and certain passages in Ezra–Nehemiah gives more weight to the idea that the Pentateuch in its present form originated during the Postexilic period within the community that was reorganizing itself around the temple of Jerusalem.

---

passages in this list mention blood or imply the presence of blood, as in the case of sacrifices. The only exception is Lev 19:8, which condemns anyone who eats a sacrifice of communion (or, offering of well-being) after two days have passed. The blood is the sacred element *par excellence* in the theology of Leviticus.

31. Ezra 7:1–6, 8:1–14; Neh 11:4–19, 12:1–26; cf. 1 Chr 1:1–9:44.

Conclusion

Despite its complexity, or perhaps because of it, the Pentateuch remains a fascinating text. After a long study of its origins, we are in a position to contemplate briefly the architecture of the city as it now presents itself to us. We need to deal with one last question: can we discover a single track leading through this variegated landscape? Or must we admit that it is impossible to speak about the final form of the text because it actually never existed and because no one ever wanted to give it the final touch?[1]

At the end of the journey, we may consider the following conclusions to be firm. The Pentateuch is not the work of a single author who composed the entire work in a relatively short time. Nor was it written by a single school of writers, at one particular time, in accord with a well-defined purpose, in a unique and recognizable style. The Pentateuch is a composite work; there is no longer the slightest doubt about this. But there remains one last question: following in the footsteps of representatives of synchronic and canonical reading, can we affirm that, despite the "fractures" of the text, it is possible to discover literary unity? It is a composite text, but it seems to have been organized with great care and art.[2] Many architects have worked on it, but the architecture is unified. The final edifice is the product of collective work, based on a single plan. So, is there a "unity" in the Pentateuch? The question, when it is put in these terms, may conceal another alternative.

The diversity of the materials that were used in the composition of the Pentateuch obliges us, when we speak about *unity*, to define the term more precisely. We need therefore to formulate the question differently: can a reader perceive in the Pentateuch a desire to organize the materials in accordance with simple principles? The final editors of the Pentateuch wanted to respect long-standing traditions, and they did not alter them. Thus, the question we must ask at this point is: did these editors integrate these traditions in an organic way, with a specific goal, into a single composition?

If it is true, as we have seen in the preceding chapter, that the Pentateuch originated within the Postexilic community that was rebuilding itself around

---

1. E. Blum, "Gibt es die Endgestalt des Pentateuch?" in *Congress Volume: Leuven, 1989* (ed. J. A. Emerton; VTSup 43; Leiden, 1991) 46–57; cf. idem, *Studien zur Komposition des Pentateuch*, 361–82.

2. See, for example, Clines, *Theme of the Pentateuch*, 5: "I am arguing that the Pentateuch is a unity—not in origin, but in its final shape"; P. R. Noble, "Synchronic and Diachronic Approaches to Biblical Interpretation," *Literature and Theology* 7 (1993) 130–48. On the implications of the redaction of the Pentateuch, see further Levinson and Zahn, "Revelation Regained," 306–10.

the temple of Jerusalem with the support of two main institutions, the priests and the elders, it should be possible to discern, in this larger structure, details that tell us something about the identity of this community. The picture may have some blurry spots, but it should be recognizable. The Postexilic community could not base its existence on a self-contradictory document, at least not for its essential points. Varying details might be permitted, but it would not have been possible to accept differences with regard to the identity of the people of Israel. For example, it would not have been possible to encounter in the Pentateuch two sets of characters contending for the privilege of being Israel's ancestors. Similarly, there is only one mediator between YHWH and his people, a unique "founder" of Israel: Moses.

The legislation contains many laws. The origin, however, was unique and shared by all: they were promulgated by the same YHWH and transmitted by the same Moses to the same Israel near Mount Sinai/Horeb or during the wanderings in the wilderness. They all bear the same seal and go back to the same "symbolic period" of history. Israel had a unique legislator because it had a unique God. This is why we must affirm that there is unity of thought in the Pentateuch. This unity, however, rather than excluding some of the diverse conceptions, included them all.

The Pentateuch was a "compromise" between various tendencies and, just like all compromises, it had to take into account different perspectives.[3] In addition, if there was indeed a compromise, this means that different groups came to an agreement that permitted them to work out together a common document that formed the basis for the Postexilic community.

What are the fundamental components of this work? Genesis 1–11 lays the "foundations," providing a universal dimension. Genesis 12–50, beginning with the ancestors, defines the people of Israel.[4] When Israel becomes a prolific people (Exod 1:1–7), Exodus–Numbers and Deuteronomy base its existence on the Covenant, which is the response and commitment of a free people to a liberating God.

Specific components emerge from this overview: the law, the cult, and the land. These three elements are usually in opposition. We all know the antitheses Law : prophets, and Law : Gospel. It is also frequently said that the Priestly tradition is not concerned with the land but only with the temple. For this reason, the Priestly Writer's work is thought to end in Exodus 40[5] or Leviticus 9.[6]

---

3. The term "compromise" is used by Blum, *Studien zur Komposition des Pentateuch*, 358; Albertz, *History of Israelite Religion*, 2.486; Zenger (ed.), *Einleitung*, 42.

4. See, among others, Blum, *Komposition der Vätergeschichte*, 505–6; and the studies by de Pury referred to in the preceding chapters.

5. Pola, *Die ursprüngliche Priesterschrift*.

6. Zenger (ed.), *Einleitung*, 94–96.

The land is the preoccupation of Deuteronomy, not of the Priestly Writer. Must cult and land therefore be in opposition to one another?

I believe that this is once again a false opposition. This topic is intended to be one of the last discussions in this introduction. I am going to set aside, for the moment, the fact that the land already appears in Gen 17:8, in the theology of the Priestly Writer (cf. Gen 28:4, 35:12, 48:4). Instead, in my analysis I am concentrating on the theology of the "tent of meeting" and the cultic institutions of P in an attempt to see whether they are conceivable without reference to the "land." The answer is no. The tent was a temporary construction, for use during a journey. It moved, as did the people in the wilderness, with the goal of arriving at the final destination of the journey—the land.

The later additions of Exod 40:36–38 highlight the close relationship between the tent and the journey. The "cloud" covers the "tent" or the "dwelling" and from this place orders all the movements of the people. This point of view is not absent from the Priestly document itself. The Levites have the task (Numbers 4*) of carrying the tent and the sacred objects. Num 10:11–12, which is usually attributed to the Priestly Writer and which is in any case of Priestly origin, describes the first departure of Israel after the construction of the tent. The order is given from the cloud. The cult is therefore that of a "journeying" people, a *populus viatorum*. Like the rest of the Pentateuch, the Priestly Writer stretches forward to the future and develops a "theology of hope." Would the God of the Priestly Writer ever forget the promise of the land when he received offerings in the desert? In P, the promise is sealed by an oath (*běrît*), an oath that God remembers when the Israelites are slaves in Egypt (Exod 2:24; 6:5–6). It is because of this oath that God swore to Israel's ancestors that he will bring them out of Egypt (Exod 6:5–6) to lead them into the land (Exod 6:8). And will the same God, when he comes to reside in a tent (Exodus 40) or when he smells the pleasing odor of the first sacrifices offered by Israel in Leviticus 9, declare himself satisfied and forsake his promise? Was the oath granting the land just a tricky way to lure Israel into the wilderness to offer sacrifices to their liberator? Does the God of P behave like some dishonest travel agent? There is a serious problem with the narrative logic of the Priestly Writer unless one integrates into P a few texts such as Numbers 14* (and 20*) that explain why a whole generation plus their leaders will not enter the land and why the fulfillment of the promise must be delayed (see especially Num 14:30; 20:12). In my opinion, P does not end in Exodus or Leviticus but in Numbers, because the problem of the land requires a firm resolution.

Actually, the whole Pentateuch is directed toward the land. YHWH promises to show it to Abraham in Gen 12:1: "Go to the land that I will show you." At the end of the Pentateuch, the same YHWH sends Moses up on Mount Nebo to "show him" this land into which Israel has not yet entered and into which the

greatest prophet will never enter (Deut 34:1).[7] This *inclusio* is meaningful.
The land remains the persistent preoccupation throughout the entire Pentateuch. Moses dies on Mount Nebo, and Joshua will complete the work that
was begun. The Pentateuch is therefore, from this point of view, an "unfinished symphony."

According to Jews, a Messiah will come one day to assemble all of the
people and found an ever-lasting "kingdom of peace." For Christians, Joshua is
Jesus—*Joshua* is the Hebrew form and *Jesus* the Aramaic form of the same
name. This is why the Gospels begin on the banks of the River Jordan, at the
very place where Moses died and where the mission of Joshua began. Jesus is
the one who, according to the Christian faith, will cross the Jordan and enter
into the "kingdom."

The conclusion of the Pentateuch remains open. Both Jews and Christians
read the same five books. But they part ways on the interpretation of the conclusion of this magnificent literary work. The division is, however, perhaps less
important than it seems to be at first. Even the structure of the New Testament
is open: it ends with the call for the Messiah's return. The Messiah, who is still
to come for the Jews, will one day come back for the Christians. All live with
this hope, which is also the final message of the Pentateuch.

Postscript

The theories advocated in this *Introduction* have recently been challenged in
several publications by John Van Seters, who considers the words *editor* and *redactor* to be anachronistic when applied to the exegesis of biblical texts.[8] For
him, the writers of biblical texts are "authors" in the full sense of the word.

In my opinion, the Canadian scholar correctly criticizes the (sometimes)
naïve application of modern concepts to biblical literature. It is obvious that
there is an important difference between ancient writers and modern "editors"
or "redactors." On the other hand, his theory is based on a somewhat narrow
understanding of language. First of all, the existence (or nonexistence) of a
word does not necessarily imply the existence (or nonexistence) of the corresponding reality. The American continent, for instance, "existed" long before
Christopher Columbus "discovered" it and Amerigo Vespucci gave it a name.

---

7. See ibid., 36.

8. See especially J. Van Seters, "The Redactor in Biblical Studies: A Nineteenth Century
Anachronism," *JNSL* 29 (2003) 1–19; idem, "An Ironic Circle: Wellhausen and the Rise of
Redaction Criticism," *ZAW* 115 (2003) 487–500; and his recent book, *The Edited Bible: The
Curious History of the "Editor" in Biblical Criticism* (Winona Lake, IN: Eisenbrauns, 2006).

People lived on this continent for centuries without knowing the name "America." Second, our words and concepts are often used in a metaphorical or analogical way. The words "editor" and "redactor," for instance, when used in biblical exegesis, cannot simply be equated with contemporary "editors" or "redactors." These words have different meanings in their contexts, based on the intentions of the scholars using them. Third, and more importantly, writers in antiquity were very different from modern authors. We have to forget our individualistic mentality and the institution of "copyright" if we are to understand ancient writers, especially those who remained anonymous and in most cases intended to be the mouthpieces of their peoples' traditions. It is of course not possible to assert that the Pentateuch is the work of "authors" who can be compared with Tolstoy, Hemingway, or Samuel Becket. And who "wrote" the Greek myths and the *Gilgamesh Epic*?

This does not mean that the ancient writers were not creative, as M. Fishbane and B. M. Levinson, for example, have amply demonstrated.[9] But these ancient writers also concealed their innovations and revisions behind their apparent faithfulness to the received tradition that in the Bible usually bore a divine seal.

To come back to the question of "editors" and "redactors," I use these words in this *Introduction* to describe the activity of the people who both put down in writing traditions they did not themselves create and also felt free to alter these writings, sometimes to a rather great extent, in order to adapt them to new circumstances.[10] What shall we call the "writers" who are responsible for these interventions? These are the main questions that I would like to raise after reading the instructive, very learned, and challenging works of John Van Seters on this crucial topic.[11]

---

9. M. Fishbane, *Biblical Interpretation in Ancient Israel* (New York: Oxford University Press, 1985); B. M. Levinson, *Deuteronomy and the Hermeneutics of Legal Innovation* (Oxford: Oxford University Press, 1997); idem, "'You Must Not Add Anything to What I Command You': Paradoxes of Canon and Authorship in Ancient Israel," *Numen* 50 (2003) 1–51.

10. Similarly, can we explain the Hebrew and the Greek forms of the book of Jeremiah without resorting to the existence "redactors" of some sort, who felt free to "edit" the book, introducing minor and major changes in the wording and in the organization of the entire work? We could ask the same question about the numerous important differences in the Pentateuchs of the Masoretic Text, the Samaritan version, the Septuagint, and the Qumran manuscripts. This also raises the question of pseudonymous attributions in antiquity.

11. For more details, see my "Plea on Behalf of the Biblical Redactors," in *Studia Theologica: Nordic Journal of Theology* 59 (2005) 4–18.

Bibliography

ABEL, F. M. *Géographie de la Palestine*. 2 vols. EB. Paris, 1933. 3rd ed., 1967.

_____ . *Histoire de la Palestine depuis la conquête d'Alexandre jusqu'à l'invasion arabe.* 2 vols. EB. Paris, 1952.

ABELA, A. *The Themes of the Abraham Narrative: Thematic Coherence within the Abraham Literary Unit of Genesis 11,27–25,18*. Malta, 1989.

ABRAMS, M. H. *The Mirror and the Lamp*. New York, 1953.

ASSOCIATION CATHOLIQUE DES ÉTUDES BIBLIQUES AU CANADA. *De bien des manières: La recherche historique biblique aux abords du XXIᵉ siècle*. LD 163. Paris, 1995.

ACHENBACH, R. *Die Vollendung der Tora: Studien zur Redaktionsgeschichte des Numeribuches im Kontext von Hexateuch und Pentateuch.* Beihefte zur Zeitschrift für altorientalische und biblische Rechtsgeschichte 3. Wiesbaden, 2003.

ALBERTZ, R. *A History of Israelite Religion in the Old Testament Period*, trans. J. Bowden. 2 vols. London, 1994. [Original: *Religionsgeschichte Israels in alttestamentlicher Zeit.* 2 vols. ATD Supplements 8/1–2. Göttingen, 1992.]

ALBERTZ, R., and BECKING, B. (eds.). *Yahwism after the Exile: Perspectives on Israelite Religion in the Persian Era* (Papers Read at the First Meeting of the European Association for Biblical Studies Utrecht, 6–9 August 2000). Studies in Theology and Religion 5. Assen, 2003.

ALBRIGHT, W. F. "Abram the Hebrew: A New Archaeological Interpretation." *BASOR* 163 (1961) 36–54.

ALETTI, J.-N. "Exégèse biblique et sémiotique." *RSR* 80 (1992) 9–28.

ALEXANDER, T. D. *From Paradise to the Promised Land: An Introduction to the Main Themes of the Pentateuch*. Grand Rapids, 1995.

_____ . "Gen 22 and the Covenant of Circumcision." *JSOT* 25 (1983) 17–22.

ALEXANDER, T. D., and BAKER, D. W. *Dictionary of the Old Testament: Pentateuch*. Leicester, 2003.

ALLISON, D. C. *The New Moses: A Matthean Typology*. Minneapolis, 1993.

ALONSO SCHÖKEL, L. "Motivos sapienciales y de alianza en Gn 2–3." *Bib* 43 (1962) 295–316.

ALT, A. "Erwägungen zur Landnahme der Israeliten in Palästina." *PJ* 53 (1939) 8–63 [= Pp. 126–75 in vol. 1 of *Kleine Schriften*.]

_____ . *Essays on Old Testament History and Religion*, trans. R. A. Wilson. Oxford, 1966. [Original: *Kleine Schriften zur Geschichte des Volkes Israel*. 2 vols. Munich, 1953–59.]

_____ . "The Formation of the Israelite State in Palestine." Pp. 223–309 in *Essays on Old Testament History and Religion*. [Original: *Die Staatenbildung der Israeliten in Palästine*. Leipzig, 1930. Repr. pp. 1–65 in vol. 2 of *Kleine Schriften*.]

_____ . "The God of the Fathers." Pp. 1–100 in *Essays on Old Testament History and Religion*. [Original: *Der Gott der Väter: Ein Beitrag zur Urgeschichte der israelitischen Religion*. BWANT 3. Stuttgart, 1929. Repr. pp. 1–77 in vol. 1 of *Kleine Schriften*.]

_____ . "The Origins of Israelite Law. Pp. 101–71 in *Essays on Old Testament History and Religion*. [Original: *Die Ursprünge des israelitischen Rechts*. Leipzig, 1934. Repr. pp. 278–332 in vol. 1 of *Kleine Schriften*.]

_____ . "The Settlement of the Israelites in Palestine." Pp. 173–221 in *Essays on Old Testament History and Religion*. [Original: *Die Landnahme der Israeliten in Palästina*. Leipzig, 1925. Repr. pp. 89–125 in vol. 1 of *Kleine Schriften*.]

ALTER, R. *The Art of Biblical Narrative*. New York, 1981.

ANBAR, M. "Genesis 15: A Conflation of Two Deuteronomic Narratives." *JBL* 101 (1982) 39–55.

_____ . "La 'reprise.'" *VT* 38 (1988) 385–98.

ANDERSON, B. W. "From Analysis to Synthesis: The Interpretation of Gen 1–11." *JBL* 97 (1978) 23–39.

ARTUS, O. *Le Pentateuque*. Cahier Évangiles 106. Paris, 1998.

ASHLEY, T. R. *The Book of Numbers*. NICOT. Grand Rapids,1993.

ASTRUC, J. *Conjectures sur les mémoires originaux dont il paraît que Moyse s'est servi pour composer le récit de la Genèse*. Brussels, 1753 = *Jean Astruc: Conjectures sur la Genèse*. Introduction and notes by P. GIBERT. Paris, 1999.

AUERBACH, E. *Mimesis: The Representation of Reality in Western Literature*, trans. W. R. Trask. Princeton, 1968. [Original: *Mimesis: Dargestellte Wirklichkeit in der abendländischen Literatur*. Berne, 1946.]

AURELIUS, E. *Der Fürbitter Israels: Eine Studie zum Mosebild im Alten Testament*. ConBOT 27. Stockholm, 1988.

AVRIN, L. *Scribes, Script and Books: The Book Art from Antiquity to the Renaissance*. Chicago, 1991.

BÄCHLI, O. *Amphictyonie im Alten Testament*. TZ Supplement 6. Basel, 1977.

BAENTSCH, B. *Exodus–Leviticus–Numeri*. HAT 1/2. Göttingen, 1903.

BARBIERO, G. *L'asino del nemico: Rinuncia alla vendetta e amore del nemico nella legislazione dell'Antico Testamento (Es 23,4–5, Dt 22,1–4, Lv 19,17–18)*. AnBib 128. Rome, 1991.

BARDTKE, H. "Henning Bernhardt Witter: Zur 250. Wiederkehr seiner Promotion zum Philosophiae Doctor am 6. November 1704 zu Helmstedt." *ZAW* 66 (1954) 153–81.

BAR-EFRAT, S. *Narrative Art in the Bible*. JSOTSup 70. Bible and Literature Series 17. Sheffield, 1989.

BARKAY, G. "The Priestly Benediction on Silver from Keteph Hinnom in Jerusalem." *Cathedra* 52 (1989) 37–76. [Hebrew]

BARRÉ, L. M. "The Riddle of the Flood Chronology." *JSOT* 41 (1988) 3–20.

BARSTAD, H. M. *The Myth of the Empty Land*. Symbolae Osloenses Fasc. Sup. 28. Oslo, 1996.

BARTHÉLEMY, D., and MILIK, J. T. *Qumran Cave I*. DJD 1. Oxford, 1955.

BARTHES, R. (ed.). *Structural Analysis and Biblical Exegesis: Interpretational Essays*, trans. A. M. Johnson Jr. Pittsburgh, 1974. [Original: *Analyse structurale et exégèse biblique*. Neuchâtel, 1971.]

BAR-ON, S. "The Festival Calendars in Exodus XXIII 14-19 and XXXIV 18-26." *VT* 48 (1998) 161-95.

BARTON, J. *Oracles of God: Perceptions of Ancient Prophecy in Israel after the Exile.* Oxford, 1986.

BAUER, U. F. W. *kl hdbrym h'lh—All diese Worte: Impulse zur Schriftauslegung aus Amsterdam. Expliziert an der Schilfmeererzählung in Exodus 13,17–14,31.* European University Studies 13. Theology 442. Berne, 1992.

BEAUCHAMP, P. *Création et séparation: Étude exégétique du premier chapitre de la Genèse.* Paris, 1969. 2nd ed., 2005.

BÉCHARD, D. P. (ed.). *The Scripture Documents: An Anthology of Official Catholic Teachings.* Collegeville, MN, 2002.

BECKWITH, R. T. *The Old Testament Canon of the New Testament Church and Its Background in Early Judaism.* Grand Rapids, 1985.

BEN ZVI, E. "The Closing Words of the Pentateuchal Books: A Clue for the Historical Status of the Book of Genesis within the Pentateuch." *BN* 62 (1992) 7–10.

_____ . "Looking at the Primary (Hi)story and the Prophetic Books as Literary/Theological Units within the Frame of the Early Second Temple: Some Considerations." *SJOT* 12 (1998) 26–43.

BERGE, K. *Die Zeit des Jahwisten: Ein Beitrag zur Datierung jahwistischer Vätertexte.* BZAW 186. Berlin, 1990.

BERLIN, A. *Poetics and Interpretation of Biblical Narrative.* Bible and Literature Series. Sheffield, 1983. [Reprinted, Winona Lake, IN, 1994.]

BLEEK, F. *Einleitung in das Alte Testament.* 3rd ed. Berlin, 1829.

_____ . *De libri Geneseos origine atque indole historica observationes.* Bonn, 1836.

BLENKINSOPP, J. "An Assessment on the Alleged Pre-Exilic Date of the Priestly Material in the Pentateuch." *ZAW* 108 (1996) 495–518.

_____ . "The Mission of Udjahorresnet and Those of Ezra and Nehemiah." *JBL* 106 (1987) 409–21.

_____ . "P and J in Genesis 1–11: An Alternative Hypothesis." Pp. 1–15 in *Fortunate the Eyes That See: Essays in Honor of David Noel Freedman in Celebration of His Seventieth Birthday,* ed. A. B. BECK et al. Grand Rapids, 1995.

_____ . *The Pentateuch: An Introduction to the First Five Books of the Bible.* ABRL. New York, 1992.

_____ . *Prophecy and Canon: A Contribution to the Study of Jewish Origins.* Notre Dame, IN, 1977.

_____ . "The Structure of P." *CBQ* 38 (1976) 275–92.

_____ . "Temple and Society in Achaemenid Judah." Pp. 22–53 in *Second Temple Studies, I: Persian Period,* ed. P. R. DAVIES. JSOTSup 117. Sheffield, 1991.

_____ . *Treasures Old and New: Essays in the Theology of the Pentateuch.* Grand Rapids, 2004.

BLUM, E. "Gibt es die Endgestalt des Pentateuch?" Pp. 46–57 in *Congress Volume: Leuven, 1989,* ed. J. A. EMERTON. VTSup 43. Leiden, 1991.

_____ . *Die Komposition der Vätergeschichte.* WMANT 57. Neukirchen-Vluyn, 1984.

_____ . "Die literarische Verbindung von Erzvätern und Exodus: Ein Gespräch mit neueren Endredaktionshypothesen." Pp. 119–56 in *Abschied vom Jahwisten: Die Komposition des Hexateuch in der Jüngsten Diskussion,* ed. J. C. GERTZ, K. SCHMID, and M. WITTE. BZAW 315. Berlin, 2002.

_____ . Review of C. LEVIN, *Der Jahwist. TLZ* 120 (1995) 786–90.

_____ . "Das sog: 'Privilegrecht' in Exodus 34,11–26: Ein Fixpunkt der Komposition des Exodusbuches?" Pp. 347–66 in *Studies in the Book of Exodus*, ed. M. VERVENNE. Leuven, 1996.

_____ . *Studien zur Komposition des Pentateuch*. BZAW 189. Berlin and New York, 1990.

BOECKER, H. J. *Law and the Administration of Justice in the Old Testament and Ancient East*. Minneapolis, 1980. [Original: *Recht und Gesetz im Alten Testament und im Alten Orient*. Neukirchener Studienbücher 10. Neukirchen-Vluyn, 1976.]

_____ . *Redeformen des Rechtslebens im Alten Testament*. WMANT 14. Neukirchen-Vluyn, 1964. 2nd ed., 1970.

BOISMARD, M.-E. *Moïse ou Jésus: Essai de Christologie johannique*. BETL 84. Leuven, 1988.

BOLIN, T. M. "When the End Is the Beginning: The Persian Period and the Origins of the Origin Tradition." *SJOT* 10 (1996) 3–15.

BOORER, S. *The Promise of Land as Oath: A Key to the Formation of the Pentateuch*. BZAW 205. Berlin, 1992.

BORGONOVO, G. "Gen 6,5–9,19: Struttura e produzione simbolica." *La scuola cattolica* 115 (1987) 321–48.

BOSCHI, B. G. *Esodo*. Nuovissima versione della Bibbia. Rome, 1978.

BOTTÉRO, J., and KRAMER, S. N. *Lorsque les dieux faisaient l'homme: Mythologie mésopotamienne*. Paris, 1989.

BOUHOUT, J.-P., and CAZELLES, H. "Pentateuque." Pp. 687–858 in vol. 7 of *DBSup*.

BOVATI, P. *Re-establishing Justice: Legal Terms, Concepts and Procedures in the Hebrew Bible*, trans. M. J. Smith. JSOTSup 105. Sheffield, 1994. [Original: *Ristabilire la giustizia: Procedure, vocabolario, orientamenti*. AnBib 110. Rome, 1986. 2nd ed., 1997.]

BRAULIK, G. *Deuteronomium 1–16,17*. NEchtB. Würzburg, 1986.

_____ . *Die Mittel deuteronomischer Rhetorik erhoben aus Deuteronomium 4,1–40*. AnBib 68. Rome, 1978.

BRAULIK, G. (ed.). *Bundesdokument und Gesetz: Studien zum Deuteronomium*. Herders Biblische Studien 4. Fribourg, 1995.

BREKELMANS, C. W. H. "Het 'Historische Credo' van Israel." *Tijdschrift voor Theologie* 3 (1963) 1–11.

BRETTLER, M. Z. "Rendsburg's *The Redaction of Genesis*." *JQR* 78 (1987) 113–19.

_____ . "Torah." Pp. 1–7 in *The Jewish Study Bible*, ed. Adele BERLIN and Marc Zvi BRETTLER. Oxford, 2004.

BRIEND, J. "Lecture du Pentateuque et hypothèse documentaire." Pp. 9–32 in *Le Pentateuque: Débats et recherches*, ed. P. HAUDEBERT. LD 151. Paris, 1992.

BRUEGGEMANN, W. *The Creative Word: Canon as a Model for Biblical Education*. Philadelphia, 1982.

BUCHHOLZ, J. *Die Ältesten Israels im Deuteronomium*. Göttinger theologische Arbeiten 36. Göttingen, 1986.

BUDD, P. J. *Numbers*. WBC 5. Waco, TX, 1984.

CAMPBELL, A. F. "The Reported Story: Midway between Oral Performance and Literary Art." *Semeia* 46 (1989) 77–85.

CAMPBELL, A. F., and O'BRIEN, M. *Sources of the Pentateuch: Texts, Introductions, Annotations*. Minneapolis, 1993.

CARDELLINI, I. *Die biblischen "Sklaven"—Gesetze im Lichte des keilschriftlichen Sklaven-rechts: Ein Beitrag zur Tradition, Überlieferung und Redaktion der alttestamentlichen Rechts-texte.* BBB 55. Bonn, 1981.

CARR, D. M. "*Biblos geneseos* Revisited: A Synchronic Analysis of Patterns in Genesis as Part of the Torah (Part One)." *ZAW* 110 (1998) 159–72; Part Two: 327–47.

_____ . *Reading the Fractures of Genesis: Historical and Literary Approaches.* Louisville, 1996.

_____ . Review of C. LEVIN, *Der Jahwist. CBQ* 57 (1995) 354–55.

_____ . *Writing on the Tablet of the Heart: Origins of Scripture and Literature.* Oxford, 2005.

CARTER, C. E. *The Emergence of Yehud in the Persian Period: A Social and Demographic Study.* JSOTSup 294. Sheffield, 1999.

CASSUTO, U. *The Documentary Hypothesis and the Composition of the Pentateuch.* London, 1961.

CAZELLES, H. "Pentateuque." Pp. 708–858 in vol. 7 of *DBSup.*

_____ . "La Torah ou Pentateuque." Pp. 95–244 in *Introduction à la Bible, II: Introduc-tion critique à l'Ancien Testament,* ed. H. CAZELLES. Paris, 1973.

CHAMPOLLION, J.-F. *Lettre à M. Dacier relative à l'alphabet des hiéroglyphes phonétiques.* Paris, 1822.

CHILDS, B. S. *Biblical Theology of the Old and New Testaments: Theological Reflection on the Christian Bible.* London, 1992.

_____ . *Exodus: A Commentary.* OTL. London, 1974.

_____ . *Introduction to the Old Testament as Scripture.* Philadelphia, 1979.

CHIRICHIGNO, G. C. *Debt-Slavery in Israel and in the Ancient Near East.* JSOTSup 141. Sheffield, 1993.

CHOLEWINSKI, A. *Heiligkeitsgesetz und Deuteronomium: Eine vergleichende Studie.* AnBib 66. Rome, 1976.

CLEMENTS, R. E. "Pentateuchal Problems." Pp. 96–124 in *Tradition and Interpretation,* ed. G. W. ANDERSON. Oxford, 1979.

_____ . *Prophecy and Tradition.* Atlanta, 1975.

CLIFFORD, R. J. *The Cosmic Mountain in Canaan and the Old Testament.* HSM 4. Cam-bridge, MA, 1972.

CLINES, D. J. A. *The Theme of the Pentateuch.* JSOTSup 10. Sheffield, 1978.

COATS, G. W. "Abraham's Sacrifice of Faith: A Form-Critical Study of Genesis 22." *Int* 27 (1973) 389–400.

_____ . *Rebellion in the Wilderness: The Murmuring Motif in the Wilderness Traditions of the Old Testament.* Nashville, 1968.

_____ . "The Wilderness Itinerary." *CBQ* 34 (1972) 135–52.

COHN, R. L. "Narrative Structure and Canonical Perspective in Genesis." *JSOT* 25 (1983) 3–16. [= Pp. 89–102 in *The Pentateuch: A Sheffield Reader,* ed. J. W. ROGER-SON. Biblical Seminar 39. Sheffield, 1996.]

COMMISSION BIBLIQUE PONTIFICALE. *L'interprétation de la Bible dans l'Église.* Paris, 1994.

CONROY, C. *Absalom, Absalom! Narrative and Language in 2 Sam 13–20.* AnBib 81. Rome, 1978.

_____ . "Reflexions on the Exegetical Task: Apropos of Recent Studies on 2 Kgs 22–23." Pp. 225–68 in *Pentateuchal and Deuteronomistic Studies: Papers Read at the XIIIth*

IOSOT Congress, Leuven, 1989, ed. C. BREKELMANS and J. LUST. BETL 94. Leuven, 1990.

COOTE, R. B. *In Defense of Revolution: The Elohist History*. Minneapolis, 1991.

CORTESE, E. "L'esegesi di H (Lev. 17–26)." *RivB* 29 (1981) 129–46.

_____. "Pentateuco: La strada vecchia e la nuova." *Liber Annuus* 43 (1993) 71–87.

_____. "La teologia del documento sacerdotale." *RivB* 26 (1978) 113–37.

_____. *La terra di Canaan nella storia sacerdotale del Pentateuco*. Supplements to RivB 5. Brescia, 1972.

CROSS, F. M. *Canaanite Myth and Hebrew Epic: Essays on the History of the Religion of Israel*. Cambridge, MA, 1973.

CRÜSEMANN, F. *Bewahrung der Freiheit: Das Thema des Dekalogs in sozialgeschichtlicher Perspektive*. Kaiser Traktate 78. Munich, 1983.

_____. "Das Bundesbuch: Historischer Ort und institutioneller Hintergrund." Pp. 27–41 in *Congress Volume: Jerusalem, 1986*. VTSup 40. Leiden, 1988.

_____. "Die Eigenständigkeit der Urgeschichte: Ein Beitrag zur Diskussion um den 'Jahwisten.'" Pp. 9–29 in *Die Botschaft und die Boten: Festschrift für Hans Walter Wolff zum 70. Geburtstag*, ed. J. JEREMIAS and L. PERLITT. Neukirchen-Vluyn, 1981.

_____. "Der Exodus als Heiligung: Zur rechtsgeschichtlichen Bedeutung des Heiligkeitsgesetzes." Pp. 117–29 in *Die hebräische Bibel und ihre zweifache Nachgeschichte: Festschrift für Rolf Rendtorff zum 65. Geburtstag*, ed. E. BLUM, C. MACHOLZ, and E. W. STEGEMANN. Neukirchen-Vluyn, 1990.

_____. *The Torah: Theology and History of Old Testament Law*, trans. A. W. Mahnke. Edinburgh, 1996. [Original: *Die Tora: Theologie und Sozialgeschichte des alttestamentlichen Gesetzes*. Munich, 1992.]

_____. *Der Widerstand gegen das Königtum*. WMANT 49. Neukirchen-Vluyn, 1978.

CRYER, F. H. "The Interrelationships of Gen 5,32; 11,10–11, and the Chronology of the Flood (Gen 6–9)." *Bib* 66 (1985) 241–61.

CULLEY, R. C. "Some Comments on Structural Analysis and Biblical Studies." Pp. 129–42 in *Congress Volume: Uppsala, 1971*. VTSup 22. Leiden, 1972.

_____. *Studies in the Structure of Hebrew Narrative*. Semeia Supplements. Philadelphia, 1976.

DANIELI, G. *Esdra–Neemia*. Rome, 1983.

DAVIES, G. F. *Israel in Egypt: Reading Exodus 1–2*. JSOTSup 135. Sheffield, 1992.

DAVIES, G. I. *The Way of the Wilderness: A Geographical Study of the Wilderness Itineraries in the Old Testament*. SOTSMS 5. Cambridge, 1979.

_____. "The Wilderness Itineraries: A Comparative Study." *TynBul* 25 (1974) 46–81.

DIEBNER, B. J. "Die Götter des Vaters: Eine Kritik der 'Vätergott'-Hypothese Albrecht Alts." *Dielheimer Blätter zum Alten Testament und seiner Rezeption in der Alten Kirche* 9 (1975) 21–51.

_____. "Neue Ansätze in der Pentateuchforschung." *Dielheimer Blätter zum Alten Testament und seiner Rezeption in der Alten Kirche* 13 (1978) 2–13.

DILLMANN, A. *Die Bücher Numeri, Deuteronomium und Josua*. 2nd ed. Leipzig, 1886.

DILLMANN, A., and RYSSEL, V. *Die Bücher Exodus und Leviticus*. 3rd ed. Leipzig, 1897.

DOHMEN, C. "Der Dekaloganfang und sein Ursprung." *Bib* 74 (1993) 175–95.

DOHMEN, C., and OEMING, M. *Biblischer Kanon: Warum und wozu?* Quaestiones disputatae 137. Freiburg, 1992.

Donner, H. "Der Redaktor: Überlegungen zum vorkritischen Umgang mit der Heiligen Schrift." *Henoch* 2 (1980) 1–30.

Dozeman, T. B. *God on the Mountain: A Study of Redaction, Theology and Canon in Exodus 19–24.* SBLMS 37. Atlanta, 1989.

Driver, G. R. "Glosses in the Hebrew Text of the Old Testament." Pp. 123–61 in *L'ancien Testament et l'Orient.* Orientalia et biblica lovaniensia 1. Louvain, 1957.

Dupont, J. "Le Magnificat comme discours sur Dieu." *La nouvelle revue théologique* 102 (1980) 321–43.

Durham, J. *Exodus.* WBC 3. Waco, TX, 1987.

Eco, U. *The Limits of Interpretation.* Bloomington, IN, 1990. [Original: *I Limiti dell'interpretazione.* Studi Bompiani. Milan, 1990.]

Eerdmans, B. D. *Alttestamentliche Studien I: Die Komposition der Genesis.* Giessen, 1908.

_____ . *Alttestamentliche Studien III: Das Buch Exodus.* Giessen, 1910.

Eichhorn, J. G. *Einleitung in das Alte Testament.* 3 vols. Göttingen, 1780–83.

Eissfeldt, O. *The Old Testament: An Introduction,* trans. P. R. Ackroyd. New York, 1965. [Original: *Einleitung in das Alte Testament.* 3rd ed. Tübingen, 1964.]

Elliger, K. "Sinn und Ursprung der priesterlichen Geschichtserzählung." *ZTK* 49 (1952) 121–42. [= Pp. 174–98 in *Kleine Schriften zum Alten Testament.* TBü 32. Munich, 1966.]

Emerton, J. A. "An Examination of Some Attempts to Defend the Unity of the Flood Narrative in Genesis." *VT* 27 (1987) 401–20; *VT* 28 (1988) 1–21.

Engnell, I. *Gamla Testamentet: En traditionshistorisk inledning.* Vol. 1. Stockholm, 1945.

_____ . "Methodological Aspects of Old Testament Study." *VT* 7 (1960) 13–30.

_____ . "The Pentateuch." Pp. 50–67 in *A Rigid Scrutiny: Critical Essays on the Old Testament,* trans. J. T. Willis. Nashville, 1969.

Eskenazi, T. C. "Torah as Narrative and Narrative as Torah." Pp. 13–30 in *Old Testament Interpretation: Past, Present, Future,* ed. J. L. Mays, D. L. Petersen, and K. H. Richards. Edinburgh, 1995.

Ewald, G. H. A. *Die Composition der Genesis kritisch untersucht.* Braunschweig, 1823.

_____ . *Geschichte des Volkes Israels bis Christus.* 2 vols. Göttingen, 1843–45. 3rd ed., 1864.

_____ . *History of Israel,* ed. Russell Martineau and J. Estlin Carpenter. Volume 1: *Introduction and Preliminary History.* Volume 2: *History of Moses and the Theocracy.* Volume 3: *The Rise and Splendour of the Hebrew Monarchy.* Volume 4: *From the Disruption of the Monarchy to the Fall.* London, 1876–86.

_____ . Review of Stähelin J. J., *Kritische Untersuchung über die Genesis.* Basel, 1830. *Theologische Studien und Kritiken* (1831) 595–606.

Eynickel, E. *The Reform of King Josiah and the Composition of the Deuteronomistic History.* OtSt 33. Leiden, 1996.

Feucht, C. *Untersuchungen zum Heiligkeitsgesetz.* Berlin, 1964.

Finkelstein, I. *The Archaeology of the Israelite Settlement.* Jerusalem, 1988.

Fischer, G. "Exodus 1–15: Eine Erzählung." Pp. 149–78 in *Studies in the Book of Exodus: Redaction—Reception—Interpretation,* ed. M. Vervenne. Leuven, 1996.

_____ . *Jahwe unser Gott: Sprache, Aufbau und Erzähltechnik in der Berufung des Mose (Ex 3–4).* OBO 91. Fribourg and Göttingen, 1989.

FISCHER, I. *Die Erzeltern Israels: Feministisch-theologische Studien zu Genesis 12–36: Redaction—Reception—Interpretation.* BZAW 222. Berlin, 1994.

FISHBANE, M. *Biblical Interpretation in Ancient Israel.* Oxford, 1985.

_____ . *Text and Texture: Close Readings of Selected Biblical Texts.* New York, 1979.

FITZMYER, J. A. *The Biblical Commission's Document "The Interpretation of the Bible in the Church": Text and Commentary.* SubBi 18. Rome, 1995.

FLANAGAN, J. W. *David's Social Drama: A Hologram of Israel's Early Iron Age.* JSOTSup 73. SWBA 7. Sheffield, 1988.

FOHRER, G. "'Amphictyonie' und 'Bund'?" *TLZ* 91 (1966) 801–16, 893–904. [= Pp. 84–119 in *Studien zur alttestamentlichen Theologie und Geschichte (1949–1966).* BZAW 115. Berlin, 1969.]

FOKKELMAN, J. P. *Narrative Art in Genesis: Specimens of Stylistic and Structural Analysis.* SSN 17. Assen, 1975. [Reprinted, Biblical Seminar 12. Sheffield, 1991.]

FOX, M. V. *The Redaction of the Books of Esther: On Reading Composite Texts.* SBLMS 40. Atlanta, 1991.

FREEDMAN, D. N. "Pentateuch." Pp. 711–27 in vol. 3 of *IDB.*

FREI, P. "Die Persische Reichsautorisation: Ein Überblick." *ZABR* 1 (1995) 1–35.

_____ . "Zentralgewalt und Achämenidenreich." Pp. 7–43 in *Reichsidee und Reichsorganisation im Perserreich,* ed. P. FREI and K. KOCH. OBO 55. Fribourg and Göttingen, 1984. 2nd ed., 1996.

FREI, P., and KOCH, K. (eds.). *Reichsidee und Reichsorganisation im Perserreich.* OBO 55. Fribourg and Göttingen, 1984. 2nd ed., 1996.

FRENDO, A. J. "Five Recent Books on the Emergence of Ancient Israel: Review Article." *PEQ* 124 (1992) 144–55.

FREVEL, C. *Mit Blick auf das Land die Schöpfung erinnern: Zum Ende der Priesterschrift.* Herders Biblische Studien 23. Freiburg i. Breisgau, 2000.

FRIEDMAN, R. E. *Commentary on the Torah, with a New English Translation and the Hebrew Text.* San Francisco, 2001.

FRITZ, V. *Tempel und Zelt: Studien zum Tempelbau in Israel und zu dem Zeltheiligtum der Priesterschrift.* WMANT 47. Neukirchen-Vluyn, 1977.

FULLER, R. C. *Alexander Geddes, 1737–1802: Pioneer of Biblical Exegesis.* Sheffield, 1984.

GARCÍA LÓPEZ, F. "De la antigua a la nueva crítica literaria del Pentateuco." *EstBib* 52 (1994) 7–35.

_____ . "Deut 34, Dtr History and the Pentateuch." Pp. 47–61 in *Studies in Deuteronomy: In Honour of C. J. Labuschagne on the Occasion of His 65th Birthday,* ed. F. GARCÍA MARTINEZ et al. VTSup 53. Leiden, 1994.

_____ . *El Pentateuco: Introducción a la lectura de los cinco primeros libros de la Biblia.* Introducción al estudio de la Biblia. Estella (Navarra), 2003.

GEDDES, A. *Critical Remarks.* London, 1800.

_____ . *The Holy Bible as the Books Accounted Sacred by Jews and Christians.* London, 1792.

GERTZ, J. C. *Tradition und Redaktion in der Exoduserzählung: Untersuchungen zur Endredaktion des Pentateuch.* FRLANT 186. Göttingen, 2000.

GERTZ, J. C.; SCHMID, K.; and WITTE, M. (eds.). *Abschied vom Jahwisten: Die Komposition des Hexateuch in der jüngsten Diskussion.* BZAW 315. Berlin, 2002.

GEORGE, J. F. L. *Die älteren jüdischen Feste mit einer Kritik der Gesetzgebung des Pentateuchs.* Berlin, 1835.

GESE, H., and RÜGER, H. P. (eds.). *Wort und Geschichte: Festschrift Karl Elliger.* AOAT 18. Kevelaer and Neukirchen-Vluyn, 1973.

GEUS, C. H. G. de. *The Tribes of Israel: An Investigation of the Presuppositions of Martin Noth's Amphictyony Hypothesis.* SSN 18. Assen, 1976.

GIBERT, P. *Bible, mythes et récits de commencement.* Paris, 1986.

–––––– . *Comment la Bible fut écrite: Introduction à l'Ancien et au Nouveau Testament.* Paris, 1995.

–––––– . "Introduction et notes" to Jean Astruc, *Conjectures sur la Genèse.* Paris, 1999.

–––––– . "Légende ou saga?" *VT* 24 (1974) 411–20.

–––––– . *Petite histoire de l'exégèse biblique: De la lecture allégorique à l'exégèse biblique.* Paris, 1989.

–––––– . *Une théorie de la légende: Hermann Gunkel (1862–1932) et les légendes de la Bible.* Paris, 1979.

GIUNTOLI, F. *L'officina della tradizione: Studio di alcuni interventi redazionali post-sacerdotali e del loro contesto nel ciclo di Giacobbe (Gn 25,19–50,26).* AnBib 154. Rome, 2003.

GOSSE, B. *La constitution du corpus des écritures à l'époque perse, dans la continuité de la tradition biblique.* Paris, 2003.

–––––– . "La tradition yahviste en Gn 6,5–9,17." *Henoch* 15 (1993) 139–54.

GOTTWALD, N. K. *The Tribes of Yahweh: A Sociology of Liberated Israel 1250–1050 B.C.E.* Maryknoll, NY, 1979.

GRABBE, L. L. *Yehud: A History of the Persian Province of Judah.* Library of Second Temple Studies 47. Volume 1 of *A History of the Jews and Judaism in the Second Temple Period.* London, 2004.

GRAF, K. H. *Die geschichtlichen Bücher des Alten Testaments: Zwei historisch-kritischen Untersuchungen.* Leipzig, 1866.

GRÄTZ, S. *Das Edikt des Artaxerxes: Eine Untersuchung zum religionspolitischen und historischen Umfeld von Esra 7,12–26.* BZAW 337. Berlin, 2004.

GRAUPNER, A. "Zum Verhältnis der beiden Dekalogfassungen Ex 20 und Dtn 5: Ein Gespräch mit Frank-Lothar Hossfeld." *ZAW* 99 (1987) 308–29.

GRAY, G. B. *Numbers.* ICC. Edinburgh, 1903.

GREENBERG, M. "The Redaction of the Plague Narrative in Exodus." Pp. 243–52 in *Near Eastern Studies in Honor of William Foxwell Albright,* ed. H. GOEDICKE. Baltimore, 1971.

–––––– . *Understanding Exodus.* New York, 1969.

GREIFENHAGEN, F. V. *Egypt on the Pentateuch's Ideological Map: Constructing Biblical Israel's Identity.* JSOTSup 361. London, 2002.

GRESSMANN, H. *Mose und seine Zeit: Ein Kommentar zu den Mose-Sagen.* FRLANT 18. Göttingen, 1913.

GRIMM, J., and GRIMM, W. *Deutsche Sagen.* Marburg, 1816–18.

–––––– . *Grimm's Fairy Tales.* New York, 1988. [Original: *Kinder- und Hausmärchen.* Marburg, 1812–15.]

GROSS, W. (ed.). *Jeremia und die "deuteronomistische Bewegung."* BBB 98. Weinheim, 1995.

GROUPE D'ENTREVERNES. *Analyse sémiotique des textes: Introduction—Théorie—Pratique.* 5th ed. Lyon, 1985.

GUILLEMETTE, P., and BRISBOIS, M. *Introduction aux méthodes historico-critiques.* Héritages et Projets 35. Montreal, 1987.

GUNKEL, H. *The Folktale in the Old Testament*, trans. M. D. Rutter. Historic Texts and Interpreters in Biblical Scholarship 5. Sheffield, 1987. [Original: *Das Märchen im Alten Testament.* Religionsgeschichte Volksbücher 2. Tübingen, 1921.]

_____ . *Genesis*, trans. M. E. Biddle. Mercer Library of Biblical Studies. Macon, GA, 1997. [Original: *Genesis.* HKAT 1/1. 3rd ed. Göttingen, 1910.]

_____ . "Die Grundprobleme der israelitischen Literaturgeschichte." *Deutsche Literaturzeitung* 27 (1906). [= Pp. 29–38 in *Reden und Aufsätze.* Göttingen, 1913.]

_____ . *Introduction to the Psalms: The Genres of the Religious Lyric of Israel*, trans. J. D. Nogalski. Mercer Library of Biblical Studies. Macon, GA, 1998.

_____ . "Die israelitische Literatur." Pp. 51–102 in *Die Kultur der Gegenwart: Die orientalischen Literaturen*, ed. P. HINNEBERG. Berlin, 1906.

_____ . *The Legends of Genesis: The Biblical Saga and History.* New York, 1964. New translation: *The Stories of Genesis.* Vallejo, CA, 1994.

_____ . *Die Psalmen.* 4th ed. Göttingen, 1926.

_____ . *Reden und Aufsätze.* Göttingen, 1913.

_____ . *Schöpfung und Chaos in Urzeit und Endzeit: Eine religionsgeschichtliche Untersuchung über Gen. 1 und Ap. Joh. 12.* Göttingen, 1894. 2nd ed., 1921.

GUNKEL, H., and BEGRICH, H. *Einleitung in die Psalmen.* Göttingen, 1933.

GUNN, D. M., and FEWELL, D. N. *Narrative in the Hebrew Bible.* Oxford Bible Series. Oxford, 1993.

GUNNEWEG, A. H. J. "Anmerkungen und Anfragen zur neueren Pentateuchforschung." *TRu* 48 (1983) 227–53; *TRu* 50 (1985) 107–31.

_____ . "ʿm hʾrṣ: A Semantic Revolution." *ZAW* 95 (1983) 437–40.

HACKETT, J. A. *The Balaam Text from Deir ʿAlla.* HSM 31. Chico, CA, 1984.

HALBE, J. *Das Privilegrecht Jahwes (Ex 34,10–26): Gestalt und Wesen, Herkunft und Wirken in vordeuteronomischer Zeit.* FRLANT 14. Göttingen, 1975.

HAMILTON, J. M. *Social Justice and Deuteronomy: The Case of Deuteronomy 15.* SBLDS 136. Atlanta, 1993.

HARAN, M. "Book-Scrolls at the Beginning of the Second Temple Period: The Transition from Papyrus to Skins." *HUCA* 54 (1983) 111–22.

_____ . "Book-Scrolls in Israel in Pre-Exilic Times." *JJS* 33 (1982) 161–73.

_____ . "On the Diffusion of Literacy and Schools in Ancient Israel." Pp. 81–95. in *Congress Volume: Jerusalem, 1986.* VTSup 40. Leiden, 1988.

_____ . *Temple and Temple-Service in Ancient Israel.* Oxford, 1979. [Reprinted, Winona Lake, IN, 1985.]

HARLAND, P. J. *The Value of Human Life: A Study of the Story of the Flood (Genesis 6–9).* VTSup 64. Leiden, 1996.

HARRISON, R. K. *Numbers: An Exegetical Commentary.* Grand Rapids, 1992.

HAUDEBERT, P. (ed.). *Le Pentateuque: Débats et recherches. XIVᵉ Congrès de l'ACFEB, Angers, 1991.* LD 151. Paris, 1992.

HELYER, L. R. "The Separation of Abraham and Lot: Its Significance in the Patriarchal Narratives." *JSOT* 26 (1983) 77–88.

HERRMANN, S. *A History of Israel in Old Testament Times*, trans. J. Bowden. 2nd ed. Philadelphia, 1981. [Original: *Geschichte Israels in alttestamentlicher Zeit.* Munich, 1973.]

_____. "Das Werden Israels." *TLZ* 87 (1962) 561–74.

HIRSCH, E. D. *The Aims of Interpretation.* Chicago, 1976.

_____. *Validity in Interpretation.* New Haven, CT, 1967.

HOSSFELD, F.-L. *Der Dekalog: Seine späten Fassungen, die originale Komposition und seine Vorstufen.* OBO 45. Fribourg and Göttingen, 1982.

_____. "Zum synoptischen Vergleich der Dekalogfassungen: Eine Fortführung des begonnenen Gesprächs." Pp. 73–118 in *Vom Sinai zum Horeb: Stationen alttestamentlicher Glaubensgeschichte,* ed. F.-L. HOSSFELD. Würzburg, 1989.

HOUTMAN, C. *Der Pentateuch: Die Geschichte seiner Erforschung neben einer Auswertung.* Contributions to Biblical Exegesis and Theology 9. Kampen, 1994.

HUGHES, J. *Secrets of the Times: Myth and History in Biblical Chronology.* JSOTSup 66. Sheffield, 1990.

HUMPHREYS, W. L. *Joseph and His Family: A Literary Study.* Columbia, SC, 1988.

HUPFELD, H. *Die Quellen der Genesis und die Art ihrer Zusammensetzung von neuem untersucht.* Berlin, 1853.

HURVITZ, A. "Dating the Priestly Source in Light of the Historical Study of Biblical Hebrew: A Century after Wellhausen." *ZAW* 100 Sup. (1988) 88–100.

_____. *A Linguistic Study of the Relationship between the Priestly Source and the Book of Ezekiel: A New Approach to an Old Problem.* CahRB 20. Paris, 1982.

HYATT, J. P. "Were There an Ancient Historical Credo and an Independent Sinai Tradition?" Pp. 152–70 in *Essays in Honor of H. G. May.* Nashville, 1970.

ILGEN, K.-D. *Die Urkunden des ersten Buchs von Moses.* Vol. 1 of *Die Urkunden des Jerusalemischen Tempelarchivs in ihrer Urgestalt, als Beytrag zur Berichtigung der Geschichte der Religion und Politik aus dem Hebräischen mit kritischen und erklärenden Anmerkungen, auch mancherley dazu gehörenden Abhandlungen.* Halle, 1798.

IRVIN, W. H. "Le sanctuaire central israélite avant l'établissement de la monarchie." *RB* 72 (1965) 161–84.

JACKSON, B. S. "Biblical Laws of Slavery: A Comparative Approach." Pp. 86–101 in *Slavery and Other Forms of Unfree Labour,* ed. L. J. ARCHER. London, 1988.

_____. *Wisdom-Laws: A Study of the Mishpatim of Exodus 21:1–22:16.* Oxford, 2006.

JACKSON, J. J., and KESSLER, M. (eds.). *Rhetorical Criticism: Essays in Honor of James Muilenburg.* Pittsburgh, 1974.

JACOB, B. *Das erste Buch der Tora: Genesis.* Berlin, 1934.

The Second Book of the Bible: Exodus. New York, 1992. [Original Hebrew: Jerusalem, 1945.]

JAMIESON-DRAKE, D. W. *Scribes and Schools in Monarchic Judah: A Socio-Archaeological Approach.* JSOTSup 109. Sheffield, 1991.

JANOWSKI, B. *Sühne und Heilsgeschehen: Studien zur Sühnetheologie der Priesterschrift und der Wurzel KPR im Alten Orient und im Alten Testament.* WMANT 55. Neukirchen-Vluyn, 1982.

_____. "Tempel und Schöpfung: Schöpfungstheologische Aspekte der priesterschriftlichen Heiligtumskonzeption." Pp. 214–46 in *Gottes Gegenwart in Israel: Beiträge zur Theologie des Alten Testaments.* Neukirchen-Vluyn, 1993.

JENKS, W. *The Elohist and North Israelite Traditions.* SBLMS 22. Missoula, MT, 1977.

JEREMIAS, J. *Theophanie: Die Geschichte einer alttestamentlichen Gattung.* WMANT 10. Neukirchen-Vluyn, 1965.

JOHNSON, M. D. *The Purpose of the Biblical Genealogies.* Society for New Testament Studies Monograph Series 8. 2nd ed. Cambridge, 1988.

JOHNSTONE, W. (ed.). *The Bible and the Enlightenment—A Case Study: Dr. Alexander Geddes, 1737–1802. The proceedings of the Bicentenary Geddes Conference held at the University of Aberdeen, 1–4 April 2002.* JSOTSup 377. London, 2004.

_____ . *William Robertson Smith: Essays in Reassessment.* JSOTSup 189. Sheffield, 1995.

KAISER, O. *Introduction to the Old Testament,* trans. J. Sturdy. Minneapolis, 1975. [Original: *Einleitung in das Alte Testament: Eine Einführung in ihre Ergebnisse und Probleme.* Gütersloh, 1969. 5th ed., 1984.]

KASWALDER, P. "L'archeologia e le origini d'Israele." *RivB* 41 (1993) 171–88.

KAUFMANN, Y. "Probleme der israelitisch-jüdischen Religionsgeschichte." *ZAW* 48 (1930) 23–43.

_____ . *The Religion of Israel: From Its Beginning until the Babylonian Exile.* Chicago, 1960.

KEARNEY, P. J. "Creation and Liturgy: The P Redaction of Ex 25–40." *ZAW* 89 (1977) 375–87.

KEEL, O., and KÜCHLER, M. *Synoptische Texte aus der Genesis.* Biblische Beiträge 8. Fribourg, 1971.

KEEL, O., and UEHLINGER, C. *Gods, Goddesses, and Images of God in Ancient Israel,* trans. A. W. Mahnke. Minneapolis, 1996. [Original: *Göttinnen, Götter und Gottessymbole: Neue Erkenntnisse zur Religionsgeschichte Kanaans und Israels aufgrund bislang unerschlossener ikonographischer Quellen.* Quaestiones Disputatae 134. Fribourg, 1992.]

KESSLER, M. "Rhetorical Criticism of Gen 7." Pp. 1–17 in *Rhetorical Criticism: Essays in Honor of J. Muilenburg,* ed. J. J. JACKSON and M. KESSLER. Pittsburgh, 1974.

KILIAN, R. "Die Hoffnung auf Heimkehr in der Priesterschrift." *Bibel und Leben* 7 (1966) 39–51.

KIRKPATRICK, P. S. *The Old Testament and Folklore Studies.* JSOTSup 62. Sheffield, 1988.

KLATT, W. *H. Gunkel: Zu seiner Theologie der Religionsgeschichte und zur Entstehung der formgeschichtliche Methode.* FRLANT 100. Göttingen, 1969.

KLEINERT, P. *Das Deuteronomium und die Deuteronomiker: Untersuchungen zur alttestamentlichen Rechts- und Literaturgeschichte.* Bielefeld and Leipzig, 1872.

KLOSTERMANN, A. "Ezechiel und das Heiligkeitsgesetz." *Zeitschrift für lutherische Theologie* 38 (1877) 401–45. [= *Der Pentateuch I.* Leipzig, 1893.]

KNIERIM, R. P. "The Book of Numbers." Pp. 155–63 in *Die hebräische Bibel und ihre zweifache Nachgeschichte: Festschrift für Rolf Rendtorff zum 65. Geburtstag,* ed. E. BLUM, C. MACHOLZ, and E. W. STEGEMANN. Neukirchen-Vluyn, 1990.

_____ . "The Composition of the Pentateuch." Pp. 393–415 in *SBL 1985 Seminar Papers.* SBLSP. Atlanta, 1985. [= Pp. 351–79 in *The Task of Old Testament Theology: Substance, Method and Cases.* Grand Rapids, 1995.]

KNOHL, I. "The Priestly Torah versus the Holiness School: Sabbath and the Festivals." *HUCA* 58 (1987) 65–117.

_____ . *The Sanctuary of Silence: The Priestly Torah and the Priestly School.* Minneapolis, 1995.

KOCH, K. *The Growth of the Biblical Tradition*, trans. S. M. Cupitt. London, 1969. [Original: *Was ist Formgeschichte? Neue Wege der Bibelexegese*. 2nd ed. Neukirchen-Vluyn, 1967.]

——. "P—kein Redaktor! Erinnerung an zwei Eckdaten der Quellenscheidung." *VT* 37 (1987) 446–67.

——. "Weltordnung und Reichsidee im alten Iran und ihre Auswirkungen auf die Provinz Jehud." Pp. 134–337 in *Reichsidee und Reichsorganisation im Perserreich*, ed. P. FREI and K. KOCH. 2nd ed. OBO 55. Fribourg and Göttingen, 1996.

KÖCKERT, M. *Vätergott und Väterverheissungen: Eine Auseinandersetzung mit Albrecht Alt und seinen Erben*. FRLANT 148. Göttingen, 1988.

KOHATA, F. "Die Endredaktion (R$_p$) der Meerwundererzählung." *AJBI* 14 (1988) 10–37.

——. *Jahwist und Priesterschrift in Exodus 3–14*. BZAW 166. Berlin, 1986.

——. "Die priesterschriftliche Überlieferungsgeschichte von Numeri xx,1–31." *AJBI* 3 (1977) 3–34.

KOOREVAAR, H. J. "De opbouw van de tien woorden in Exodus 20:1–17." *Acta Theologica* 15 (1995) 1–15.

KRAPF, T. M. *Die Priesterschrift und die vorexilische Zeit: Yehezkel Kaufmanns vernachlässigter Beitrag zur Geschichte der biblischen Religion*. OBO 119. Fribourg and Göttingen, 1992.

KRATZ, R. G. *The Composition of the Narrative Books of the Old Testament*. London, 2005. [Original: *Die Komposition der Erzählenden Bücher des Alten Testaments: Grundwissen der Bibelkritik*. Uni-Taschenbücher 2157. Göttingen, 2000.]

——. "Der Dekalog im Exodusbuch." *VT* 44 (1994) 205–38.

——. *Das Judentum im Zeitalter des Zweiten Tempels*. FAT. Tübingen, 2004.

——. *Translatio imperii*. WMANT 63. Neukirchen-Vluyn, 1987.

KRAUS, H.-J. *Geschichte der historisch-kritischen Erforschung des Alten Testaments*. 3rd ed. Neukirchen-Vluyn, 1982.

KREUTZER, S. *Die Frühgeschichte Israels in Bekenntnis und Verkündigung des Alten Testaments*. BZAW 178. Berlin, 1989.

KUENEN, A. "Critische bijdragen tot de geschiedenis van den Israëlitischen godsdienst. V: De priesterlijke bestandsdeelen van Pentateuch en Josua." *Theologisch Tijdschrift* 4 (1870) 391–426, 487–526.

——. *Historisch-kritisch onderzoek naar het ontstaan en de verzameling van de boeken des Ouden Verbonds*. Leiden, 1861.

KUHL, C. *Die drei Männer im Feuer*. BZAW 55. Berlin, 1930.

——. "Die "Wiederaufnahme": Ein literarkritisches Prinzip." *ZAW* 64 (1952) 1–11.

LAGHI, P.; GILBERT, M.; and VANHOYE, A. *Chiesa e Sacra Scrittura: Un secolo di magistero ecclesiastico e di studi biblici*. SubBi 17. Rome, 1994.

LAGRANGE, M.-J. *L'Écriture dans l'Église: Choix de portraits et d'exégèse spirituelle, 1890–1937*. LD 142. Paris, 1990.

——. *Historical Criticism and the Old Testament*, trans. E. Myers. ATLA Monograph. London, 1905. [Original: *La méthode historique surtout à propos de l'Ancien Testament*. EB. Paris, 1903.]

LANG, B. "A Neglected Principle in Ezekiel Research: Editorial Criticism." *VT* 29 (1979) 39–44.

LASSERRE, G. "Quelques études récentes sur le Code de l'alliance." *RTP* 125 (1993) 267–76.

LEIMAN, S. Z. (ed.). *The Canon and Masorah of the Hebrew Bible: An Introductory Reader.* Library of Biblical Studies. New York, 1974.

LEMAIRE, A. *Les écoles et la formation de la Bible dans l'ancien Israël.* OBO 39. Fribourg and Göttingen, 1981.

LEMCHE, N. P. "The Chronology in the Story of the Flood." *JSOT* 18 (1980) 52–62.

––––––. "The 'Hebrew Slave.'" *VT* 25 (1975) 129–44.

––––––. "The Manumission of Slaves—The Fallow Year—The Sabbatical Year—The Jobel Year." *VT* 26 (1976) 38–59.

LEVENSON, J. *Sinai and Zion: An Entry into the Jewish Bible.* San Francisco, 1985.

LEVIN, C. "Der Dekalog am Sinai." *VT* 35 (1985) 165–91.

––––––. "Das israelitische Nationalepos: Der Jahwist." Pp. 63–85 in *Grosse Texte alter Kulturen: Literarische Reise von Gizeh nach Rom,* ed. M. HOSE. Darmstadt, 2004.

––––––. *Der Jahwist.* FRLANT 157. Göttingen, 1993.

––––––. "Das System der zwölf Stämme Israels." Pp. 163–78 in *Congress Volume: Paris, 1992,* ed. J. A. EMERTON. VTSup 61. Leiden, 1995.

LEVINE, B. A. *Numbers 1–20* and *Numbers 21–36.* AB 4A–4B. New York, 1993–2000.

LEVINSON, B. M. "The Birth of the Lemma: Recovering the Restrictive Interpretation of the Covenant Code's Manumission Law by the Holiness Code (Lev 25:44–46)." *JBL* 124 (2005) 617–39.

––––––. "The Case for Revision and Interpolation within the Biblical Legal Corpora." Pp. 37–59 in *Theory and Method,* ed. B. M. LEVINSON.

––––––. *Deuteronomy and the Hermeneutics of Legal Innovation.* New York, 1997.

––––––. "Deuteronomy." Pp. 356–450 in *The Jewish Study Bible,* ed. Adele BERLIN and Marc Zvi BRETTLER. Oxford, 2004.

––––––. "Goethe's Analysis of Exodus 34 and Its Influence on Julius Wellhausen: The *Pfropfung* of the Documentary Hypothesis." *ZAW* 114 (2002) 212–23.

––––––. *L'herméneutique de l'innovation: Canon et exégèse dans l'Israël biblique,* trans. Vincent Sénéchal and Jean-Pierre Sonnet. Le livre et le rouleau 24. Brussels, 2006.

––––––. "The Human Voice in Divine Revelation: The Problem of Authority in Biblical Law." Pp. 35–71 in *Innovation in Religious Traditions,* ed. M. A. WILLIAMS, C. COX, and M. S. JAFFEE. Religion and Society. Berlin, 1992.

––––––. "Is the Covenant Code an Exilic Composition? A Response to John Van Seters." Pp. 272–325 in *In Search of Pre-exilic Israel: Proceedings of the Oxford Old Testament Seminar,* ed. J. DAY. JSOTSup 406. London, 2004.

––––––. "The Manumission Laws of the Pentateuch as a Challenge to Contemporary Pentateuchal Theory." Pp. 281–324 in *Congress Volume: Leiden 2004,* ed. A. LEMAIRE. VTSup 109. Leiden, 2006.

––––––. "'The Right Chorale': From the Poetics of Biblical Narrative to the Hermeneutics of the Hebrew Bible." Pp. 129–53 in *"Not in Heaven": Coherence and Complexity in Biblical Narrative,* ed. J. P. ROSENBLATT and J. C. SITTERSON. Bloomington, IN, 1991.

––––––. "Textual Criticism, Assyriology, and the History of Interpretation: Deuteronomy 13:7a as a Test Case in Method." *JBL* 120 (2001) 211–43.

––––––. "'You Must Not Add Anything to What I Command You': Paradoxes of Canon and Authorship in Ancient Israel." *Numen: International Review for the History of Religions* 50 (2003) 1–51.

LEVINSON, B. M. (ed.). *Theory and Method in Biblical and Cuneiform Law: Revision, Interpolation and Development.* JSOTSup 181. Sheffield, 1994.

LEVINSON, B. M., and DANCE, D. "The Metamorphosis of Law into Gospel: Gerhard von Rad's Attempt to Reclaim the Old Testament for the Church." Pp. 83–110 in *Recht und Ethik im Alten Testament,* ed. B. M. LEVINSON and E. OTTO. Münster, 2004.

LEVINSON, B. M., and ZAHN, M. M. "Revelation Regained: The Hermeneutics of כי and אם in the Temple Scroll." *Dead Sea Discoveries* 9 (2002) 295–346.

LICHT, J. *Storytelling in the Bible.* Jerusalem, 1978. [= *La narrazione nella Bibbia.* Studi biblici 101. Paideia, 1992.]

LIPIŃSKI, E. "עַם *ʿam.*" Pp. 163–77 in vol. 11 of *TDOT.* [= "*ʿam.*" Pp. 177–94 in vol. 6 of *TWAT.*]

LIPSCHITS, O., and BLENKINSOPP, J. (eds.). *Judah and the Judeans in the Neo-Babylonian Period.* Winona Lake, IN, 2003.

LODS, A. *Histoire de la littérature hébraïque et juive.* Paris, 1950.

————— . "Un précurseur allemand de Jean Astruc: Henning Bernhard Witter." *ZAW* 43 (1925) 134–35.

LOHFINK, N. "Die Abänderung der Theologie des priesterlichen Geschichtswerks im Segen des Heiligkeitsgesetzes: Zu Lev. 26,9.11–13." Pp. 129–36 in *Wort und Geschichte: Festschrift für Karl Elliger zum 70. Geburtstag,* ed. H. GESE and H. P. RÜGER. AOAT 18. Kevelaer and Neukirchen-Vluyn, 1973. [= Pp. 157–68 in *Studien zum Pentateuch.*]

————— . "Die Ältesten Israels und der Bund: Zum Zusammenhang von Dtn 5,23; 26,17–9; 27,1.9f und 31,9." *BN* 67 (1993) 26–41.

————— . "Bund als Vertrag im Deuteronomium." *ZAW* 107 (1995) 215–39.

————— . "Der Bundesschluss im Lande Moab: Redaktionsgeschichtliches zu Dt 28,69–32,47." *BZ* n.s. 6 (1962) 32–56. [= Pp. 53–82 in vol. 1 of *Studien zum Deuteronomium.*]

————— . "Deutéronome et Pentateuque: État de la recherche." Pp. 35–64 in *Le Pentateuque: Débats et recherches,* ed. P. HAUDEBERT. LD 151. Paris, 1992. [= "Deuteronomium und Pentateuch: Zum Stand der Forschung." Pp. 13–38 in vol. 3 of *Studien zum Deuteronomium.*]

————— . "Die Erzählung vom Sündenfall." Pp. 81–101 in *Das Siegeslied am Schilfmeer: Christliche Auseinandersetzung mit dem Alten Testament.* Frankfurt, 1965.

————— . "Freizeit: Arbeitswoche und Sabbat im Alten Testament, insbesondere in der priesterlichen Geschichtsdarstellung." Pp. 190–208 in *Unsere grossen Wörter: Das Alte Testament zu Themen dieser Jahre.* Freiburg-im-Breisgau, 1977.

————— . "Gab es eine deuteronomistische Bewegung?" Pp. 91–113, 335–47 in *Jeremia und die "deuteronomistische Bewegung,"* ed. W. GROSS. BBB 98. Weinheim, 1995.

————— . "'Ich bin Jahwe, dein Arzt' (Ex 15,26): Gott, Gesellschaft und menschliche Gesundheit in der Theologie einer nachexilischer Pentateuchbearbeitung (Ex 15,25b.26)." Pp. 11–73 in *"Ich will euer Gott werden": Beispiele biblischen Redens von Gott,* ed. H. MERKLEIN and E. ZENGER. SBS 100. Stuttgart, 1981. [= Pp. 91–155 in *Studien zum Pentateuch.*]

————— . "Die Priesterschrift und die Geschichte." Pp. 189–255 in *Congress Volume: Göttingen, 1977,* ed. W. ZIMMERLI. VTSup 29. Leiden, 1978. [= Pp. 213–54 in *Studien zum Pentateuch.*]

_____ . "Der Schöpfergott und der Bestand von Himmel und Erde: Das Alte Testament zum Zusammenhang von Schöpfung und Heil." Pp. 15–39 in *Sind wir noch zu retten? Schöpfungsglaube und Verantwortung für unsere Erde*, ed. G. ALTNER et al. Regensburg, 1978. [= Pp. 191–211 in *Studien zum Pentateuch*.]

_____ . *Studien zum Deuteronomium und zur deuteronomistischen Literatur*. Vol. 1. Stuttgarter biblische Aufsatzbände: Altes Testament 8. Stuttgart, 1990.

_____ . *Studien zum Deuteronomium und zur deuteronomistischen Literatur*. Vol. 2. Stuttgarter biblische Aufsatzbände: Altes Testament 12. Stuttgart, 1991.

_____ . *Studien zum Deuteronomium und zur deuteronomistischen Literatur*. Vol. 3. Stuttgarter biblische Aufsatzbände: Altes Testament 20. Stuttgart, 1995.

_____ . *Studien zum Deuteronomium und zur deuteronomistischen Literatur*. Vol. 4. Stuttgarter biblische Aufsatzbände: Altes Testament 31. Stuttgart, 2000.

_____ . *Studien zum Deuteronomium und zur deuteronomistischen Literatur*. Vol. 5. Stuttgarter biblische Aufsatzbände: Altes Testament 38. Stuttgart, 2005.

_____ . *Studien zum Pentateuch*. Stuttgarter biblische Aufsatzbände: Altes Testament 4. Stuttgart, 1988.

_____ . "Die Ursünden in der priesterlichen Geschichtserzählung." Pp. 38–57 in *Die Zeit Jesu: Festschrift für Heinrich Schlier*, ed. G. BORNKAMM and K. RAHNER. Freiburg-im-Breisgau, 1970. [= Pp. 169–89 in *Studien zum Pentateuch*.]

_____ . *Die Väter Israels im Deuteronomium: Mit einer Stellungnahme von Thomas Römer*. OBO 111. Fribourg and Göttingen, 1991.

_____ . "Zum 'kleinen geschichtlichen Credo' Dtn 26,5–9." *Theologie und Philosophie* 46 (1971) 19–39.

_____ . "Zur Dekalogfassung von Dt 5." *BZ* 9 (1965) 17–32 [= Pp. 193–209 in vol. 1 of *Studien zum Deuteronomium*.]

LONG, B. O. "Framing Repetitions in Biblical Historiography." *JBL* 106 (1987) 385–99.

LONGACRE, R. E. *Joseph: A Story of Divine Providence*. Winona Lake, IN, 1989. 2nd ed., 2003.

_____ . "Who Sold Joseph into Egypt?"Pp. 75–91 in *Interpretation and History: Essays in Honour of Allan A. MacRae*, ed. R. L. HARRIS et al. Singapore, 1986.

LOZA, J. *Las Palabras de Yahve: Estudio del Decálogo*. Biblioteca Mexicana. Mexico City, 1989.

LUBAC, H. DE. *Medieval Exegesis: The Four Senses of Scripture*. 2 vols., trans. Mark Sebanc and E. M. Macierowski. Grand Rapids, MI / Edinburgh, 1998–2000. [Original: *Exégèse médiévale: Les quatre sens de l'Écriture*. 2 vols. Paris, 1959–64.]

_____ . *Scripture in the Tradition*, trans. Luke O'Neill. New York, 2000. [Original: *L'Écriture dans la tradition*. Paris, 1966.]

LUST, J. "Exodus 6,2–8 and Ezechiel." Pp. 209–24 in *Studies in the Book of Exodus*, ed. M. VERVENNE. Leuven, 1996.

MARCONI, N. "Contributi per una lettura unitaria di Gen 37." *RivB* 39 (1991) 277–303.

MATHYS, H.-P. "Bücheranfänge und -schlüsse." Pp. 1–29 in *Vom Anfang und vom Ende: Fünf alttestamentliche Studien*. Beiträge zur Erforschung des Alten Testaments und des antiken Judentum 47. Frankfurt am Main, 2000.

MAYES, A. D. H. "The Theory of the Twelve Tribe Israelite Amphictyony." Pp. 297–308 in *Israelite and Judaean History*, ed. J. H. HAYES and J. M. MILLER. OTL. Philadelphia, 1977.

McCarthy, D. J. "Moses' Dealings with Pharaoh: Exod 7:8–12:27." *CBQ* 27 (1965) 336–47.

———— . *Treaty and Covenant: A Study in Form in the Ancient Oriental Documents and in the Old Testament*. AnBib 21A. Rome, 1978.

McDonald, L. M. *The Formation of the Christian Biblical Canon*. 2nd ed. Peabody, MA, 1995.

McEvenue, S. E. "The Elohist at Work." *ZAW* 96 (1984) 315–32.

———— . *The Narrative Style of the Priestly Writer*. AnBib 50. Rome, 1971.

———— . "The Speaker(s) in Ex 1–15." Pp. 220–36 in *Biblische Theologie und gesell-schaftlicher Wandel: Für Norbert Lohfink SJ*, ed. G. Braulik, W. Gross, and S. McEvenue. Freiburg-im-Breisgau, 1993.

McKnight, E. V. *Postmodern Use of the Bible: The Emergence of Reader-Oriented Criticism*. Nashville, 1988.

Meier, S. A. *Speaking of Speaking: Marking Direct Discourse in the Hebrew Bible*. VTSup 46. Leiden, 1992.

Mendelsohn, I. *Slavery in the Ancient Near East*. New York, 1949.

Mendenhall, G. E. "Change and Decay in All Around I See: Conquest, Covenant and *The Tenth Generation*." *BA* 39 (1976) 152–57.

———— . "Covenant Forms in Israelite Tradition." *BA* 17 (1954) 50–76. [= *Law and Covenant in the Ancient Near East*. Pittsburgh, 1955.]

———— . "The Hebrew Conquest of Palestine." *BA* 25/3 (1962) 66–87. [= Pp. 100–120 in vol. 3 of *The Biblical Archaeologist Reader*. Garden City, NY, 1970.]

———— . *The Tenth Generation: The Origins of the Biblical Tradition*. Baltimore, 1973.

Mettinger, T. N. D. *In Search of God: The Meaning and Message of the Everlasting Names*. Philadelphia, 1987.

Meynet, R. *L'analyse rhétorique: Une nouvelle méthode pour comprendre la Bible*. Initiations. Paris, 1989.

———— . "Les dix commandements, loi de liberté: Analyse rhétorique d'Ex 20,2–17 et Dt 5,6–21." *Mélanges de l'Université Saint-Joseph* 50 (Beirut, 1984) 405–21.

———— . *"E ora scrivete per voi questo cantico": Introduzione pratica all'analisi retorica*. Rome, 1996.

Michaud, R. *Débats actuels sur les sources et l'âge du Pentateuque*. Montreal, 1994.

Milgrom, J. *Leviticus*. 2 vols. AB 3–3A. Garden City, NY, 1991.

———— . *Numbers*. JPS Torah Commentary. New York, 1989.

Minor, M. *Literary-Critical Approaches to the Bible*. West Cornwall, CT, 1992.

Mittmann, S. "Num 20,14–21: Eine redaktionelle Kompilation." Pp. 143–49 in *Wort und Geschichte: Festschrift Karl Elliger*, ed. H. Gese and H. P. Rüger. AOAT 18. Kevelaer and Neukirchen-Vluyn, 1973.

Moberly, R. W. L. *At the Mountain of God: Story and Theology in Exodus 32–34*. JSOTSup 22. Sheffield, 1983.

———— . "The Earliest Commentary on the Akedah." *VT* 38 (1988) 302–23.

Moore, G. F. "Tatian's *Diatessaron* and the Analysis of the Pentateuch." *JBL* 9 (1890) 201–15. [= Pp. 243–56 in *Empirical Models for Biblical Criticism*, ed. J. Tigay. Philadelphia, PA, 1985.]

Morgan, D. F. *Between Text and Community: The "Writings" in Canonical Interpretation*. Minneapolis, 1990.

Mowinckel, S. *Le décalogue*. Paris, 1927.

_____ . *Erwägungen zur Pentateuchquellenfrage*. Oslo, 1964.

_____ . *Tetrateuch—Pentateuch—Hexateuch: Die Berichte über die Landnahme in den drei altisraelitischen Geschichtswerken*. BZAW 90. Berlin, 1964.

MUILENBURG, J. "Form Criticism and Beyond." *JBL* 88 (1969) 1–18.

NEEF, H.-D. *Die Heilstraditionen Israels in der Verkündigung des Propheten Hosea*. BZAW 169. Berlin, 1987.

NEGRETTI, N. *Il settimo giorno: Indagine critico-teologica delle tradizioni presacerdotali e sacerdotali circa il sabato biblico*. AnBib 55. Rome, 1973.

NEU, R. *Von der Anarchie zum Staat: Entwicklungsgeschichte Israels vom Nomadentum zur Monarchie im Spiegel der Ethnosoziologie*. Neukirchen-Vluyn, 1992.

NEUFELD, E. "The Prohibitions against Loans at Interest in Ancient Hebrew Laws." *HUCA* 26 (1955) 355–412.

NICHOLSON, E. W. "The Interpretation of Exodus xxiv 9–11." *VT* 24 (1974) 77–97.

_____ . "The Pentateuch in Recent Research: A Time for Caution." Pp. 10–21 in *Congress Volume: Leuven, 1989*, ed. J. A. EMERTON. VTSup 43. Leiden, 1991.

_____ . *The Pentateuch in the Twentieth Century: The Legacy of Julius Wellhausen*. Oxford, 1998.

NIDITCH, S. *Underdogs and Tricksters: A Prelude to Biblical Folklore*. San Franciso, 1987.

NIEHR, H. "פָּרַשׁ *pāraš*." Pp. 124–28 in vol. 12 of *TDOT*. [= "*pāraš*." Pp. 782–87 in vol. 6 of *TWAT*.]

NIELSEN, E. *Oral Tradition*. London, 1954.

_____ . "The Tradition-Historical Study of the Pentateuch since 1945, with Special Emphasis on Scandinavia." Pp. 11–28 in *The Production of Time: Tradition History in Old Testament Scholarship*, ed. K. JEPPESEN and B. OTZEN. Sheffield, 1984.

NIEMANN, H. M. *Herrschaft, Königtum und Staat: Skizzen zur soziokulturellen Entwicklung im monarchischen Israel*. FAT 6. Tübingen, 1993.

NOBLE, P. R. *The Canonical Approach: A Critical Reconstruction of the Hermeneutics of Brevard S. Childs*. Biblical Interpretation Series 16. Leiden, 1995.

_____ . "Synchronic and Diachronic Approaches to Biblical Interpretation." *Literature and Theology* 7 (1993) 130–48.

NORTH, C. R. "Pentateuchal Criticism." Pp. 48–83 in *The Old Testament and Modern Study*, ed. H. H. ROWLEY. Oxford, 1951.

NOTH, M. *Das Buch Josua*. HAT 1/7. Tübingen, 1938. 2nd ed., 1953.

_____ . *1 Könige*. BKAT 9/1. Neukirchen-Vluyn, 1969.

_____ . *Exodus*, trans. J. S. Bowden. OTL. Philadelphia, 1962. [Original: *Das zweite Buch Mose: Exodus*. ATD 5. Göttingen, 1957. 5th ed., 1973.]

_____ . *History of Israel*. 2nd ed. New York, 1960. [Original: *Geschichte Israels*. Göttingen, 1960. 6th ed., 1966.]

_____ . *A History of Pentateuchal Traditions*. Englewood Cliffs, NJ, 1972. Reprinted, Chico, CA, 1981. [Original: *Überlieferungsgeschichte des Pentateuch*. Stuttgart, 1948. Reprinted, Darmstadt, 1960.]

_____ . *Numbers*, trans. J. D. Martin. Philadelphia, 1968. [Original: *Das vierte Buch Mose: Numeri*. ATD 7. Göttingen, 1966.]

_____ . *Das System der zwölf Stämme Israels*. BWANT 52. Stuttgart, 1930.

_____ . *Überlieferungsgeschichtliche Studien: Die sammelden und bearbeitenden Geschichtswerke im Alten Testament*. Tübingen, 1943. 2nd ed., 1957.

OEMING, M.; SCHMID, K.; and WELKER, M. (eds.). *Das Alte Testament und die Kultur der Moderne.* Münster, 2004.

OGDEN, R. A. "Intellectual History and the Study of the Bible." Pp. 1–18 in *The Future of Biblical Studies,* ed. R. E. FRIEDMAN and H. G. M. WILLIAMSON. Semeia Studies. Atlanta, 1987.

OLIVA, M. "Interpretación teológica del culto en la perícopa del Sinaí de la Historia Sacerdotal." *Bib* 49 (1968) 348–51.

OLSON, D. T. *The Death of the Old and the Birth of the New: The Framework of the Book of Numbers and the Pentateuch.* BJS 71. Chico, CA, 1985.

OTTO, E. "Aspects of Legal Reforms and Reformulations in Ancient Cuneiform and Israelite Law." Pp. 160–96 in *Theory and Method in Biblical and Cuneiform Law: Revision, Interpolation and Development,* ed. B. M. LEVINSON. JSOTSup 181. Sheffield, 1994.

_____ . "Biblische Rechtsgeschichte: Ergebnisse und Perspektiven der Forschung." *TRev* 91 (1994) 283–92.

_____ . "Del Libro de la Alianza a la Ley de Santidad: La reformulación del derecho israelita y la formación del Pentateuco." *EstBib* 52 (1994) 195–217.

_____ . *Das Deuteronomium in Pentateuch und Hexateuch: Studien zur Literaturgeschichte von Pentateuch und Hexateuch im Lichte des Deuteronomiumsrahmen.* FAT 30. Tübingen, 2000.

_____ . *Das Deuteronomium: Politische Theologie und Rechtsreform in Juda und Assyrien.* BZAW 284. Berlin, 1999.

_____ . "Gesetzesfortschreibung und Pentateuchredaktion." *ZAW* 107 (1995) 373–92.

_____ . *Gottes Recht als Menschenrecht: Rechts- und literaturgeschichtliche Studien zum Deuteronomium.* Beihefte zur Zeitschrift für altorientalische und biblische Rechtsgeschichte 2. Wiesbaden, 2002.

_____ . "Das 'Heiligkeitsgesetz': Leviticus 17–26 in der Pentateuchredaktion." Pp. 65–80 in *Altes Testament: Forschung und Wirkung. Festschrift für Henning Graf Reventlow,* ed. P. MOMMER and W. THIEL. Frankfurt am Main, 1994.

_____ . "Kritik der Pentateuchkomposition." *TRu* 60 (1995) 163–91.

_____ . "Die nachpriesterschriftliche Pentateuchredaktion im Buch Exodus." Pp. 61–111 in *Studies in the Book of Exodus,* ed. M. VERVENNE. Leuven, 1996.

_____ . "Die Paradieserzählung Genesis 2–3: Eine nachpriesterschriftliche Lehrerzählung in ihrem religionshistorischen Kontext." Pp. 167–92 in *"Jedes Ding hat seine Zeit . . .": Studien zur israelitischen und altorientalischen Weisheit—Diethelm Michel zum 65. Geburtstag,* ed. A. A. DIESEL et al. BZAW 241. Berlin, 1996.

_____ . "פָּסַח *pāsaḥ*; פֶּסַח *pesaḥ*." Pp. 1–24 in vol. 12 of *TDOT*. [Original: "*Pæsaḥ*." Pp. 659–82 in vol. 6 of *TWAT*.]

_____ . *Der Pentateuch.* Erträge der Forschung. Darmstadt, 2004.

_____ . "Stehen wir vor einem Umbruch in der Pentateuchkritik?" *Verkündigung und Forschung* 22 (1977) 82–97.

_____ . *Theologische Ethik des Alten Testaments.* Theologische Wissenschaft 3/2. Stuttgart, 1994.

_____ . "Town and Rural Countryside in Ancient Israelite Law: Reception and Redaction in Cuneiform and Israelite Law." *JSOT* 57 (1993) 3–22.

_____ . "Von der Programmschrift einer Rechtsreform zum Verfassungsentwurf des Neuen Israel: Die Stellung des Deuteronomiums in der Rechtsgeschichte Israels."

Pp. 93–105 in *Bundesdokument und Gesetz: Studien zum Deuteronomium*, ed. G. BRAU-LIK. Herders biblische Studien 4. Fribourg, 1995.

OTTO, E., and ACHENBACH, R. (eds.). *Das Deuteronomium zwischen Pentateuch und Deuteronomischem Geschichtswerk*. FRLANT 206. Göttingen, 2004.

PAAP, C. *Die Josephsgeschichte Genesis 37–50: Bestimmungen ihrer literarischen Gattung in der zweiten Hälfte des 20. Jahrhunderts*. Europäische Hochschulschriften 23. Frankfurt, 1994.

PARUNAK, H. V. D. "Oral Typesetting: Some Uses of Biblical Structure." *Bib* 62 (1981) 153–68.

PATTE, D. *What Is Structural Exegesis?* Philadelphia, 1976.

PEDERSEN, J. "Passahfest und Passahlegende." *ZAW* 52 (1934) 161–75.

PERLITT, L. *Bundestheologie im Alten Testament*. WMANT 36. Neukirchen-Vluyn, 1969.

_____ . *Deuteronomium-Studien*. FAT 8. Tübingen, 1994.

_____ . "Hebraismus—Deuteronomismus—Judaismus." Pp. 279–95 in *Biblische Theologie und gesellschaftlicher Wandel: Für Norbert Lohfink SJ*, ed. G. BRAULIK, W. GROSS, and S. MCEVENUE. Freiburg-im-Breisgau, 1993.

_____ . "Priesterschrift im Deuteronomium?" *ZAW* 100 Supplement (1988) 65–88 [= Pp. 123–43 in *Deuteronomium-Studien*. FAT 8. Tübingen, 1994.

_____ . *Vatke und Wellhausen*. BZAW 94. Berlin, 1965.

PETERSEN, D. L. "Israelite Prophecy: Change versus Continuity." Pp. 191–203 in *Congress Volume: Leuven, 1989*, ed. J. A. EMERTON. VTSup 43. Leuven, 1991.

PETTINATO, G. *La saga di Gilgamesh*. Milan, 1992.

PHILLIPS, A. "The Laws of Slavery: Ex 21,2–11." *JSOT* 30 (1984) 51–66.

PLOEG, J. P. M. VAN DER. "Slavery in the Old Testament." Pp. 72–87 in *Congress Volume: Uppsala, 1971*. VTSup 22. Leiden, 1972.

POLA, T. *Die ursprüngliche Priesterschrift: Beobachtungen zur Literarkritik und Traditionsgeschichte von P^g*. WMANT 70. Neukirchen-Vluyn, 1995.

POLAND, L. M. *Literary Criticism and Biblical Hermeneutics: A Critique of Formalist Approaches*. American Academy of Religion Academy Series 48. Atlanta, 1985.

POLKA, B. *The Dialectic of Biblical Critique: Interpretation and Existence*. New York, 1986.

POWELL, M. A. *The Bible and Modern Literary Criticism: A Critical Assessment and Annotated Bibliography*. New York, 1992.

_____ . *What Is Narrative Criticism?* Minneapolis, 1992.

PROCKSCH, O. *Das nordhebräische Sagenbuch: Die Elohimquelle*. Leipzig, 1906.

PURY, A. DE. "Dos leyendas sobre el origen de Israel (Jacob y Moisés) y la elaboración del Pentateuco." *EstBib* 52 (1994) 95–131.

_____ . "Osée 12 et ses implications pour le débat actuel sur le Pentateuque." Pp. 175–207 in *Le Pentateuque: Débats et recherches*, ed. P. HAUDEBERT. LD 151. Paris, 1992.

PURY, A. DE, and RÖMER, T. (eds.). *Le Pentateuque en question: Les origines et la composition des cinq premiers livres de la Bible à la lumière des recherches récentes*. Le monde de la Bible 19. Geneva, 1989. 3rd ed., 2002.

PURY, A. DE; RÖMER, T.; and MACCHI, J.-D. (eds.). *Israel Constructs Its History: Deuteronomistic Historiography in Recent Research*. JSOTSup 306. Sheffield, 2000. [Original: *Israël construit son histoire: L'historiographie deutéronomiste à la lumière des recherches récentes*. Le monde de la Bible 34. Geneva, 1996.]

QUICK, P. A. "Resumptive Repetition: A Two-Edged Sword." *Journal of Translation and Textlinguistics* 6 (1993) 289–316.

RABENAU, K. VON. *Die beiden Erzählungen vom Schilfmeerwunder in Exod. 13,17–14,31.* Theologische Versuche 1. Berlin, 1966.

RAD, G. VON. "The Form-Critical Problem of the Hexateuch." Pp. 1–78 in *The Problem of the Hexateuch and Other Essays.* New York, 1966. [Original: *Das Formgeschichtliche Problem des Hexateuch.* BWANT 6/26. Stuttgart, 1938 = Pp. 9–86 in *Gesammelte Studien zum Alten Testament.* TBü 8. Munich, 1958.]

_____ . *Genesis: A Commentary,* trans. J. H. Marks. Philadelphia, 1972. [Original: *Das erste Buch Mose: Genesis.* ATD 2–4. Göttingen, 1949. 9th ed., 1972.]

_____ . *Holy War in Ancient Israel,* trans. M. J. Dawn. Grand Rapids, 1991. [Original: *Der Heilige Krieg im alten Israel.* ATANT 20. Zurich, 1951.]

_____ . "Josephsgeschichte und ältere Chokma." Pp. 120–27 in *Congress Volume: Copenhagen, 1952.* VTSup 1. Leiden, 1953. [= Pp. 272–80 in *Gesammelte Studien zum Alten Testament.* TBü 8. 2nd ed. Munich, 1961.]

_____ . *Old Testament Theology,* trans. D. M. G. Stalker. Vol. 1. Edinburgh, 1962. [Original: *Theologie des Alten Testaments.* Vol. 1. 4th ed. Munich, 1962.]

REINDL, J. "יצב/נצב *nṣb/yṣb.*" Pp. 519–29 in vol. 9 of *TDOT.* [Original: "*nṣb/jṣb.*" Pp. 555–65 in vol. 5 of *TWAT.*]

RENAUD, B. "La figure prophétique de Moïse en Ex 3,1–4,17." *RB* 93 (1986) 510–34.

_____ . "La formation de Ex 19–40: Quelques points de repère." Pp. 101–33 in *Le Pentateuque: Débats et recherches,* ed. P. HAUDEBERT. LD 151. Paris, 1992.

_____ . "Les généalogies et la structure de l'histoire sacerdotale dans le livre de la Genèse." *RB* 97 (1990) 5–30.

_____ . *La théophanie du Sinaï—Ex 19–24: Exégèse et théologie.* CahRB 30. Paris, 1991.

RENDSBURG, G. A. *The Redaction of Genesis.* Winona Lake, IN, 1986.

RENDTORFF, R. "Between Historical Criticism and Holistic Interpretation: New Trends in Old Testament Exegesis." Pp. 298–303 in *Congress Volume: Jerusalem, 1986.* VTSup 40. Leiden, 1988.

_____ . *Canon and Theology.* OBT 30. Minneapolis, 1994.

_____ . "Directions in Pentateuchal Studies." *Current Research: Biblical Studies* 5 (1997) 43–65.

_____ . "The Future of Pentateuchal Criticism." *Henoch* 6 (1984) 1–15.

_____ . "Gen 8,21 und die Urgeschichte des Jahwisten." *KD* 7 (1961) 69–78.

_____ . "Jakob in Bethel: Beobachtungen zum Aufbau und zur Quellenfrage in Gen 28,10–22." *ZAW* 94 (1982) 511–23.

_____ . "Literarkritik und Traditionsgeschichte." *EvT* 27 (1967) 138–53.

_____ . *The Old Testament: An Introduction,* trans. J. Bowden. London, 1985. [Original: *Das Alte Testament: Eine Einführung.* Neukirchen-Vluyn, 1983. 3rd ed., 1988.]

_____ . "The Paradigm Is Changing: Hopes and Fears." *BibInt* 1 (1993) 34–53.

_____ . "Traditio-Historical Method and the Documentary Hypothesis." Pp. 5–11 in *Ancient Near-East as Related to the Bible and the Holy Land.* Vol. 1 of *Proceedings of the Fifth World Congress of Jewish Studies.* 2 vols. Jerusalem, 1969.

_____ . *Das Überlieferungsgeschichtliche Problem des Pentateuch.* BZAW 147. Berlin, 1976.

_____ . "The "Yahwist" as Theologian? The Dilemma of Pentateuchal Criticism." *JSOT* 3 (1977) 2–9. [Original: "Der "Jahwist" als Theologe? Zum Dilemma der Pentateuchkritik." Pp. 158–66 in *Congress Volume: Edinburgh, 1974.* VTSup 28. Leiden, 1975.]

REUSS, E. *Die Geschichte der Heiligen Schriften des Alten Testaments.* Braunschweig, 1881.

RICHTER, W. "Beobachtungen zur theologischen Systembildung in der alttestamentlichen Literatur anhand des 'kleinen geschichtlichen Credo.'" Pp. 175–212 in *Wahrheit und Verkündigung* (FS W. Schmaus). Munich, 1967.

_____ . *Exegese als Literaturwissenschaft: Entwurf einer Literaturtheorie und Methodologie.* Göttingen, 1971.

RIEHM, E. *Die Gesetzgebung Mosis im Lande Moab.* Gotha, 1854.

ROBINSON, R. B. "The Literary Function of the Genealogies of Genesis." *CBQ* 48 (1986) 595–608.

ROFÉ, A. *The Book of Balaam.* Jerusalem, 1979.

_____ . "An Inquiry into the Betrothal of Rebekah." Pp. 27–40 in *Die Hebräische Bibel und ihre zweifache Nachgeschichte: Festschrift für Rolf Rendtorff zum 65. Geburtstag,* ed. E. BLUM, C. MACHOLZ, and E. W. STEGEMANN. Neukirchen-Vluyn, 1990.

_____ . *Introduction to the Composition of the Pentateuch.* Biblical Seminar 58. Sheffield, 1999.

ROGERSON, J. W. *The Bible and Criticism in Victorian Britain: Profiles of F. D. Maurice and William Robertson Smith.* JSOTSup 201. Sheffield, 1995.

_____ . *Old Testament Criticism in the Nineteenth Century: England and Germany.* London, 1984.

_____ . *W. M. L. de Wette: Founder of Modern Biblical Criticism. An Intellectual Biography.* JSOTSup 126. Sheffield, 1992.

RÖMER, T. "Exode et Anti-Exode: La nostalgie de l'Égypte dans les traditions du désert." *Dielheimer Blätter zum Alten Testament und seiner Rezeption in der Alten Kirche* 12 (*Lectio difficilior probabilior? L'exgèse comme expérience de décloisonnement* [FS F. Smyth-Florentin], ed. T. RÖMER; 1991) 155–72.

_____ . "La formation du Pentateuque: Histoire de la recherche." Pp. 67–84 in *Introduction à l'Ancien Testament,* ed. T. RÖMER, J.-D. MACCHI, and C. NIHAN. Le monde de la Bible 49. Geneva, 2004.

_____ . *Israels Väter: Untersuchungen zur Väterthematik im Deuteronomium und in der deuteronomistischen Tradition.* OBO 99. Fribourg and Göttingen, 1990.

_____ . "La narration, une subversion: L'histoire de Joseph (Gn 37–50*) et les romans de la diaspora." Pp. 17–30 in *Narrativity in Biblical and Related Texts,* ed. G. J. BROOKE and J. D. KAESTLI. Leuven, 2000.

_____ . "Nouvelles recherches sur le Pentateuque: À propos de quelques ouvrages récents." *Études théologiques et religieuses* 77 (2002) 69–78.

_____ . "Le Pentateuque toujours en question: Bilan et perspectives après un quart de siècle de débat." Pp. 343–74 in *Congress Volume: Basel, 2001,* ed. A. LEMAIRE. VTSup 92. Leiden, 2002.

RÖMER, T., and BRETTLER, M. "Deuteronomy 34 and the Case for a Persian Hexateuch." *JBL* 119 (2000) 401–19.

RÖMER, T., and NIHAN, C. "Le débat actuel sur la formation du Pentateuque." Pp. 85–113 in *Introduction à l'Ancien Testament,* ed. T. RÖMER, J.-D. MACCHI, and C. NIHAN. Le monde de la Bible 49. Geneva, 2004.

ROOKER, M. F. *Biblical Hebrew in Transition: The Language of the Book of Ezekiel.* JSOTSup 90. Sheffield, 1990.

ROSE, M. "La croissance du corpus historiographique de la Bible: Une proposition." *RTP* 118 (1986) 217–326.

_____ . *Deuteronomist und Yahwist: Untersuchungen zu den Berührungspunkten beider Literaturwerke.* ATANT 67. Zurich, 1981.

_____ . "Empoigner le Pentateuque par sa fin! L'investiture de Josué et la mort de Moïse." Pp. 129–47 in *Le Pentateuque en question: Les origines et la composition des cinq premiers livres de la Bible à la lumière des recherches récentes,* ed. A. DE PURY. Le monde de la Bible. Geneva, 1989. 2nd ed., 1992.

ROST, L. "Das kleine geschichtliche Credo." Pp. 11–25 in *Das kleine geschichtliche Credo und andere Studien zum Alten Testament.* Heidelberg, 1964.

ROUILLARD, E. *La péricope de Balaam (Nombres 22–24): La prose et les "oracles."* EB 4. Paris, 1985.

ROWLEY, H. H. *The Growth of the Old Testament.* London, 1950.

RUDOLPH, W. *Der "Elohist" von Exodus bis Josua.* BZAW 68. Berlin, 1938.

RUPPERT, L. "Die Aporien der gegenwärtigen Pentateuchdiskussion und die Josefserzählung der Genesis." *BZ* 29 (1985) 31–48. [= Pp. 89–109 in *Studien zur Literaturgeschichte.*]

_____ . *Genesis: Ein kritischer und theologischer Kommentar,* vol. 1: *Gen 1,1–11,26.* Forschung zur Bibel 70. Würzburg, 1992.

_____ . *Studien zur Literaturgeschichte des Alten Testaments.* Stuttgarter Biblische Aufsatzbände 18. Stuttgart, 1994.

RUPRECHT, E. "Die Religion der Väter: Hauptlinien der Forschungsge-schichte." *Dielheimer Blätter zum Alten Testament und seiner Rezeption in der Alten Kirche* 11 (1976) 2–29.

RÜTERSWÖRDEN, U. "Die Persische Reichsautorisation der Tora: Fact or fiction?" *ZABR* 1 (1995) 47–61.

SACCHI, P. *Storia del Secondo Tempio: Israele tra VI secolo a.C. e I secolo d.C.* Turin, 1994.

SÆBØ, M. (ed.). *Hebrew Bible. Old Testament: The History of Its Interpretation,* vol. 1: *From the Beginnings to the Middle Ages (until 1300).* Part 1: *Antiquity.* Göttingen, 1996.

SAILHAMER, J. H. *Introduction to Old Testament Theology: A Canonical Approach.* Grand Rapids, 1995.

SAKENFELD, K. D. *Journeying with God: A Commentary on the Book of Numbers.* International Theological Commentary. Grand Rapids, 1995.

SANDERS, J. A. "Adaptable for Life: The Nature and Function of Canon." Pp. 531–60 in *Magnalia Dei: Essays on the Bible and Archeology in Memory of G. Ernest Wright.* Garden City, NY, 1976.

_____ . "Canon." Pp. 837–52 in vol. 1 of *ABD.*

_____ . *Canon and Community: A Guide to Canonical Criticism.* Philadelphia, 1984.

_____ . *From Sacred Story to Sacred Text: Canon as Paradigm.* Philadelphia, 1987.

_____ . "The Integrity of Biblical Pluralism." Pp. 154–69 in *"Not in Heaven": Coherence and Complexity in Biblical Narrative,* ed. J. P. ROSENBLATT and J. C. SITTERSON. Indianapolis, 1991.

_____ . *Torah and Canon.* Philadelphia, 1972.

SAUSSURE, F. DE. *Course in General Linguistics,* trans. R. Harris; ed. C. Bally and A. Sechehaye. 3rd ed. LaSalle, IL, 1983. [Original: *Cours de linguistique générale.* Geneva, 1915. Reprinted, Paris, 1969.]

SAVOCA, G. *Iniziazione all'analisi biblica strutturalista: Teoria e applicazioni.* Messina, 1989.

SCHARBERT, J. *Numeri.* NEchtB 27. Würzburg, 1992.

SCHART, A. *Mose und Israel in Konflikt: Eine redaktionsgeschichtliche Studie zu den Wüstenerzählungen.* OBO 98. Fribourg and Göttingen, 1990.

SCHENKER, A. Review of BARBIERO G., *L'asino del nemico. Bib* 73 (1992) 263–65.

SCHMID, H. H. "Auf der Suche nach neuen Perspektiven für die Pentateuchforschung." Pp. 375–94 in *Congress Volume: Vienna, 1980*, ed. J. A. EMERTON. VTSup 32. Leiden, 1981.

_____ . "In Search of New Approches in Pentateuchal Research." *JSOT* 3 (1977) 33–42.

_____ . *Der sogenannte Jahwist: Beobachtungen und Fragen zur Pentateuchforschung.* Zurich, 1976.

_____ . "Vers une théologie du Pentateuque." Pp. 361–86 in *Le Pentateuque en question: Les origines et la composition des cinq premiers livres de la Bible à la lumière des recherches récentes*, ed. A. DE PURY. Le monde de la Bible. Geneva, 1989. 3rd ed., 2002.

SCHMID, K. *Erzväter und Exodus: Untersuchungen zur doppelten Begründung der Ursprünge Israels innerhalb der Geschichtsbücher des Alten Testaments.* WMANT 81. Neukirchen-Vluyn, 1999.

_____ . "Die Josephsgeschichte im Pentateuch." Pp. 83–118 in *Abschied vom Jahwisten: Die Komposition des Hexateuch in der jüngsten Diskussion*, ed. J. C. GERTZ, K. SCHMID, and M. WITTE. BZAW 315. Berlin, 2002.

SCHMIDT, L. *Beobachtungen und Fragen zu der Plagenerzählung in Exodus 7,14–11,10.* StudBib. Leiden, 1990.

_____ . "Jakob erschleicht sich den väterlichen Segen: Literarkritik und Redaktion in Genesis 27,1–45." *ZAW* 100 (1988) 159–83.

_____ . *Literarische Studien zur Josephsgeschichte.* BZAW 167. Berlin, 1986.

_____ . *Studien zur Priesterschrift.* BZAW 214. Berlin, 1993.

_____ . "Väterverheissungen und Pentateuchfrage." *ZAW* 104 (1992) 1–27.

_____ . "Weisheit und Geschichte beim Elohisten." Pp. 209–25 in *"Jedes Ding hat seine Zeit": Studien zur israelitischen und altorientalischen Weisheit. Diethelm Michel zum 65. Geburtstag.* BZAW 241. Berlin, 1996.

_____ . "Zur Entstehung des Pentateuch: Ein kritischer Literaturbericht." *Verkündigung und Forschung* 40 (1995) 3–28.

SCHMIDT, W. H. *Einführung in das Alte Testament.* Berlin, 1979. 5th ed., 1995.

_____ . "Elementäre Erwägungen zur Quellenscheidung im Pentateuch." Pp. 22–45 in *Congress Volume: Leuven, 1989*, ed. J. A. EMERTON. VTSup 43. Leiden, 1991.

_____ . *Exodus 1,1–6,30.* BKAT 2/1. Neukirchen-Vluyn, 1988.

_____ . "Die Intention der beiden Plagenerzählungen (Exodus 7–10) in ihrem Kontext." Pp. 225–43 in *Studies in the Book of Exodus*, ed. M. VERVENNE. Leuven, 1996.

_____ . "Plädoyer für die Quellenscheidung." *BZ* 32 (1988) 1–14.

_____ . "Ein Theologe in salomonischer Zeit? Plädoyer für den Jahwisten." *BZ* 25 (1981) 82–102.

SCHMIDT, W. H.; DELKURT, H.; and GRAUPNER, A. *Die Zehn Gebote im Rahmen alttestamentlicher Ethik.* Erträge der Forschung 281. Darmstadt, 1993.

SCHMITT, H.-C. "Dtn 34 als Verbindungsstück zwischen Tetrateuch und Deuteronomischem Geschichtswerk." Pp. 181–92 in *Das Deuteronomium zwischen Pentateuch und Deuteronomischem Geschichtswerk*, ed. E. OTTO and R. ACHENBACH. FRLANT 206. Göttingen: Vandenhoeck & Ruprecht, 2004.

_____ . "Die Hintergründe der 'neuesten Pentateuchkritik' und der literarische Befund der Josefsgeschichte." *ZAW* 97 (1985) 161–79.

_____ . *Die nichtpriesterliche Josephsgeschichte*. BZAW 154. Berlin, 1980.

_____ . "'Priesterliches' und 'prophetisches' Geschichtsverständnis in der Meerwundererzählung Ex 13,17–14,31: Beobachtungen zur Endredaktion des Pentateuch." Pp. 138–55 in *Textgemäss: Aufsätze und Beiträge zur Hermeneutik des Alten Testaments* (FS E. Würthwein), ed. W. ZIMMERLI. Göttingen, 1979.

_____ . "Redaktion des Pentateuch im Geiste der Prophetie: Beobachtungen zur Bedeutung des 'Glauben'-Thematik innerhalb der Theologie des Pentateuch." *VT* 32 (1982) 170–89.

_____ . "Die Suche nach der Identität des Jahweglaubens im nachexilischen Israel: Bemerkungen zur theologischen Intention des Pentateuch." Pp. 259–78 in *Pluralismus und Identität*, ed. J. MEHLHAUSEN. Munich, 1995.

SCHNIEDEWIND, W. M. *How the Bible Became a Book: The Textualization of Ancient Israel.* Cambridge, 2004.

SCHRAMM, B. *The Opponents of Third Isaiah: Reconstructing the Cultic History of the Restoration*. JSOTSup 193. Sheffield, 1994.

SCULLION, J. J. "*Märchen, Sage, Legende*: Towards a Clarification of Some Literary Terms Used by Old Testament Scholars." *VT* 34 (1984) 321–36.

SEEBASS, H. "À titre d'exemple: Réflexions sur Gen 16//21,8–21//26,1–33." Pp. 215–30 in *Le Pentateuque en question: Les origines et la composition des cinq premiers livres de la Bible à la lumière des recherches récentes*, ed. A. DE PURY. Le monde de la Bible. Geneva, 1989. 3rd ed., 2002.

_____ . "Biblisch-theologischer Versuch zu Num 20,1–13 und 21,4–9." Pp. 219–29 in *Altes Testament: Forschung und Wirkung—Festschrift für Henning Graf Reventlow*, ed. P. MOMMER and W. THIEL. Frankfurt, 1994.

_____ . "Gehörten Verheissungen zur ältesten Bestand der Vätererzählungen?" *Bib* 64 (1983) 189–210.

_____ . *Genesis I: Urgeschichte (1,1–11,26)*. Neukirchen-Vluyn, 1996.

_____ . *Genesis II/1: Vätergeschichte I (11,27–22,24)*. Neukirchen-Vluyn, 1997.

_____ . *Genesis II/2: Vätergeschichte II (23,1–36,43)*. Neukirchen-Vluyn, 1999.

_____ . *Genesis III: Josephgeschichte (37,1–50,26)*. Neukirchen-Vluyn, 2000.

_____ . "Que reste-t-il du Yahwiste et de l'Élohiste?" Pp. 199–214 in *Le Pentateuque en question: Les origines et la composition des cinq premiers livres de la Bible à la lumière des recherches récentes*, ed. A. DE PURY. Le monde de la Bible. Geneva, 1989. 2nd ed., 1992.

SEELIGMANN, I. L. "Hebräische Erzählung und biblische Geschichtsschreibung." *TZ* 18 (1962) 305–25.

SEGAL, B. Z. (ed.). *The Ten Commandments in History and Tradition*. Jerusalem, 1990.

SEIDEL, B. "Entwicklungen der neueren Pentateuchforschung im 20. Jahrhundert." *ZAW* 106 (1994) 476–85.

_____ . *Karl David Ilgen und die Pentateuchforschung im Umkreis der sogenannten Urkundenhypothese: Studien zur Geschichte der exegetischen Hermeneutik in der späten Aufklärung*. BZAW 213. Berlin, 1993.

SELLIN, E., and FOHRER, G. *Einleitung in das Alte Testament*. 9th ed. Heidelberg, 1965.

SHEPPARD, G. T. "Canonical Criticism." Pp. 861–66 in vol. 1 of *ABD.*

SHILOH, M. "And He Said . . . and He Said." *Sefer Korngreen*. Tel Aviv, 1963. [Hebrew]

SIMIAN-YOFRE H. "Diacronia: I Metodi storico-critici." Pp. 79–119 in *Metodologia dell'Antico Testamento*, ed. H. SIMIAN-YOFRE. Bologna, 1994.

SIMON, R. *Histoire critique des versions du Nouveau Testament*. Paris, 1690.

_____ . *Histoire critique du texte du Nouveau Testament*. Paris, 1689.

_____ . *Histoire critique du Vieux Testament*. Paris, 1678. [Reprinted, Rotterdam, 1685.]

SKA, J.-L. "L'appel d'Abraham et l'acte de naissance d'Israël (Gn 12,1–4a)." Pp. 367–89 in *Deuteronomy and Deuteronomic Literature: Festschrift C. H. W. Brekelmans*, ed. M. VERVENNE and J. LUST. BETL 133. Leuven, 1997.

_____ . "Biblical Law and the Origins of Democracy." Pp. 146–58 in *The Ten Commandments: The Reciprocity of Faithfulness*, ed. W. P. BROWN. Library of Theological Ethics. Louisville, 2004.

_____ . "Il canone ebraico e il canone cristiano dell'Antico Testamento." *Civiltà cattolica* 148/3 (1997) 213–25.

_____ . *Il codice dell'alleanza: Il diritto biblico e le leggi cuneiformi. Esegesi di Es 21,2–32*. Rome, 1996.

_____ . "Dal Nuovo all'Antico Testamento." *Civiltà cattolica* 147/2 (1996) 14–23.

_____ . "De la relative indépendance de l'écrit sacerdotal." *Bib* 76 (1995) 396–415.

_____ . "Essai sur la nature et la signification du cycle d'Abraham (Gn 11,27–25,11)." Pp. 153–77 in *Studies in the Book of Genesis: Literature, Redaction and History*, ed. A. WÉNIN. BETL 155. Leuven, 2001.

_____ . "Ex 19,3–8 et les parénèses deutéronomiques." Pp. 307–14 in *Biblische Theologie und gesellschaftlicher Wandel: Für Norbert Lohfink SJ*, ed. G. BRAULIK, W. GROSS, and S. MCEVENUE. Freiburg-im-Breisgau, 1993.

_____ . "Exode 19,3b–6 et l'identité de l'Israël postexilique." Pp. 289–317 in *Studies in the Book of Exodus: Redaction—Reception—Interpretation*, ed. M. VERVENNE. BETL 126. Leuven, 1996.

_____ . "Genèse xviii 6a—intertextualité et interprétation: 'Tout fait farine au bon moulin.'" Pp. 61–70 in *Congress Volume: Oslo 1998*, ed. M. SÆBØ and A. LEMAIRE. VTSup 80. Leiden, 2000.

_____ . *Introduzione al Deuteronomio: Struttura, storia, teologia*. Rome, 1995.

_____ . "Il lavoro nella Bibbia." *Firmana* 8 (1995) 47–62.

_____ . "Nel segno dell'arcobaleno: Il racconto biblico del diluvio (Gen 6–9)." Pp. 41–66 in *La natura e l'ambiente nella Bibbia*, ed. M. LORENZANI. Studio biblico teologico aquilano. L'Aquila, 1996.

_____ . "Un nouveau Wellhausen?" *Bib* 72 (1991) 253–63.

_____ . "La "nouvelle critique" et l'exégèse anglo-saxonne." *RSR* 80 (1992) 29–53.

_____ . *"Our Fathers Have Told Us": Introduction to the Analysis of Hebrew Narratives*. SubBib 13. Rome, 1990.

_____ . *Le passage de la mer: Étude de la construction, du style et de la symbolique d'Ex 14,1–31*. AnBib 109. Rome, 1986. 2nd ed., 1997.

_____ . "Le Pentateuque: État de la recherche à partir de quelques nouvelles 'Introductions.'" *Bib* 77 (1996) 245–65.

_____ . " 'Persian Imperial Authorization': Some Question Marks." Pp. 161–82 in *Persia and Torah: The Theory of Imperial Authorization of the Pentateuch*, ed. J. W. WATTS. SBLSymS 17. Atlanta, 2001.

_____ . "La place d'Ex 6,2–8 dans la narration de l'exode." *ZAW* 94 (1982) 530–48.

_____ . "Les plaies d'Égypte dans le récit sacerdotal (Pg)." *Bib* 60 (1979) 23–35.

_____ . "A Plea on Behalf of the Biblical Redactors." *Studia Theologica: Nordic Journal of Theology* 59 (2005) 4–18.

_____ . "Quelques remarques sur Pg et la dernière rédaction du Pentateuque." Pp. 95–125 in *Le Pentateuque en question: Les origines et la composition des cinq premiers livres de la Bible à la lumière des recherches récentes*, ed. A. DE PURY. Le monde de la Bible. Geneva, 1989. 3rd ed., 2002.

_____ . "Récit et récit métadiexégétique en Ex 1–15: Remarques critiques et essai d'interprétation de Ex 3,16–22." Pp. 135–71 in *Le Pentateuque: Débats et recherches*, ed. P. HAUDEBERT. LD 151. Paris, 1992.

_____ . "El relato del diluvio: Un relato sacerdotal y algunos fragmentos redaccionales posteriores." *EstBib* 52 (1994) 37–62.

_____ . "Le repas de Ex 24,11." *Bib* 74 (1993) 305–27.

_____ . Review of C. LEVIN, *Der Jahwist*. *Bib* 77 (1996) 425–28.

_____ . Review of J. VAN SETERS, *The Life of Moses*. *Bib* 76 (1995) 419–22. [= *CBQ* 58 (1996) 140–41.]

_____ . "Séparation des eaux et de la terre ferme dans le récit sacerdotal." *La nouvelle revue théologique* 103 (1981) 512–32.

_____ . "Sincronia: Analisi narrativa." Pp. 139–70, 223–34 in *Metodologia dell'Antico Testamento*, ed. H. SIMIAN-YOFRE. StudBib 25. Bologna, 1994. 2nd ed., 1997.

_____ . "La sortie d'Égypte (Ex 7–14) dans le récit sacerdotal (Pg) et la tradition prophétique." *Bib* 60 (1979) 191–215.

_____ . "La structure du Pentateuque dans sa forme canonique." *ZAW* 113 (2001) 331–52.

_____ . "The Yahwist, a Hero with a Thousand Faces: A Chapter in the History of Modern Exegesis." Pp. 1–23 in *Abschied vom Jahwisten: Die Komposition des Hexateuch in der jüngsten Diskussion*, ed. J. C. GERTZ, K. SCHMID, and M. WITTE. BZAW 315. Berlin, 2002.

SKINNER, J. *Genesis*. ICC. Edinburgh, 1910.

SMEND, R. *Deutsche Alttestamentler in drei Jahrhunderten*. Göttingen, 1989.

_____ . *Die Entstehung des Alten Testaments*. Theologische Wissenschaft 1. Stuttgart, 1978.

_____ . "Gehörte Juda zum vorstaatlichen Israel?" Pp. 57–62 in vol. 1 of *Fourth World Congress of Jewish Studies*. 2 vols. Jerusalem, 1967.

_____ . *Jahwekrieg und Stämmebund: Erwägungen zur ältesten Geschichte Israels*. FRLANT 84. Göttingen, 1963.

SNAITH, N. H. *Leviticus and Numbers*. Century Bible. London, 1967.

SOGGIN, J. A. *Introduction to the Old Testament*. 3rd ed. OTL. London, 1989. [Original: *Introduzione all'Antico Testamento*. 4th ed. Brescia, 1987.]

SONNET, J.-P. *The Book within the Book: Writing in Deuteronomy*. Biblical Interpretation 14. Leiden, 1997.

SPARKS, K. L. *The Pentateuch: An Annotated Bibliography*. Institute for Biblical Research Bibliographies. Grand Rapids, 2002.

SPINOZA, B. *Tractatus teologico-politicus*. Amsterdam, 1670.

STAMM, J. J. *Der Dekalog im Lichte der neueren Forschung*. Berne, 1958.

_____ . "Zum Altargesetz im Bundesbuch." *TZ* 1 (1945) 304–6.

STECK, O. H. *Der Abschluss der Prophetie im Alten Testament: Ein Versuch zur Frage der Vorgeschichte des Kanons.* Biblische Studien 17. Neukirchen-Vluyn, 1991.

———. "Aufbauprobleme in der Priesterschrift." Pp. 287–308 in *Ernten was man sät: Festschrift für Klaus Koch zu seinem 65. Geburtstag,* ed. D. R. DANIELS, U. GLESSMER, and M. RÖSEL. Neukirchen-Vluyn, 1991.

STEINMANN, J. *Richard Simon et les origines de l'exégèse biblique.* Paris, 1959.

STEINS, G. "Die Bücher Esra und Nehemia." Pp. 175–83 in *Einleitung in das Alte Testament,* ed. E. ZENGER. StB 1/1. Stuttgart, 1995.

STERNBERG, M. *The Poetics of Biblical Narrative: Ideological Literature and the Drama of Reading.* Indiana Literary Biblical Studies. Bloomington, IN, 1985.

STEURENAGEL, C. *Deuteronomium und Josua.* Göttingen, 1900.

STORDALEN, T. "Genesis 2,4: Restudying a *locus classicus.*" *ZAW* 104 (1992) 163–71.

STRUPPE, U. *Die Herrlichkeit Jahwes in der Priesterschrift: Eine semantische Studie zu k^{e}bôd JHWH.* Österreichische Biblische Studien 9. Klosterneuburg, 1988.

SUTHERLAND, D. "The Organisation of the Abraham Promise Narratives." *ZAW* 95 (1983) 337–43.

TALMON, S. "The 'Desert Motif' in the Bible and in Qumran Literature." Pp. 31–63 in *Biblical Motifs: Origins and Transformations,* ed. A. ALTMANN. Cambridge, MA, 1966.

———. "The Presentation of Synchroneity and Simultaneity in Biblical Narrative." Pp. 9–26 in *Studies in Hebrew Narrative Art throughout the Ages.* Scripta Hierosolymitana 27. Jerusalem, 1978. [Reprinted in *Literary Studies in the Hebrew Bible: Form and Content—Collected Studies.* Jerusalem, 1993.]

———. "The Three Scrolls of the Law That Were Found in the Temple Court." *Textus* 2 (1962) 14–27. [= Pp. 455–68 in *The Canon and Masorah of the Hebrew Bible: An Introductory Reader,* ed. S. Z. LEIMAN. Library of Biblical Studies. New York, 1974.]

TENGSTRÖM, S. *Die Toledotformel und die literarische Struktur der priesterlichen Erweiterungsschicht im Pentateuch.* Lund, 1982.

THIEL, W. "Erwägungen zum Alter des Heiligkeitsgesetzes." *ZAW* 81 (1969) 40–72.

———. "Vom revolutionären zum evolutionären Israel? Zu einem neuen Modell der Entstehung Israels." *TLZ* 113 (1988) 401–10.

THOMPSON, T. L. *Early History of the Israelite People: From the Written and Archaeological Sources.* Studies in the History of the Ancient Near East 4. Leiden, 1992.

———. *The Historicity of the Patriarchal Narratives: The Quest for the Historical Abraham.* BZAW 133. Berlin, 1974.

TIGAY, J. H. "An Empirical Model for the Documentary Hypothesis." *JBL* 94 (1975) 329–42.

———. *The Evolution of the Gilgamesh Epic.* Philadelphia, 1982.

———. "The Evolution of the Pentateuchal Narratives in the Light of the Evolution of the *Gilgamesh Epic.*" Pp. 21–52 in *Empirical Models.*

———. "The Significance of the End of Deuteronomy (Deuteronomy 34:10-12)." Pp. 137–43 in *Texts, Temples, and Traditions: A Tribute to Menahem Haran,* ed. M. V. FOX et al. Winona Lake, IN, 1996.

TIGAY, J. H. (ed.). *Empirical Models for Biblical Criticism.* Philadelphia, 1985.

TOSATO, A. *Il matrimonio israelitico: Una teoria generale.* AnBib 100. Rome, 1982.

TREBOLLE BARRERA, J. "Redaction, Recension, and Midrash in the Books of Kings." *BIOSCS* 15 (1982) 12–35.

TUCH, J. C. F. *Commentar über die Genesis.* Halle, 1838. 2nd ed., 1871.

TURNER, L. A. *Announcements of Plot in Genesis.* JSOTSup 96. Sheffield, 1990.

UTZSCHNEIDER, H. *Das Heiligtum und das Gesetz: Studien zur Bedeutung der sinaitischen Heiligtumstexte (Ex 25–40, Lev 8–9).* OBO 77. Fribourg and Göttingen, 1988.

VAN SETERS, J. *Abraham in History and Tradition.* New Haven, CT, 1975.

_____ . "Cultic Laws in the Covenant Code (Exodus 20,22–23,33) and Their Relationship to Deuteronomy and the Holiness Code." Pp. 319–45 in *Studies in the Book of Exodus*, ed. M. VERVENNE. Leuven, 1996.

_____ . *The Edited Bible: The Curious History of the "Editor" in Biblical Criticism.* Winona Lake, IN, 2006.

_____ . *In Search of History: Historiography in the Ancient World and the Origins of Biblical History.* New Haven, CT, 1983. [Reprinted, Winona Lake, IN, 1997.]

_____ . "An Ironic Circle: Wellhausen and the Rise of Redaction Criticism." *ZAW* 115 (2003) 487–500.

_____ . *Der Jahwist als Historiker*, ed. H. H. Schmid. Theologische Studien 134. Zurich, 1987.

_____ . "The Law of the Hebrew Slave." *ZAW* 108 (1996) 534–46.

_____ . *The Life of Moses: The Yahwist as Historian in Exodus–Numbers.* Contributions to Biblical Exegesis and Theology 10. Louisville, 1994.

_____ . *Prologue to History: The Yahwist as Historian in Genesis.* Louisville, 1992.

_____ . "Recent Studies on the Pentateuch: A Crisis in Method?" *JAOS* 99 (1979) 663–73.

_____ . "The Redactor in Biblical Studies: A Nineteenth Century Anachronism." *JNSL* 29 (2003) 1–19.

_____ . "The Religion of the Patriarchs in Genesis." *Bib* 61 (1980) 220–33.

VATER, J. S. *Commentar über den Pentateuch.* 3 vols. Halle, 1802–5.

VATKE, W. *Die biblische Theologie wissenschaftlich dargestellt.* Berlin, 1835.

VAULX, J. DE. *Les Nombres.* SB. Paris, 1972.

VAUX, R. DE. *The Bible and the Ancient Near East*, trans. D. McHugh. Garden City, NY, 1971. [Original: *Bible et Orient.* Cogitatio Fidei 24. Paris, 1967.]

_____ . *Early History of Israel*, trans. D. Smith. Philadelphia, 1978. [Original: *Histoire ancienne d'Israël 1: Des origines à l'installation en Canaan* and *Histoire ancienne d'Israël 2: La période des Juges.* EB. Paris, 1971–73.]

_____ . "The Twelve Tribes of Israel: The Theory of the 'Israelite Amphictyony.'" Pp. 695–715 in *Early History of Israel.* [Original: "La thèse de l'amphictyonie israélite." *HTR* 64 (*Studies in Memory of Paul Lapp*; 1971) 415–36 = Pp. 19–36 in *Histoire ancienne d'Israël 2: La période des Juges.*]

VEIJOLA, T. "Das Opfer des Abraham: Paradigma des Glaubens aus dem nachexilischen Zeitalter." *ZTK* 85 (1988) 129–64.

VERMEYLEN, J. "La formation du Pentateuque à la lumière de l'exégèse historico-critique." *RTL* 12 (1981) 324–46.

_____ . "Les premières étapes de la formation du Pentateuque." Pp. 149–97 in *Le Pentateuque en question: Les origines et la composition des cinq premiers livres de la Bible à la lumière des recherches récentes*, ed. A. DE PURY. Le monde de la Bible. Geneva, 1989. 3rd ed., 2002.

_____ . "Le vol de la bénédiction paternelle: Une lecture de Gen 27." Pp. 23–40 in *Pentateuchal and Deuteronomistic Studies*, ed. C. BREKELMANS and J. LUST. BETL 94. Leuven, 1990.

VERVENNE, M. "The Protest Motif in the Sea Narrative (Ex 14,11–12): Form and Structure of a Pentateuchal Pattern." *ETL* 63 (1987) 257–71.

_____. "The Sea Narrative Revisited." *Bib* 75 (1994) 80–98.

VERVENNE, M. (ed.). *Studies in the Book of Exodus: Redaction—Reception—Interpretation.* BETL 126. Leuven, 1996.

VERVENNE, M., and LUST, J. (eds.). *Deuteronomy and Deuteronomic Literature: Festschrift C. H. W. Brekelmans.* BETL 133. Leuven, 1997.

VOGELS, W. *Abraham et sa légende: Genèse 12,1–25,11.* Lire la Bible 110. Paris, 1996.

_____. *Moïse aux multiples visages: De l'Exode au Deutéronome.* Lire la Bible 112. Paris, 1998.

VOLZ, P., and RUDOLPH, W. *Der Elohist als Erzähler: Ein Irrweg der Pentateuchkritik?* BZAW 63. Giessen, 1933.

VORLÄNDER, H. *Die Entstehungszeit des jehowistischen Geschichtswerkes.* Europäische Hochschulschriften 23. Theologie 109. Frankfurt, 1978.

_____. *Mein Gott: Die Vorstellung vom persönlichen Gott im Alten Orient und im Alten Testament.* AOAT 23. Kevelaer and Neukirchen-Vluyn, 1975.

WAGNER, N. E. "Abraham and David?" Pp. 117–40 in *Studies in the Ancient Palestinian World Presented to Professor F. V. Winnett,* ed. J. W. WEVERS and D. B. REDFORD. Toronto Semitic Texts and Studies. Toronto, 1972.

_____. "Pentateuchal Criticism: No Clear Future." *Canadian Journal of Theology* 13 (1967) 225–32.

WAGNER, V. "Zur Existenz des sogenannten 'Heiligkeitsgesetzes.'" *ZAW* 86 (1974) 307–16.

WAHL, H. M. *Die Jakobserzählungen: Studien zur ihrer mündlichen Überlieferung, Verschriftung und Historizität.* BZAW 258. Berlin, 1997.

WATSON, D. F., and HAUSER, A. J. *Rhetorical Criticism of the Bible: A Comprehensive Bibliography. With Notes on History and Method.* Biblical Interpretation Series 4. Leiden, 1994.

WATTS, J. W. (ed.). *Persia and Torah: The Theory of Imperial Authorization of the Pentateuch.* SBLSymS 17. Atlanta, 2001.

WEIDMANN, H. *Die Patriarchen und ihre Religion im Licht der Forschung seit Julius Wellhausen.* FRLANT 94. Göttingen, 1968.

WEIMAR, P. *Die Berufung des Mose: Literaturwissenschaftliche Analyse von Exodus 2,23–5,5.* OBO 32. Fribourg and Göttingen, 1980.

_____. *Die Meerwundererzählung: Eine redaktionskritische Analyse von Ex 13,17–14,31.* Ägypten und Altes Testament 9. Wiesbaden, 1985.

_____. "Sinai und Schöpfung: Komposition und Theologie der priesterschriftlichen Sinaigeschichte." *RB* 95 (1988) 138–62.

_____. "Struktur und Komposition der priesterschriftlichen Geschichtsdarstellung." *BN* 24 (1984) 81–134; *BN* 24 (1984) 138–62.

_____. *Untersuchungen zur priesterschriftlichen Exodusgeschichte.* Forschung zur Bibel 9. Würzburg, 1973.

_____. *Untersuchungen zur Redaktionsgeschichte des Pentateuch.* BZAW 146. Berlin, 1977.

WEIMAR, P., and ZENGER, E. *Exodus: Geschichten und Geschichte der Befreiung Israels.* Stuttgarter Bibelstudien 75. 2nd ed. Stuttgart, 1975.

WEINBERG, J. P. "Die Agrarverhältnisse in der Bürger-Tempel-Gemeinde der Achämenidenzeit." Pp. 443–46 in *Wirtschaft und Gesellschaft im Alten Vorderasien*, ed. J. HARMATTA and G. KOMORÓCZY. Budapest, 1976.

_____ . *The Citizen-Temple Community.* JSOTSup 151. Sheffield, 1992.

WEINFELD, M. "Sabbath, Temple, and the Enthronement of the Lord: The Problem of the *Sitz im Leben* of Gen 1:1–2:3." Pp. 501–12 in *Mélanges bibliques et orientaux en l'honneur de M. Henri Cazelles*, ed. A. CAQUOT and M. DELCOR. AOAT 212. Neukirchen-Vluyn and Kevelaer, 1981.

WEISS, M. *The Bible from Within: The Method of Total Interpretation.* Jerusalem, 1984.

WELLHAUSEN, J. *Die Composition des Hexateuchs und der historischen Bücher des Alten Testaments.* Berlin, 1866. 2nd ed., 1889. 3rd ed., 1899.

_____ . *Prolegomena to the History of Israel.* Reprints and Translation Series. Altanta, 1994. [With a reprint of the article "Israel" from *Encyclopaedia Britannica.* Preface by W. Robertson Smith. Original: *Prolegomena zur Geschichte Israels.* Berlin, 1883.]

WENHAM, G. J. "The Coherence of the Flood Narrative." *VT* 28 (1978) 336–48.

_____ . *Genesis 1–15.* WBC 1. Waco, TX, 1987.

_____ . *Genesis 16–50.* WBC 2. Dallas, 1994.

_____ . "Method in Pentateuchal Criticism." *VT* 41 (1991) 84–109.

WESTBROOK, R. "What Is the Covenant Code?" Pp. 15–36 in *Theory and Method in Biblical and Cuneiform Law: Revision, Interpolation and Development*, ed. B. M. LEVINSON. JSOTSup 181. Sheffield, 1994.

WESTERMANN, C. *Genesis 1–11*, trans. J. J. Scullion. Minneapolis, 1984. [Original: *Genesis 1–11.* BKAT 1/1. 3rd ed. Neukirchen-Vluyn, 1984.]

_____ . *Genesis 12–36*, trans. J. J. Scullion. Minneapolis, 1985. [Original: *Genesis 12–36.* BKAT 1/2. Neukirchen-Vluyn, 1981.]

_____ . *Genesis 37–50*, trans. J. J. Scullion. Minneapolis, 1986. [Original: *Genesis 37–50.* BKAT 1/3. Neukirchen-Vluyn, 1982.]

_____ . "Die Herrlichkeit Gottes in der Priesterschrift." Pp. 227–49 in *Wort, Gebot, Glaube: Beiträge zur Theologie des Alten Testaments. Walther Eichrodt zum 80. Geburtstag*, ed. H. J. STOEBE. ATANT 59. Zurich, 1970. [= Pp. 115–37 in vol. 2 of *Forschung am Alten Testament: Gesammelte Studien.* TBü 55. Munich, 1974.]

WETTE, W. M. L. DE. *Beiträge zur Einleitung in das Alte Testament.* Halle, 1806–7.

_____ . *Dissertatio critica qua Deuteronomium diversum a prioribus Pentateuchi libris, alius cuiusdam recentioris autoris opus esse demonstratur.* Jena, 1805.

WHYBRAY, R. N. *Introduction to the Pentateuch.* Grand Rapids, 1995.

_____ . *The Making of the Pentateuch: A Methodological Study.* JSOTSup 53. Sheffield, 1987.

WIEDER, A. "Ugaritic-Hebrew Lexicographical Notes." *JBL* 84 (1965) 160–64.

WIENER, H. M. *The Composition of Judges II 11 to 1 Kings II 46.* Leipzig, 1929.

WIESEHÖFER, J. "'Reichsgesetz' oder 'Einzelfallgerechtigkeit'? Bemerkungen zu P. Freis These von der Achämenidischen 'Reichsautorisation.'" *ZABR* 1 (1995) 36–46.

WILLIAMSON, H. G. M. *Ezra and Nehemiah.* OTG. Sheffield, 1987.

_____ . *Ezra, Nehemiah.* WBC 16. Waco, TX, 1985.

_____ . *Studies in Persian Period History and Historiography.* FAT 38. Tübingen, 2004.

WILSON, R. R. *Genealogy and History in the Biblical World.* New Haven, CT, 1977.

_____ . "The Old Testament Genealogies in Recent Research." *JBL* 94 (1975) 169–89.

WINNETT, F. V. *The Mosaic Tradition.* Toronto, 1949.

———. "Re-examining the Foundations." *JBL* 84 (1965) 1–19.

WOLDE, E. J. VAN, *A Semiotic Analysis of Genesis 2–3: A Semiotic Theory and Method of Analysis Applied to the Story of the Garden of Eden.* SSN 25. Assen, 1989.

WOLFF, H. W. "Das Kerygma des Jahwisten." *EvT* 24 (1964) 73–98. [= Pp. 345–73 in *Gesammelte Studien zum Alten Testament.* TBü 22. Munich, 1964.]

———. "Zur Thematik der elohistischen Fragmente in Pentateuch." *EvT* 29 (1969) 59–72. [= Pp. 402–17 in *Gesammelte Studien zum Alten Testament.* TBü 22. Munich, 1973.]

WRIGHT, D. P. "The Laws of Hammurabi as a Source for the Covenant Collection (Exodus 20:23–23:19)." *MAARAV* 10 (2003) 11–87.

WUELLNER, J. "Where Is Rhetorical Criticism Taking Us?" *CBQ* 49 (1987) 448–63.

WYNN-WILLIAMS, D. J. *The State of the Pentateuch: A Comparison of the Approaches of M. Noth and E. Blum.* BZAW 249. Berlin, 1997.

YARDENI, A. "Remarks on the Priestly Blessing on Two Ancient Amulets from Jerusalem." *VT* 41 (1991) 176–85.

ZAHN, M. "Revelation Regained: The Hermeneutics of כי and אם in the Temple Scroll." *Dead Sea Discoveries* 9 (2002) 295–346.

ZAMAN, L. R. *Rendtorff en zijn "Das überlieferungsgeschichtliche Problem des Pentateuch": Schets van een Maccabeër binnen de hedendaagsche Pentateuchexegese.* Brussels, 1984.

ZENGER, E. "Auf der Suche nach einem Weg aus der Pentateuchkrise." *TRev* 78 (1982) 353–62.

———. *Gottes Bogen in den Wolken: Untersuchungen zu Komposition und Theologie der priesterschriftlichen Urgeschichte.* Stuttgarter Bibelstudien 112. Stuttgart, 1983.

———. *Israel am Sinai: Analysen und Interpretation zu Exodus 17–34.* Altenberge, 1982.

———. *Die Sinaitheophanie.* Forschung zur Bibel 3. Würzburg, 1971.

———. "Le thème de la 'sortie d'Égypte' et la naissance du Pentateuque." Pp. 301–31 in *Le Pentateuque en question: Les origines et la composition des cinq premiers livres de la Bible à la lumière des recherches récentes,* ed. A. DE PURY. Le monde de la Bible. Geneva, 1989. 3rd ed., 2002.

———. "Wie und Wozu die Tora zum Sinai kam: Literarische und theologische Beobachtungen zu Exodus 19–34." Pp. 265–88 in *Studies in the Book of Exodus,* ed. M. VERVENNE. Leuven, 1996.

ZENGER, E. (ed.). *Einleitung in das Alte Testament.* Studienbücher Theologie 1/1. 4th ed. Stuttgart, 2004. [= *Introduzione all'Antico Testamento,* trans. F. DELLA VECCHIA. Brescia, 2005.]

———. *Die Tora als kanon für Juden und Christen.* Herders Biblische Studien 10. Freiburg, 1996.

ZIMMERLI, W. *Gottesoffenbarung: Gesammelte Aufsätze zum Alten Testament.* TBü 19. Munich, 1969.

———. "'Heiligkeit' nach dem sogenannten Heiligkeitsgesetz." *VT* 30 (1980) 493–512.

———. "Sinaibund und Abrahambund: Ein Beitrag zum Verständnis der Priesterschrift." *TZ* 16 (1960) 268–80. [= Pp. 205–16 in *Gottesoffenbarung: Gesammelte Aufsätze zum Alten Testament.*]

ZUBER, B. *Vier Studien zu den Ursprüngen Israels.* OBO 9. Fribourg and Göttingen, 1976.

Index of Authors

Index of Scripture

New Testament

Deuterocanonical Literature